BHOTAN

AND THE STORY OF THE DOOAR WAR

BHOTAN

AND THE STORY OF THE DOOAR WAR

INCLUDING

SKETCHES OF A THREE MONTHS' RESIDENCE IN THE HIMALAYAS, AND NARRATIVE OF A VIST TO BHOTAN IN MAY 1865

BY

SURGEON RENNIE, M.D.

20TH HUSSARS

AUTHOR OF 'THE BRITISH ARMS IN NORTH CHINA AND JAPAN' AND 'PEKING AND THE PEKINGESE'

GYAN

Published by

GYAN

Gyan Publishing House
5, Ansari Road
Daryaganj, New Delhi-110002
Phone: 011-47034999, 9811692060
E-mail: books@gyanbooks.com

Distribution Network
gyanbooks.com
India, USA, Canada, UK, Australia, France

ISBN : 978-81-212-2925-8 (PB)
First Published, 1866

2nd Impression 2021

Printed at: Gyan Press, Delhi.

Bhotan and the Story of the Dooar War
Author: Surgeon Rennie

BHOTAN

AND THE STORY OF

THE DOOAR WAR

INCLUDING

SKETCHES OF A THREE MONTHS' RESIDENCE IN THE HIMALAYAS, AND NARRATIVE OF A VISIT TO BHOTAN IN MAY 1865

BY

SURGEON RENNIE, M.D.

20TH HUSSARS

AUTHOR OF 'THE BRITISH ARMS IN NORTH CHINA AND JAPAN' AND 'PEKING AND THE PEKINGESE'

BHOTANESE HORSEMAN AND ATTENDANT

LONDON

JOHN MURRAY, ALBEMARLE STREET

1866

VIEW OF THE SNOWY RANGE AND PEAK OF KENCHINJUNGA.

[From a Photograph taken at Darjeeling.]

Dedication

TO

COLONEL HAWKES

AND

THE OFFICERS OF THE 80TH REGIMENT

This Volume is Inscribed

IN RECOLLECTION OF MUTUAL GOOD FEELING

AND OF MUCH KINDNESS

RECEIVED BY THE AUTHOR DURING THE PERIOD HE SERVED

WITH THE CORPS ON

THE NORTH-EASTERN FRONTIER OF INDIA

PREFACE.

THERE is probably no country in the world that, until within the present year, has been less a subject of interest than Bhotan, and as a natural consequence, probably no one, that there is less generally known about. In fact, it may be said without exaggeration, that, until recently, comparatively few but those who made Asiatic geography a special study ever heard its name. Nevertheless, hidden as Bhotan has been from public notice, a great deal of official information has been on record about it, and from its proximity to the north-eastern frontier of our possessions in India, the Government of that country has had frequent troubles with it; the earliest of which dates as far back as the year 1772. These troubles have related chiefly to raids into British territory (plundering cattle, &c., and carrying off natives to be used as slaves) which having been punished in a variety of mild ways without producing any good effect, ultimately decided the Indian Government on annexing in 1864 the portion of the Bhotan frontier from which the predatory incursions were made. In the course of the narrative however it will be shown that grounds exist for believing that the faults were not altogether on the side of the Bhotanese, and that a certain lawlessness of action has prevailed on both sides of the frontier; pretty much as existed on the borders of England and Scotland in former years.

The first chapter is devoted to a sketch of the country, its inhabitants, and form of government, sufficiently detailed to enable the reader at starting to understand who the Bhotanese really are, and the relation in which they stand to Thibet, and thus, indirectly, to our old friends the Chinese. In preparing this sketch, I have drawn freely on the official records having latest reference to the subject, and have also, in some measure been aided by my own observation. The second chapter refers to the commencement of British intercourse with Bhotan in 1772, and brings our acquaintance with the country up to the year 1815. The third treats of the troubles consequent on the annexation of Assam in 1828, and the assumption by the Government of India of the relations which had previously existed between the Assamese and the Bhotanese. Reference is also briefly made in this chapter to the first regular mission sent to Bhotan by the Indian Government in 1837, and to the train of events (details being given in the form of an Appendix) which in 1862 determined the Governor-General, Lord Canning, to send a second. This mission was that of the Honourable Ashley Eden, and its failure having been the immediate cause of the Dooar war—so called from the name of the territory belonging to Bhotan that it was deemed necessary* to annex as a preventive of further aggression—a more than passing notice is required of it. Chapters four and five are therefore devoted to an account of Mr. Eden's journey from Darjeeling to Poonakha, the capital of Bhotan, in 1864. Chapter six treats of negotiations at that place, and of the peculiar circumstances under which they were conducted. While the two previous chapters are a *précis* of a portion of a very interesting report furnished the Government of India by Mr. Eden on his return, this chapter (the sixth) is the substance in detail, but little altered from the original text, of a special communication addressed to the Government, and to which publicity has only recently been given. The character of the remainder of the narrative may be gathered from the following statement of the circumstances under which it has been written.

Early in October 1864, when the organisation of the field force about to operate against Bhotan was in progress, the 80th Regiment, at the time at Jhansi, was detailed to form a portion of it. A staff-surgeon was required to take medical charge of it; the surgeon of the corps being at the time in England. I volunteered for this duty, but as I was at the time specially employed I was not considered available. As matters however turned out, a staff-surgeon was not at the period wanted, the left Wing only of the regiment going to Darjeeling on the north-eastern frontier as a support—while the head-quarters were brought down to Dum Dum, near Calcutta; so as to be at hand, in the event of further support being required. Shortly after this occurred, my services having been placed at the disposal of the Commander-in-Chief, I thought it likely, that, from my local position, should the head-quarters of the 80th Regiment have to proceed to the scene of hostilities, I should have to accompany it. This led to my making myself acquainted with the train of events which had rendered operations against Bhotan necessary, and with a view of having a connected record of events in the event of ultimately having opportunities for personal observation, I also collected such information relating to the opening of the campaign as my residence in Calcutta enabled me to do.

At the commencement of December 1864, the British troops entered the Bhotan territory, and the annexation measures, which had been previously determined on, were carried out, almost without resistance, and the year 1865 opened with the whole affair apparently terminated; orders being issued by the Government for the break-up of the field force. Before however these orders could be acted upon, the aspect of affairs on the frontier was completely changed—the Bhotanese came down in force, and attacked our troops in the positions they were holding in the lower range of the Himalayas of Bhotan, from two of which they succeeded in dislodging them ; one of the columns losing its guns and some of its sick in retreating to the plains.

Immediate preparations were made by the Government for repairing these disasters, and large reinforcements—including two batteries of Royal Artillery, the 55th and 80th Regiments—were despatched in February to the north-eastern frontier. I was placed in medical charge of the latter corps, which formed the reserve of the Left Brigade of the Dooar Field Force, and served with it in the Himalayas until the termination of active operations, and the adoption for the time being, of a purely defensive policy.

Though the 80th Regiment was not required to advance beyond Darjeeling, and consequently was not actively engaged, I was nevertheless favourably situated for obtaining information regarding the few operations which were carried on, and I was also able to see something of Bhotan and the recently annexed Dooars.

In June 1865, I was ordered to England in charge of troops, and with the view partly of beguiling the tediousness of a four months' voyage round the Cape of Good Hope—made for the fifth time—partly in the hope of furnishing some information about a country almost altogether unwritten about, so far as I am aware, except in Government reports not available to the reading public generally, I set myself the task now completed, in the course of which I have endeavoured to give such a sketch of the recent military operations and their results as brings our acquaintance with Bhotan up to the latest date:—the campaign against it having become invested with a degree of interest more the result of its cost (£800,000)* and the expenditure of life and health from climatic causes by which it has been attended, than of the more exciting incidents of warfare; the minimum of what is usually called military glory having accrued from it.

In the course of that portion of the narrative which relates to my residence at Darjeeling, I have endeavoured to throw some light on the origin of the Mongolian tribes forming the bulk of the population of the Sikim Himalayas—a subject upon which but little has been written, and that little, I am inclined to think of doubtful accuracy. Whatever my views relating thereto may be worth, in forming them, I have had the advantage of a moderately intimate previous acquaintance with the physical and other characteristics of a variety of subdivisions of the great Mongolian family, and particularly of the one from which, in my opinion, is descended the section of the Sikim population, concerning whose origin obscurity exists. That my observations on

* The sum quoted above, was that which the Dooar war was known to have cost when I left Calcutta on the 17th of June 1865. Now however, it must be represented by much higher figures; consequent on the unfinished character of the campaign and the extensive preparations which have since been made for a renewal of hostilities.

this subject and other points relating thereto might be better arranged than they are, I am fully sensible, but I have preferred making them in a somewhat desultory manner rather than deviate from the plan I have followed throughout of recording my personal experiences in the order of their occurrence.

The arranging and re-writing of my notes and shaping the work into its present form were commenced in the Bay of Bengal, and finished off the Azores—for its shortcomings, therefore, I trust allowance will be made; a cuddy table in a sailing troop ship presenting a combination of circumstances the reverse of favourable to a literary undertaking.

The following are the sources from which those portions of the narrative (Appendix included) relating to events prior to the commencement of the military operations, as yet unfinished, have chiefly been compiled—Captain Turner's Embassy to Thibet, Kishenkant Bose's account of his visit to Bhotan, and the reports of Captain Pemberton, Dr. Griffiths, and the Honourable Ashley Eden.

TROOP SHIP 'RINALDO,' AT SEA:
October 11*th*, 1865.

POSTSCRIPT.

With respect to the illustrations, I have to state that having casually brought home a few photographs from Darjeeling, it was thought as well to engrave them, and also introduce a few woodcuts from Dr.

Hooker's journal of his visit to the Sikim Himalayas; the woodcuts thus borrowed, being so far illustrative of what is described in the portions of the narrative where they have been introduced, as to be useful to the reader.

I may also state that at the conclusion of the narrative, I have been able to append a note containing a brief summary of our relations with Bhotan up to the latest date; which renders the work more complete than it otherwise would be.

December 18*th*, 1865.

CONTENTS.

CHAPTER IV.

CHAPTER V.

CHAPTER VI.

CHAPTER VII.

CHAPTER VIII.

CHAPTER IX.

CHAPTER X.

CHAPTER XI.

CHAPTER XII.

CHAPTER XIII.

CHAPTER XIV.

CHAPTER XV.

CHAPTER XVI.

CHAPTER XVII.

CHAPTER XVIII.

CHAPTER XIX.

CHAPTER XX.

CHAPTER XXI.

CHAPTER XXII.

CONTENTS OF APPENDIX B.

Which contains a Narrative of the Relations existing between the Government of India and the Bhotanese between the Years 1828 *and* 1861, *a Summary only of which appears in the body of the Work at Pages* 50 *and* 51.

LIST OF ILLUSTRATIONS.

GUIDE

TO THE

PRONUNCIATION OF LOCAL NAMES.

Ambaree	Am-bah-ree	Kenchinjunga	Ken-shin-jun-gah
Assooraghur	As-soor-ah-ghur	Kursiong	Kur-see-ong
Balgatchie	Bal-gatch-ee	Kyrantee	Ky-ran-tee
Bhaugulpore	Baw-gul-pore	Labah	Lahb-ah
Bhotan	Boat-awn	Leebong	Lee-bong
Bullabaree	Bul-lah-bah-ree	Lepcha	Lep-chah
Carragola	Cah-rah-go-lah	Libra	Leeb-rah
Chamoorchee	Chaw-moor-chee	Luchmeepoor	Lutch-mee-poor
Chitreepeer	Chit-ree-peer	Mahanuddy	Mah-hah-nud-dee
Darjeeling	Dar-jee-ling	Mechi	Metch-ee
Dewangiri	Day-wan-ghee-ree	Mynagoorie	Mine-ah-goo-ree
Dhalimkote	Dah-lim-kote	Narrain	Nar-rain
Dhamonee	Dah-moan-ee	Pacheem	Pah-cheem
Darungah	Dar-un-gah	Parseebutty	Par-see-butty
Dhumsong	Dum-song	Punkabaree	Punk-kah-bah-ree
Dinagepore	Di-nage-pore	Pushok	Push-ok
Dooars	Doo-ars	Putlakowa	Putt-la-cow-ah
Fallacottah	Fallah-cottah	Poonakha	Poon-ack-ah
Goalpara	Go-al-pah-rah	Rajmahal	Raj-mah-hawl
Gozal	Go-zawl	Rungeet	Run-gheet
Goorkha	Goor-kah	Rungnoo	Rung-noo
Gooroogaon	Goo-roo-gah-on	Saleeka	Sal-ee-kah
Gopaulgunge	Go-paul-gunge	Senchal	Sen-shawl
Gowhatty	Gow-hatty	Sikim	Sick-im
Jullapahar	Julla-pah-har	Silligoorie	Silly-goo-ree
Julpigorie	Jul-pi-go-ree	Soubah	Soob-ah
Julpesh	Jul-paish	Tasagong	Tah-sah-gong
Kalimpoong	Kah-lim-poong	Terai	Ter-i
Koomrekatta	Koom-re-kah-tah	Titalyah	Tit-ah-lee-ah
Kishengunge	Kishen-gunge	Uchaka	U-chaw-kah

BHOTAN

AND

THE DOOAR WAR.

CHAPTER I.

Geographical Position and Extent of Bhotan—Nature of the Country—Meaning of the term Dooar—Origin of the word Bhotan—Source from which its Inhabitants have sprung—The term Bhoteah synonymous with that of Thibetian—Obscurity connected with the early History of Bhotan—Traditions with reference thereto—Political Relations with Thibet and China—Nature of the Government—Constitution of the Council—The Dhurma and Deb Rajas—The Penlows, Jungpens, and their Subordinates—Revenue and Judicial Systems—Religion—Language—Military Resources.

THE country to which the name of Bhotan is usually given in modern maps is situated on the north-eastern frontier of our Indian Empire, between the parallels of 26° 30′ and 28° of north latitude and from 88° 45′ to 92° 25′ of east longitude. It extends from the southern declivities of the great central ridge of the Himalaya Mountains to the level ground in front of that portion of their inferior chain which constitutes the natural northern boundary of the Assam Valley and the north-eastern one of the plains of Bengal.

In length Bhotan is two hundred and twenty miles. Its breadth varies a good deal, and may be stated as averaging about ninety miles. It is bounded on the north by Thibet, on the south by Bengal, the protected State of Cooch Behar, and Assam. On the west by the Teesta River, which separates it from Sikim (the territory intervening between Bhotan and Nepaul), and on the east by the Dhunseeree River, separating it from the hill districts ruled over by the Towang Raja; a priest subordinate to the Grand Lama—the ecclesiastical ruler of Thibet.

With the exception of a strip of land varying in breadth from ten to thirty miles, situated at the foot of the inferior heights—but not properly belonging to Bhotan; having been acquired by aggression from the Mogul dynasty, the whole of the country presents a succession of as rugged and lofty mountain scenery as is to be found in the world. The area of Bhotan Proper, namely, the portion included between the higher and lower Himalayan ranges, has been estimated at 19,800 geographical miles. The level ground at the foot of the latter, wrested from the Moguls, runs along the whole length of the country, and separates the British frontier from the subordinate chain of the Bhotan hills. Communication between this plain and the interior of Bhotan takes place through a series of mountain passes, locally known as Dooars, a word derived from the Hindoostanee *dwār*, a gate or entrance. This name has been inappropriately applied to the level tract upon which these passes open, and thus a much wider meaning has become attached to the word Dooar than that which etymologically belongs to it. These Dooars, which consist of a rich and fertile soil capable of high cultivation, will be more fully described in connexion with the history of British intercourse with Bhotan.

Though the Bhoteahs, by which name it has become the custom to designate the inhabitants of intra-montane Bhotan,* are as distinct from the natives of Hindoostan as the African Negro is from the Chinaman, the appellation, nevertheless, by which their country is known to us, owes its origin to a Hindoostanee source—the word Bhotan simply meaning the country of the Bhots or Thibetians. More correctly, it should be spelt Bhotstan—*stan* in the Persian and Arabic meaning place, as *istan* does in the Sanscrit: hence Hindoostan, Afghanistan and Beloochistan, the places respectively of the Hindoo, the Afghan, and the Belooch. The Bhoteahs and the Thibetians are in fact the same people; the former being what may be termed a colonial branch of the latter, who have become alienated in a considerable measure from the mother country, by attempting the independent government of hill territory, originally acquired by Thibetian enterprise, but, from its unproductiveness, apparently given up by the Government to such adventurers as chose to remain in it.

The proofs of identity between the terms Thibetian and Bhoteah are the following. In the first place, the word Thibet is not only unknown in the country portrayed under that name in European maps, but is a word respecting the origin of which we have no authentic knowledge. Williams, in noticing Thibet in his work called "The Middle Kingdom," states—

* I make use of the term intra-montane Bhotan, as distinctive of Bhotan Proper; inasmuch as the Dooar portion of the country is inhabited by an Indianic race altogether distinct from the Bhoteahs, and held in vassalage by them.

"The name Tibet or Tubet is corrupted from *Tu-po*, the country of the Tu, a race which over-ran it in the sixth century; another name, according to Turner, is Pue Koachim, signifying 'the snowy country of the north,' but Csoma,* who lived there some years, says the people called it Pot, or Bod, or Bod Yul, the land of Bod. The Chinese call the whole country Si Tsang, and divide it into Tsien Tsang, or Anterior Tibet, and Hang Tsang, or Ulterior Tibet." That the word Bot, variously pronounced Bhote, Bod, Pot, Poot, is the name by which Thibet is locally known, I am able to testify from personal knowledge, and that such is the case would also seem to be recognised by certain geographers, inasmuch as in many modern maps the country is designated by the words "Thibet or Bot." I am not myself inclined to adopt the words *Tu Po* as those from which Thibet is derived; being of opinion that it more probably owes its origin to a source somewhat similar to that to which the word Typhoon is to be traced, namely, a corruption of the two Chinese words *Ta* and *Fung*; the former signifying great, the latter wind. Though Bot may not be the name by which Thibet is commonly known in China, it does not appear to me to preclude the possibility of the local name of Bot having received the Chinese affix of *Ta*, as indicative

* The Csoma here referred to by Williams is Csoma de Korosi, a Hungarian who resided several years at Lassa, the capital of Thibet, studying the language. He composed a Thibetian grammar and dictionary, the publication of which he superintended at Calcutta, and, unfortunately, while on the way back to the scene of his philological labours, was overtaken by sickness, which terminated fatally at Darjeeling in 1842. A tombstone in the burial-ground of that remote station, bearing a highly eulogistic inscription, marks his last resting-place.

of the greater division of the country from the lesser, and thus that the two words Ta Bot, corrupted into Thibet, may have been adopted by foreigners as generic for the whole. That there is a subdivision of the country called Great Thibet is supported by the evidence of Csoma de Korosi, who says that the country is divided by the inhabitants into Kham Yul or Eastern Thibet, called also Pot-Chen or Great Thibet, Wei Tsang or Thibet Proper, and Ari or North-western Thibet. In the second place, at Darjeeling, which is one of the great points of rendezvous between the Indo-Chinese races, the word Thibet is unintelligible, though Thibetians abound in the place; the term Bhoteah, however, is generally understood and in no way restricted to the inhabitants of Bhotan. At Darjeeling it is a matter of every-day occurrence at the present time to see groups of men belonging to the Mongolian race in conversation, who, while bearing a general resemblance to each other, nevertheless differ in many respects, such as the mode of wearing the hair, the nature of their garments and dialect. Many of them understand a little Hindoostanee, a knowledge of which is very useful to them in the course of the petty trading transactions in which they are engaged. On going up to groups of this kind, as I have often done, and pointing out a particular man, asking if he is a Bhoteah, the reply may be "Ney Bhoteah, Lepcha;" meaning that the man is not a Thibetian, but a Lepcha, the name by which a Mongolian tribe that forms a large proportion of the population of Sikim Proper, and British Sikim or the Darjeeling territory, is known.*

* The Lepchas and their probable origin will be found more fully alluded to in another part of the work.

Indicating a second man, and enquiring if he is a Bhoteah, the answer may be in the affirmative, and then the interrogator has to find out what Bhoteah he is; one man may be a "Sikim Bhoteah," another a "Nepaul Bhoteah," or Thibetians who have emigrated to and settled in these countries; while a third may be a "Dhurma Bhoteah," or inhabitant of Bhotan Proper; so called from the country being presided over by an ecclesiastical ruler known as the Dhurma Raja. Another of the group may admit himself a Bhoteah, but deny belonging to any of these countries, and reply, "Cheen Ka Bot;" meaning that he is a Bhoteah of China, or what we call a Thibetian. In the group there may be one or more other men, who, though quite distinct from the natives of Hindoostan, still are equally distinct from the Lepchas and the different classes of the Bhoteahs. Their features are decidedly those of the Malay race, and they are known under the generic name of Paharees, or hill-men. They may be either natives of Nepaul, or a cross between them and the Bengalee. Many of them, no doubt, are sprung from the aborigines of that portion of the Himalayan range which is now inhabited chiefly by Mongolian tribes.

Having thus shown the wide signification locally attached to the term Bhoteah, I shall in the course of the ensuing narrative avoid using it, and in lieu thereof substitute Bhotanese, as distinctive of the inhabitants of Bhotan.*

* In explanation of the mode adopted by me of spelling this word, I may as well state that it is based on no rule whatever. I have merely adopted it from observing that it is the one most commonly followed in modern maps and atlases, and therefore the one most familiar to European geographers, and quite as correct as Bootan, the other way in which the

With respect to the early history of Bhotan we have little or no reliable information, what is known on the subject being for the most part traditional and hurriedly acquired in the course of the diplomatic relations which the Government of India has, on two occasions within the last twenty-five years, unsuccessfully endeavoured to establish with the Bhotanese Government. The latest and most detailed account we have is that contained in the Report of the Honourable Ashley Eden, the failure of whose mission to Bhotan, in 1864, led to the military operations that will hereafter be referred to. According to the data furnished Mr. Eden, Bhotan has not been in the possession of Thibetians for much more than two centuries, and is stated to have belonged to a tribe that the Bhotanese call Tephoo, who are believed to have been the people of Cooch Behar. Of the conquest of the Tephoo territory (Bhotan), and the establishment therein of an organised form of government, Mr. Eden gives the following account—

"About two hundred years ago some Thibetian sepoys were sent from Kampa* by the orders of the Lassa Government to look at the country; a fight ensued; the Tephoos gave way and went down to the plains, with the exception of a few who remained in

word is usually spelt. I have adopted the same principle with reference to the word Sikim, and shall adhere to it throughout the narrative, except where it appears as a quotation.

* Kampa is the name given to that portion of Thibet lying between the southern bank of the Tsan Po River and the snowy ridges which separate it from the northern limit of Bhotan. According to Pemberton, it is the portion of Thibet to which the knowledge of the Bhotanese is almost entirely confined, as he could discover few people in the country who had visited Lassa.

a menial capacity with the Bhoteahs, and whose descendants are to be found still holding the lowest offices about the forts, and their appearance clearly indicates their plains origin. The Kampa sepoys took such a fancy to the country that they refused to return, and, remaining, formed a little colony without organisation or government. After a time they were visited by a travelling Lama from Lassa, named Sheptoon La-pha. He acquired great influence over the little colony, and they eventually made him their king, under the title of Dhurma Raja. He was a good and wise ruler, kept the country in good order, was beneficent to his subjects, and was supported entirely by voluntary contributions. There was at this time in a monastery of Kain, to the south-east of Lassa, a certain Lama named Farchoo Doopgein Sheptoon; he was a very religious man, but was not bound by vows of celibacy, and had a large family. A few years after the election of Sheptoon La-pha to be Dhurma Raja, Doopgein went to Lassa to see his tutor and religious guide, but on arriving there found he was dead. The other disciples of the deceased Lama told him that, just before dying, he had said, 'Tell my disciple, Farchoo Doopgein, that if he journeys to the Lah-Lumpa (south country) he will become a great man.' He accordingly came to the conclusion that the south country must be Bootan, and went there and settled down quietly. By degrees he acquired a great reputation for piety and learning, people flocked to him, and his wishes were more cared for than those of the Dhurma Raja, Sheptoon La-pha. La-pha began to fear that the people would dethrone him and place Doopgein on the throne, and so he wrote him a letter requesting him to leave the country. Doopgein refused. On this the Dhurma Raja sent him an order banishing him from the country, on the ground that a married Lama was a scandal to the religion of Buddh. This letter he sent by a one-eyed messenger, a proceeding which, according to the Thibetian notions of etiquette, is a gross insult. Doopgein, however, interpreted it otherwise, and sent back the following message to him: 'You have tried to insult me by sending me a message by a one-eyed man; but I see a good omen in this—it clearly indicates that you will soon have difficulty in seeing the country you now govern.' This was taken as a declaration of war. Doopgein claimed the Rajaship, the people flocked to him, and La-pha was abandoned by his followers, and, being reduced to starvation, ran away into Thibet to a place called Kongoo.* . . . . Doopgein Sheptoon was the only good ruler the Booteahs ever had. It was he who built the forts of Angdu Forung, Poonakh, and lastly, Paro. He made a code of laws for the protection of the ryots (agricultural peasantry), forbidding the levy of anything beyond voluntary contributions. He appointed Penlows and Jungpens (governors respectively of provinces and forts) to administer the country, but kept them under control, and limited the number of their followers to twenty-five for each chief.†

* According to the traditionary account from which the above is taken, Sheptoon La-pha was well received at Kongoo by some Thibetian merchants, who assessed themselves in a fixed sum annually for his support, in consideration of services he had rendered them while in Bhotan by facilitating their communication with Bengal.

† The same tradition states that—" When Doopgein Sheptoon became Dhurma Raja, he separated from his family; their descendants are still distinguished as the clan of Chu-jē, the chief family of Lamas in Bhotan.

The next Dhurma Raja, considering that temporal and spiritual powers were incompatible, confined himself entirely to the latter, and appointed a Dewan or Vizier to wield the former. This Dewan by degrees became the Deb Raja and temporal ruler of Bootan. There is no further trace of the history of Bootan till some eighty or ninety years ago, when a certain Deb, Jeedah, distinguished himself by his aggressive foreign policy."

The account here given of the origin of the Bhotan Government was obtained by Mr. Eden from Cheeboo Lama, whose information, it is stated, was derived from books from Thibetian monasteries. Cheeboo Lama is a native of Sikim, of the Lepcha tribe, who, though a priest by profession, resides at Darjeeling as the political representative of the Sikim Raja, with whom the British Government is at present on friendly terms. He accompanied Mr. Eden's mission to Bhotan as Thibetian interpreter. From some little personal knowledge, however, I have of him, I should not feel inclined to place implicit reliance on the correctness of information furnished by him on matters

They are up to the present time exempted from all taxation and payment of revenue, and are entitled to special marks of distinction on entering any of the forts; they manage all the affairs of the Dhurma Raja. When Lama Doopgein Sheptoon died he said that if his body was preserved he would reappear again in Bhotan. His body is to the present day kept in the Fort of Poonakh, in a silver tomb called Sheptoon Machee (or the first Sheptoon), and tea and rice are daily put into the tomb. Three years after the death of Doopgein, his incarnation reappeared at Lassa in the person of a little child, who, before it ought to have been able to speak, announced itself as the Dhurma Raja of Bhotan. It was brought in great state to Bhotan, and having had the late Raja's cooking utensils put before it, and similar articles belonging to other persons, it identified the Raja's property, thus satisfactorily establishing its own identity as the promised incarnation."

relating to local history or philology; having found his statements on certain points, connected with these subjects, that he might have been supposed to be quite competent to give a reliable opinion upon, altogether wrong. There are several inconsistencies in what he has stated to Mr. Eden, amongst others, that the Thibetian sepoys should have made the travelling Lama their ruler under the title of Dhurma Raja, the words being of purely Hindoostanee origin, and their meaning, "The King of Virtue"—the Thibetian language being at the same time as distinct from the Hindoostanee as the latter is from the English. It may have been that it was by terms synonymous in Thibetian to Dhurma Raja in Hindoostanee that Sheptoon La-pha was raised to the sovereignty of Bhotan—still that such was the case is not stated.*

* The following extract from the Travels of Ralph Fitch, a merchant of London, who in the year 1583 visited Bengal, is interesting, from showing that at that time the country we now call Bhotan was in the possession of Thibetians, and also that the term Bhoteah was then in use as well as the Hindoostanee word Dhurma as indicative of the Ruler of Bhotan:—"There is a country four days' journey from Cuch or Quichue, before mentioned, which is called Bootanter and the city Bhoteah; the king is called Durmain, the people whereof are very tall and strong; and there are merchants which come out of China, and they say out of Muscovia or Tartary, and they come to buy [sell?] musk, cambals, agates, silk, pepper, and saffron of Persia. The country is very great—three months' journey. There are very high mountains in this country, and one of them is so steep that when six days' journey off it he may see it perfectly. Upon these mountains are people which have ears of a span long; if their ears be not long they call them apes. They say that when they be upon the mountains they see ships in the sea sailing to and fro; but they know not whence they come nor whither they go. There are merchants which come out of the east, they say from under the sun, which is from China, which have no beards; and they say there it is something warm. But those who have come from the other side of the mountains, which is from the north, say there it is very cold. The northern merchants are apparelled with woollen cloth and hats, white

Considering these inconsistencies, and the absurdities connected with the incarnation of the Doopgein Sheptoon, which are circumstantially detailed by Cheeboo, I am inclined to think that, in the absence of specific data on which to form a judgment, the following brief notice of the subject in the account given by Captain Pemberton of his mission to Bhotan in 1838 is likely to be found the more correct—

"There is a tradition current in Bootan that the country was once ruled by Thibetian officers resident in it, and that all the palaces and castles now occupied by the Deb and Dhurma Rajas, Penlows, and Jungpens were originally constructed by Chinese and Thibetian architects for the accommodation of those provincial governors; but that after holding the country for some time, and finding it totally unprofitable, the officers were withdrawn, and the Booteahs were allowed to govern themselves; still, however, agree-

hozen close, and boots which be of Muscovia or Tartary. They report that in their country they have very good horses, but they be little; some men have four, five, or six hundred horses or kine; they live with milk and flesh. They cut the tails of their kine, and sell them very dear, for they be in great request and much esteemed in those parts: the hair of them is a yard long. They use to hang them for bravery upon the heads of their elephants; they be much used in Pegu and China; they buy and sell by scores upon the ground. The people are very swift on foot." This description of the trade between Thibet, Bhotan, and Bengal closely resembles what it is at the present day, and from the reference made to Cooch Behar, it may be inferred that in those days it was the place where the traders chiefly assembled. Fitch's travels are contained in Hakluyt's Collection of Voyages, and he seems to have been engaged in the Levant trade, and to have reached India *viâ* Tripoli, Syria, Ormuz, and thence to Goa. After a short residence amongst the Portuguese, he sailed to Bengal, Pegu, Siam, and Molucca, visiting the island of Ceylon and the cities of Cochin and Calicut; he then returned to Ormuz, whence he proceeded overland to Tripoli, where embarking he reached England in 1591.

CHEEBOO LAMA.

[From a Photograph taken at Darjeeling in May 1865.]

ing to the payment of an annual tribute, and recognising the continued supremacy of the Emperor of China in secular, and that of the Delai (Grand) Lama in spiritual, affairs. The style of these buildings, which unites the peculiarities of Thibetian and Chinese architecture, greatly tends to confirm this current belief; and that the Thibetian influence did extend far more to the southward between the seventh and tenth centuries than it has done since is proved from a fact mentioned by Monsieur Landress in the introduction to the translation made by him and Messrs. Klaproth and Abel Remusat of the Chinese work Foe-Koue-Ki, where, speaking of the Thibetians, he says that 'during the Tsang dynasty, from the seventh to the commencement of the tenth century, they issued forth as conquerors from their original limits; waged an almost incessant war against China; and following the course of their rivers, which issuing from the south-eastern corner of their valleys opened a route to India, extending their conquests in this direction to the Bay of Bengal, to which they gave the name of the Thibetian Sea.' At what period the withdrawal from Bootan took place I have not the means of forming a probable conjecture; but it appears quite certain from the result of the enquiries made during my residence in the country, that the power of China is regarded with considerable respect by the authorities in Bootan, and a very marked deference is shown to the supposed views and wishes of the authorities resident in Lassa, both Chinese and Thibetian."

With reference to the existence at the present day of direct political relations between the Bhotanese and the Governments of China and Thibet, there is no proof that the former actually takes place, while it is equally certain that the latter does, though to no very important extent. On this point Mr. Eden states—"To Thibet Bootan is nominally subject, but the Thibetians avoid all intercourse with their unruly tributaries. Every year a formal feudatory payment of a fee as acknowledgment of subjection, consisting of a few pieces of cloth, silk, and some rice is made; but if the Bhotanese omitted to send the annual instalment, it is pretty certain that the Thibetians would not take the trouble to remind them of the omission; for the presentation of this tribute is made the excuse for a series of robberies and outrages of various sorts in Thibet by the party of Booteahs who escort it. So violent are these men in their conduct, that for years past it has been customary to disarm all Booteahs sent to Lassa, and for the last few years the Thibetians have made the Booteahs deliver their tribute on the frontier. No Thibetian official or trader ever trusts himself across the Bootan frontier, and their relations with the country generally are in a very unsatisfactory footing. The Thibetians invariably refuse to aid the Booteahs in any of their wars." Though the Bhotanese do not procure military assistance from the Thibetian Government, either secretly or overtly, as far as we know, nevertheless, from facts which have lately come to my knowledge, and to which reference will be made hereafter, there is considerable reason to doubt their not having lately received aid from within the Thibetian frontier.*

* According to the following remarks by Captain Pemberton, the relations of Bhotan with China and Thibet would appear to have been, a few years ago, of a much more intimate nature than the above extract

In theory there is said to be an excellent system of government in Bhotan, while in practice there is little or none. As the Government now exists, there is no doubt that it has two nominal heads, known to us and to the neighbouring hill-tribes under the Hindoostanee names of the Dhurma and the Deb Rajas,* though called by other names, as I am given to understand, by the Bhotanese themselves. The former is the spiritual head, the latter the temporal one. The theory of government, in fact, is framed somewhat on the same principle as now exists in Japan, which is ruled over by a spiritual king (the Mikado), who is not supposed to interfere in temporal matters, but to leave them to the care of a chief executive

from Mr. Eden's report would imply. Captain Pemberton states:—"The only occasion on which anything approaching to regular communication takes place is once a year, when orders are received from Lassa; on this occasion, it is said, messengers arrive bearing an imperial mandate from China addressed to the Deb and Dhurma Rajas of Bootan, and the Penlows and Jungpens under their orders. It is written on fine cambric in large letters, and generally contains instructions to be careful in the government of the country, to quell promptly all internal tumult or rebellion, and to report immediately, on pain of the infliction of a heavy fine, any apprehended invasion from external foes. A reply is despatched by special messengers who are always attended by twenty-three coolies bearing loads of a particularly fine description of rice grown in Assam, and called Malbhoge; other goods to the estimated value of 3,000 rupees per annum are also sent, consisting principally of Assam erendi silks, of a white ground with red borders, six cubits long and three broad; cotton cloths, twelve cubits long and three broad; and choora, made of a very fine rice grown in Assam." On one of these occasions it is stated that the orders contained in the imperial mandate were neglected, and a fine equal to five thousand rupees was in consequence imposed on the Bhotan Government, which was paid by three instalments in three years.

* While, as already mentioned, Dhurma Raja in Hindoostanee means the King of Virtue, the word Deb is a corruption of Dev, which, in the same language, is the Deity himself.

officer—the Tycoon. In Bhotan, however, the relative position of the temporal ruler differs from that of the Tycoon in Japan; the Tycoon possessing real power, while the Deb Raja is believed to have none—at least at the present day, as our latest intercourse with his Government has fully established.

The Dhurma and Deb Rajas are supposed to be aided in conducting the affairs of state by a ministerial Council styled the Lenchen, composed of the following permanent members: The Lam Zimpen, or chief secretary to the Dhurma Raja; the Donnai Zimpen, or prime minister; the Tassishujung, the Poonakha, and Angdu Forung Jungpens, or the governors respectively of the forts of Tassishujung, Poonakha, and Angdu Forung; the Deb Zimpen, or chief secretary to the Deb Raja; and the Joom Kalling, or chief judge.

In addition to the foregoing seven ordinary members of the Lenchen, there are three extraordinary members who attend council when they happen to be at the seat of government, and who are liable to be called on to attend at any period of emergency. These are the Paro, the Tongso, and the Daka Penlows—the governors respectively of Western, Eastern, and Central Bhotan. When they are present, the Council receives the collective title of Chenlah.

The Dhurma Raja is looked upon by the Bhotanese in the same light as the Grand Lama of Thibet is viewed by his subjects, namely, as a perpetual incarnation of the Deity, or Buddha himself in a corporeal form. During the interval between his death and reappearance, or, more properly speaking, until he has reached an age sufficiently mature to ascend his spiritual throne, the office of Dhurma Raja is filled by proxy from amongst the priesthood.* The first signs of the reappearance of the Dhurma Raja are supposed to be indicated by the child refusing his mother's milk and displaying a preference for that of the cow. He is also supposed to articulate a few words distinctly and convey his meaning in an intelligible manner by certain signs. As soon as the news of these miraculous indications reach the court, a deputation composed of the principal Lama priests proceed to the spot where the young Dhurma is reported to have reappeared, taking with them all the articles that in his former state of existence he had been in the habit of using. These are spread before

* On comparing the accounts given by Captain Pemberton and Mr. Eden respecting the manner in which the officiating Dhurma Raja is appointed, I find that a very marked discrepancy exists between them. The former states: "The Dhurma Raja, like his great prototype of Lassa (the Grand Lama), is supposed to be Buddh himself, clothed in human form, and by successive transmigrations from one corporeal frame to another, to escape the ordinary lot of humanity. On the death or temporary withdrawal of the Dhurma from the sublunary scene of his existence, his office remains vacant for a twelvemonth, during which time the senior Gylong, or priest, regulates the religious observances of the country." Whereas the latter states: "The Dhurma Raja succeeds by incarnation. During the interval between his death and re-appearance, or rather until he has arrived at years of discretion after his last birth, the office is held by a spiritual chief named Lam Thepoo. This officer is supposed to be the incarnation of one Choler Tigou, who had, a century ago, claimed to be the avatar (representative) of the body of Doopgein Sheptoon, whilst the Dhurma Raja was the avatar of his spirit. The two avatars fought a pitched battle, and after much loss of life they came to a compromise, Choler Tigou, under the name Lam Thepoo, being made head of the Lamas, and being allowed a perpetual regency through his avatars, during the periodical disappearance from this world of the Dhurma Raja, while the Dhurma Raja remained supreme spiritual head of the country." The Dhurma Raja who was officiating at the time of Mr. Eden's visit to Poonakha is believed to have been the Lam Thepoo, and not the true incarnation.

the child, mixed up with some others made to resemble them, with the view of testing the infallibility of the newly-born deity, who, as a matter of course, always selects the proper ones; and the priests declare their conviction that he is their former spiritual head, and convey the child with great ceremony to Poonakha, at which place all installations of either the Dhurma or the Deb Rajas must be made, otherwise they are not valid. At the period of Captain Pemberton's visit, the Dhurma was a child of nine years of age, whereas, on the recent occasion of Mr. Eden's mission, the office was filled by a shy-looking youth of eighteen, who was a mere puppet with whom the form of consultation was not even gone through by the Council. He was officiating until the reappearance of one who died in 1861.

The Deb Raja is supposed to be elected by the council of permanent ministers, and to be chosen from amongst the principal officers of the country, who are eligible for seats in the Council. At the present day, however, in practice the government of the country has fallen in reality into the hands of the Penlows of Eastern and Western Bhotan, who are usually at war with one another, and the Deb, now merely the nominee of whichever of the two happens to be for the time the most powerful—though in theory they (the Penlows) are supposed to be nominated by the Deb—the practice, however, being that they fight their way to power. The Deb Raja is consequently a mere puppet who exercises no influence whatever in Government matters. Mr. Eden observes—"There are generally some three or four Debs or ex-Debs in the country. The Paro Penlow nominates a Deb and places him on the throne; a few months afterwards the Tongso

Penlow ejects him and substitutes his own puppet. He is in his turn ejected by the Paro Penlow, and so this perpetual struggle goes on, and has gone on without interruption for the last fifty years. Bhotan has not known within that period an interval of six months' peace and freedom from civil war; at least so say the agricultural classes, and their statement is entirely borne out by such knowledge as we have of the affairs of the country."

Though there are nominally three Penlows, the one who is supposed to govern Central Bhotan has, now-a-days, no influence of any kind. Formerly he was an official of authority, but the successive ministries have by degrees so pruned his territory, that it is now reduced to an insignificant extent, and consists of a small tract of barren hill-land to the south of Paro; the headquarters of the Penlow of Western Bhotan. The Tongso and Paro Penlows exercise the power of life and death, and are virtually independent, though they admit a sort of nominal subordination to the Deb Raja, while actually they care nothing for any orders that either he or the council may issue. They generally commence their public careers as common soldiers; and, by distinguishing themselves for the diplomatic talents which, according to Mr. Eden, lead to most speedy advancement in Bhotan—namely, fraud and treachery—gradually rise through the various subordinate grades, until they reach the office of Zimpen or Chief Secretary to the Penlow they are serving under. By this time they usually have their chiefs so completely in their power as to render it an easy matter for them to secure the succession to the office for themselves; for instance, when the one Penlow finds himself hard pressed by the other, it is common for him to promise his Zimpen, that, if he will get him out of the trouble, he will retire in his favour within a certain fixed period. Should some such opportunity not offer, and the Zimpen see no other mode of getting promotion, he does not scruple, it is alleged, either to murder or depose his master: it was in the latter way that the Paro and Tongso Penlows in power at the period of Mr. Eden's mission attained their positions. A certain proportion of the revenues they draw from their territories is paid to the Council; but it is stated to be done more from a superstitious dread that the Lama priests might starve were it withheld, than from any sense of subordination or duty.

Next in importance to the Penlows are the Jungpens; the word being derived from *jung*, a fort, and *pen*, a keeper or governor. By us they are usually called Soubahs, a corruption of a Hindoostanee word. These Jungpens are appointed by the Penlows usually from amongst their own followers; and, as a natural consequence, any change in the Penlowship is accompained by a corresponding change of all the subordinate district officers. The Paro Penlow, for instance, had under him in the Dooars, until our recent occupation of them, the Jungpen or Soubah of Dhalimkote, who managed the district bordering on the frontiers of Sikim Proper, of British Sikim (Darjeeling) and on the Julpigorie frontier, the river Teesta separating the whole;—also the Katma of Mynagoorie, who until lately managed the Dooar of that name, belonging to Bhotan, about nine miles from the British frontier at Julpigorie. When a Penlow has been overthrown, his subordinates who have been ejected with him take up their quarters in the neighbourhood of the forts or other places over which they have held jurisdiction; and, coincident with the attempt being made to turn out the ruling Penlow, a similar attempt is made by the ex-Jungpens to oust his followers from the forts. The three Jungpens who have seats in council, namely, those of Poonakha, Tassishujung and Angdu Forung, have independent charges, and rank nearly as high as the Penlows, though they exercise but little power.

The officers immediately subordinate to the Jungpens are the Nieboos. They act as their deputies; and are the class of men who, while employed in charge of small stockades in the Dooars (where they usually go under the name of Katmas), have, by organizing raids into our territory, brought about hostilities between the British Government and Bhotan.

It is clear from the sketch I have endeavoured to give of the present state of government in Bhotan, collected from the report chiefly of Mr. Eden, that in reality none whatever exists; the country being portioned off into two great and several small divisions, for the possession of which continuous struggles are being carried on by successive adventurers, the claims of one being apparently as good as those of the other, and hence might, as it were, legitimately occupies the place of right. In reference to this point, Mr. Eden remarks—"There is no man in the country who is capable of making his authority felt by any other man, and there is no man in authority whose office, or even his life, is worth one year's purchase: it is therefore futile to suppose that we can, by any agreement, or treaty, or promise, secure the good neighbourhood of the Bootanese; for however, well disposed towards us the people actually making an engagement might be, their word would not be held binding by the officials generally, and it is a matter of certainty that a term of three years would see every man in office changed." I myself am inclined to think that the absence of any systematic form of government in Bhotan admits of explanation by reference to the tradition already mentioned, relating to the country having been formerly ruled over by a provincial Government appointed from Thibet, but which was withdrawn in consequence of the unremunerating character of the possession; and that a colonial Government, in imitation of that of the mother country, was formed by those who remained, but which, from some cause unknown, they would seem gradually to have become unable to conduct according to the principles which usually constitute an established system of government. Most probably it is to the want of any legitimate mode of succession to supreme rank in the country, that the utter disorganisation into which the government of Bhotan has gradually fallen is to be traced; and I incline to the opinion, that, but for the direct authority exercised over it by China, the ecclesiastical government of Thibet, would, ere this, have assumed a similar chaotic state.

Where such a state of government exists as is now found in Bhotan, the revenue and judicial systems must necessarily be in a very imperfect condition. With respect to the former, it is chiefly obtained from contributions furnished respectively by the Bengallee inhabitants of the Dooars, and the people of Bhotan Proper. Mr. Eden has thus epitomised the manner of collecting it—"The only limit on the demand being the natural limit of the power of the official to extort more;" while with reference to the latter he states—"The Bootanese have no laws, either written or of usage. Where there are no rights of property, and the hereditary system is unknown, there is no need of civil law; and where crime is the only claim to distinction and honour, there can be no criminal law. There is no police.* The Jungpens are supposed to exercise powers of life and death, but these powers are only used for purposes of extortion. No one dares to complain of an offence, for if the person charged pays a sufficient bribe he is sure of obtaining his revenge by having his accuser heavily fined and probably robbed of all his possessions. For robbing the goods of a Penlow or Jungpen, or plotting against his life, a man is sometimes capitally punished. This is done by placing him on a drop projecting over the river; he is allowed here any indulgence he wishes,

* Mr. Eden, though the latest authority on Bhotan, can hardly be expected to be the most impartial—personal insult and political failure being fresh in his recollection at the period of his writing his report, and I think a tendency is sometimes apparent in the document to overstate Bhotanese defects. For instance, though in the above extract he states—"There is no police," he himself adduces evidence in the course of his report that police do exist in the country, inasmuch as he alludes to several disputes which the members of his Mission had with a police official in charge of the market-place at Paro (see chapter v.). It would seem doubtful, also, whether the Bhotanese mode of collecting their revenue from the Dooars was so unsystematic as Mr. Eden's notice of it implies; because, since our recent annexation of them, it has been determined, in the first instance, to continue collecting it in the same manner as the inhabitants had been accustomed to under Bhotanese rule. This remark may possibly induce the reader to suspend his judgment of the Bhotanese as a people generally, until he has perused the whole narrative: towards its termination will be found some statements, the result of observation during the recent hostilities, calculated in some degree to modify the unfavourable impression conveyed in Mr. Eden's account.

however immoral it may be, and the indulgence which is customary on the occasion is of the most indecent description. His hands are then tied, and he is dropped into the river. The only jails in the country are the dungeons under the forts, in which political offenders are confined, and in which ryots are locked up when undergoing a process of extortion." The only code of laws Bhotan appears ever to have possessed is that referred to as having been drawn up by Doopgein Sheptoon for the protection of the agricultural peasantry; but beyond the assertion that it once existed, nothing now-a-days is known of it. The only trace of anything relating to laws now remaining pertain to etiquette, such, for instance, as that a man must not pass a certain place on horseback, or appear with the head covered within a certain distance of a fort.

From what has been already stated in connexion with the circumstances under which one Dhurma Raja succeeds the other, it will have been understood that the form of Buddhism, presided over by the Grand Lama of Thibet, is the faith practised by the Bhotanese. Their religious exercises, however, are for the most part confined to the propitiation of evil spirits, and the routine recital of a few stereotyped sacred sentences; also a mechanical form of praying by a process analogous to that of telling the beads.*

The language spoken by the Bhotanese is a dialect of the Thibetian, more or less intermixed with words

* Rotatory cylinders made of metal constitute the mechanism usually employed. They are of various sizes, some being small, admitting of being carried in the hand like a child's toy, while others are ponderous fixtures in temples and forts.

from the languages of the countries near it. On the southern frontier of Bhotan many words and idioms have been adopted from the Assamese, Bengallee and Hindoostani, while on the northern frontier the dialect is said to be nearly pure Thibetian.

The military resources of Bhotan have hitherto been considered very insignificant: no properly organised force or semblance of a regular army having been seen, with the exception of a few hundred men who are kept as guards about the different forts. Their arms consist of matchlocks, jingals, bows and arrows, heavy straight swords, and large knives. Catapults are also used, and stones of considerable size thrown by them. Some of the Bhotanese soldiers wear chain armour, while others wear heavy iron helmets of a semi-globular shape, padded inside with quilted cotton, and generally having a flap of the same material attached to the back part, and hanging down behind, thus affording a not indifferent protection to the neck against the effects of a sword cut. Those who are in attendance on officers of the higher grades usually carry circular shields made of thick buffalo hide well varnished and studded with brass knobs, and bound by a strong rim of the same metal. The Bhotanese have heretofore been looked upon as a very contemptible enemy: events, however, which have transpired in the course of our recent experience on the Bhotan frontier have tended to show that the estimate formed of their military resources and individual courage has been on the whole undeservedly low.

Having thus given a general description of what the Bhotan government is, I shall reserve such remarks as I have to make connected with the appearance of the country, its cultivation and products, the manners and customs of its people, &c., until I come to that part of the narrative referring to my personal knowledge of it, and shall now proceed to lay before the reader an account of the history of British intercourse with Bhotan, some acquaintance with which is indispensable to the right understanding of the train of events which have gradually embroiled us in a war with the country.

CHAPTER II.

Commencement of British Intercourse with the Bhotanese—Invasion of Cooch Behar by the latter—Hostile Measures taken by the East India Company—The Regent of Thibet intercedes for the Bhotanese A Treaty concluded—The Governor-General of India sends a Mission to Thibet *viâ* Bhotan under Mr. Bogle—Its Progress, Reception, and Result—A second Mission under Captain Turner sent to Thibet—An Envoy from Bhotan visits Calcutta—Invasion of Thibet by the Nepaulese—Retributive Measures adopted by the Emperor of China —Intercourse with Thibet closed—Dispute with Bhotan about the Bijnee Raja—Visit of Kishen Kant Bose to Bhotan.

British intercourse with Bhotan commenced in 1772, prior to which period there is nothing on record to show that we had any political relations with the country. In that year, however, the Bhotanese invaded Cooch Behar,* which state became a dependency of the East India Company's Government shortly after its sovereignty was established in Bengal, and carried off the Raja and his brother, intending to govern the country by a ruler of their own. The Cooch Behar family applied to the Government of India for aid, which was granted; and a small force, consisting of four companies of sepoys and two guns, under the command of Captain Jones, proceeded to the town of Cooch Behar, then in the possession of the Bhotanese. This little force took the town by storm, and not only

* The native state of Cooch Behar is situated on the north-eastern frontier between Bengal and Assam. It is separated from the highlands of Bhotan by the Dooars, and is still ruled over by its own Raja, subject to the supervision of a British resident.

drove the Bhotanese beyond the frontier, but followed them up across the Dooars, and, entering the hills, captured the forts of Passakha and Dhalimkote, as well as the stockade of Chichacotta, in the Buxa Dooar, near the Cooch Behar frontier, at which latter place a somewhat determined resistance was made.

These successes so pressed the Bhotanese that they immediately applied for assistance to the Thibetian Government, at the time presided over by the Teeshoo Lama,* who was acting as regent during the minority of the Grand or Delai Lama. The Teeshoo Lama responded to their appeal, and addressed a letter, couched in a friendly spirit, to the then Governor-General of India, the celebrated Warren Hastings, requesting a cessation of hostilities against Bhotan, and the restoration of the lands that had been taken possession of. This letter was read in Council on the 29th of March, 1774; and while the Teeshoo Lama characterised the Bhotanese as a rude and ignorant race, who fully deserved punishment, he hinted that they had been sufficiently chastised, and urged that, as Bhotan formed a dependency of Thibet, a prosecution of hostilities against it might irritate the Grand Lama and his subjects against the British Government. The Teeshoo Lama concluded his letter by saying, "I have reprimanded the Deb for his past conduct, and I have admonished him to desist from his evil practices in future, and to be submissive to you in all things. I am persuaded he will conform to the advice I have given him; and it will be necessary for you to treat

* The Teeshoo Lama is the Buddhist official next in rank to the Grand Lama. He resides usually at Teeshoo Loomboo, and rules over the portion of Thibet of which it is the chief town.

him with compassion and clemency. As for my part, I am but an hereditary priest, and it is the custom of my sect, with rosary in our hands, to pray for the welfare of all mankind, and especially for the peace and happiness of the inhabitants of this country; and I do now, with my head uncovered, entreat you will cease from all hostilities against the Deb in future." This letter, which was accompanied by presents to the Governor-General,* produced a very favourable impression; and after some negotiation a treaty of peace was entered into and ratified, on the 25th April 1774, between the Government of India and that of Bhotan.†

The impression produced by the letter of the Teeshoo Lama was not only sufficiently favourable to effect the object for which it was written, but also to create a desire on the part of the Government of India to become more intimately acquainted with its author, as a probable means of establishing extended commercial intercourse. A mission to the Court of the Teeshoo Lama was accordingly organised, and placed under the charge of Mr. George Bogle, "a gentleman of distinguished ability and remarkable equanimity of temper." Mr. Bogle was accompanied by Mr. Hamilton as Medical Attendant, and the mission left Calcutta on the 6th of May 1774, taking with it

* It is stated in Mr. Eden's report, that, "This letter was conveyed to Calcutta by a Hindoostanee pilgrim named Porungher Gossein, who some years later accompanied Captain Turner on his mission to Thibet, and a Thibetian named Paima. They were charged to deliver certain presents to the Governor-General, amongst which were sheets of gilt leather stamped with the Russian eagle, showing that even at that period there was commercial intercourse between Russia and Central Asia."

† A copy of this Treaty will be found in Appendix A.

as presents a selection of philosophical instruments, cloth manufactures of Britain and India, cutlery, hardware, and firearms. These were sent as specimens of the articles our productive industry was capable of furnishing; and to them were added some more valuable tokens of the Governor-General's esteem for the Teeshoo Lama, in the form of strings of pearls, corals, brocades, and shawls.*

Mr. Bogle proceeded through Cooch Behar and entered Bhotan, where he was detained at Tassishujung, its summer capital, for some time, waiting for passports. Thence he went on to the frontier post called Phagri, which separates Bhotan from Thibet, and on the 12th of October, 1774, reached Desheripgay, where the Court of the Teeshoo Lama was at the time established. Mr. Bogle succeeded completely in the objects of his mission, and resided at Desheripgay and Teeshoo Loomboo until April 1775, when he returned to Bengal. He does not seem to have been charged with any political mission to Bhotan, and of his progress through that country and residence in Thibet there are no records amongst the archives of the Government of India, with the exception of a few notices on the trade of Thibet, and a single letter written from Desheripgay, where the Teeshoo Lama was residing in December 1774, and addressed to the Governor of Bengal. This letter represented the Lama's reception of him as most gracious, and testified to his readiness to establish unrestricted commercial intercourse between his subjects and those of Bengal; that the Lama was about to return to his capital of Teeshoo Loomboo, and that he postponed

* Pemberton's Report.

entering into any definite arrangements until his arrival there, when he intended consulting with the resident merchants; also that he had written to the authorities at Lassa on the subject; and that, from the very high estimation in which he appears to have been regarded, there was every prospect of a successful issue to the negotiations.

It would appear that at this time special circumstances tended to invest the Teeshoo Lama with unusual influence. He had discovered the reigning Grand Lama and installed him at Botala, the mountain at Lassa on which the monastery of Potrang-Marbu stands, the ecclesiastical palace of the Grand Lama. He was also known to be a favourite with Kien-lung, the reigning Emperor of China,* from whom he had received many proofs of esteem, and his influence had been materially increased by his being appointed President of the Council of five members, to whom, during the minority of the Grand Lama, the government of the country was entrusted, subject apparently to supervision from Peking, as it is stated that at this time there were two Chinese officers resident at Lassa, who were relieved every three years, and who appeared to exercise considerable control over the proceedings of the Council. The great expectations, however, which had been formed of the results likely to ensue from the success of Mr. Bogle's mission were not realised, in consequence of the deaths of both that gentleman and the Teeshoo Lama: the latter died in 1780 from smallpox at Peking, where he was at the time on a visit.†

* Kien-lung was the Emperor who received Lord Macartney's Embassy to China in 1795.

† No stronger proof can be adduced of the confidence with which Mr.

Even after Teeshoo Lama's death, a spirit of friendly intercourse seems to have been maintained between the Governments of Thibet and India because in 1781 letters were addressed to Warren Hastings by the Regent Teeshoo Lama, and by Soopoon Choomboo, the favourite cupbearer and minister of the deceased Lama, detailing the melancholy circumstances attending his death, and evidently written under the conviction that the Governor-General would fully sympathise with them in the loss they had sustained, and which was thus feelingly expressed by the Regent—"The measure of his existence was filled up, and the lip of the cup of life was overflowed, and he retired from this perishable world to the everlasting mansions on the first day of the month of the Rugjub, in the year of the Hijeree 1194 (5th July, 1780). To us it was as if the heavens had been precipitated on our heads, as if the splendid and glorious orb of day had been converted into utter darkness. The multitude lifted up, on all sides, the voice of sorrow and lamentation; but what availed it? For fortune, treacherous and deceitful, had determined against us, and we all bent down on the knee of funeral affliction, and performed the holy obsequies such as were due. And we now supplicate with an united voice the return of the hour of transmigration; that the bodies may be speedily exchanged, and our departed Lama again be restored to our sight. This is our only object, our sole employment: may the

Bogle had succeeded in inspiring the Teeshoo Lama, than the fact that a short time after his visit, the latter entrusted to him a considerable sum of money to be expended in the erection of a temple on the banks of the Hooghly, immediately opposite Calcutta, for which purpose a piece of land had been granted by the Government of India.

Almighty God, who listeneth to the supplications of his servants, accept our prayers!"* Shortly after the receipt of this communication, intelligence reached Calcutta that the incarnation of the deceased Teeshoo Lama had been effected, and the Governor-General deemed it an eligible opportunity for re-opening direct communications with Thibet; and accordingly a second mission was determined on, for the purpose of conveying the congratulations of the Governor-General on the successful consummation of an event so pregnant with interest to the subjects of the Teeshoo Lama.

This mission was entrusted to Captain Turner, of the Bengal army, who received his instructions on the 9th of January 1783, and left Calcutta shortly afterwards, accompanied by Lieutenant Davis, of the Bengal Engineers, as Surveyor, and Mr. Robert Saunders as Surgeon. The mission traversed the plains of Bengal *viâ* Moorshedabad, Rungpore, and Cooch Behar, and arrived at Chichacotta, a Bhotanese frontier post in the Dooars, on the 11th of May. From this place it followed the same route as Mr. Bogle took in 1774, namely, that through the Buxa Dooar, and reached Tassishujung on the 1st of June, where they were detained some time; permission to proceed nearer towards Thibet being withheld until the Regent Teeshoo Lama had been communicated with. After a delay of upwards of three months, the required authority arrived for the mission to continue its journey through Bhotan to Teeshoo Loomboo, but coupled with the condition that it was not to exceed two officers. This deprived the mission of the ser-

* Turner's Embassy, Appendix, page 450.

vices of Lieutenant Davis, who returned to Bengal. On the 8th of September, 1783, Captain Turner, accompanied by Mr. Saunders, proceeded on his journey, and in due course reached Teeshoo Loomboo, where, according to his report, the important object of establishing an extended commercial intercourse was fully obtained as far as the Regent Teeshoo Lama was capable of granting it. In his official report he states that he found in the Regent "the best disposition for encouraging and assisting, by the authority he possesses, the proposed plans of commercial intercourse; but being neither so able nor decided in his character as the former Lama, he is cautious of avowedly and publicly sanctioning a measure which might possibly raise up some inveterate enemies against him in the Chinese administration." Subsequent events, however, demonstrated that an over-hopeful estimate had been formed by Captain Turner of the probable results of his mission.*

Though Captain Turner's mission, like that of Mr. Bogle's, was undoubtedly one to Thibet—its object being the conveyance of the Governor-General's pro-

* Though, as will be shown hereafter, nothing resulted from this mission, considerable expectations nevertheless were at one time entertained, and which seemed to be based on reasonable grounds, as shown by the fact that in February 1786, a native named Poorungeer, "to whose intelligence and fidelity Captain Turner had previously avowed his obligations," arrived in Calcutta from Thibet; and, in reply to questions put to him by orders of Sir John Macpherson, who was then officiating as Governor-General, it appeared that merchants had already found their way from Bengal to Teeshoo Loomboo, where the markets were represented as being well supplied with English and Indian manufactures. In proof of the estimation in which they were held, it was also stated that the gold dust and silver with which they had been purchased had undergone a considerable fall in exchangeable value in favour of the goods.

fessed satisfaction at hearing of the incarnation of his former correspondent Teeshoo Lama, there is an incidental remark made by Captain Turner in his report, which tends to show that so far back as 1783 questions were arising of a territorial nature, rendering it necessary that political communication should be reopened between the Indian Government and Bhotan. The remark in question occurs at page 79 of his report, when speaking of some Zinkaffs or Bhotanese Government messengers, for whose neglect of orders he was endeavouring to pacify the Deb Raja, and is to the following effect—"Having urged everything that occurred to me in extenuation of their crime, apparently without effect, I was obliged at last to own that the Zinkaffs had yielded to the advice of Mr. Goodlad and myself, and not acted of their own accord. I observed that I had taken upon myself thus much to answer for, being charged with particular despatches from the Governor-General, and entrusted with a confidential communication upon the business of their (the Zinkaffs') mission, which respected the ancient boundary between the Company's Province and Bootan." No records, however, are to be found throwing any light upon the specific nature of the diplomatic instructions Captain Turner would seem to have been charged with to Bhotan; with the exception, that from the few documents remaining to which reference can now be made, it appears that he was authorised to cede, and did cede, to the Bhotan Government the district of Ambaree Fallacottah, which was at the time unquestionably British territory.

Of any further intercourse, political or otherwise, with Bhotan, we have no information until 1787, in which year the Dhurma and Deb Rajas sent the Jungpen of Tassishujung to Calcutta, as an envoy, for the adjustment of certain boundary questions which were a source of dispute between the Bhotanese and the Zemindars (native land proprietors) on the frontier, and which resulted, as shown by an entry in the proceedings of the Collector of Rungpore, in the Government of India directing the district of Jelpaish (now known as Julpesh) to be made over to the Bhotanese. This district, as well as that of Ambaree Fallacottah, ceded in 1784 by Captain Turner, formed a portion of the extensive Zemindaree of Bykantpore, and the justness of their cession, especially of the former, to the Bhotanese, would seem to have been very questionable; inasmuch as, in a report called for by the Government before taking action in the matter, the Collector of Rungpore expressed himself strongly in favour of the right of possession of the Zemindar of Bykantpore, and stated that nothing could be clearer, from documents produced by him, bearing the seal of the Council of Dinagepore, and registered at Calcutta, that the claim of the Deb Raja was unfounded. With reference to this transaction Mr. Eden states—"I am afraid that on this occasion the friendship of the Bootanese was purchased at the expense of the Bykantpore Zemindar, and the unfortunate Bengallee ryots living in these mehals (estates), who were thus practically handed over as serfs to the barbarous rulers of the hill tract to their north, had just cause of complaint in the transfer thus so hastily made." Referring to the testamentary proof placed before Government in favour of the Zemindar of Bykantpore, by the Collector of Rungpore, Mr. Eden continues—"How, in the face of such documents, the Government of the day reconciled it to their sense of justice to give up these lands to the Booteahs is not easy to understand. The Bykantpore Zemindar received a remission of revenue for the lands thus taken from him. Why this remission was made, if it was believed that the mehals really belonged to Bootan, is not clear." From my personal acquaintance with the position of the two estates in question, both of which I have visited, I should say that, at the period under discussion, there could be little doubt that, while Ambaree Fallacottah, from being situated some miles from the west bank of the Teesta, was within the British frontier, there was equally little doubt that Jelpaish, from being about nine miles inland from the eastern bank of the same river, was, at the time, territory subject to the jurisdiction of Bhotan, though no doubt legally possessed by the Zemindar of Bykantpore, as proved by the fact of its being the site of the ancestral temple of the Bykantpore family.

I now come to the consideration of the circumstances which led to the hopes entertained of commercial intercourse with Thibet through Bhotan, consequent on Bogle's and Turner's missions, being doomed to disappointment. About the year 1790, a refugee priest from Lassa, named Sumhur Lama, visited Nepaul, and by an exaggerated account of the wealth contained in the palace of the Teeshoo Lama at Teeshoo Loomboo, so excited the cupidity of the ruler of that country, then known as the Goorkha Raja, that in 1791 he despatched a force, consisting, it is said, of 18,000 men, into Thibet, for the purpose of plundering the monastery referred to, which object it effected.

On intelligence of this aggression and sacrilege reaching the Emperor of China (Kien-lung), an envoy was sent by him to the Court of Nepaul demanding satisfaction for the injuries inflicted, an indemnity equal to 5,200,000*l.* sterling for the property plundered, the surrender of Sumhur Lama, and the liberation of a Wuzeer of Lassa, who had been carried away captive by the Nepaulese army on its return from invading Thibet. The demands of the Emperor of China were refused, and his ambassador treated with indignity. On the latter returning to Peking, and narrating the unsuccessful result of his mission, an army amounting to 70,000 men was despatched, which entered Nepaul in two divisions, and after repeatedly defeating the Goorkha (Nepaulese) forces, arrived at within twenty miles of Khatmandoo, the capital.* The Nepaulese Raja, now thoroughly worsted, applied to Lord Cornwallis, then Governor-General of India, for assistance; and at the same time the Grand Lama wrote begging that none might be granted, and entered into a narrative of the unprovoked outrage through which the Nepaulese had brought upon themselves the chastisement they were receiving from the Emperor of China. Lord Cornwallis declined to afford material aid, but offered to mediate—a proposal, however, out of which nothing came, as the Nepaulese submitted to the terms of the Chinese commander.

The practical results of this invasion of Nepaul are thus described by Captain Pemberton—"The Chinese forces, after reducing the Nepaulese to submission, retired to Teeshoo Loomboo and Lassa, establishing a chain of military posts, however, along

* Kirkpatrick's Nepaul, Appendix No. 2, page 347.

the whole southern frontier of Thibet, and giving the most unequivocal proof of their determination openly to assume the sovereignty of a country which had for years been virtually subject to their rule." After referring to a statement made by Captain Turner, to the effect that the Chinese military occupation extended into Sikim, but the correctness of which appears to be doubtful, Captain Pemberton goes on to say—"Whether the frontier posts extended into Sikim or not is, however, of little consequence. The great object of prohibiting all intercourse between the inhabitants of British India and the extensive tribes who dwell in the lofty regions of Thibet was then effectually accomplished." Thus ceased the attempts which had been made by the Government of India, between the years 1774 and 1784, to open and preserve direct intercourse with Thibet through Bhotan.

While such were the political relations of China, Thibet, and Nepaul, about the same time, namely 1792, the Indian Government found itself again embroiled with that of Bhotan, the latter having shown a determination, if possible, to exercise a controlling influence in the affairs of Bijnee, a small state, the Raja of which was nominally under the protection of both the British and Bhotan Governments. The Bijnee throne had become vacant by the assassination of the—Raja, Novindra Narrain, and, without any reference to the Governor-General of India, the Bhotan authorities appointed a successor. The Indian Government ordered an investigation, the results of which established the fact that the right of nomination unquestionably rested with it. The Government of India, however, for some reason or other which does not appear, did not press its claim, and allowed the nominee of the Bhotan Government to retain the Rajaship.

Coeval with the closing of Thibet to enterprise from Bengal, a similar cessation of intercourse with Bhotan would seem to have taken place for nearly a quarter of a century, as there is no record of any event of importance having characterised the relations of the Indian and Bhotan Governments from the period of the Bijnee dispute until 1815. In that year a native official, named Baboo Kishenkant Bose, was deputed by Mr. David Scott, the judge of Rungpore, on whose establishment he was, to the Deb Raja, for the purpose of arranging some fresh boundary disputes with Bhotan. The appointment of this native gentleman as envoy was made with the sanction of Government. He entered Bhotan from the Assam frontier, going from Goalpara to Bijnee, thence to Sidlee and Cherrung, and from there up the valley of the Patchoo Matchoo Rivers to Poonakha. Kishenkant Bose wrote an account of his observations while in Bhotan, a portion of which was translated and published in the fifteenth volume of the 'Asiatic Researches'; but of the special results of his mission I have been unable to find any record.* A good deal of information was collected

* As a proof of the ignorance at the time existing in Calcutta with reference to Bhotan, Captain Pemberton cites the fact that, in Hamilton's East India Gazette, a publication founded on official documents, Kishenkant Bose is represented as having been deputed to Lassa by the Bengal Government, to negotiate some boundary arrangements with the Deb Raja, but which he could not effect in consequence of being unable to get further than Bhotan, where he was detained about a year. From this it would seem that time had so dimmed the recollection of our previous intercourse with Thibet, as to obscure the fact that the Grand Lama, and not the Deb Raja, was the reigning power at Lassa.

by him, some of which, however, is of very questionable accuracy; Kishenkant having been either somewhat ready in booking as facts statements told him in joke by the inhabitants, or else slightly prone to draw on his own imagination. For instance, he states—"In Bhotan lightning does not descend from the clouds as in Bengal, but rises from the earth. This was not actually seen, but the holes in the earth were inspected, and it is universally reported to be the case by the inhabitants. In Bootan it never thunders, nor do the clouds ever appear of a black colour, but merely resemble mist. The rain which falls is also exceedingly fine." Whatever may have been the state of the meteorology of Bhotan in 1815, that the rain fell in torrents in 1865, and that thunder and lightning occurred in the ordinary way, I had sufficient experience during the short time I was in the country.

Though the illustration just given shows that all Kishenkant Bose's statements are not of a reliable character, the following sketch of the state of government is not unlikely to have been a correct one, being in some respects in accordance with what has been more recently ascertained. He states—"The Booteahs enjoy the revenues of their country by mutual concurrence in the following manner. They first become Zinkaffs or Poes (messengers or soldiers), then Tumas, then Zimpes under the Pillos (Penlows) or other officers; after that Soubahs of Passes; after that Zimpe, then Pillo, and at length they may become Deb Raja. The last Deb was in fact originally a Zinkaff. If a man, however, possess extraordinary abilities or interest, he may get on more quickly, and become at once a Zimpe from being a Zinkaff. Where a person gets a good appointment, he is not allowed to keep it long, but at the annual religious festivals frequent removals and appointments take place. The Deb Raja himself, after a time, is liable to be thrust out on some such pretence as that of his having infringed established customs; and unless he have either Tongso or Paro Pillo on his side, he must, if required to do so, resign his place, or risk the result of a civil war: on this account the Deb strives by removals and changes at the annual festivals to fill the principal offices with persons devoted to his interest. . . . The practice of the courts is that if a man complain he can never obtain justice, but he may be subject to a fine if he fails to establish his claim. If a merchant has a demand against any one, and can by no means get paid, he can only go to the Deb Raja, or some other judge, and say, 'Such a man owes me so much; pray collect the amount and use it as your own.' The defendant is then summoned, and, if the demand is proved to be just, the money is realised for the use of the judge, who, on the other hand, if the claim is not established, takes the amount demanded from the plaintiff." Of the origin of the Bhotan Government, Kishenkant Bose also gives a legend, which, though it differs entirely in its details from the traditional account furnished Mr. Eden by Cheeboo Lama, so far agrees with it, as to specify the people of Cooch Behar as those who originally possessed the country now known as Bhotan, and to indicate Thibet as the place from which the first Dhurma Raja came. Like Cheebo Lama's tradition however, it contains so much of the marvellous as to render it of little value, as compared with the less precise but more probable account given by Captain Pemberton.

CHAPTER III.

The Annexation of Assam reopens political Relations with Bhotan—Description of the Dooars—Conditions on which the Bhotanese retained those of Assam—Disputes respecting the Payment of Tribute for them—Aggressions within the British Frontier of Assam—Pemberton's Mission—The Assam Dooars taken possession of by the Indian Government—Troubles connected with the Bengal Dooars—Ambaree Fallacottah taken under British Management—Raids continue—Punitive measure adopted—Predatory Incursions into Sikim—Darjeeling threatened—Troops ordered to the Frontier—The Bhotanese retire—A Second Mission to Bhotan decided on—The Hon. Ashley Eden appointed Envoy—Nature of his Instructions.

For upwards of twelve years subsequent to the visit of Kishenkant Bose our intercourse with Bhotan appears to have been so unimportant as not to have called for record; inasmuch as, no traces of any communication with the country are to be found until after the first Burmese War, when the Government of India was forced into the occuption of Assam, which the Burmese had conquered and nearly depopulated. On the expulsion of the Burmese from the country being effected by the British Forces, it became indispensable, as a means of protecting our frontier, that we should assume the government of Lower Assam which its native rulers were unable to administer, and in thus, in 1828, acquiring possession of this province, the Indian Government had also to assume the very unsatisfactory relations which had for some time previously existed between the Assamese princes and their neighbours—more especially the Bhotanese.

On this point, quoting from Captain Pemberton—"Surrounded as the valley of Assam is on three sides by tribes but little removed from a state of absolute barbarism, it was to be expected that during the imbecile rule of its princes, and the anarchy which followed its conquest by the ruthless forces of Ava, every border tribe would endeavour to extend its possessions, by an appropriation of as large a portion of the lands at the foot of the mountains as it had power to retain. . . . . As soon as the cessation of hostilities with Ava afforded leisure for an examination into the nature of the relations which had existed between the Princes of Assam and the bordering hill states and tribes, it was discovered that the latter had obtained possession of several tracts of land in the plains, the occupation of which had been tolerated by the rulers of Assam, from inability to expel the intruders, and an apprehension of more extended evil, should they excite the angry passions of tribes whom they were unable to pursue into their fastnesses amongst the mountains, and who could at any time descend and sweep the country with impunity, from the foot of the lower ranges of hills to the banks of the Berhampooter." The Bhotanese it appears, had more than any other of the surrounding tribes benefitted by those encroachments, and as it is to their possession, thus acquired, of the Dooars or plains at the foot of the hills that the gradual extension of the relations of the British Government with their country is to be chiefly traced, it here becomes necessary to give some account of them in detail and of the tenures by which they are held, before proceeding to narrate the various acts of aggression on the part of the Bhotanese, which, since the establishment of British rule in Assam, have frequently endangered the amicable relations of the two Governments, and ultimately resulted in the war to which this narrative owes its origin.

The Dooars, as has already been explained, are embraced in a narrow tract of country extending along the foot of the lower range of the Himalaya mountains, and separating the British territory from Bhotan Proper. The breadth of the Dooars varies from ten to thirty miles,* and their extreme length may be estimated at two hundred and twenty miles. The northern portion, or that immediately bordering on the hills, presents a rugged irregular sloping surface, caused by spurs and inferior heights projecting into the plains from the more lofty ones behind. It consists of forest land and thickets of dense vegetation abounding with elephants, deers, tigers, rhinoceros, buffaloes, and various other wild animals, including boa constrictors. The southern portion again, consists of a rich black soil, extremely fertile and capable of producing luxuriant crops of rice, cotton and tobacco. A good deal of the former is grown there, especially in the neighbourhood of our frontier, and considering the comparatively small amount of land under cultivation, a fair amount of the two latter is also raised; the Dooars in fact being the main source from which the Bhotanese obtain their tobacco.

The climate of the Dooars is very unhealthy, both in the cultivated and uncultivated portions, but

* Both Pemberton and Eden give twenty miles as the extreme breadth of the Dooars. This, however, is an under-estimate, and has arisen, I presume, from the forest and jungle land, known as the "Terai," at the immediate base of the hills, not having been included in the measurement.

especially in the latter, where it is so injurious to the human system, as to render it almost impossible for any one to remain long exposed to it without contracting serious and frequently fatal disease; so pestilential is the malaria. The inhabitants chiefly consist of a tribe called the Mechis, who appear to be the only people so constituted as to be capable of permanently enduring the climate. The Bhotanese themselves dread it, and as a general rule carefully avoid the Dooars during the rains. Those however, who, from their official employment, have had to reside there the whole year round, have done so at places a considerable distance from the foot of the hills, and as close to the British frontier as possible; as shown by the position of the stockades at Mynagoorie and Dhamonée.

Upon this tract of country a number of passes open from the Bhotan hills, each pass being under the control of a Soubah (Jungpen), who has also control of a certain proportion of the level ground underneath, and to which, in some instances, the same name is given as that borne by the pass through which it is entered: hence, as explained at page 2, the term Dooar, which properly should be confined to the mountain gorges, has become extended to the plains with which they communicate. These Dooars are eighteen in number, eleven of them being situated on the frontier of the Rungpore district and Cooch Behar territory in Bengal, between the rivers Teesta and the Monass, and the remaining seven on the Assam frontier, between the Monass and the Dhunseeree rivers. The Bengal Dooars are those of Dhalimkote, Mynagoorie (formerly called Zumerkote), Chamoorchee (known in Bhotan as

Sumchee), Luckee, Buxa (Passaka), Bhulka, Bara, Goomar, Reepo, Cherrung, and Bagh, also known as Chota or little Bijnee. Of the seven Assam Dooars, two border on the Durrung district, and are known as the Booree Goomah, and the Kalling Dooars; the remaining five border on the Kamroop district, and are called the Shurkolla, Banska, Chappagoorie, Chapkahama, and Bijnee Dooars.

It would seem to have been supposed that each of these eighteen, so called, Dooars, have special passes opening upon them from which they take their names—such at least I take to be the inference conveyed in the following notice of them by Mr. Eden: "There is a narrow slip of land varying in breadth from ten to twenty miles which runs along the lower range of the Bootan hills from the Darjeeling district to the frontier of Upper Assam. . . . . Entering into this tract from the hills are eighteen passes; each pass is under the authority of a Jungpen, or, as we call them, Soubahs, and under the administration of each Jungpen is a certain division of territory which bears the name of the pass to which it is attached, and thus the whole locality came to be known as the *Athara Dooar* or Eighteen Passes or Dooars." Some little personal knowledge, however, which I have of the Bengal Dooars warrants me in saying that this is incorrect, or at least not now-a-days applicable. For instance the Zumerkote or Mynagoorie Dooar is situated some twenty miles to the south of Dhalimkote, the pass through which it is reached—hence it may be reasonably asserted that the relation said to exist between the number of districts into which the level ground at the foot of the hills has been divided, and the number of passes by which they are reached, is erroneous.

Though possession of the Assam Dooars by the Bhotanese was practically complete, in theory they were not their absolute property, as those of Bengal were. They had managed however so to harass the rulers of Assam by continual acts of aggression, that the latter were glad to obtain a prospect of security, by making over to them the seven Dooars, in consideration of receiving annually a tribute in the form of Yak tails, musk, gold dust, ponies, blankets, and knives, to the amount of 4,785 Narrain rupees*—an arrangement, happily described by Captain Pemberton, as a mutual compromise between conscious weakness and barbarian cunning.

The British Government, on assuming the rule of Assam, adopted the relations then existing between that country and Bhotan; the arrangements about the Dooars being confirmed and renewed. These however were of so complicated a nature, that it is difficult to see how they could be expected to terminate otherwise than in mutual misunderstanding; for instance, the two Dooars on the Durrung frontier were held alternately by the British and Bhotan

* Previous to the invasion of Cooch Behar by the Bhotanese, they not only had no systematic coinage, but are believed to have had a prejudice against one. On the conquest however of Cooch Behar in 1772 they got possession of the dies used for coining the Narrain rupee; the current coin of the Cooch Behar Raja of that name, and introduced a coin into Bhotan, which became known as a Deb rupee. The purity of this coin however being entirely dependent on the honesty of the Bhotanese officials, its standard value was found to be so variable, that it was soon rejected as a circulating medium by the inhabitants of the Dooars and the Plains, and the Narrain or Cooch Behar rupee used instead of it.

Governments during the year: the former having jurisdiction from July to November, and the latter for the remaining eight months. The other five Dooars, on the contrary, were held exclusively by the Bhotanese, and the Indian Government neither exercised any control over them, nor was allowed to interfere in any way in their internal management, during any portion of the year. The origin of this difference in the mode of tenure of the Durrung and Kamroop Dooars has never been satisfactorily explained; but as it was in existence on our taking over Assam, notwithstanding the great inconvenience attending the arrangement, it was considered the more expedient course to allow it to continue, than to endanger the tranquillity of the frontier by altering a practice which had received the sanction of custom for years. At the time these engagements were entered into, others of a similar nature were entered into with some other hill tribes who had also been encroaching on Assam, but as they have no special reference to Bhotan, it is not necessary to allude to them.

Such is a general sketch of the relations originally existing between the British and Bhotan Governments —the train of events which have gradually led to their being altered now come under narration.

The first cause of trouble was the annual payment of the tribute for the Assam Dooars, which, being in kind, was a fruitful cause of dispute. Officials called Sizawals were appointed on the frontier to receive the articles from the Bhotanese, which, on the one hand, it was alleged they (the Sizawals) were in the habit of changing for substitutes of inferior value, while on the other it was alleged that the tribute sent by the Bhotanese was not of the value agreed upon. Be that as it may, the articles composing it on being sold by auction systematically failed to realise their nominal value, and each year's tribute fell short of the sum fixed—consequently, from the very beginning, a gradually increasing balance was shown against the Bhotanese. Payment of arrears was demanded, but refused on the ground that the articles were sold at unnecessarily low prices—a not unreasonable argument; as it seems to me absurd to have entertained the probability, that, in the disposal by auction of articles of the nature in question, either their real value, or any fixed sum for them, could be regularly secured. Coincident with the claim for arrears of tribute being preferred, predatory acts within our territory and that of Cooch Behar, as well as the abduction of natives under British protection, became common from the Bhotan frontier.

From this period incursions of a like nature continued more or less frequent until 1837, when the Government of India, under the belief that the Bhotan Government was ignorant of what was going on on the frontier, sent Captain Pemberton as an envoy to Bhotan to adjust the then existing difficulties. This mission, though well received, failed in effecting the object for which it was sent, and as the only means of protecting the frontier from aggression the East India Company determined to annex the Assam Dooars, and pay the Bhotanese Government an annual sum of 10,000 rupees for the loss of revenue thus sustained by the control of the Dooars passing out of its hands. This measure was carried out in 1841, and proved on the whole successful in putting a stop to raids within the British frontier of Assam; though incursions from the hills into the annexed Dooars themselves continued for many years.

The year following the attachment of the Assam Dooars, the large estate of Ambaree Fallacottah, referred to as having been taken from the Zemindar of Bykantpore and made over to Bhotan in 1784, was, at the request however of the Bhotanese themselves, taken under the management of the East India Company; the latter holding itself responsible to the former for the net annual proceeds of the property.

Outrages similar to those referred to as having taken place on the Assam side, now became common in the vicinity of the Bengal Dooars, hardly a year passing without their occurrence. The aggressors, it was believed, being either the Bhotan frontier officials, or robbers protected them. Repeated representations were made by the Government of India to that of Bhotan, but without any good resulting, and in 1860 it was determined to withhold the rental of Ambaree Fallacottah as a mild punishment;—the Bhotanese at the same time being given to understand that the payment would recommence on their complying with the demands of the Indian Government relative to the surrender of certain natives who had been carried off into Bhotan from under British protection. This measure was productive of no good result, and though aggressions still continued, the Bengal Government, not feeling satisfied that the central Government of Bhotan was really cognisant of the misconduct of its frontier officials, recommended that a second mission should be sent, and that a British agent should be appointed to reside at the Bhotan court.*

* While a detailed account of the various acts of aggression committed by the Bhotanese within the British and Cooch Behar frontiers,

These views, slightly modified were adopted by Lord Canning, whose general concurrence in them was thus communicated to the Bengal Government by the Secretary to the Foreign Department (Colonel Durand) in a letter dated the 23rd of January, 1862—"His Excellency in Council desires me to state that it is very expedient that a mission should be sent to Bootan to explain what our demands are, and what we shall do if they are not conceded; and to make our arrangements with Sikhim clearly understood by the Booteahs. But His Excellency in Council is doubtful as to placing an agent in Bootan, and it will be better to leave this question to be decided after the result of the mission is known." Lord Canning also pointed out that his Agent in Assam (Major Hopkinson) should be called upon to state what arrangements he considered necessary for the security of the mission.

While this correspondence regarding the appointment of a mission was going on a raid was made into Sikim by the Bhotanese, on the grounds that it was through that country becoming embroiled with the British the previous year, that Ambaree Fallacottah had been taken from Bhotan.* This raid was organised by the Jungpen of Dhalimkote, and resulted in thirteen men and women and twenty-three head of

and of the train of events resulting therefrom, between the years 1828 and 1861, might prove tedious to many, there are others who may be desirous of having more precise information than that which is conveyed in the brief summary given above. I have, therefore, felt that the work will be incomplete without a narrative of the events in question, more in detail, and have accordingly prepared one, which forms Appendix B, and includes a notice of Pemberton's mission to Poonakha and description of Tongso, the residence of the Penlow of that name.

* In the year 1861, some disturbances (to which allusion will be made in detail hereafter) occurred on the Sikim frontier, which rendered the

cattle being carried off—the latter valued at 495 rupees. This occurred in January 1862, and the following month the Bhotanese again turned their attention to Cooch Behar and committed several outrages. The Raja of that state now claimed British protection under the treaty of 1773, on the grounds that owing to the aggressive conduct of the Bhotanese, the talooks* of Cooch Behar adjoining the Dooars would probably soon be deserted. The British Government recognised his claim for military protection, and two companies of infantry were ordered to proceed to Cooch Behar for that purpose. As the rainy season however was close at hand, and as raids were not to be expected during that period of the year, the Cooch Behar Raja ultimately came to the conclusion that there was no necessity for the presence of British troops within his territory, and accordingly they were not sent.

Though there was at this time a lull on the Cooch Behar frontier, the scene had changed to that of Darjeeling; information having been received from four distinct sources of an intended attack on that district, which was verified by the appearance of a considerable force of armed Bhotanese on the frontier, and by their making preparations for crossing the Teesta. Detachments were immediately pushed on to the frontier from the regiment at Julpigorie, and two companies of Her Majesty's 38th Regiment, and one

sending of a British force into the country necessary, and resulted in the conclusion of a Treaty of Amity—offensive and defensive—with the Sikim Raja.

* The term talook is applied to divisions of land rented for agricultural purposes, and is synonymous with the word farm, as commonly used by ourselves.

company of the 10th Native Infantry were moved up in support. Coincident with this demonstration against Darjeeling, insolent demands were made by the Jungpen of Dhalimkote for the arrears of the Ambaree Fallacottah rents, due since its attachment in 1860. On the appearance of the troops however he withdrew his force from the frontier.

Shortly after this affair, the Deputy Magistrate at Julpigorie, received a communication from the Bhotan official at Mynagoorie, requesting an interview; as he wished to hand over to him for punishment four British subjects, whom he had made prisoners, in consequence of their having committed aggressions against Bhotanese property. The interview was granted, but the Mynagoorie official declined to surrender the men, unless an enemy of his, who had taken refuge within the British territory was given up in return, and there the matter ended. This official admitted to the magistrate having likewise in his possession several elephants taken from natives within the British frontier.

The impression held by the Government that in a country so imperfectly governed as Bhotan, the frontier officials acted very much as they chose—an impression which had materially influenced it in forbearing from the adoption of extreme measures—received some degree of confirmation at this time, from the fact that an officer of rank, denominated a Durpun Raja, was sent by the Deb Raja to the Governor-General's agent at Gowhatty to receive the rents of the Assam Dooars, and, if possible, have the amount annually paid increased—the despatches of which he was the bearer, are thus referred to in the Bengal Administration Report for 1862—

"No mention was made in these despatches of the outrages we had complained of. The Rajah (the Durpun) had merely been sent for the purpose of receiving the annual allowance we make to Bhootan for certain Dooars, amounting to about 10,000 rupees, and, if possible, to obtain an increase of two or three thousand rupees to the allowance. Nothing transpired respecting the stoppage of rents of Ambaree Fallacottah. There is reason, therefore, for suspecting that they had never been remitted to the Deb Raja, but appropriated by the Soubah of Dalimkote, and our failing to obtain redress from the Bhootan Government by withholding them is thus easily explained. During the Conference the agent spoke of the outrages of the Bhootanese on our territory, and the evasive replies of the Deb Raja to our demands for redress. The Durpun Raja replied, that no complaints from the agent (Governor-General) had reached the Deb Raja. He observed—'there were a great many Dooars, and a great many kinds of people in them who made mischief in them, and that the Deb Raja really did not know what went on in the Dooars. What goes on in the Dooars is concealed from the Deb Raja.' There is every reason to believe that this is a correct representation of the condition of the administration of Bhootan. It is probable that the revenue of Ambaree Fallacottah is annually appropriated by the Dalimkote Soubah, and that the Deb Raja is thus unaware of its attachment. The letters that purported to be replies from the Deb Raja to our demands for redress were doubtless the spurious productions of some of the Soubahs through whom our communications to the Bhootan Government are transmitted." The reason assigned by the

Deb for wanting an increase to the Assam compensation money, was that 10,000 rupees was insufficient to cover the religious ceremonies to which it was applied, and therefore that the addition requested was necessary.

The sending of a mission to Bhotan having been definitely settled, a messenger named Mokundo Sing, was, in July 1862, dispatched from Assam to the court of the Deb Raja, bearing letters announcing the intention of the Governor-General to send an envoy to confer with them on such matters as required explanation and settlement between the two Governments. The Bhotan authorities were also requested to indicate the route which the mission should take, and to make the necessary arrangements for facilitating its reaching the capital.

This messenger did not get back to Gowhatty until the beginning of December, having been delayed on his journey, owing to obstructions caused by the frontier officers. His wants were supplied at Poonakha, which he reached in seven days' march from Cherrung: otherwise his reception does not appear to have been very friendly, and the reply he brought back from the Deb Raja was unsatisfactory and contradictory. The latter commenced his letter by stating—"You ask an interview; that is good; I want to speak to you about the Dooars;" and then went on to admit that he had received numerous complaints from the British authorities regarding the misconduct of his subjects on the frontier, and suggested the following very simple course for their adjustment—"With regard to the quarrels of the frontier authorities, they are not important enough to be heard by the Dhurma Raja, and if your sahibs (officials) do the same, the

East India Company also should not listen to them either"—a recommendation pretty suggestive of the amount of latitude the supreme powers in Bhotan are either inclined or obliged to accord, to their subordinates. With regard to the coming of the mission, he concluded his letter by saying—"You want an interview, but now it would be attended with much trouble, owing to the cold, and bad state of the roads; moreover, the Dhurma Raja does not wish such an interview. If you want to come for the settlement of any quarrel, I have not informed the Dhurma Raja that such is the case. I had intended to send Zinkaffs to you, with your men, for the adjustment of quarrel, but on account of the heat I cannot do so now. Afterwards, in the month of Magh, I shall send over two or three Zinkaffs, who will settle disputes according to our order." The Lieutenant Governor of Bengal (Mr. Cecil Beadon) recommended that the mission should be dispatched at once; but the Government of India thought that as the Bhotanese authorities had been asked to select the route for the mission and promised to send Zinkaffs, it was better to wait and hear what they had to say—the more so as the cold season was already so far advanced.

The Zinkaffs never came, and this breach of promise taken in connexion with the evasive nature of the reply sent by the hands of Mokundo Sing, decided the Indian Government in dispatching the mission without further reference to Bhotan, and by whatever might appear to be the most convenient route.

The Honourable Ashley Eden, one of the most able officers of the Bengal Civil Service, was selected as envoy; an appointment he was peculiarly suited for; having displayed remarkable tact and judgment when employed in a similar capacity two years previously, in adjusting the difficulties then existing between the British Government and the Sikim Raja, and which resulted in his negotiating a treaty distinguished alike by moderation and good sense, and the practical working of which, has proved in every respect satisfactory.

On August 11, 1863, Mr. Eden received his instructions, which were to the following general effect—matters of detail being left to his discretion.

1stly. To explain in a friendly and conciliatory spirit to the Bhotan Government, the circumstances which had rendered it necessary to occupy Ambaree Fallacottah, and withhold its revenues, and to inform it, that, in the event of the demands of the British Government being complied with, the occupation would cease, and that though the management of the estate would continue as formerly in the hands of the latter, the rents would be paid to Bhotan.

2ndly. To demand the surrender of all captives carried off, and the restoration of property taken from British, Cooch Behar and Sikim territories.

3rdly. With reference to the aggressions on the part of British and Cooch Behar subjects, complained of by the Bhotanese, proof to be required, and such redress given as the circumstances may call for.

4thly. To endeavour to effect some satisfactory arrangement for the rendition of criminals by the British and Bhotan Governments respectively.

5thly. The Bhotan Government to be made fully aware of the position in which the protected states of Cooch Behar and Sikim stand to the British Government, and that any aggression committed on them by Bhotan would be viewed as unfriendly conduct towards the British Government.

6thly. To secure, if practicable, free commercial intercourse between Bengal and Bhotan, as well as protection to traders and travellers.

7thly. To obtain all the information possible respecting the nature, population and resources of the country.

8thly. To try and secure the results of the mission in the form of a Treaty, a draft of such as would be desirable being furnished.

A sum of ten thousand rupees was placed at Mr. Eden's disposal for the purchase of presents for the Dhurma and Deb Rajas, and such other members of the Bhotan Cabinet as it might be deemed expedient to propitiate. The route to be taken by the mission was determined by the Indian Government, and that *viâ* Darjeeling, was selected as the preferable one; owing to the facilities it was supposed to afford for the mission organising its own means of hill transport, and thus, to a certain extent, being independent of the Bhotan authorities.

CHAPTER IV.

Mr. Eden prepares to start from Darjeeling—Delay there and its Causes—Departure of the Mission—Arrival in Bhotan—Reception by the Natives—A Monastery—Fort of Dhumsong—Arrival at Dhalimkote—Visit from the Jungpen—Scene connected with flogging Coolies—Difficulties encountered—Part of Escort left behind—Reach Sipchoo—Story of Nimba Kazee—The Tulélah Pass—The Jungpen of Tsangbe—Coolies frost-bitten—A Miller operated on under Chloroform—Officials arrive and try to make Mr. Eden return—Village Omen—Ascent of the Taigonlah Mountain—Arrival at Hah Tampien—Friendly Reception by the Jungpen—Coolies die in the Snow—Dangers of the Cheulah Pass—A second Attempt made to stop the Mission—Arrival at Paro.

Early in November 1863, Mr. Eden arrived at Darjeeling, our Himalayan station on the north-eastern frontier, and commenced to organise the transport of his mission; the constitution of which had been determined on as follows—Captain Goodwin Austen, of the Bengal Staff Corps, as Assistant to the Envoy and Surveyor, Captain Lance, of the same corps, to command the escort, Dr. Simpson, of the Bengal Army as Medical Attendant, and Cheeboo Lama, to whom reference has already been made, as Thibetian interpreter. Mr. Power of the Uncovenanted Service was also detailed to accompanying the mission as an Assistant to Mr. Eden. The escort was to consist of one hundred men, half Seiks, half Sappers of the Sebundy corps.

As no reply had been received from the Bhotan authorities to a communication which had been addressed to them on the 10th of September previously, by the Lieutenant Governor of Bengal, notifying the intended departure of the mission, and requesting that some officer might be deputed to meet it on the banks of the Teesta, and guide it to Poonakha, Mr. Eden himself addressed the Bhotan Government from Darjeeling on the 10th of November, intimating his arrival there, and requesting that the Jungpen of Dhalimkote might be instructed to meet him on the frontier and aid him in conveying his baggage and camp—adding that if this was not done, he should be compelled to report to his Government that no arrangements had been made, and which would be considered as indicating an absence of friendly feeling.

Shortly after this letter was despatched, it came to Mr. Eden's knowledge, that in fact there was at the time no recognised Government in Bhotan; the whole country being in a state of anarchy and confusion, owing to a rebellion that had broken out a few months previously—and regarding which the following particulars were ascertained. It appeared that the Jungpen of Poonakha had obtained a promise from the Deb Raja while the court was at Tassishujung, its summer residence, that if he assisted him in a crisis which seemed imminent, he should be rewarded by promotion to the office of Jungpen of the Fort of Angdu Forung; a situation much coveted, from its being a sort of small Penlowship. The crisis passed over, and the Deb Raja broke his promise, by conferring the appointment on another. The Poonakha Jungpen felt himself aggrieved, and when the Court returned to Poonakha for the winter months, he admitted all the Deb Raja's retinue into the fort or palace, but shut the Deb out himself, and immediately appointed a nominee of his own to the Debship. The dethroned Deb Raja fled to Tassishujung, where his case was taken up by the Paro Penlow, which secured him the aid of Western Bhotan. This compelled the Jungpen of Poonakha to invoke that of Eastern Bhotan, by calling for the assistance of the Tongso Penlow, who readily responded, and was joined by all the members of the Council except the Paro Penlow. The rebels then invested Tassishujung, and commenced the siege by cutting off the supply of water from the fort, through which they succeeded in obtaining all the money the besieged had, by allowing them to come three times a week and draw water on payment of 300 rupees for each indulgence. As soon as the funds of the garrison were exhausted, thirst compelled the Deb Raja's followers to surrender, and the Deb himself was permitted to retire into private life in the monastery of Simtoka.

While this rebellion was going on in the interior, one on a smaller scale was prevailing in the immediate vicinity of the British frontier, headed by the Jungpen of Dhalimkote. This official was a follower of one of the members of Council, who was taking a prominent part in the other rebellion, but in his post at Dhalimkote, he was subordinate to the Paro Penlow, who sent an official to supersede him. He refused to surrender the fort, and a force was dispatched to compel him to do so. The siege continued for several months, but was raised by the besiegers, on their hearing that Mr. Eden's mission was about visiting the place.

While Mr. Eden was thus detained at Darjeeling,

the Jungpen of Dhalimkote sent messengers to him on several occasions, assuring him that the delay in answering the letters of the Governor-General, and in making arrangements for the reception of the mission arose solely from the disorganised state of the country, and from no unwillingness to receive a representative of the British Government. He begged him to wait patiently, and promised to give him every assistance in his power. Towards the end of November, he requested an interview with Cheeboo Lama, to explain to him how matters stood at head-quarters. Cheeboo met him at the Teesta, and they had a conference which extended over several days. His desire was evidently that Mr. Eden should enter into negotiations with him. He professed great friendship, and went the length of hinting, that, if a reply did not soon come to the letter Mr. Eden had addressed on the 10th of November to the Deb and Dhurma Rajas, he would, provided he received a present, aid the mission in entering the country—even if in so doing, he should incur the displeasure of his Government.

Mr. Eden reported the state of affairs to the Government of India, and was informed that the Governor-General (Sir William Dennison, acting until the arrival of Sir John Lawrence) was of opinion —"that as the rebellion had been successful, and a substantive Government had apparently been re-established," and as the Jungpen of Dhalimkote had promised to assist, there was no reason why the advance of the mission should be longer postponed—the more so, as it appeared to the Indian Government, that the new Deb Raja might be desirous of cultivating a good understanding with the British

Government, in order to strengthen himself in his position. On the receipt of these orders, Mr. Eden made immediate preparations to advance, and wrote to the Jungpen of Dhalimkote that he was on the point of starting, and requested that men might be sent to meet him at the Teesta.

Difficulties were now encountered by Mr. Eden in procuring the necessary transport for the baggage of the mission; as the Darjeeling coolies* were unwilling to enter Bhotan, the inhabitants of which are not looked upon with favour by the other hill residents. Through the assistance of Cheeboo Lama a number of coolies were collected sufficient to enable the baggage of the mission to be dispatched to the frontier on the 1st of January 1864. On the 4th of the month, the mission left Darjeeling, and the same day overtook the coolies just as they arrived at the Teesta, twenty-two miles from Darjeeling, and upwards of 6,000 feet below it. There the coolies left in considerable numbers, being afraid to cross the frontier. Mr. Eden was again relieved from his difficulties by Cheeboo Lama, who procured assistance through his own tenants,† and after a delay of three days, succeeded in getting his camp established on the Bhotan side of the Teesta, which had to be crossed on bamboo rafts.

The mission then commenced the ascent of the

* The word commonly used in the East, as indicative of the class of men who live by general labour; its source being *Kuli*, the Hindoostanee for labourer.

† The British Government, in consideration of services rendered by Cheeboo Lama in adjusting difficulties which had arisen between it and his own Sovereign, the Sikim Raja, gave him a present of a large tract of hill land out of that which was annexed from Sikim.

mountains of Bhotan, and reached a hamlet called Kalimpoong, 3,733 feet above the level of the sea. "Here," observes Mr. Eden, "we were obliged to halt one day to muster the coolies and re-arrange the baggage, which had got into confusion in consequence of frequent desertions. Whilst here, we visited a number of villages; the inhabitants seemed delighted to see us, and made us presents of eggs, fowls, oranges, and vegetables. This part of the country is very fairly cultivated, and has a number of inhabitants; it is so close to our frontier that the villagers set their chiefs at defiance, and are the only people under the Bootan Government who are able to carry on any sort of trade. They were vehement in their abuse of their own Government, and loud in their praise of our administration in Darjeeling; their only wish seemed to be that they should come under our rule. Nearly every household had some members resident in our territory. We visited a monastery in the neighbourhood; the Lamas were absent, but we were shown over it by two nuns, who pointed with pride to an English vessel which was placed on the altar as a receptacle for holy water, but which in other countries is used for a very different purpose.* There were fine orange groves in the neighbourhood of the monastery, but the people dared not sell the oranges for fear of the Lamas. At the unaccustomed sight of money, however, their fear of their priests vanished, and they not only sold, but afterwards gave us a large quantity of oranges." At Kalimpoong,

* On visiting this monastery sixteen months after Mr. Eden did, a green-coloured European finger glass was standing on the altar, which I presume was the English vessel to which he refers.

Mr. Eden was met by a very surly old official, the ex Nieboo of Dhumsong—"here as everywhere else there being two officers in the appointment, one in power and one out of power." He at first requested Mr. Eden not to proceed further into the country, but ultimately gave guides to show the road to Dhalimkote.

On the 9th of January, the mission continued its progress, and after a long march reached Paigong. On the road a number of the coolies deserted, leaving their loads behind them, which necessitated a quantity of the baggage being stored in the village.*

The next day, only a few miles' advance was made as far as Paiengong, the mission having gone off the road for a few miles to visit the fort of Dhumsong, a small quadrangular building built of stones and mud, situated on a bluff, about 5,000 feet high, jutting out into the valley of the Teesta, between Sikim and Bhotan. Mr. Eden describes the view from the place as magnificent. He states—"The snows of the Choolah, Nitai, and Yaklah passes were all quite close; on three sides of us were the different snowy ranges of Bootan, Sikhim, and Nepaul; we could see within a space of sixteen miles the four countries of Thibet, Sikhim, Bootan, and British Sikhim. The view was very extended. Darjeeling was plainly visible, and below was the beautiful and fertile valley of Rhinok in Sikhim; we

* Amongst the baggage thus left behind was a box of arsenical soap; this was never sent after the mission, and the authorities denied that it could have been stolen. On the return however of the mission from Poonakha, it was admitted that the box had been opened, and its contents being mistaken for some peculiar food for horses, cattle had been fed on it and seven of them had died.

could see for many miles the road from the Thibet Passes to the Runjeet River on the Darjeeling frontier, the route followed by the Thibetian traders who annually visit Darjeeling." The officer in charge of the Dhumsong fort was a little dirty old man, who closed the doors, and insolently refused Mr. Eden admission.

On the 11th of January, the party reached the top of the mountain of Labah, a height of 6,620 feet, and the next day descended from there by a very steep and difficult path to a rapid stream, which Mr. Eden describes as one of the branches of the Durlah River, but which, on the occasion of my visiting it the following year, I was told goes by the name of the Chale River. On arriving here, the mission was met by musicians, ponies, and mules, sent by the Jungpen of Dhalimkote, out of compliment to whom, and in accordance with the custom of the country, some of the members of the mission availed themselves of the transport sent, "and had a very uncomfortable ride on high Tartar saddles on very fidgety and vicious mules." The mission now ascended from the bed of the Chale River, and, preceded by the musicians performing a noisy and monotonous national air on silver flageolets and brass cymbals, reached the valley of Ambiok, 2,922 feet high, situated immediately below the fort of Dhalimkote, from which, in honour of the occasion, a constant fire of matchlocks was kept up during the day.

Notwithstanding, however, the demonstrative character of the mission's reception, and the external indications of friendship which accompanied it, on Mr. Eden's sending to the Jungpen for a supply of rice for the camp followers, in accordance with a promise he had made to furnish the necessary supplies, he declined to give it unless he was paid in advance at the rate of seven rupees (fourteen shillings) per maund (eighty pounds), when at the time it was known as a fact, that the price of the article at the place from which the Jungpen procured it was only ten annas, or the equivalent of fifteen pence English money, per maund.

On the 14th of January, after having given this illustration of his commercial abilities, the Jungpen paid Mr. Eden a visit; and came accompanied by a disorderly band of about two hundred followers, consisting of musicians, matchlockmen, and standard bearers—the latter carrying boards with inscriptions on them, which shows that the Bhotanese still retain some of the external formalities of the race from which they are sprung. Those familiar with China will recollect how invariably inscription-bearing boards form an accompaniment of all officials of rank on paying visits of ceremony. The interview and its results Mr. Eden describes as follows—"As they approached our camp the whole party halted every twenty yards and gave loud shouts, apparently in imitation of a pack of jackals. A similar cry is used on advancing to fight. Whilst the screaming was going on, the Jungpen put down his head and shook himself in his saddle; the same practice was observed on other occasions, but I could obtain no explanation of it except that it was an 'old custom.' The Jungpen on arriving at my tent, was seized by the legs by some of his followers, and after being twirled round in the air twice was carried to the tent, as it was thought below his dignity to walk. The ceremony was, however, very far from dignified, for the Jungpen attempted to get down, and was brought to my tent, kicking violently and abusing his men. He was a fat, uncouth, boorish, ignorant man. He assumed airs of great dignity for a time, but was unable to resist asking for some brandy. On receiving this he became very talkative; his chief topic, however, was the quantity of spirits he could drink; he repeatedly called for more brandy, and finding that it was taking effect upon him, I gave him leave to go; nothing, however, would induce him to leave; he stayed for four or five hours, and at length was taken away forcibly by his servants, who saw that I was annoyed. But even then he could not be persuaded to return to the fort, but went to the tent of Cheeboo Lama, and sat there drinking. Later in the day he left the camp; but whilst going through it he saw some coolies, who after receiving large advances of pay had deserted us and had been brought back, being flogged. He insisted on their being released. Captain Lance and Dr. Simpson, who were present, said they could not do so without my orders; he then drew his knife and rushed into the ring with his followers, threatening to cut down the Commissariat-sergeant who was in attendance, and behaving with great violence. The men of the escort ran to their arms and fell in, and the bullying and violence of the Jungpen and his followers was immediately changed to abject fear. Seeing me approaching, he ran to meet me, trembling with fear, and begged for forgiveness. I ordered him out of camp, and the whole party ran off to the fort in a most undignified manner. I declined to receive any further visits from him until he sent me a written apology for his conduct, and this he did the next day." How far this flogging of the coolies, here alluded to, was either a justifiable or an expedient measure, appears to me open to question, inasmuch as it is clear from the commencement that there was a great indisposition on their part to come, and that a constant amount of pressure had to be employed to induce any of them to start. The exception taken by the Jungpen to the course adopted certainly seems to me the least objectionable trait in his proceedings on the day in question.

Finding it impossible to procure supplies at Dhalimkote, or the villages in its neighbourhood, for the large number of natives composing his camp, Mr. Eden sent Captain Austen through the Dooars to the frontier station of Julpigorie for the purpose of purchasing rice. While Mr. Eden was waiting the return of Captain Austen, he received a letter from the Deb Raja, simply instructing him to let the Dhalimkote Jungpen know what he had come about, and he would arrange about the interview required. Mr. Eden explained fully to the Jungpen the object of the mission. He displayed a friendly spirit, and impressed Mr. Eden with the belief that he was really anxious to forward his progress—the more so as he himself was a party having a considerable interest in the success of the mission; the attached rents of Ambaree Fallacottah forming a portion of the Dooar revenue over which he had control. At the same time he was evidently unwilling that Mr. Eden should proceed without specific authority from the Deb Raja, whose letter appeared to be written under the impression that the mission was still within the British frontier. He complained of the conduct of his Government, and proved to Mr. Eden that he had repeatedly written for instructions as to what he was to do on the arrival of the mission, and that he had received evasive replies, evidently so shaped as to hold him responsible for either the mission coming or going back. He was told that the Deb Raja did not understand the object of the Governor-General in sending an envoy, and that it was caused by some complaint against him, which he must settle himself, and in so doing take care not to give offence. Mr. Eden replied to the Deb Raja's letter, and distinctly stated to him that his business was with the supreme Government, and not with the Jungpen of Dhalimkote; also requesting a specific answer as to whether he wished to receive him or not, as, in the event of his decision being in the negative, he should at once return and report the same to the Governor-General.

The description which Mr. Eden now gives of the state of the mission transport is not such as to favour the view that the flogging system had been attended with any practical benefit, but rather the contrary: "It was impossible for me to move without the help of the Darlingcote (Dhalimkote) authorities, for the Nepalese and Sikhim coolies, seeing the very questionable manner in which we were received, had run away in great numbers, and we had not enough left to carry on even our necessary baggage, though reduced to the smallest limits, and in addition to this we had now to carry on rice for the coolies themselves. I had built a large godown (storehouse) at Ambiok, and intended to leave a considerable store of rice there to be sent on to us from time to time, but still each cooly required for the march nearly a maund of rice, or another cooly's load. My only hope was in obtaining people of the country, who could feed themselves at their own villages, and could carry some extra rice for own men. The Jungpen made the greatest difficulty about procuring these men, and certainly he had been placed by his own Government in an awkward position." At this juncture information was received from Captain Austen that the necessary supplies had been procured at Julpigorie, and were on their way to Dhalimkote.

Mr. Eden now told the Jungpen that he must either make up his mind to aid him in going on, or take the responsibility of his going back. Under a promise of payment, he ultimately consented to assist, and to take charge of such stores, tents, men, and baggage, as transport could not be found for.

On the 29th of January Captain Austen having returned, Mr. Eden moved on, leaving behind nearly all his tents and most of his baggage and stores; as it was impossible to get coolies enough to carry them, as well as to carry food for themselves. Half the escort also had to be left behind in charge of the native officer, a Soubadar; the carriage available not admitting of more than fifty Seiks and a few sappers going on. Before leaving, Mr. Eden visited the Jungpen and was received with great civility. Refreshments were offered him, and in the course of being shown over the fort, he was taken into a small temple adjoining the Jungpen's residence, where a number of Lamas were at the time chanting prayers for the safe journey of the mission.

From Dhalimkote the course of the mission lay in the first instance in a south-easterly direction for about four miles, necessitating a descent of 1,500 feet, which brought it to the Sukyamchoo River, a narrow shallow stream that runs round the spur on which the fort of Dhalimkote stands. Here the mission halted for the night, the place having a malarious appearance, and the feeding-ground apparently of wild elephants.

The next day's march extended over eleven miles, and lay through heavy forests. About half way, a large river, the Nurchoo, was crossed, and about six miles further on, the mission encamped near a smaller one, called the Mochoo; the waters of which abounded with fish, and its banks with wild animals of every description.

The journey the following day was also through forest land. Near the end of it the Dechu, a deep, swift river, had to be crossed before reaching the halting-place at Sipchoo, ten miles from the Mochoo. A delay of some hours occurred at the Dechu, over which a bridge had to be thrown before the mission could cross. After this had been effected, a steep wooded cliff had to be ascended to a height of about 1,500 feet. Here Mr. Eden was met by some Bhotanese officials in a state of intoxication, as they are stated usually to be, who said there was a large fort in the neighbourhood, full of men, and begged him not to encamp within a mile of it; for fear the soldiers might come out, and while under the influence of liquor attack his party—adding that it was the wish of the officer in charge of the fort to prevent any harm occurring. Mr. Eden however did not believe them, and on going on found that the fort and the soldiers were equally imaginary. The whole town of Sipchoo consisted of two huts, three or four cattle sheds, and a few men and women. The Bhotanese were not in the least degree abashed by the detection of the untruth they had told, but treated the matter as a joke, and said that their only object in having given this false information was that it might be the means of inducing Mr. Eden to select a better encamping ground nearer to the river.*

The coolies shipped at Dhalimkote had only agreed to come as far as Sipchoo, Mr. Eden being given to understand that the places were thickly populated, and that there would be no difficulty in procuring fresh relays. This proved a deliberate falsehood, there being only five houses in the whole neighbourhood, and not a coolie to be got. The official in charge

* Mr. Eden mentions the following incident which occurred at this period of the journey:—"One of the first persons who came forward to greet us was Mimba Kazee. This man's history is a curious one: he was for many years in our service, and was in receipt of, for a Booteah, a large salary, as translator of the Darjeeling Court. He was Dr. Campbell's right-hand man for years, was with that gentleman and Dr. Hooker when they were imprisoned by the Sikhim Raja in 1851, and is specially mentioned under the name of Nimbo in Dr. Hooker's Journal (page 233) as having broken away from captivity and found his way into Darjeeling, swimming the Teesta with "a large iron ring on each leg, and a link of several pounds' weight attached to one." When Dr. Campbell, at the end of 1860, entered Sikhim, this man was with him and behaved well, receiving several rewards for bravery. In 1861, when I relieved Dr. Campbell of the charge of our relations with Sikhim, Mimba was made over to me as a trustworthy guide and spy; he had not been with me more than a week before I had reason to suspect him of intriguing with the enemy. He found out that I was watching him, and the day we crossed the frontier he fled into Bootan, taking with him sixty or seventy of his ryots, his cattle and all the property he could remove. I afterwards found that he had been endeavouring to induce the Bootanese to join the Sikhimese against us. He had a valuable estate in Darjeeling, this was of course forfeited to the State, and is now called the "Mimba Kazee Tea Plantation," in the hands of a European Company. He seems to have offered the Paro Penlow rupees 2,000, to make him Jungpen of Darlingcote. The Penlow led him on until he got all his money out of him, and then refused to give him any employment higher that of a private soldier. He came to me at Sipchoo, smiling as if nothing had happened: he entreated to be taken into our employ, and his great wish evidently was to be allowed to return to Darjeeling. He joined our camp, and was on the whole useful, though I was not able to trust him to any great extent."

of the Sipchoo district was a Nieboo, or Jungpen's deputy, who called on Mr. Eden the day after his arrival. He declared his inability to give him any assistance, stated that it was out of the question the mission going on without the aid of Government, that he had received no communications about it, but that if it remained at Sipchoo for a few weeks, it was possible orders might come, and coolies be procurable. He treated the matter with perfect indifference, and as he clearly had no intention of giving himself any trouble about it, Mr. Eden determined on his own course of action: his choice lying between returning at once to British territory, or going on, leaving behind him the greater portion of the reduced camp equipage and escort that he had brought on to Sipchoo. With the precedents of Bogle's, Turner's, and Pemberton's missions before him; all of which had gone on with but a limited number of attendants, he made up his mind to push on as little encumbered as possible. He accordingly left behind all the heavy baggage and stores, all the escort except fifteen Seiks and ten Sebundy sappers, the latter for road-clearing, bridge-making, &c. Also Mr. Power, his uncovenanted assistant, the Commissariat sergeant, the moonshee (literary assistant in Hindoostanee), the native doctor, and every camp follower who could be spared.

Having made arrangements for the encamping and halting of those thus left behind, Mr. Eden moved on a distance of seven miles on the 2nd of February, to Tsigong, a fine open plain at an elevation of 5,756 feet, just below the Tulélah Pass, and reached by a continuous ascent up a mountain spur, where notwithstanding its great height, the marks of wild elephants were seen. At this place the mission was again harassed by the desertion of coolies, whose natural repugnance to the work they seem to have been forced into, was increased on the day's march by alarming accounts given them by the people they met on the road as to the depth of the snow in some of the passes, and which as results showed were not exaggerated.

On the morning of the 3rd of February the Tulélah Pass was entered, and shortly afterwards the party came to snow, through which it had to march until dark, the depth varying from one and a-half to two feet. The night was spent at a place called Thlungchoo, at an elevation of 8,198 feet. The snow was deep, but the men managed to light fires, and protected themselves completely from the cold.

On the 4th of February the Tulélah Pass was crossed at an elevation of 10,000 feet. From that a descent of 2,500 feet was made with much difficulty through the snow to Dongachuchoo. The snow here was not very deep, but the men were all thoroughly exhausted and desponding, and nothing but the fear of again crossing the snows prevented the great majority of the coolies running off and leaving the mission in the jungle. The next day Mr. Eden determined to give them a rest, and went only a few miles down to the bottom of the valley and encamped on the bank of the river Am Mochoo (3,849 feet);* here the sun was hot, and the coolies' spirits improved.

On the 6th of February the mission continued its

* The following description of this river is given by Mr. Eden:—"The Mochoo is a very beautiful river, deep, very rapid, and broad; it is full of enormous boulders, which makes the river one continuous line of white foam. It was spanned by a curious and ingenious

journey, and after going for a few miles up a very steep ascent, came to a perfectly level path, well wooded and watered. Proceeding along this for eight miles, a precipitous descent had to be made to a small stream, which was crossed, and a second ascent made to Tsangbe (6,143 feet elevation). Here a very pretty little hamlet of some four or five houses was found, with a number of small villages and monasteries scattered about the neighbourhood. The villagers were very friendly, and flocked round the camp with presents of eggs, milk, and fowls, and professed to be anxious to come under British rule. The ground in the vicinity of the village was well cultivated, and the fields neatly fenced with loose stone walls. Tillage was carried on with the plough, and not with the hand, as at Darjeeling; the crops being barley, buckwheat, millet, and turnips. At Tsangbe, which is

bridge. Advantage had been taken of a great rock to throw across from one bank some eight or ten large beams, the ends of which were weighed down by large heaps of stones and earth supported by a revetment. Across these beams were placed a row of thick logs, then another set of beams projecting far beyond the first layer and similarly weighed down with stones and earth, then some logs, and so on till a sufficient length of beam was projected across the river to support a platform thrown from these beams to other small beams built into the rock in the river. On the other side the span was much greater, and in addition to the beams thrown out from the bank and from the rock, the platform was supported by canes and small creepers; it was in fact a compound of a suspension and a pier bridge. It was neatly boarded throughout, and was some four or five feet broad. The height from the centre span to the water was thirty feet, and the breadth of the span ninety feet. The Mochoo comes from Phagri in Thibet, and passes close under the Sikhim Raja's Thibet Palace at Choombi, and runs through Bootan into the Berhampooter. If the country had been in any hands but those of the Booteahs a road into Thibet would have been taken up this valley, and would have opened communication with the plains, avoiding all snowy passes."

eight miles distant from the Am Mochoo, the mission halted.

On the 7th of February, the Jungpen of Tsangbe called on Mr. Eden, and told him that he had received no communication from Government about him, and could neither give him any assistance himself, nor allow the villagers to do so. Also, that it was not the custom of the country to allow persons to pass the forts without orders; but that, as he had not a sufficient number of men to stop the mission, Mr. Eden could go on if he chose to do so, but that he would not give him a single coolie. When asked if he would take the responsibility of saying that the Deb Raja declined to receive the mission, he said he had no authority to say anything of the kind, as he had no doubt that if Mr. Eden went on, he would be well received, but at the same time thought it desirable that he should remain where he was until he (the Jungpen) communicated with Government. Mr. Eden pointed out to him that the Deb Raja had had ample time to communicate his intentions to his various subordinates, and said that he might write to the effect that he (Mr. Eden) was unwilling to turn back, knowing how serious the consequences would be to the Bhotan Government, unless he was aware for certain, that it was not intended he should be received, and that if only distinctly told so, he should go back at once.

On examining the coolies at this place, it was found that nearly all the Nepaulese ones had been more or less frost-bitten in crossing the Tulélah pass, and some of them very badly. "We therefore," says Mr. Eden, "purchased a number of hides and pieces of woollen cloth, and compelled them all to make boots for themselves, according to the fashion of the country." The oversight of not—while forcing men on a distasteful service of this kind—having made provision for such a contigency as here referred to, will be self evident.

Mr. Eden, seeing that it was quite hopeless entertaining the idea of bringing on the portion of his camp left at Sipchoo, sent instructions to Mr. Power to return as soon as he could to Darjeeling, taking with him all the extra stores and baggage, as well as the Seiks and sappers left at Dhalimkote, with the exception of five of the latter to remain as a guard over the things left with the Jungpen of that place. He was instructed also to leave with the Nieboo of Sipchoo a store of rice for the party on its return, and all the presents from the Governor-General for the Bhotan Court, which, from want of carriage, Mr. Eden had been unable to bring on with him. He then arranged with the Jungpen of Tsangbe and the Nieboo of Sipchoo to keep the mission's communication open with Darjeeling by a line of dawk (postal) runners, and to give protection to people passing backwards and forwards thus employed. This they both agreed to do, on receiving a present, with a promise of a further one, on the completion of their engagement.*

* On the way to Tsangbe the mission passed a flour-mill worked by a water-wheel. The miller in charge of it, an old man, had a large tumour on his lip, which entirely concealed his mouth and lower part of his face, and seriously interfered with his taking food. Dr. Simpson told him that he would remove it for him if he came to where the mission was going to encamp. He did so while it halted at Tsangbe, and had the tumour excised under the influence of chloroform, to the great astonishment of a large number of spectators. The results of this operation would seem to have spread with rapidity through the

On the 9th of February the mission left Tsangbe, passing the fort of that name on the way—a small building of rubble stone with a wooden roof, and remarkable only for the beauty of its situation. After going a few miles, a steep descent had to be made to a small river, the Sukchu, which was crossed by a good wooden bridge. The opposite side of the valley was then ascended by a steep zigzag, "evidently made several years ago at a considerable expense." On the way a beautiful waterfall was passed: the supply of water was not large, but it fell from a considerable height, and was scattered like rain. On reaching the top of the ascent a number of villagers collected and paid the mission the compliment due to all persons of distinction travelling through the country; namely, setting fire to little heaps of wormwood as they pass. They seem to be under the impression that Mr. Eden and his party had come to take possession of the country, and were undisguised in their abuse of their own Government. The halting-place for this day was Saybee, described as "a very fine little village," with some cultivation and good houses; its elevation being 6143 feet, and its distance from Tsangbe about ten miles.

On reaching this place, Mr. Eden was informed that some Government messengers (Zinkaffs) had recently arrived, and had given out that they were charged with instructions to turn him back. Hearing that these men said they had letters for him,

country, as Mr. Eden states with reference thereto: "The operation seemed to have attracted the attention of the Bootanese in a very singular manner, for, at every village through which we passed, and on our arrival at the Durbar (state reception) one of the first questions asked, was, 'Which was the Doctor who had removed the tumour?'"

Mr. Eden sent for them, but they made excuses for not coming. On threatening to have them punished, they at last came. The interview with them will be best given in Mr. Eden's own words—"It turned out that they had no letters for me: they said they had letters to the Darlingcote Jungpen, instructing him to turn me back. I replied that as they had nothing for me they might go. They told me that if I went on I might be opposed. I pointed out to them that I could not act upon the information of petty messengers like themselves, and unless they could show written authority from the Deb to forbid my coming on, I would have nothing to say to them. They gave me the letters to the Darlingcote Jungpen, and told me to read them, as they were intended to have reached him whilst I was there, and were instructions regarding me. I opened the cover and found two letters, according to the Booteah custom; one full of professions of friendship for the British Government, and instructing him to do everything he could to satisfy me and settle any dispute I might have with him regarding the frontier, but not a word about my going back. This letter was evidently intended to be shown to me. The second was a most violent and intemperate production, threatening the Jungpen with forfeiture of life for having allowed me to cross the frontier, ordering him to pay a fine of rupees seventy to each of the messengers sent him, and abusing him in the grossest terms; at the same time, telling him on no account to allow me to go away angry, but to try and entice me across the frontier again, adding, however, that if he could not get rid of me without offending me, he should send me on to the Durbar by the Sumchee and Dhone road, and should see that proper arrangements were made for furnishing supplies. The Zinkaffs, after reading the letters, said it was clear that I should go back and enter the country by the Sumchee road. I pointed out that two days more would bring me into the Sumchee road, and that to go back would take me fifteen days. They said that the Amla (council) had shown such folly in not giving proper orders for my reception, that they should not trouble themselves in the matter, and that I might go which way I liked. I asked one of them to return with me; he agreed at first, but then said he must go on to Darling (Dhalimkote) to get his share of the fine; but they gave me guides from the village, and supplied us with fodder, &c., for the horses."

While at Saybee, the villagers and their headmen came to Mr. Eden, and begged to be allowed to accompany his party back to Darjeeling. They were told that they were at liberty to go and settle there if they liked, but they explained that the difficulty they had to overcome was to get away from their own country, where they were so watched as to be unable to escape without leaving their families behind them, and that the lives of the families of runaways were looked upon as forfeited. They repeated what it appears had been mentioned to the mission some marches back, namely, that from three European children having been born in the village, it was an omen that the country would pass into the hands of the British, and that they had been expecting the fulfilment of this omen for some time, and now that people of that nation had come to the village, they felt it was true. At the request of Mr. Eden, the children in question were brought to the camp—they had no claims to

European origin, but were Albinos. This was explained to the villagers, but they could not be made to understand that there was not something mysterious about their birth, and that it was connected with the advent of the mission; as they said they had never heard of any other children of similar appearance having been born in the country.

On the 10th of February the mission left Saybee, first making a slight descent to the River Saychoo, and then an ascent by a very steep zigzag up the commencement of the Taigonlah Mountain, over the top of which it had to pass. About the middle of the day, an open grassy plain, at a height of 9256 feet, named Bhokur, was reached. Here there was a little snow, and a magnificent herd of yaks or Chowrie cattle, that apparently had been driven down from the higher pass by the heavy snow. As there was a doubt about finding a supply of water further on, and the snow was found to be deep, the mission terminated its day's journey here, hoping to clear the pass the next day. On the morning of the eleventh it again started, but made slow progress, owing to the steepness of the ascent and depth of the snow: both horses and men making their way with difficulty. Here the whole aspect of the country changed; instead of the usual forests of rhododendron, magnolia, oak, chestnut, &c., the party suddenly passed into an entirely new vegetation, nothing being seen but pines of various descriptions, and which was found to be a forest much more pleasant to travel in than that through which it had hitherto been passing: being thinner and cleaner from undergrowth. Towards evening a stone rest house, erected for the shelter of travellers overtaken in the snow, was passed. "In the evening," says Mr. Eden, "we halted at Shafebjhee; the snow was deep, but the men made themselves, and us, tolerably comfortable by collecting large quantities of juniper and laying it over the snow, and the juniper and pine boughs made splendid fires which they kept up all night. The height of the camp was 11,800 feet: the thermometer registered 13°, yet with some two hundred persons, some Sikhs, others Bengallees, not a man suffered from the cold." At this place a heavy mist completely obscured the view, and as Captain Austen was desirous of being able to fill into his map observations made from so commanding a position, he determined to remain behind, and catch the mission up two marches ahead.

On the 12th of February Mr. Eden went on, leaving Captain Austen and his Assistants in a little rest house close to the pass, made partly out of the face of the rock, partly of stones. The descent from the pass was found very steep, the snow apparently increasing—in place of decreasing in depth as the elevation became less. The road lay alongside a pretty little stream, which had to be crossed ten times by small wooden bridges—"the men had some difficulty in making a road through the snow, and in places where there had been water-courses there were large sheets of ice very trying for men with a maund weight on their backs; in several places, little waterfalls had frozen, and there were large icicles twenty feet high." Some hours' marching brought the mission into the Hah valley, through some scenery described as very lovely and park-like, and here it encamped for the night, at Dorika; a small plain on the banks of the Hachoo River. A few miles before arriving at this place, the party had struck, and passed along the Sumchee and Dhone road: the route usually taken to the Dooars and plains of Bengal from Paro and Western Bhotan generally.

On the 13th of February, the camp was struck at Dorika, and the party crossed the Hachoo by a strong wooden bridge, and marched along a good level road up a very beautiful valley along the banks of the river. On the way some fine villages containing strong three storied houses were passed; many of them however were in ruins, the rest were empty; the occupants having gone down to spend the winter at Sumchee (Chamoorchee). The scenery as the mission advanced became magnificent, immediately facing it were the high peaks of the Thibet mountains, the sides of the valley for about a quarter of a mile perfectly flat, with the clear stream of the Hachoo, about sixty yards wide, creeping slowly along, and presenting a marked contrast to the boisterous torrents that had recently been passed. The fields on both sides of the river were neatly fenced like those at Tsangbe, and water was conducted over them by a system of small channels. The land was terraced and revetted with stones, and each village had a good bridge across the river.

Early in the day Hah Tampien was reached. As it was approached large flocks of black sheep, yaks, and cattle were grazing below the snow line. This place was found to be the residence of a Jungpen, the villages in its neighbourhood were inhabited, and the people came out in a crowd to receive the mission. Their appearance in common with that of the inhabitants of the pine forest tracts generally is represented as not prepossessing; as they keep large fires burning in their houses day and night, which having no chimneys, leads to a thick deposit of soot being left on their faces, which, as they never wash, does not improve the expression of their countenances. Here, however, the mission seems to have met with the first indications of spontaneous civility; as the Jungpen, immediately on its arrival, sent down a supply of fire-wood, forage for the horses, and buckwheat flour.

The next day the Jungpen called on Mr. Eden, who thus describes him—"he was a very fine and well mannered old man; he gave us a hearty welcome, and brought with him his family; his wife is a daughter of the Paro Penlow: they stayed a long time in our camp, looking at such curiosities as we had with us, and he entreated me so earnestly to stay one day that I could not refuse him, especially as I was anxious that Captain Austen should rejoin us here. The Paro Penlow's wife, who was on a visit to her daughter, called and assured me that we should be received in a very friendly manner by her husband." The fort under the charge of this Jungpen was a very pretty four storied little building, commanded, as is the case with most Bhotanese fortifications, by an outpost, higher than itself, about eighty yards distant. One of the Jungpen's servants had lately mutinied and taken possession of this outpost, and set his master at defiance. About two miles from the fort there is a fine monastery, and in its immediate neighbourhood is a black temple dedicated to the tutelary deity of the poisoners, "one of the chief favourites in the Bhotean pantheon." Some distance up the valley are a number of fine villages, the inhabitants of which are said to be the richest in Bhotan, but have the reputation of being very lawless, and great robbers. Their proximity to Thibet places them in a more independent position, for being within a few miles of that frontier, if ill treated they have only to run across the path and are safe from pursuit. They appeared to Mr. Eden more civil, obliging and truthful than the people of the country generally. Close to the camp there was a medicinal spring, held in repute by the inhabitants, as a cure for skin diseases and rheumatism. It was heated like the mineral springs in Sikim, by throwing hot stones into the water.

During the night heavy snow fell, and in the morning it was two feet deep all over the camp. At daybreak the Jungpen, with his wife, children and all his followers, came again to the camp; their object being to see that the mission had not suffered from the cold. They brought with them straw and fir poles, with which they constructed tents for the sepoys, and took all the camp followers and coolies to the village to give them better shelter. The snow continued to fall all the 15th and 16th, and prevented any of the party moving from their tents. On the latter date Captain Austen returned. Considerable anxiety had been experienced about him; the more so, as rumours reached the mission, through the villagers, that some of the people with him had died of the cold, and which proved to be true.

Captain Austen, it appeared, had remained where the mission left him for the first day of the snow, thinking that it was only of a local and temporary character, and that on its ceasing, he would be able to continue his observations. Finding that it was becoming continuous he determined to descend, and in so doing found the snow in many places breast deep. This, combined with the fact of its snowing heavily at the time, led to his party getting separated; and on arriving at Dorika, in the valley, four men were found missing. Captain Austen sent back to seek for them. Two were found dead at the top of the pass, where they had lain down to die shortly after starting. The other two had been picked up by the ex-Jungpen of Tsangbe, who happened to be passing at the time. He had helped himself to the property found with the dead bodies, and had also broken open the boxes carried by the coolies that he had saved. Some difficulty was experienced in getting him to give up the property he had thus acquired.

On the 17th of February the weather cleared, but it was impossible to move, owing to the depth of the snow, and the extreme cold; the thermometer standing at 11°. Mr. Eden now heard that a deputation from the Government was on its way to stop his progress. He determined to frustrate this movement, and leave Hah Tampien as soon as practicable, and make his way to Paro, and there personally ascertain how the Penlow of that place, usually one of the most influential men in the country, was disposed towards him. He kept his intention secret from the Jungpen, and, judging that two days of sun must have reduced the depth of the snow, he made up his mind to start on the 19th of February. Accordingly at daylight, Captain Austen and Dr. Simpson started with Cheeboo Lama's servants, and twenty strong men that had been sent by the Sikim Raja a few days before, to aid the mission. This party was to tread a path through the snow, which Mr. Eden, with the remainder of the camp, was to follow. Some hours after they had started, Mr. Eden sent on the baggage and tents. The Jungpen, now perceiving the intention to leave, came down with all his men, and stated in a violent manner that the mission could not go on; as he had orders from the Government to stop it; until the deputation referred to arrived. He was asked to show his orders, but could not do so. Mr. Eden then informed him that half the camp had gone on several hours, and were by that time half way to Paro, and that he could not delay a moment longer. He was very angry, but became so far soothed by a present as to give guides and the aid of some sepoys, on Mr. Eden's promising not to mention having received any assistance from him.

Mr. Eden overtook the advanced party under Captain Austen at three o'clock in the afternoon; the ascent, from the untrodden state of the snow, having proved one of great difficulty, and very trying to the impaired strength of the coolies. The end of the pass appeared not more than half a mile distant, and from the information given him, Mr. Eden was led to believe that, once across the pass, a village could be reached where shelter for the night would be found. It was therefore decided to push on — the snow, however became deeper and deeper; varying from three to eight feet. The horses and mules were continually sinking over their backs in it, and much delay was experienced. At six o'clock the top of the pass was reached, and Mr. Eden concluded that the day's difficulties were over, and sent on Dr. Simpson and Captain Austen with the advanced party; while he waited behind to see the rear one across; especially as some of the coolies were trying to lie down in the snow and fall asleep. Several of them had to be carried, so prostrated had both their mental and physical powers become, from the combined effects of over fatigue and cold. The expectations with reference to the day's troubles being at an end proved premature; because, as the party advanced, the snow became of greater and greater depth, and both mules and horses were continually sinking up to their necks. "Evening," states Mr. Eden, "began to draw on whilst we were still on the pass, and the coolies became frightened and desponding, and many wanted to be allowed to lie down and die. A halt would have involved the death of every man in the camp; for there was no going to the right or left. We drove and encouraged the men on, but our progress was not more than a quarter of a mile an hour; fortunately the weather was clear, and there was a bright moon. At about eleven o'clock at night we reached some forest, which afforded shelter from the wind, and the snow was less deep in places. The coolies were getting sick and faint, and I therefore gave them permission to bivouac in gangs of not less than twelve, with a Sirdar (headman) with each gang, who was to see that the men kept close together, and that a fire was burning all night. I gave those who could do so permission to go on, leaving their loads piled under trees, whence they could be fetched next morning. They readily took advantage of this permission, and we went on with greatly reduced numbers. The horses and mules struggled through the snow in the most wonderful manner, sinking over their hocks at every step, constantly rolling on their backs, and yet keeping up with us." If such were the difficulties encountered by the lower animals in keeping their equilibrium, and making their way through the snow, what must have been the difficulties experienced by worn-out frost-bitten coolies, burdened with upwards of two-thirds of a hundredweight on their backs?

Midnight passed without any signs of the village appearing which Mr. Eden supposed was just below the Pass. At one A.M., however, of the 20th February, its proximity was indicated to them by the baying of a Thibetian watch-dog, and they shortly afterwards reached the place, 'perfectly exhausted, not having tasted food since nine o'clock the previous morning, and having been marching through the snow continuously for fifteen hours.' Shelter in good houses was procured. When morning came all the coolies who had been left behind turned up in safety with their loads. The height of the Cheulah Pass (that which had just been crossed) was 12,490 feet, and the height of the village 10,067 feet. An advanced portion of the deputation sent to arrest the progress of the mission was found in this village. They had attempted to force the Pass during the snow storm, so as to get to Hah Tampien before Mr. Eden left it, but could not succeed, and had to return. On hearing of the arrival of the mission at the village they took their departure, making a great noise, and, in the confusion which at the time prevailed, stealing everything they could lay their hands on, including one of the Seik's muskets.

Early in the forenoon of the 20th, the deputation itself arrived, having been detained seven days in a neighbouring monastery, in consequence of the snow. They made themselves very disagreeable, and turned a number of the mission followers out of the houses in which they had taken shelter. Their servants crowded round the baggage; and before the sentry had time to see what they were about, they bolted with some cooking utensils, and whatever else they could conveniently lay their hands on. In the course of the day the deputies (Zinkaffs) waited on Mr. Eden, and delivered a letter to him from the Deb Raja. They told him that their instructions were to return with him to the frontier, for the purpose of re-arranging the boundary, and receiving charge again of the resumed Assam Dooars. After this the demands of the British Government were to be enquired into; and if they (the Zinkaffs) considered it necessary, Mr. Eden was to be allowed to proceed to Poonakha, for the purpose of having an interview with the Deb and Dhurma Rajas. The letter from the Deb Raja was of the same evasive character as all his previous communications. In reference to Mr. Eden's threat to return to Darjeeling, he said that he should not speak of doing that, as he had never declined to receive him; "but that it would be well to investigate complaints on the frontier, and that the surplus collections of the Assam Dooars and of Ambaree Fallacottah ought to be paid to the Bhotan Government." Mr. Eden declined to enter into any negociations with the Zinkaffs, and said that he would either return to Darjeeling, or go on to Poonakha. They begged him not to do the former, and undertook to go forward and make arrangements for his reception at the latter place. They accordingly took their departure professedly for this purpose.

Mr. Eden followed them on the morning of the 21st February, and was met on the road by some messengers, who requested him to defer entering Paro that day; but to halt a few miles from the place, as the Penlow was desirous of receiving him with great honour, and required time to make the necessary preparations.

The mission accordingly halted for the day, and on the 22nd of February went on to Paro, where, far from any arrangements having been made for its reception, it was kept standing on a sandy plain for two hours, with a strong wind blowing, without being allowed to pitch its tents—every place that was proposed as the site of the camp being objected to for some such reason as its being sacred to a wood sprite or a river demon. After considerable delay some officers came out of the fort, and pointed out one of the spots that had been previously objected to as that on which the mission was to encamp. A few oranges and pieces of Thibetian bread were sent as a present from the Penlow; but none of the customary friendly ceremonials were gone through.

CHAPTER V.

The Paro Authorities send for Cheeboo Lama—The Mission treated with Insolence—Mr. Eden's Interview with the Penlow and Ex Penlow of Paro—Fort, Town, and Market Place of Paro—Dispute with a Police Official—Valley of Paro—Proximity to Thibet—Monasteries—Paro Annual Festival and Races—The Master of the Horse—Departure for Poonakha—Government Messengers meet the Mission and endeavour to stop it—The Ex Deb Raja—The Dokiew Lah Pass and its traditionary Mark—Approach to Poonakha.

On the 23d of February the Paro Penlow, accompanied by his father-in-law, the ex Paro Penlow*, sent for Cheeboo Lama, and in the first place threatened him for daring to bring Englishmen into the country—in the course however of further conversation, he admitted the probability of good resulting

* This ex-official is the Paro Penlow referred to in the sketch given of the state of the country at the time the mission reached Darjeeling, as the one who had taken up the cause of the Deb Rajah, dethroned by the Jungpen of Poonakha for not promoting him to the governorship of Augdu Forung. The Paro Penlow again, his stepson, was the son of a previous Penlow of Paro, of whom the ex Penlow in question had been chief officer, and whom on his death he succeeded—the succession including also the wife and family; the Paro Penlow who figures above being one of the children. This young man, through his own father, being related to the Jungpen of Augdu Forung and some other influential members of Government, his stepfather, when the tide of fortune was turning against him during the late rebellion, hit on the happy expedient of saving his position by abdicating in favour of his stepson, in hopes that the young man's connexions would prevent Paro being attacked. At the same time however, he retained all the real power in his own hands, while he allowed his stepson to assume the dignity of the office, and occupy the State apartments in the fort.

from the mission, but that the Government had positively prohibited them from allowing it to proceed; and that if Mr. Eden would wait at Paro, pending a reference to Poonakha, which would take only four days, the mission would be made comfortable and treated with respect. They added that there was no object in the mission going on to Poonakha; as the Deb Raja had no authority, and that the Paro Penlow, as Ruler of Western Bhotan, was the proper officer to deal with. The latter proposition was not entertained, as Mr. Eden states that he "declined to open any negotiations with any one but the supreme authority, whether real or nominal"—he agreed however to remain four days, pending a reference to Poonakha.

Notwithstanding the promise which the Penlows had made, that in the event of the mission's remaining at Paro it would be treated with respect, the practice was the contrary. The mission was ordered to remain in camp until further orders, and on declining to do so was treated with insolence. The Penlow's soldiers crowded round the camp, stole whatever was within their reach, jeered the coolies and followers, called them slaves, and drew their knives upon them, on their making any attempt at reply. The mission servants were fined for going about with their heads covered, and attempts were made to make Mr. Eden and the higher officers dismount from their ponies on nearing the residence of the police officer of the place. The villagers also were punished who were detected selling provisions or holding any communication with the camp. As the insolence was increasing, and also as the messengers the Penlow had promised to send to Poonakha, had not even been started, Mr. Eden sent to him to say, that he would no longer brook such treatment, and that unless he adopted a different course towards him, he should either go at once to Poonakha or back to Darjeeling.

This threat proved successful; the Penlow dispatched the messengers to Poonakha, and had an interview with Mr. Eden, at which he wished to make it appear that the unfriendly course which had been pursued was attributable to the ex Penlow—who, he stated, having voluntarily abdicated, should not in future be allowed to interfere. This explanation Mr. Eden characterises as a mere subterfuge adopted by him, to get out of a false position. The annoyances however decreased, and in a few days the ex Penlow requested Mr. Eden to call and see him, which he did, and was received in a friendly manner. After this interview he became civil and communicative, and gave the mission a good deal of information about the present state of Government. He explained that, though for the sake of appearances, hostilities had been suspended during the visit of the mission to the country, he did not recognise the existing Government; as the ex Deb had been forcibly dethroned, and all authority usurped by the Tongso Penlow, in whose hands the present Deb and Dhurma Rajas were mere puppets. Also, that there was no man either of ability or position in the Council, and that all the places about the court were being filled by creations of the Tongso Penlow. He likewise informed Mr. Eden that the confidential adviser of the latter was a Hindostanee, who came to Bhotan after the Bengal mutiny, bringing with him papers purporting to bear the seals of "The Kings of Delhi, Lahore and Nepaul," and that he had proposed to the Bhotan Government to join a general war for the purpose of driving the English from India. All this, as will be seen hereafter, proved to be true. He begged Mr. Eden to bear in mind, that, whatever the Government then in power might do, he was not responsible for it, and had refused to stop the progress of the mission by force—also, that if any violence was attempted to it at Poonakha, he would render it assistance.

Paro Fort, the residence of both the Penlow and the ex Penlow, is described as a very striking building, far surpassing the expectations which had been formed of Bhotanese architecture. "It is a rectangular building surrounding a hollow square, in the centre of which is a high tower of some seven stories, surrounded by a large copper cupola. The outer building has five stories, three of which are habitable; the two lower stories being used as granaries and stores are lighted with small loopholes, whilst the upper stories are lighted with large windows, opening in most cases into comfortable verandahs. The entrance to the fort is on the east side by a little bridge over a narrow ditch; the gateway is handsome, and the building alone is much higher than the rest of the outer square; it is ornamented and painted, and has a number of well-executed inscriptions engraved on stone and iron, some of them gilt. At the gateway are a row of cages, in which are kept four enormous Thibetian mastiffs." The gates are lined with iron plates, studded with nails, and the thresholds also are covered with iron. The first thing which catches the eye on entering the fort is a large cylinder, about ten feet high, turned by a crank, so arranged that on each rotation, a bell is rung. This is used for the mechanical recitation of holy sentences—praying by machinery in fact. The visitor on entering the court is surprised to find himself at once on the third story; "for the fort is built on a rock which is overlapped by the lower stories, and forms the ground base of the courtyard and centre towers." Thus shot striking anywhere lower than the verandahs, would not find its way into the court, but only pass through the store-room and be arrested by the rock. After passing through a dark passage which turns first to the left and then to the right, a large well-paved and scrupulously clean courtyard is reached; the first set of rooms on the left is devoted to the relatives of the ladies of the palace. Beyond these rooms is a second small gateway, and the first set of rooms on the left hand were occupied by the ex Penlow. They were reached by a steep staircase opening into a long open vestibule, in which his followers lounge. This again leads into a large hall where his soldiers mess, and in which one of his secretaries is always in waiting. "Below the hall is the Penlow's state room; it is somewhat low, but of great size and really very striking, for the Bootanese have derived from their intercourse with Thibet and China in old days very considerable taste in decoration. The beams are richly painted in blue, orange, and gold, the Chinese dragon being the most favourite device; the roof is supported by a series of carved arches, and all round the room and on the arches are suspended bows, quivers, polished iron helmets, swords, matchlocks, coats of mail, Chinese lanterns, flags and silk scarves consecrated by the Grand Laama of Thibet, arranged with the most perfect taste."

The walls of the fort are very thick, and are composed of rubble stone, gradually sloping from the base to the top. The garrison consisted, at the time Mr. Eden visited it, of about two hundred and fifty soldiers, but its strength is nominally four hundred. "Each village has to send a certain number of men, who are bound to serve seven years, and can only escape this servitude by purchasing their discharge for rupees seventy. In point of fact, they never wish for their discharge, for though they receive no pay, they have food and clothing for nothing, and a general license to plunder and extort from the rest of the inhabitants of the country." These men are represented as having no knowledge of drill, even of the rudest description, and to be but imperfectly acquainted with the use of their own fire-arms. "They are employed in repairing and building the forts, embanking rivers, &c., and in this respect their work is really very creditable." The fort is approached by a handsome bridge, the entrances to which are paved with large slabs of stone, and at each end there is a large, strongly built stone tower in which a guard remains at night under the warder of the bridge. "The bridge is very neatly boarded with deal planks, and about fifteen yards is a wooden arch, handsomely painted, and covered with the mystic sentence.* These arches support a wooden roof." The road from the bridge to the fort is paved throughout, and about half way is a flag beyond which no one is allowed to go on horseback; not even the Penlow himself. Restrictions similar to this, exist, in the vicinity of some of the Imperial and Buddhistic buildings in Peking—the limit to equestrians being indicated by large stone

* The words—"Om Manee Padme Hom;" the mystic and sacred sentence of Thibet.

slabs, bearing inscriptions usually in the Chinese, Manchu, Mongolian and Thibetian languages. Inside the fort there is a monastery, containing about seventy monks, who seemed to be treated with little respect; the only use to which the mission saw them put, was playing the band at the Paro annual races. They receive food and clothing gratis. Above the large fort there are six smaller ones, intended to be outposts, but the whole of which command the lower and principal fort.

During the mission's detention at Paro, a good deal of topographical information was picked up about the neighbourhood. The town was found to be situated within a quarter of a mile of the fort, and to consist of about thirty good three-storied stone houses; having a market-place, in the form of a large open stony square near the river, where every evening between two and three hundred people collected. In the centre of the square there is a small ornamented building, in which a police official sits during the market time to prevent fighting. "No one," states Mr. Eden, "is allowed to enter the market with the head covered or on horseback. We had several misunderstandings with the Darogah (police official) because we refused to dismount." The course here reported as having been adopted by the mission, affords a very fair illustration of the way in which troubles frequently arise between ourselves and semi-civilized nations; from the feeling, which, it is to be regretted, forms one of the characteristics of the Englishman abroad, that it is his right and mission to disregard the prejudices, and ride rough-shod over the time-honoured customs of Orientals. If it was the established rule of Paro market-place, that horsemen were not admitted, I am aware of no reasonable grounds why it should have been deliberately broken through by the gentlemen constituting this mission:—if they considered it derogatory to conform to the market rule, it became their duty to put a check on their curiosity, and refrain from visiting a place, where an observance was demanded, compliance with which was felt to be incompatible with a proper regard for what was due to their position, in place of adopting a course which might have led to violence being shown them.

In the vicinity of the market-place there is a curious old gateway, the walls and ceilings of which are covered with Chinese frescoes, apparently executed many years ago. This gateway stands on a road which leads to Phagri, a large commercial town in Thibet. It passes up the valley of the Patchoo River, and is the road by which Turner's mission reached Thibet. It is easy for pack cattle throughout, and the distance can be done in two days by laden coolies. "Paro," observes Mr. Eden, "from its situation should be one of the largest cities in the East; situated in a perfectly level plain, easy of access from the low country, surrounded by land capable of producing great quantities of wheat and rice, only two easy marches by an excellent road from one of the chief marts in Thibet, it ought to be the *entrepôt* of the trade of Thibet, Tartary, China, and India. It should be full of depots of broad cloth, cotton goods, cutlery, rice, corals, tea, spices, kincoles, leather, and miscellaneous articles of European manufacture brought there to be exchanged for rock salt, musk, gold dust, borax, and silk, but under its present rulers not a Thibetian ever ventures across the frontier, and there is not only no trade, but no communication between Thibet and Paro. On the Thibet road, about seven miles from Paro, is the fort of Dakya Jung, which is intended to act as a defence against invasion from the Thibet side. The lower and level portion of the valley is richly cultivated with rice, which is procurable in considerable quantities at two rupees a maund; the higher portion of the valley grows a very fine, full-grained wheat and barley. We rode on one occasion down the valley some ten miles, nearly to where the Patchoo joins the Thimpoo or Tchinchoo River, along the bank of which is the Buxa Dooar route taken by Pemberton and Turner; the Paro valley is a perfectly level plain: to this point, the road was an excellent unmade grass ride, along the river banks, with an avenue of weeping willows; both sides of the river are well studded with pretty villages, and their unusually prosperous look was, we found, attributable to the fact that they belonged to the sepoys and officials of the fort; we ascertained that every evening the whole garrison of the fort was allowed to leave and remain in their homes for the night; many of them on a sort of furlough and were permitted to remain in the villages for months together, and during harvest and seed time, the men are nearly all absent at their little farms. There must have been some six or seven hundred houses in the valley, all of three or four stories. Cattle were numerous, and the people seemed, compared with the rest of the Bootanese, tolerably contented." The soil in the neighbourhood of Paro would seem to be charged with iron to a singular extent; as shown by the fact that a magnet placed on the ground anywhere in the valley became immediately covered with a kind of ferruginous dust, also that on collecting a heap of sand and working it with the magnet, "a very large per-centage of iron was separated from the sand." There is an iron mine two days' journey from Paro, from which lead in small quantities is stated also to be obtained.

"The tops of the mountain ridges all around Paro are dotted with monasteries. On the Eastern range is the celebrated monastery of Dongâlah; it is said to have a number of good frescoes on its walls by Thibetian artists. During our stay at Paro, the mountain on which it is situated was one mass of snow, and we could not therefore visit it. Close to Paro, on the western side of the valley is Gorikha; the monastery is small, but is much venerated by the people. Above this monastery is a large, level, grass plateau about 9000 feet high, with a magnificent view of the Thibetian snowy range, and immediately fronted by the splendid cone-shaped Chumularhi, a sacred mountain in Thibet, 23,944 feet high, which is visible from Baugulpore and other stations hundreds of miles away in the plains. The plateau under any Government but that of Bootan would be used as the summer palace of Paro, and as summer quarters for troops; for though Paro is 7,741 feet high, higher indeed than any of our sanatoria,* the sun has great power there, notwithstanding the strong breeze which blows up the valley regularly from 10 A.M. to 5 P.M. On a bleak hill on the north-west of Paro valley is a place of pilgrimage

* Mr. Eden is hardly correct here; because Senchal the cantonment of Darjeeling is 8,600 feet high—Julla Pahar however, where the Convalescent Depot is, is about 1000 feet lower.

held in much esteem by the Buddhists, the temple and monastery of Tuckshung (the Tiger's Cave). It is cut of, and built into the rock, and overhangs a fearful precipice. The venerated Goraknath is said to have visited the spot, ejected the tigers, and resided there. Cheeboo Lama, and nearly all the Sikhimese were highly delighted at the opportunity afforded them of visiting this celebrated place, and some of our Sirdars (headmen of coolies) spent all their money in the purchase of butter to burn in votive lamps. Those with barren wives, who desired heirs, anticipated the most beneficial results from their pilgrimage to the shrine."

Towards the close of the mission's stay at Paro, the annual festival began; but Mr. Eden could not stay to see more than the races, with which it commenced—"A long string of ponies was brought each being ornamented with ribbons and coloured streamers, mounted by men with very little clothing on except a long coloured scarf hanging from the head. In front of the riders was the Tah-pen, or Master of the Horse. It is curious that this functionary who is a high officer of the Court, should have a title so precisely similar to one of our own Court officials, but Master of the Horse is a literal translation of his title (*tah*, a horse; *pen*, a master). On arriving at the starting-post all the riders dismounted; sepoys armed with long whips rushed amongst the crowd, and cleared a road with great brutality and violence. At a given signal the ponies were one by one flogged by a number of men with whips into a gallop; the riders had to run holding on by the mane until the pony was well off, and then vault up to their seats. Many showed considerable dexterity, vaulting backwards and forwards over the ponies whilst at a gallop, lying down full length on the ponies' backs. No saddles or pads of any sort were used. The ponies were started one after another, and there was no attempt at testing their speed; the skill of the rider alone was on the trial. After going a certain distance they halted, and were started again in the same manner; some six different starts must have been made before the course was completed. At the end of the course the riders were all entertained at the expense of the Penlow, and they then went back to the palace in the same manner. The Tah-pen was lifted off and on to his horse on each occasion with a great parade, for it is contrary to Booteah notions of dignity for a man to mount and dismount from his horse himself." The old Penlow, though the *ex* one in name, in reality possessed all authority, and was very anxious that Mr. Eden should remain and see the festivities to an end—and though in the first instance he objected to sketching and photography, he offered in the event of Mr. Eden's staying, to allow the camera to be brought into the palace (fort) and the whole scenes taken from there. He also offered to dress himself in armour, and have his own likeness taken. Mr. Eden's anxiety to bring his mission to a conclusion at Poonakha, and get back to Bengal before the setting in of the rains prevented his accepting the offer.

Sixteen days having elapsed since the mission arrived at Paro, and no communication having been received from the Bhotan Government, though such could have been easily sent in two days, Mr. Eden informed the Penlow that he must either return to Darjeeling or go on without further delay. The Penlow admitted that the mission had been treated with inexcusable neglect, but said that nothing better could be expected from such a ministry as was then in power, "and that there was no accounting for anything it did." He, however, recommended Mr. Eden to go on; as he thought if he once got to head-quarters all would go well. On Mr. Eden's taking leave of the old Penlow before starting, he was very friendly, and warned him to keep a constant watch on the Council, as it was composed of treacherous and ignorant men.*

On the 10th of March the mission left Paro by a steep ascent up a fair road winding amongst the detached outworks of the fort. On reaching the top of the pass (11,164 feet) a little snow was found—also a fort called the Bieylah Jung, having a garrison of a few men. From here, by a gradual descent of eight miles down the opposite side, through smooth grass and pine forest filled with all sorts of game. The mission then came to a village named Pemethong, distinguished by a few houses and an empty monastery and fort, where it encamped on a fine open flat, at an elevation of 8,499 feet. A good many of the inhabitants were Bengallees, apparently from Cooch Behar, who had been abducted many years before, and retained but confused ideas of the country from which they had come.

* This warning was *bonâ fide*; as it came to light afterwards that the Paro Penlow had been requested to seize Cheeboo Lama, and send the rest of the mission back. He refused to do this, but said that if the Government sent him a written order to prevent the mission coming on, he would put it in force, but not practise any treachery. The Government, however, declined to take the responsibility of giving him the order.

Whilst the mission was encamped at this place, Government messengers—some of whom were the same as met it at Hah Tampien—arrived from Poonakha, and said they had orders from the Deb Raja, to the effect that the mission was to return at once with them to Paro, and after hearing all Mr. Eden had to say, if they thought it necessary, higher officers would be sent to treat with him. Exactly the same scene was repeated here as took place on the 2nd of February, when the deputation met the mission shortly after it left Hah Tampien: Mr. Eden offering to go back to Darjeeling if they would say that the Deb declined to receive him, and they on the other hand refusing to commit themselves to any such statement, and winding up by telling him that if he would not return to Paro, and wait until some further course of action was decided on, he had better then continue his journey to Poonakha. Mr. Eden requested them to accompany him to the capital or go on in advance and explain what he had said—this they positively declined to do—saying they had received orders to go to Paro and must obey them.*

The mission now continued its course towards Poonakha, and shortly after leaving Pemethong came on the Buxa Dooar road, which runs along the valley of the Thimpoo River, so called, after the district of that name; the chief town of which is Tassishujung.

* It was afterwards ascertained that these men had been instructed to levy a fine on the Paro Penlow, as a punishment for his having allowed the mission to enter his territory. Showing that though the so-called Government would not take upon itself the responsibility of openly declining to receive the mission, it nevertheless systematically punished the local officers who had allowed the mission to progress towards the capital.

All the houses in the valley were remarkably good, and the mission halted at Chalamafee, a large village situated where the roads to Poonakha and Tassishujung meet: the latter place being only two miles off.

The following day, shortly after starting, the mission came to the monastery of Simtoka, where the Deb Raja, who had lately been dethroned, was found to be residing. Cheeboo Lama requested to be permitted to call upon him, but he declined seeing him, on the grounds that he had no power to assist the mission, and that the mere fact of any one connected with it, holding communication with him, might be prejudicial to its interests.

The party now passed along a narrow valley with a pine forest on either side, and gradually ascended the Dokiew Lah Pass 10,019 feet elevation; the incline to which was so gradual as scarcely to render the ascent perceptible. On the top of the pass there are the remains of a fort, some obelisks, and a wall bearing a sacred inscription. A few yards from the highest peak of the pass, there is a small indentation which the Bhotanese regard with veneration, as the mark of the hoofs of Doopgein Sheptoon's horse, who, already mentioned, tradition indicates as one of the founders of the Bhotan ecclesiastical dynasty. The view from the top of the Dokiew Lah Pass is represented as very magnificent, the whole of the Poonakha valley and vast extent of the snowy range of Thibet being seen immediately in front.

The mission being now within a short march of Poonakha, halted just above the village of Telagong, a place chiefly inhabited by monks, who were found to be living comfortably in substantial houses, many of them coloured and ornamented with wood carving.

The cultivation round this village consisted of wheat, barley, turnips, mustard and chillies, and is described as having been really fine. From Telagong Poonakha is reached by descending a valley, and, after crossing a small river, ascending the opposite side for a short distance, where there is a nearly level road leading to it; the elevation being about 5,000 feet. The country in the neighbourhood is perfectly open, and no trees are to be seen near the line of road.

CHAPTER VI.

Arrival of Mr. Eden at Poonakha—Two Natives taken from under his Protection—The Council send for Mr. Eden—Indignities from the Mob—Draft Treaty submitted—Interview with the Dhurma and Deb Rajas—The Tongso Penlow demands the Assam Dooars—Mr. Eden prepares to depart—Terms on which he consents to re-open Negotiations—Their Progress—The Tongso Penlow's Hindostanee adviser—Mr. Eden attends Council with the Treaty and is insulted—He endeavours to leave, but is not allowed until he signs a Document assigning over to Bhotan the Assam Dooars—He is then treated with Civility—Difficulties offered to his leaving—Poonakha Fort—The Mission succeeds in getting away and returning to Paro, and from thence to Darjeeling.

On the 15th of March the mission reached Poonakha, and though Mr. Eden had sent several men to announce his approach, and had also written to the Deb Raja to say when he would arrive, the only notice taken of his communications was a message sent by a sepoy, to say that the mission could not approach by the ordinary road, but must go down the side of the hill and come in by a back way. Mr. Eden prudently determined to give them no excuse for picking a quarrel and turned off by the route indicated, though it was so precipitous that the party had great difficulty in making the descent.

At first no notice whatever was taken of the mission or of any one connected with it, except that small quantities of very inferior rice were sent by the Jungpen of Poonakha, and that a demand was made by the

Tongso Penlow for the delivery of two British subjects, residents of the village of Kishengunge in the district of Purneah, who had taken refuge in the camp of the mission. One of these men Mr. Eden had detained with the sanction of the Paro Penlow, and the other was a slave at Poonakha, who, meeting Mr. Eden's party on the road, and seeing his brother employed as a coolie with it, had also joined it. Mr. Eden protested against this demand, claiming the men as British subjects. He was told in reply that they should be returned to him at once, but that it was necessary to make inquiries from them regarding the circumstances of their captivity, in order that proper measures should be taken for punishing those who had seized them. Mr. Eden allowed them to go away for this purpose, but instead of returning them, the Tongso Penlow sent them away from Poonakha to be slaves at a monastery. Mr. Eden made frequent demands for their return, and was at first met by evasion, but ultimately was plainly told that they would not be given up.

After the lapse of a day or two the Council sent for Cheeboo Lama and abused him in unmeasured terms for bringing the mission into the country, accusing him also of having planned it for his own good, and telling him that whatever resulted from it would be on his head. On the 17th of March they sent for Mr. Eden, who went down and was told that the Council would receive him in a house near the fort. He had to pass through a disorderly crowd of sepoys and servants, who were extremely insolent, and several stones and pieces of wood were thrown at him and his attendants. On approaching the house, they were told that the Council was not ready, and were kept standing out on a plain in a strong sun, exposed to the ridicule of several hundred persons. The members of the Council who had assembled to meet Mr. Eden, were the Tassishujung Jungpen, the Poonakha Jungpen, the Deb Rajah's Dewan, the Deb Zimpen (chief officer), and the Tongso Penlow, who had lately appointed himself also Zimpen, or chief officer to the Dhurma Rajah. The members of the Council who were absent, were the Koom Kulling or Chief Kazee (Judge), and the keeper of the Fort of Angdu Forung.*

On the mission being admitted to the presence of the council, the Tongso Penlow, though by right only an extraordinary member of the Council, occupied the seat of honour, took upon himself the office of spokesman, and would not allow any of the other members to take any part in the proceedings, or even to converse with any of the mission. The Council were on this occasion civil, though the manner of the Tongso Penlow was very supercilious, and no objections were

* This officer previously held the office of Jungpen of Poonakha, and is the person referred to at page 61, as having originated the rebellion which took place shortly before the mission visited Bhotan, and which resulted in the removal of the then ruling Deb Raja, and the appointment of an insignificant Lama to that office. To effect this, as stated by the Paro Penlow, the aid of the Tongso Penlow had been called in, and on his arrival with a large force, the scale was at once turned against the Government; but having done this, the Penlow instead of returning to Tongso, took up his residence at head-quarters, and appointed his own creatures and relatives to places of trust. Through him the Lama was put in as a puppet Deb Rajah, and by appointing himself Zimpen to the Dhurma Raja, he practically secured all authority in his own person; the other members of the Council being powerless in his hands, and much irritated by his remaining at Poonakha, with the exception, however, of the Tassishujung Jungpen, who was his son-in-law, and the Angdu Forung Jungpen, who was his chief supporter.

made to the mission bringing in their chairs with them and sitting down during the interview. None of the customary friendly ceremonies however were observed, the visit being characterised by cold formality. The Council said, that as the mission did not understand Bhoteah, and that as the Council did not understand Hindoostanee, the best way of conducting negotiations would be by Cheeboo Lama being made acquainted with Mr. Eden's views, and that they would make him (Cheeboo) similarly acquainted with theirs, and that he should go to them every day, and on his return inform Mr. Eden of what had passed and take further instructions from him; it being understood that they would receive all he said as coming direct from the British Envoy, who again was to receive all he said as coming from the Council. This proposal was readily agreed to by Mr. Eden, and the interview ended.

The draft treaty was then sent to them, and the 18th and 19th of March passed in discussions between Cheeboo Lama and the Tongso Penlow with reference to its provisions. The other members of the Council seemed to take no interest in the matter, and with difficulty could be persuaded to listen to the clauses of the draft, no objections were raised to any portion of the treaty except the eighth and ninth articles relating to the appointment of an agent at Poonakha and to free commercial intercourse between the two countries. Some slight hints were thrown out regarding the return of the Assam Dooars, but on Cheeboo Lama pointing out that that had nothing to do with the matter the British Envoy had come to settle, the subject was not further discussed.

Mr. Eden at this time remonstrated with regard to

the delay which had taken place in appointing a day for an interview with the Deb and Dhurma Rajas. He was at first told that there was no necessity for his seeing them at all. He insisted, however, and on the 20th of March was told that these dignitaries were waiting to receive him. Mr. Eden and the other members of the mission accordingly went, and every opportunity was taken of treating them with indignity. On the occasion of previous missions to Bhotan, the Envoys were allowed to sit and were received with respect by the Deb and Dhurma Rajas inside the palace; on the occasion in question however the mission was taken on to a plain behind the palace, and hustled into a tent a few feet square and made of thin cotton, the heat being almost unbearable, and the tent so pressed upon by the mob outside that it seemed in constant danger of coming down on the top of them. After being detained in this tent for about half an hour, they were told that the Council wished to see them, and they accordingly went to a small tent where the Council was seated. The mission had been accorded permission to bring their chairs—the servants however were forbidden to bring them into the tent. Mr. Eden remonstrated, but was told that he and his attendants must adapt themselves to the habits of the country. The whole interior of the tent was occupied by the Council, so the mission had to sit outside on mats in the sun. Under the impression that their intentions were friendly, and that there was a prospect of the treaty being agreed to, Mr. Eden avoided raising difficulties, and attributed their conduct to ignorance rather than to an intention to insult, and made excuses to the other officers of the mission, who were becoming somewhat intolerant of the treatment to which they were being exposed. Mr. Eden was asked for the Governor-General's letters to the Deb and Dhurma Rajas, and replied that he would deliver them himself. The Tongso Penlow said that this was not usual, and that he would receive them. They were then given to him and he placed them on the ground.

The mission was now told to go to the Deb Raja, and was pushed through a crowd to a little canopy in which the Deb Raja was sitting. Mr. Eden and the others were made to stand outside with uncovered heads in the sun, while the Governor-General's letter was brought in by a common coolie and put down before the Deb Raja, who seemed much frightened and did not speak. The Tongso Penlow acted as spokesman, and informed Mr. Eden, as if from the Deb Raja, that he (Tongso Penlow) would conduct with the mission the business for which it had come to Poonakha. The members of the mission were then pushed rudely on one side to make way for the Deb Raja to leave the tent, and were then ordered to follow him to another little canopy in which the Dhurma Raja, a boy of about eighteen, was seated. The same course was followed here, and Mr. Eden informed by the Tongso Penlow that the Dhurma Raja also referred the mission to him in like manner as the Deb had done; though in fact the Dhurma never opened his lips during the interview. The mission was then taken back to the little tent into which it had been first conducted. Mr. Eden complained of the heat and requested permission to return to his camp, but was told that the mission must remain where it was until the Council had leisure to to see it again. The Dhurma and Deb Rajas now returned to the palace, and the mission was kept waiting for an hour in the tent, during which period its members were exposed to the insolence of the sepoys in attendance on the Rajahs and the Council, who mustered in considerable numbers round the tent pushing one another against its sides. On one occasion they lifted the sides of the tent up and threw a man inside of it. Mr. Eden and his party were quite helpless, as an objection had been raised to their bringing the escort with them. They protested against this conduct to some officials who were near, but without the slightest effect.

At the expiry of an hour they were again taken to the Council, and it was agreed to go through the draft treaty clause by clause. After reading the two first articles having reference respectively to the continuance of peace and friendship between Great Britain and Bhotan, and that in consideration of the latter country using its utmost endeavours to restrain depredations, and also to restore British subjects carried off into captivity, the British Government will consent to pay an annual rent for the portion of the Dooars known as Ambaree Fallacottah, which it would continue to occupy, the Tongso Penlow said that a clause must be added to the effect that the resumed Assam Dooars should at once be made over to Bhotanese officers, and that after this had been done all other matters in dispute could be arranged; but that until it was done, there was no use in discussing the surrender of captive British subjects or of plundered property, as these were matters of no importance and could be settled at any time. Mr. Eden was much startled at this proposal, as well as by the overbearing manner which the Tongso Penlow now assumed, and proceeded to explain to the Council that it was on account of outrages on British territory that the Dooars in question had been resumed many years ago, and that other proceedings had since been threatened. He distinctly informed the Tongso Penlow that the question of the Assam Dooars was one that had been closed for many years; that his instructions did not permit him even to discuss the subject; that he knew nothing of any claims ever having been made by the Bhotanese for a resettlement of the question; that the compensation agreed upon had been regularly paid by the British Government and received by that of Bhotan, and that the only question connected with the return of land which he was empowered to deal with was the attachment of Ambaree Fallacottah. The Tongso Penlow then became violent, and Mr. Eden endeavoured to convince him, that even supposing he entered into any negotiation regarding the Assam Dooars the Governor-General would not ratify his engagements, and that it would do the Bhotan Government more harm than good to press the matter—but that at the same time if they thought otherwise, he would be the bearer of any letter they wished to address to the Government on the subject—at the same time telling them plainly that he was quite certain that these Dooars never would, under any circumstances be returned, and that it was better to dismiss all consideration of that subject from their minds, and take measures to prevent the loss of further lands, which would be a sure consequence of a refusal to comply with the moderate and just demands of the British Government—whilst on the other hand, compliance with these demands would be immediately followed by the release of the tract

(Ambaree Fallacottah) then under attachment. In reply, the Tongso Penlow took up the draft treaty, crumpled it up and said, 'Then we will have war; you are nobody; you have no authority from the Governor-General; we do not want Ambaree Fallacottah, and as to the demands of the Government of India, a Chupprassee (office messenger) might have been sent to settle them; I will have nothing more to do with you; go!' This was said with great vehemence in a haughty threatening manner. Mr. Eden, addressing himself to the other members of the Council, said that he had come in spite of great obstacles which had been thrown in his way for the sole purpose of securing a friendly understanding between the two countries; that he had done all in his power to bring this about, but that he now saw that it was useless; that he was in no way to blame for the result; that of course it was optional for them to adopt an unfriendly course if they saw fit to do so, and that the consequences of their so doing rested with themselves, and that he should at once return and report to the Governor-General what had occurred. No notice was taken of what he said, and he returned to camp and made immediate preparations for leaving, it being his opinion as well as that of his officers, that after what had occurred it was clear that no good could result from the mission longer remaining.

As soon as the Council learned from the spies who were always kept in the camp of the mission, that Mr. Eden was preparing to depart, messenger after messenger came to him from them, entreating him to remain for one day more to enable the members to explain their views, saying that they deplored what had occurred; that the Tongso Penlow had no authority to speak as he had done; that they all approved of the draft treaty which had been submitted, and that they did not wish for the return of the Assam Dooars; that the Tongso Penlow had appropriated the whole of the revenue of these Dooars, and had paid nothing in for three years to the Deb and Dhurma Rajas; that he was now endeavouring to usurp the whole Government, and that if Mr. Eden would only stay he should be resisted and all would be settled amicably: adding that his going away would end in a disturbance.*

Mr. Eden consented to remain a day or two and hear what they had to say, on the distinct understanding that the Assam Dooars should not again be alluded to, and that the Tongso Penlow should not be present at any future interview. In coming to this decision, Mr. Eden was influenced by the knowledge of the fact, that most of the Council were really opposed to the Tongso Penlow, on account of the manner in which he had set their authority aside, and had bestowed office on all his relatives and dependants; but he was not then aware how entirely they were in his power.

At this stage of the proceedings, with the view of obtaining some written acknowledgment from the Government that the Assam Dooars should not again be alluded to, and of affording the Council an opportunity of publicly and officially expressing their dissent from the course of policy pursued by the Tongso

* This allusion to the probability of a disturbance was explained by a message brought to Cheeboo Lama from the Tongso Penlow, to the effect that if Mr. Eden attempted to withdraw his mission without settling all that he (the Penlow) wanted, his so doing would be prevented by force.

Penlow, Mr. Eden addressed a letter to the Government, stating that the Tongso Penlow had declined to enter into any negotiation until the Assam Dooars were returned; that he had no authority to enter into any discussion on that subject, and that he should therefore return and report what had passed to the British Government. No reply to this was received, but next day the Tongso Penlow sent to ask what Mr. Eden meant by using a red seal,—though he had always previously used one without any objections being raised; adding that it had been agreed that there should be no written negotiations, but that they should be conducted verbally through Cheeboo Lama. Relying on the friendly assurances of the Council previously received, Mr. Eden took no notice of this communication. After this, the Angdu Forung Jungpen arrived, and sending for Cheeboo Lama abused him as the others had done for bringing the mission into the country, and warned him that he was responsible for all that might happen in consequence.

On the 22nd of March, the Council sent to say that everything had been settled as Mr. Eden wished, and requested him to attend. He consented on the understanding that the mission should not be exposed to the insults of a mob, and that the Tongso Penlow should not be present. The mission however had to pass through a disorderly crowd, precisely as on previous occasions, and a few stones were thrown. The two members of the Council who had been hitherto absent had returned, and were now present. The mission had not long been seated with the Council when the Tongso Penlow walked in and took his seat at their head. The draft treaty was read, article by article, and was agreed to with the exception of the eighth and ninth ones already referred to. They would not enter into any argument regarding their objections to these articles, but said plainly that it was no use discussing the subject; for that nothing could ever make the Deb and Dhurma Rajas agree to them, but that if Mr. Eden would consent to abandon these, they would at once agree to the rest of the treaty. Mr. Eden, finding that argument was useless, as they would not attend to what he was saying, and feeling convinced, from what he had seen, that no British representative could reside with safety in Bhotan, nor trader be safe, whatever the Bhotanese Government might promise, consented to the omission of the articles in question. The Council then asked him to have the treaty copied as soon as possible; as the season was advancing, and it would be difficult for him to return, and also because some of the Council had journeys to make, which would be attended with difficulty if deferred a little later in the season. The interview terminated without the question of the Assam Dooars being mooted.

After this interview, the Tassishujung Jungpen, whom at this time Mr. Eden did not know was a son-in-law of the Tongso Penlow, sent a message of congratulation to him on the auspicious turn affairs had taken, and claimed for himself the credit of having prevented the Penlow's alluding any further to the Assam Dooars, in consideration thereof asking for a present.

Mr. Eden now undertook to have the treaty translated, and four copies of it and of the list of British subjects and plundered property demanded by the Indian Government ready within two days. While these papers were in course of preparation the Council sent repeatedly to Mr. Eden urging him to use greater dispatch, insinuating that he was needlessly delaying the business for which he had come; though the two days had not expired. During this period the Hindoostanee to whom reference has been already made was continually coming to the camp speaking seditiously to the sepoys of Mr. Eden's escort, and making them presents of money. His proceedings were duly reported to Mr. Eden by the Jemadar of the escort from time to time. He represented himself to the Bhoteahs as being General Nundanum Singh, son of Attaram Singh, and grandson of Runjeet Singh, "the old one-eyed lion of Lahore." Mr. Eden found out that he had been in the habit of procuring arms and ammunition in small quantities from a Bengalee named Lutchmun Baboo, said to reside within seven days' march from Dhalimkote. He was, as the Paro Penlow had previously informed Mr. Eden, the confidential adviser of the Tongso Penlow. He was always close to him, and at the interviews he took up his position behind Mr. Eden's chair. He was dressed as a Bhotanese, but had regular Hindostanee features. He was apparently about forty-five or fifty years of age, and his hair, which was cut quite close, was grey. He was constant in his abuse of the British Government, and Mr. Eden was inclined to view the misconduct of the Tongso Penlow as being mainly attributable to his counsels. He went so far as to induce him to claim some of Mr. Eden's Seik escort as Bhotanese subjects—this claim, however, was not formally preferred.

On the 24th of March, the treaty and lists being duly prepared, the mission was directed to attend with them at the Council, that they might be signed.

The tents of the Council were on this occasion brought across to the side of the river on which the mission camp was pitched. On arriving at the place of interview, the mission was shown into an empty tent, and was detained there an hour whilst the members of Council amused themselves by examining the arms of the escort, and joking with the sepoys and crowd. Though this conduct did not look very friendly, Mr. Eden was unwilling to think the neglect shown him was premeditated or intentional, as that morning he had been urged to make haste and get the treaty ready for signature. At last the members seated themselves in the tent, and on the mission entering, at first the conversation was friendly, and tea and rice were handed round, but even whilst this apparent civility was going on, several things were done which the mission found it difficult to bear patiently. The treaty was at length taken up for the purpose of comparing the two copies. After the two first articles were read, the Tongso Penlow proposed to add that the Assam Dooars should be given up to him as soon as the treaty was signed, and that the whole of the revenues collected from them since the date of resumption, calculated at three lacs rupees per annum, should be paid over to him by the Governor-General's Agent in Assam. Mr. Eden was naturally astounded at this proposal after all that had passed on the subject, and looked towards the Council, expecting them to interfere, but with the exception of the Angdu Forung Jungpen, they all pretended not to know what was passing, and occupied themselves in eating pawn, and talking in a trivial childish manner to the other officers of the mission. Mr. Eden called upon them to listen, and said that he now formally repeated once for all what he had already said on a previous occasion, to the effect that he had no authority to enter into negotiations on the subject, and positively refused to discuss it—also that if the Tongso Penlow insisted on pressing the matter, he would at once withdraw, as he had proposed a few days previously, but had foregone his intention on the distinct promise that the matter should not again be referred to. He pointed out to the Council that their conduct in agreeing to a treaty, continually urging him to have it copied and signed, and then at the last moment rejecting it, was quite incomprehensible, and he again explained to them that his powers were confined to the draft treaty that had been already submitted. While Mr. Eden was thus addressing the Council, its members were all laughing and talking, and not paying the least attention to what he was saying. The Tongso Penlow, however, replied that they had never agreed to the draft treaty, but had only requested a fair copy to be made of it; that that did not bind them, that he had never consented to it and would never consent to that or any other treaty until the Assam Dooars were returned—also, that Mr. Eden had chosen to come there, and that if he had no authority to treat on all matters, he should not have come at all, but having done so, that he could not now be allowed to depart without settling the only matter in which he (the Penlow) had any interest. The mission was now directed to adjourn with the Council to another tent pitched in a more public position, and surrounded by an immense crowd. After this the tone and manner of the Tongso Penlow and the Angdu Forung Jungpen became every moment more offensive. The former took up a large piece of wet dough, rubbed

Mr. Eden's face with it, pulled his hair, slapped him on the back, and committed other acts of very great insolence. On Mr. Eden showing signs of impatience and remonstrating, he smiled, and deprecating anger pretended that it was all the familiarity of friendship, much to the amusement of a large assemblage of bystanders. He continued urging the surrender of the Assam Dooars, saying how wrong Mr. Eden was to have come to Bhotan if he had no power to restore them. Mr. Eden made no reply, his object now being to avail himself of the first opportunity of getting away without risking a disturbance. The Angdu Forung Jungpen now surpassed the Tongso Penlow in insolence, by taking some pawn leaf, which he had chewed, from his mouth, and requesting Dr. Simpson to eat it, throwing it angrily in his face on his refusing to do so. As matters seemed now becoming serious, the members of the mission debated whether to withdraw at once or to await a better opportunity. The latter course was decided on. Dr. Simpson sat perfectly still without wiping the pawn from his face. The Angdu Forung Jungpen next seized Cheeboo Lama's watch-ribbon from his neck, and with great violence wrenched away the watch that been given him by the Governor-General, passing it to one of the other members of Council who secreted it in his dress. The Council now observing the mission consulting together and looking for the escort, apparently thought they had gone too far. Cheeboo Lama's watch was returned, and Dr. Simpson was requested to wipe the stain from his face, which he declined to do. Taking advantage of this change, Mr. Eden appealed to the Council, reminding them that on the previous occasion they declared that they did not want the Assam Dooars back, and that they deplored the Tongso Penlow's conduct—calling upon them to repeat now what they had then told him. Most of the members however pretended not to hear, the others said that they agreed with the Tongso Penlow. Mr. Eden then said that it was clear that no understanding could be come to, as they required him to do that which he had neither power nor authority to execute, even if he wished to do it, and that he must therefore take leave of them, asking for safe conduct back to Darjeeling. The Tongso Penlow called out, "I want nothing but the Assam Dooars, and if I don't get them, it is better to have war than a treaty; I will write to the Governor-General." The mission having gradually worked its way outside the tent, got back to camp again without further molestation.

It being too late to leave that night, the mission having no supplies, Mr. Eden made up his mind to leave next day, if he saw any chance of getting away unmolested. The next morning, (March 25th), at day-break, Joom Kulling, one of the Council who always had been friendly, being opposed to the Tongso Penlow, and likely to benefit by the return of Ambaree Fallacottah, came out of the fort and sent for Cheeboo Lama, saying that he had something of importance to communicate, but the moment the Lama started, Tongso Penlow's sepoys came out and forbade his holding any communication with any one except the Penlow's son-in-law (the Tassishujung Jungpen). Joom Kulling, though nominally of higher rank than the Penlow, was at the same time guarded and prevented from communicating with the mission. He sent a message to Mr. Eden to say that he was anxious to come to him but dared not do so. It was now clear to the mission that Tongso Penlow had cast aside his mask, and had determined openly to set aside the Government altogether. Knowing that he had gained his present position by unscrupulous measures, the position of the mission became very unpleasant, especially as the other members of the Council evidently had neither the power nor the will to protect it. They sent messages, however, entreating Mr. Eden not to thwart the Tongso Penlow too much; their friendly messages however being generally accompanied by demands for presents.

Cheeboo Lama was now sent for by the Tassishujung Jungpen, and after some conversation with the latter, was taken to the Council, where a paper was given to him in which it was stated that the Government of India should readjust the whole boundary between the two countries, return the Assam Dooars, pay compensation at the rate of three lacs of rupees for each year since the resumption, and deliver up all runaway slaves and political offenders who had taken refuge within British territory. This paper Cheeboo Lama brought to Mr. Eden, who, taking it to be the letter the Tongso Penlow had said he meant to write to the Governor-General, kept it, and said it would be duly delivered, and requested that arrangements might be made for furnishing the mission with supplies and a passport, as he wished to return at once. Cheeboo Lama returned to the fort with this message, and was abused and insulted by the Tongso Penlow, who told him to inform Mr. Eden that he must sign and seal the paper. Mr. Eden replied that his signature was of no use—that he would say all that was wished to the Governor-General, but could do nothing more. At this time Cheeboo Lama told him that from the manner of the Council he saw no hope of the mission ever coming to any sort of amicable settlement; that they were becoming more abusive than ever, and that a sharp watch must be kept over their proceedings, as they seemed disposed to act with violence. On receiving Mr. Eden's second message, the Tongso Penlow threw off all pretence of friendship, told Cheeboo Lama that he had brought the mission to the country for his own ends, and should suffer for it; that he was now convinced that Mr. Eden was a person of no authority or position, and not even of rank equal to a servant of the Governor-General's servants; that unless he at once agreed to sign the paper, and give an order for the surrender of the Assam Dooars, he would seize and imprison both him and Cheeboo Lama, and confine them in the stocks in the dungeon of the fort—adding that they had come without any invitation, and having done so, must take the consequences—also, that they should now see that they could not "sit on the heads" of the Bhotanese. The Angdu Forung Jungpen went further, and said in Cheeboo Lama's hearing, that as there was sure to be war, it would be better to commence it by killing all those who were then in their hands.

The mission determined to say nothing more that day, but to consult during the night how it could get away with the least risk. Mr. Eden was at this time suffering from fever, brought on by exposure to the sun on the occasion of his visits to the Council tent, and this was urged as an excuse for not sending a reply that day. The mission, however, was not allowed to remain quiet, Cheeboo Lama being again sent for, and Mr. Eden told him to repeat his previous reply with reference to his want of authority, and desire at once to return. On hearing this, the Tongso Penlow said to the Lama that further discussion was useless—that Mr Eden must sign, and that if he again sent to say that he had no authority, he should confine him till some one came vested with power to make over the Assam Dooars. Cheeboo Lama said that he would bring Mr. Eden's answer in the morning, and he found out through friendly Bhotanese that the Tongso Penlow and the Angdu Forung Jungpen had made up their minds to attempt the seizure of the mission, and that it was not a mere idle threat.

In the evening, Mr. Eden assembled all the members of the mission, including Cheeboo Lama, and held a long consultation as to the best course to adopt under the circumstances. It being clear that a friendly treaty, even if it had been desirable to enter into one after what had occurred, was now out of the question, what remained for the mission to determine, was how it could best get back to British territory with the least embarrassment to the Government. The Deb and Dhurma Rajas and the majority of the Council were helpless, if even they had been friendly, being mere puppets in the hands of "two treacherous and notoriously unscrupulous robber chiefs," who had virtually seized on the Government. The mission could not stay where it was, for it had no supplies but those procured from time to time from the fort, and sentries were placed all round to prevent communication with the villagers. The mission decided that one of three courses only could be adopted—namely, either to allow the Bhotanese to retain Mr. Eden and Cheeboo Lama, on condition that the rest of the camp was allowed to withdraw in safety, or to make an attempt to escape by night, or sign the paper as requested by the Tongso Penlow. The first proposition was rejected on the grounds that if Mr. Eden and Cheeboo Lama were detained, the Government would have had to sent a force at once to release them, which, at that advanced season of the year, it would have been very difficult to have brought into the country, in consequence of many of the rivers becoming impassable, and the valleys uninhabitable from malaria—also, because the moment a force entered the country the probabilities were that the lives of the prisoners would be threatened unless it was immediately withdrawn, and the Government consequently placed in a very difficult position. The second proposition, the mission at first felt disposed to accept, as, with the escort there was some chance of evading pursuit and of escaping down the Buxar Dooar road to the plains, or of taking refuge with the Paro Penlow. On mature consideration, however, with 150 coolies to protect, some of them sick and scarcely able to stand, it was decided that flight should only be resorted to as a last expedient. The only course left was to pretend compliance with their demands, and though extremely repugnant to the feelings of the mission, no other means of avoiding the serious difficulty in which it was placed was apparent. After the repeated assurances given by Mr. Eden of his want of authority, and the threats held out to him of imprisonment if he attempted to leave, he decided that any engagement entered into by him was not binding on the Indian Government; moreover, he had seen quite enough to convince him that there was not a man in the country who had any sort of idea of the nature of a treaty, and that the Bhotan Government never had had any intention of abiding by any engagement involving the surrender of British subjects or property if even a treaty had been properly entered into. Taking therefore all the circumstances into consideration it was decided that Mr. Eden should express his willingness to sign the paper that had been submitted to him, but, as it seemed probable that even after this, he might be detained as a guarantee, it was decided that if, after signing, any further obstacles were thrown in the way of the departure of the mission, it should go off by night and trust to the Paro Penlow for protection.

Mr. Eden, however, determined to make one final attempt to avoid the distasteful alternative and obtain leave to go, so he sent Cheeboo Lama again to say that it was no use his signing the engagement proposed by the Tongso Penlow; that independently of want of authority, the engagement provided for the rendition of runaway slaves; that the British laws did not recognize slavery; that on the contrary we considered it a serious crime, and that the Governor-General would never listen to such a proposal. It being also insisted that the paper should be signed by Cheeboo Lama, on the grounds that the engagement would likewise be binding on Sikim and Cooch Behar, Mr. Eden pointed out that Cheeboo Lama had come at his request, and not a representative of Sikim, and that his signature was useless, but the Tongso Penlow would not even listen to what Cheeboo Lama was saying, and sent him back after grossly abusing him, telling him to remind Mr. Eden of his previous threats, and to return at once with his consent to sign.

Farther argument being obviously useless, Mr. Eden sent word to say that he would sign as they liked, and must then return at once to British territory. The Council then said that they wished to have a fair copy made of the engagement, and it was given to them for that purpose, but when what purported to be the fair copy was brought to Mr. Eden the following day, he found that it had been entirely changed; that the condition regarding the payment of the three lacs of rupees per annum had been omitted, evidently under the conviction that it would show on the face of the treaty that it had been extorted, and an absurd paragraph had been added, to the effect that if we ever encroached on Bhotan, we were to submit to be punished by the Bhotanese, Sikimese, and Cooch Behar Governments acting together, all slaves were to be returned, as well as all Dooars, including that of Julpigorie, within the British frontier proper. As there was no object in pointing out the difference between the original and the copy, Mr. Eden said he would sign it whenever they chose to fix a day, and attempted to obtain permission to do so in his own tent, and start at once for Darjeeling. This they would not agree to, as the presents sent by the Governor-General, which Mr. Eden had been unable to bring on with him on account of the refusal of the local officers to supply coolies, had not arrived, though they were expected to arrive that day. It was evident they were determined to have the presents, as men were sent three or four times a day to see if they had arrived, and at length Mr. Eden was accused of having appropriated them by an officer sent by the Tongso Penlow, who said that the Governor-General's letter contained a long list of cloth and other articles sent through him, and that if he did not give them up according to that list it would not be well. Mr. Eden asked who had read the Governor-General's letter and was told that it was in Bengalee, and had been read by an interpreter. This Mr. Eden knew to be false, for the letter was in English, as he had been desired to translate it and had purposely avoided doing so, because, observing how suspicious they were, he thought that if a translation was appended in Cheeboo Lama's handwriting, they would declare it a forgery, and he had no one else with him who could write the Bhotanese character. Mr. Eden at once taxed the messengers with this falsehood, but they persisted in their demand in a threatening impertinent manner. The same day, however, the presents arrived, and the moment the news reached the Council they became clamorous to possess them. Fearing that the mission camp would be plundered if the presents were withheld, Mr. Eden promised to give them up as soon as he received supplies, and that proper arrangements were made for his leaving on a certain day. It was then agreed that the mission should meet the Council on the 27th March, and should be allowed to go the following day, supplies were also sent. Mr. Eden accordingly distributed the presents, keeping back some small articles of jewellery which could be easily concealed, and the guns, which latter he did not think it expedient to give them. In making an inventory of the presents given to the Rajas, the Tongso Penlow entered some beautiful pearl earrings as "glass ornaments set in brass," and represented all the other articles to be imitation or of inferior manufacture—at the same time taking all the most valuable presents off to his own house, instead of to the Deb Raja's treasury.

On the day appointed, the mission went to the Council, hoping that the engagement would be signed, and that it would be at once allowed to leave. This hope was not realised; the Council however having now got their own way, behaved with much greater civility than on any of the former occasions. The members of the mission were allowed the use of their chairs, and the usual ceremonies were now for the first time observed. No one was allowed to press on them or come near them; they were received in a house instead of in tents, were addressed with courtesy and respect, and exposed to no insults. The Hindoostanee was in the verandah of the room, and was constantly consulting with the Tongso Penlow.

On the 28th of March the Council professed to be engaged in making preparations for the mission taking leave of the Deb and Dhurma Rajas. Some of the Council came to the camp of the mission. Mr. Eden was ill at the time, and occupying a leaf hut. They requested permission to go and sit in his tent: this he objected to, from the fear that they would steal everything they could lay their hands on. After some questions regarding the Kings of Lahore and Delhi, their sons, and their power as compared with that of the British, questions evidently asked with reference to information they had received from the Hindostanee, they insisted upon going into Mr. Eden's tent, though he was unable to accompany them. He therefore had to bring up all the Seiks of the escort to watch them and prevent them plundering.*

* Mr. Eden afterwards found out at Paro that these statesmen had been sent by the Tongso Penlow to see if there was anything in the camp which it was worth while to plunder, as if so, it was his intention to organise a night robbery. This was not carried out, the report of

On the 29th March, Mr. Eden and the other members of the mission were asked to attend and take leave of the Deb and Dhurma Rajas, and to sign the agreement. They were received in tents, but the people were made to treat them with respect. The mission was first taken to the Council tent, where the Tongso Penlow produced three copies of the agreement; none of them were signed by any one on the part of the Bhotanese Government. The seal of a late Dhurma Raja, and one purporting to be that of the Deb Raja, had been affixed to one copy but not to the others, and this was even not done in the presence of the mission. They made Mr. Eden sign and seal two copies, and made Cheeboo Lama do the same. Mr. Eden put the words "under compulsion" on each copy, to prevent the agreement being sent down to Assam and made use of before he had time to communicate with the Government. The third copy was then handed to Mr. Eden and the Tongso Penlow asked him to sign it for him. He refused to do so, and appealed to the Council to say whether the Penlow was entitled to have a copy signed by him any more than the other members of the Council were. They agreed with Mr. Eden, and the Penlow seeing that he could not obtain this without a fresh dispute gave way.* The mission was then taken to the tents of the Dhurma and Deb Rajas, by whom its members had white scarfs placed on their necks—a compliment which ought to have been paid them

the members of Council being unfavourable; as the members of the mission fortunately had secured all their valuables on seeing them approaching.

* Appendix C contains a translation of the document signed by Mr. Eden.

on the occasion of their first visit, and the omission to do so, showed the intention to behave in an unfriendly manner. The mission was then informed that the demon Mohakul would be put on the heads of all present, and that if anything was then done to injure the Bhotanese, that demon would at once take notice of it. A large wooden four-headed demon was then carried round, and every one near the tent received a knock from it. A letter was then given for the Governor-General, three ponies were presented, and a few pieces of silk. The mission then returned to the Council House, and Mr. Eden said that he intended to leave at once. The Tongso Penlow said that there was no occasion for such haste, and that he had better wait; but, on Mr. Eden's repeating that he could not delay longer, he raised no further objection and took leave of the mission.

As soon as Mr. Eden left the Council, the Tongso Penlow started off to his own territory, attended by a large procession. The Hindoostanee accompanied him, dressed in robes of honour, and riding on a pony next to the Penlow himself. Immediately on the departure of the latter, the mission struck their tents, but the moment the coolies started, Bhotanese sepoys rushed out and stopped the road, while others came up and asked what the mission meant by daring to go without orders, and that it could not leave until the Angdu Forung Jungpen, who had gone to his own fort, had returned, which he would do in the course of a few days. Mr. Eden positively refused to stay a day longer—the men became very violent, and Cheeboo Lama then volunteered to go to the fort and explain that Mr. Eden was too ill to remain in such a hot place, and that if anything happened to him in consequence of the delay they would be held responsible. The mission then pushed past these sepoys, and got up the hill on to the road, so as to be in a better position, whatever might happen. At this time one of the Council sent out word to the mission to go on and wait for no one, and take no notice of any orders sent by his colleagues. Mr. Eden then sent the camp on, telling the coolies to remain a few miles down the road for the evening, whilst he remained behind with the Seik escort, waiting the return of Cheeboo Lama; being apprehensive that they might seize him. Just as it became dark, the Lama sent to Mr. Eden to say that he was safe and that he had better go on. He did not, however, arrive in camp until it was late, Mr. Eden having become very anxious on his account, and not without reason as it turned out, for he had been detained and told that he should be kept a prisoner until Mr. Eden returned. Joom Kulling, however, managed to get him away on pretence of giving him some dinner, and then got him outside the fort. Joom Kulling expressed great regret at the conduct of the Tongsò Penlow, and considerable apprehension with reference to the course the Indian Government would adopt on seeing the engagement that Mr. Eden had been forced into and on hearing all that had passed. He declared that the Assam Dooars were not wanted by any one but the Tongso Penlow, and that of late years no one had ever derived any benefit from the compensation paid by the Government of India annually for that tract. When Cheeboo Lama went to the fort he found most of the Council exceedingly angry, and there was evidently a violent dispute going on amongst them—some were for detaining the mission, others for letting it go*.

In the middle of the night some officers, with seven or eight men, arrived at the camp of the mission, forbidding it to move farther, until the Angdu Forung Jungpen returned. Mr. Eden positively refused to wait, telling them that by their conduct the

* The fort of Poonakha and palace of the Dhurma and Deb Rajas is described as a much inferior building to that of Paro, being, at the time of Mr. Eden's visit to its vicinity, in a tumble-down condition, and having a dirty and mean appearance. It is situated on a sandy stony delta formed by the junction of the rivers Patchoo and Matchoo, and is built in the form of a rectangle enclosing a court-yard, in the centre of which there is a six-storied tower. On the southern aspect of the palace there is a monastery, containing about 300 Lamas. On the west side, raised higher than the other buildings is the residence of the Deb Raja, while in the centre tower is that of the Dhurma Raja. While Mr. Eden's mission was at Poonakha, the east side was occupied by the governor of the fort, the members of the Council, and temporarily by the Tongso Penlow. The palace has two bridge entrances, one across the Patchoo and the other across the Matchoo. These consist of broad covered ways open at the side and entered by a large gateway passing under a tower. Scarcely a habitation was to be seen in the neighbourhood, though there were the remains of some supposed to have been destroyed from time to time in the course of fights to obtain possession of the fort. The Court resides at Poonakha from November to the end of April, and at Tassishujung, sixteen miles distant, during the remainder of the year; its support having to be defrayed by the governors respectively of the two places during its period of residence with them. Whilst the Court is absent the fort of Poonakha is left in charge of a few servants. The valley in which it stands is 4,534 feet elevation, very level, and produces a good deal of rice. The soil like that of Paro is highly ferruginous. The communication with the plains it is inferred must be tolerably level as the rivers (Patchoo and Matchoo) have a hundred miles to flow before reaching there. Both of these rivers are swift and deep streams—the Matchoo rises from the foot of the snowy mountains of Ghassa, while the Patchoo has a more easterly sourse. After their junction at Poonakha they flow down to the Berhampooter under the united name of the Patchoo Matchoo or Father and Mother River.

Bhotanese showed that they attached no importance to the engagement entered into that morning, that he was determined to go on, and would only be stopped by force. They declared that the Angdu Forung Jungpen had something of great importance to communicate, and that if the mission would only wait for six hours on the road the next day, he would come by a cross road and meet it. Mr. Eden agreed to this, but next morning sent the camp on with instructions to try and get across the pass before dark, and waited himself at the place appointed with the other officers of the mission and a portion of the escort.

About eleven o'clock on the forenoon of the 30th March, the messenger who had been sent returned, saying that the Angdu Forung Jungpen was furious, and had sent to say that he would not see Mr. Eden unless he returned, that he had gone away without his leave, that he would catch him before he got to Paro, and that he (Mr. Eden) would be responsible for the result if he went on. Mr. Eden now determined to try his utmost to get out of their hands, and gave the order to move forward. The Bhotanese officers then declared that they could not allow Cheeboo Lama to go, and that they must take him back with them. This Mr. Eden positively refused to allow. They persisted; but, observing that Mr. Eden was determined to use force, they became unsettled in their purpose, and suggested that a letter should be written to the Angdu Forung Jungpen, explaining that Mr. Eden should have taken leave of him if had been at Poonakha, but could not await his return; also, that he had waited for him some time on the road, and could not wait any longer. With this letter, and a present of money for themselves, they said that they would arrange that the mission should reach Paro without any interference; as they would delay returning and reporting its departure until it had got well on the way. The mission now pushed on, and crossing the pass before dark, halted on the opposite side.

During the night a Zinkaff arrived and demanded the surrender of Cheeboo Lama. He kept the whole camp awake for some hours with his vociferations, but became quiet on Mr. Eden threatening to have him turned out. It then appeared that he was armed with a perwannah (order) from one of the Council, which, failing all attempts at intimidation, he was under instructions to produce—this perwannah being in fact a passport through the valley the mission was then entering, which was under this official, and Mr. Eden was asked to bear in mind that, whatever the other members of Council had done, the sender of this passport had treated him in a friendly manner. A white scarf was also sent by Joom Kulling, with a request that the mission would bear in mind that he had never behaved in an unfriendly manner, and that he was not on good terms with the Tongso Penlow.

The mission continued its journey the same night by moonlight, and by a forced march reached the border of the Paro Penlow's territory on the evening of the 31st March, and the following morning entered Paro. The ex Paro Penlow was friendly and attentive, listened to all that had passed, said that he had been very apprehensive regarding the safety of the mission, that he had kept a constant watch on the proceedings of the Council, and that if violence had actually been resorted to, he should have marched over, with all the men at his disposal, for the release of the mission. Of course it is impossible to say whether this was really his intention or not, but Mr. Eden thinks that it very probably was; because he was a far-seeing shrewd old man, had been for many years the enemy of the Tongso Penlow, and avowedly did not recognise the authority of the person who was then called Deb Raja at Poonakha; consequent on his being an adherent of the Deb who had been recently dethroned. The young Paro Penlow was also professedly friendly; but Mr. Eden represents him as a most importunate beggar, who tried to obtain possession of everything the mission had, and who, there is a fear, had he not been restrained by his stepfather, would not have hesitated to obtain his end by force. He was moreover, as has been already shown, a relation, on his father's side, of the Angdu Forung Jungpen, and it was a source of satisfaction to the mission to know that he exercised no real authority at Paro. Mr. Eden remained there but one day, and made an attempt to procure the release of some Bengalees who claimed British protection. The old Penlow, however, friendly as he was in other respects, would not hear of this being done.

The mission left Paro on the 2nd of April; and, just as it was starting, a passport for it arrived from the Council at Poonakha. After leaving Paro the only difficulty encountered was the re-crossing of the Taigonlah Pass, where the snow was still four or five feet deep, and the lower stratum having melted, the ponies and mules sank up to their girths. So great was the difficulty in getting them through, that some had to be left behind; including two old mules that the Paro Penlow had presented to Mr. Eden.

On the way through the Taigonlah Pass, a messenger arrived from the Paro Penlow to inform the mission that hostilities had recommenced against the existing Government, and that an engagement had already taken place between the ex Deb and the Tassishujung Jungpen. At Dhalimkote further news was obtained of its progress and of the plan of operations, which were stated to be the following—The Jungpen of Byagur, a subordinate of the Tongso Penlow's, was to seize on that official's fort (Tongso) during his absence, and exclude him from it, while the ministers combined with the Paro Penlow to exclude him from the Council, and eject his son-in-law from the fort of Tassishujung. The Tongso Penlow again was said to have a plan of his own, which was to resign the Penlowship in favour of his brother, and turn out the Deb he had lately appointed, and assume the office himself.

The mission reached Darjeeling in thirteen marches from Paro, without meeting with any further mishaps than those which have been mentioned.

CHAPTER VII.

Remarks on Mr. Eden's Mission—Question of the Propriety of sending it—Darjeeling unsuited as a Starting-place—Objections to abandoning the Escort—Also to pushing on in the face of continued Discouragement—Management of Negotiations at Poonakha—Signing under Compulsion justified—Measures against Bhotan proposed by Mr. Eden on his Return—Steps adopted by the Government of India—A Bhotanese Dispatch addressed to Cheeboo Lama—Note referring to Remark therein—Proclamation annexing the Dooars and a Portion of the Hill Territory of Bhotan—Detail of the Force assembled to carry it out.

WITH the return of Mr. Eden's mission to British territory our friendly relations with Bhotan ceased, and, as might be expected under the circumstances, the policy adopted by the Envoy became the subject of much controversy, and for the most part of acrimonious comment: the British name being alleged by some to have suffered a degradation at his hands, such as it never previously had been subjected to in the East. In collating the sketch of British intercourse with Bhotan, which has just been brought to a conclusion, my endeavour has been to divest it of a polemical character by avoiding, as much as possible, the introduction of observations of my own—holding however the opinion that there is much to justify that portion of Mr. Eden's proceedings against which censure has been chiefly directed; namely, his allowing himself to be coerced into signing the document making over to Bhotan British territory. A few remarks on the subject of the mission generally may not be out of place.

With the *resumé* given—partly in the body of the work, partly in Appendix B—of our diplomatic intercourse with Bhotan fresh in my recollection, I find it difficult to avoid the conclusion that it was a mistake ever thinking of sending a mission into the country, or entertaining the idea, that in the event of its apparent success any treaty obligations entered into by the Bhotanese either would or could be respected; it seeming to me as if the determination to send an Envoy to the Court of Bhotan had been arrived at without a sufficiently careful study of the political state of the country—though data, having reference to the chaotic condition of the Government, amply sufficient for forming a judgment on, as well as considerable local facilities for procuring additional information, appear to have been available—also, that if our police and military establishments on the frontier were unequal to the protection of the natives under our rule, action and not diplomacy was the course which the antecedents of the Bhotanese should have indicated as the only one to be adopted in dealing with them:—a people unruly and semicivilised, towards whom our intercourse had been marked for many years by a degree of forbearance, which can hardly be said to be our custom to extend to Orientals generally.

That Bhotan was not in a state suited either to receive or to benefit by a diplomatic mission, facts have been sufficiently demonstrative; and, while therefore, the mission originated in an erroneous conception of the power and responsibility of the nominal heads of the central Government of the country—erroneous conceptions seem to me, for the most part, to have characterised its progress. The first error, in my opinion, committed after the mission had been determined on, was the selection of Darjeeling as the starting-place, owing to the extremely steep and mountainous nature of the country that had to be traversed before reaching Dhalimkote—a mountain march in fact extending over nearly seventy miles of about as bad road for travelling on, especially with an extensive baggage train, as perhaps is to be found in the world. Whereas, had Julpigorie, our frontier station on the plains, due south of Dhalimkote, and only forty miles distant from it, been made the starting-point from British territory, the whole of the transport of the mission might have been conveyed on pack animals over thirty-two miles of perfectly level country, intersected by a few narrow and shallow streams admitting of being easily crossed, to the foot of the hills, and from thence by a very gradual ascent and moderately good pathway, to the valley of Ambiok immediately underneath the fort of Dhalimkote. The mission once established at this place, and with easy communication with its base of operations, would have been more favourably situated in reference to procuring the necessary transport, and preserving its entirety than was the case, arriving as it did from Darjeeling with coolies over-loaded, worn-out, discontented, and endeavouring to escape. This arrangement, as already mentioned, was made under the supposition that the mission would be able at Darjeeling to get the necessary means of transport for the whole journey, and thus be so far independent of the Bhotan Government. That this however would be an easy matter at Darjeeling, where labour of the nature in question is both scarce and valuable, must have been a conclusion arrived at somewhat hurriedly, and without due calculation of the difficulties likely to be encountered in getting several hundred men to enter a country they view with disfavour, and isolate themselves from their homes and their families for an indefinite period, especially from a place where employment more congenial to their tastes than that required by the mission, was both easily procured and well remunerated. I have a strong suspicion, that, if the facts connected with the manner in which the coolies were collected at Darjeeling, through whose aid the mission was originally able to start, were known—it would be found that a degree of coercion, bearing a close approximation to temporary slavery, had to be employed before the mission baggage was got to the banks of the Teesta—else why should the coolies have commenced to run away in considerable numbers before even they had quitted British territory? The starting from Julpigorie for Dhalimkote need not have interfered with the procuring from Darjeeling of such coolie transport as might have been voluntarily available, and thus the disorganisation of the mission train, which commenced from its very starting, would probably have been averted.

Mr. Eden appears in some measure to have foreseen the troubles in store for the mission, and at one time to have doubts about the expediency of going on; inasmuch as, it will be remembered he placed the state of matters before the Indian Government in the end of November at Darjeeling, and in reply was told that the political state of Bhotan at the time did not appear to the Governor-General (Sir William Dennison officiating), to contra-indicate the advance of the mission, leaving him, consequently, no option but to go on. At Dhalimkote again in January, he made a second representation of his position, and of the difficulties which surrounded him, and was told that the Governor-General (Sir John Lawrence), "did not think the state of affairs unfavourable to a successful issue" of the mission. Here again but little option was left Mr. Eden, but to make the best of the means at his disposal, and prosecute his journey onwards, even at the sacrifice he had to make of half his escort and a portion of his baggage. On reaching Sipchoo however, and finding that he had no means of replacing the large number of coolies who there left him, it appears to me that in place of abandoning nearly all his escort and baggage, he ought to have made a third reference to the Government of India before taking that step; seeing that from want of transport it had become impossible for him to give effect to what the Government had decided was essentially necessary should be the characteristic of the mission on its coming in contact with the Bhotanese authorities; namely—"that the mission should be organised on a scale calculated to impress the Court with the importance which the British Government attaches to the establishment of clear and decisive relations with the Government of Bootan, and the adoption of some means whereby the present unsatisfactory state of affairs on the frontier may be put a stop to, and the mutual rendition of persons charged with the commission of heinous crimes may be secured." * Hence it was that Mr. Eden's mission was organised on so large a scale, and with a military escort so much in excess of what previous

* Communication from the Lieutenant-Governor of Bengal to the Government of India, dated 11th October, 1862.

diplomatic experience of the country had shown to be actually necessary. The opinion expressed by the Lieutenant Governor of Bengal, and acted on by the Supreme Government of India, would seem to have been fully endorsed by Sir John Lawrence, whose responsibility as Governor-General commenced on the 12th January 1864; as he states in a dispatch to the Secretary of State for India, dated 1st June 1864, having reference to the failure of the mission, "with such a people as the Bhootanese, if an envoy were to go at all into the country, he should have moved with such a force as to have commanded respect"—an expression of opinion unequivocally conveying disapproval of the manner in which the escort was wholesale abandoned, and rendering it the more likely that had a third reference been made, authority to proceed would have been withheld, and either the withdrawal of the mission from the country ordered, or its halt at Sipchoo until such time as it could move under circumstances more commanding, and better calculated to give effect to the object in view.

From the period of the mission's leaving Sipchoo until its arrival at Poonakha, Mr. Eden's policy appears to me to have been somewhat headstrong and not over consistent: his narrative containing repeated expressions of readiness to go back if only sure that he was not to be welcome at head-quarters, and yet, notwithstanding constant proof that such was the case, steadily pushing on in the face of the greatest physical obstacles, and at times when due consideration for the condition of his means of transport, ought to have indicated rest as most desirable. In fact the idea of making a treaty would seem to have become a sort of *ignis fatuus* alluring him on to Poonakha, though from a very early period it must or ought to have been evident to him—who, from his local position, was so much better able to judge of the matter than any one connected with the Government of India—that no possible good could come from any negotiations entered into under such a condition of misrule as Bhotan was then labouring under. It would have been well then, if the moral courage which Mr. Eden displayed at Poonakha in extricating himself from the trap into which the moral 'Jack o' lantern' had led him, had been exercised at an earlier period after leaving Dhalimkote—if only to the extent of halting and communicating with Calcutta—the probable result of such a reference, may be inferred from the following extract from a letter addressed to Mr. Eden by the Government of India dated 13th July 1864—" His Excellency in Council is of opinion that it would have been well had you given up your mission, particularly after your arrival at Paro. It was clear at the outset that the Bhootanese had no intention of receiving you. They did much to deter you from marching forward, almost from the very first, and the behaviour of even the Paro Pillo (Penlow), was anything but encouraging and friendly. But, having once determined to press on and reach the capital of Bhootan, your conduct was as resolute, and dignified as under the trying circumstances in which you were placed it probably could be; and in regard to the proposed treaty, though it would under the circumstances have been more judicious to have had no allusion to Articles VIII. and IX.,* his Ex-

* The articles relating to the residence of a British Envoy at the seat of government in Bhotan, and to free trade and commercial intercourse between the countries.

cellency in Council does not think that in any case your treatment would have been different." While thus judging after the fact, and freely commenting on the course adopted by Mr. Eden in pushing on to Poonakha, it is but fair to recollect that the primary responsibility of the untoward advance into Bhotan rests not with Mr. Eden, but with the supreme Government at Calcutta: the reply to two representations of the difficulties attending the progress and prospects of the mission having been instructions to go on. Mr. Eden's position, therefore, it must be admitted, became one of undoubted difficulty and embarrassment, and certainly not favourable to independent action based on clear views of circumstances as at the time existing.

With reference to the career of the mission at Poonakha, it appears to me that after the manner in which Mr. Eden was treated immediately after his arrival at that place, by having two British subjects removed from his camp by subterfuge, and their return refused by the Tongso Penlow, he was wrong in opening negotiations as he did, in place of giving the Bhotanese Government the alternative of surrendering them, or of abiding by the consequences of the mission at once departing, consequent on an act of unfriendship. Convinced as Mr. Eden must have been long before he reached Poonakha, that the Tongso Penlow was in reality the Government for the time being, what possible good could be expected from entering into negotiations—one of the chief objects to be attained by which being the giving up of all British subjects held in bondage by the Bhotanese, when they were thus openly taken from under the protection of the British Envoy himself, and their surrender openly refused? A second error, I think, was committed by Mr. Eden in not adhering to the resolve he made on consenting to defer his departure after the second interview with the Council; namely, that the Tongso Penlow was not to be present on any future occasion of his meeting the Council. This was the proviso on which negotiations were resumed, and yet at the very next interview it was set at naught; the Tongso Penlow not only being present, but the Presidency of the Council assumed by him, apparently without remonstrance by Mr. Eden, who continued discussing the terms of the treaty, in place of insisting on the resolution he had made being adhered to—had this been done, it is probable that the insulting consequences which followed would have been avoided, and likewise also the Dooar war; as it is by no means unlikely that the Tongso Penlow, from finding the British Envoy thus pliant on one point that he had apparently determined to resist, may have conceived the idea of making him equally pliant on other matters, regarding which, he was desirous that his acquiescence—willing or unwilling—should be obtained.

With reference to that portion of Mr. Eden's proceedings upon which public censure has more severely fallen; namely, his purchasing the safe retreat of his mission by conforming to terms incompatible with the national honour, the course pursued by him admits not only of the fullest justification, but calls for commendation, characterised as it was by a praiseworthy anxiety to safely withdraw from a position of questionable security those entrusted to his charge —disregardless as to whether the means by which it was effected might or might not be fatal to his own official reputation. Mr. Eden sufficiently warned the Tongso Penlow of the worthlessness of the document he was exacting, and there can be no reasonable doubt, that the course Mr. Eden adapted was in accordance with both the dictates of common sense and discretion, and at the same time the one least calculated to embarrass his Government. With such a people as the Bhotanese, and especially with such a representative Government as that presided over by the Tongso Penlow and his ministers, utterly unacquainted with international intercourse and diplomatic obligation, it would seem to have been a matter of very little consequence what means were resorted to, provided they were successful, for the purpose of getting a number of British subjects out of a doubtful position, that it is clear they ought never to have been placed in. However much the soundness of the judgment which dictated the pushing on from Sipchoo, or the manner in which it was done may be open to question, there can be no doubt about the energy and courage which were displayed in carrying it out, and in surmounting the many difficulties, physical and moral, which had to be encountered after leaving that place, and in bringing these remarks to a conclusion, I cannot do so more appositely than by quoting the following observations, having reference to the signing under compulsion, from an article which appeared in the Calcutta Review, on Mr. Eden's mission, shortly after its return. "The treaty was signed, with the words 'under compulsion' attached to the signature, and it is needless to point out that a treaty obtained in such circumstances, signed by an envoy having no authority to agree to such terms, and unratified by the Government, is no more than waste paper. . . . The Indian Government, therefore, are in no way embarrassed by their envoy having had to sign such a treaty, and on the other hand they have learnt what is the real nature of the Bhootan Government, and how utterly futile it is to attempt to treat with them, according to the forms used amongst civilised nations, or to suppose that any treaty which they may enter into will bind them. By the course which Mr. Eden adopted, agreeing, that is to say, to sign the treaty, and signing it under compulsion, he has succeeded in obtaining the two objects, which we have pointed out, the circumstances of the mission rendered of paramount importance. He succeeded in bringing back his whole party safely to Darjeeling, and the Government are now in all respects in an infinitely better position for dealing with the Bhootan Government than they were before. They know that the Bhootan Government are responsible for, and cognisant of, the continually recurring aggressions on our territory, and the captivity of our subjects; they know that to expect redress or compensation from such a Government is futile, that they despise our forbearance, and regard our leniency as weakness, that our rights must be maintained by force and not by threats, and that anything like friendly intercourse with the disintegrated concourse of robbers that forms the Government of Bhootan is utterly out of the question. To Mr. Eden, of all men, such a proceeding as signing a treaty the provisions of which would be disgraceful, were they not so utterly absurd, must have been most repulsive. It is repugnant to the ordinary instinct of British courage to do anything under compulsion, and a thousand times over must it be repugnant, when the compulsion is applied by a set of contemptible barbarians, and the thing to be done is *per se* in any way discreditable. That Mr. Eden did nevertheless keep this natural feeling of repugnance, and his regard for his own personal reputation (for he must have foreseen the kind of criticism to which he would be exposed), subordinate to his duty to his Government, and to his care for the other members of the mission; that he preferred to act according to the dictates of prudence and sagacity, rather than those of pride and passion, entitles him, we consider, to our highest respect, and to the gratitude and support of Government. He avoided rashness in a position where instinct and temper and habits of thought must all have prompted him to act rashly, because he saw that a single rash step would be fatal, not only to himself, but to those who were under his guidance; and in his signing the treaty when he did, no less than in advancing in the first instance in the face of all the obstacles which the cunning of a barbarian Government had placed in his way, we consider that he displayed the truest and highest species of courage, in that he manfully did his duty by the Government which had employed him, regardless alike of personal danger and personal reputation." If not to the full extent, with the general tenor at least, of these remarks, I think most people who take a moderate and unprejudiced view of the affair will be inclined to concur. Others no doubt will dissent, and hold to the opinion that has been pretty freely expressed; to the effect that Mr. Eden should have hazarded any amount of physical inconvenience rather than have appended his signature to a document containing terms which were discreditable. Had Mr. Eden only had himself to think of, the probabilities are, that an instinctive sense of national honour and pride would have indicated that as the course for him to follow, but with the interest of between two and three hundred people in a measure depending upon him, the moral courage he displayed in adopting the course he did, entitles him to the fullest measure of praise.

On the 21st of April, immediately after his return to Darjeeling, Mr. Eden addressed a communication to the Government, confined chiefly to a detailed narrative of events at Poonakha, and the substance of which document has been placed before the reader in the preceding chapter. This communication was followed by a lengthy memorandum dated the 7th of May, containing Mr. Eden's views with reference to the adoption of the means best calculated to secure the frontier from further Bhotanese aggression. The following was the choice of measures he proposed—

"1st. The permanent occupation of the whole country.

"2nd. The temporary occupation of the country, to be followed by the withdrawal of the occupying force after destroying all the forts and letting the people see and feel our power to reach them at any future time.

"3rd. The permanent annexation of that tract at the foot of the hills called the Dooars and Jelpesh, which formerly and naturally belonged to Bengal, but which was partly wrested from the Mahomedan Rulers of Bengal, and partly ceded by us at the end of last century."

In the event of the latter proposition being adopted, Mr. Eden pointed out that on the lowest range of the

Bhotan Hills, at elevations from 2,000 to 3,500 feet above the Dooars, there existed a regular series of small forts in which the Bhotanese officers resided who had charge over the Dooars, and that it would be necessary to take possession of them and occupy them; incorporate the hill territory, in fact, in which they are, with the Dooars, and make it the frontier. He also strongly recommended the annexation of the portion of Bhotan between Darjeeling and Dhalimkote; on the grounds that if this mountain tract remained in the hands of the Bhotanese after the occupation of the Dooars, the Sikim and Darjeeling frontiers would be constantly exposed to raids.

The Government of India, however, was inclined to act more leniently towards the Bhotanese, and in the first instance it was determined only to permanently annex Ambaree Fallacottah, and withhold for the future the annual compensation for the Assam Dooars—these measures being as a punishment for the insult offered the British Envoy. At the same time, however, a demand was made to the Bhotan Government, requiring the surrender of all British and Cooch Behar subjects held in captivity, failing which, the annexation of the Bengal Dooars was determined on, as well as the adjoining hill territory proposed by Mr. Eden. A certain time was given the Bhotanese to comply with this demand, they failed to do so, and preparations were immediately made for giving effect to the measures just mentioned; which necessitated the advance of the British frontier for a depth varying from twenty to forty miles, throughout a length of one hundred and eighty miles—the most western position in the hills to be occupied being Dhalimkote and the most eastern one

Dewangiri—the intermediate ones from west to east being Chamoorchee, Balla, Buxa (Passakha) and Bishensing; the level ground at the foot of this line of hill posts being the eleven Bengal Dooars, and five out of the seven Assam ones, namely those in the Kamroop District, situated between the Monass and the Bor Rivers.

For the annexation of this territory a force in round numbers amounting to 10,000 men was collected on the Bengal, Cooch Behar and Assam frontiers, and divided into four columns; so as to advance from four different points and act independently.

The Bhotan Government hearing that preparations for hostilities were in course of being made, addressed a letter to Cheeboo Lama, through the Jungpen of Dhalimkote, a curious production of which the following is a translation—"The British say you were interpreter to the mission, we do not know what you said and Eden did not know what we said, but you know whether the treaty was not agreed to. We used no force, if we had, it should have been mentioned at the time, and you should not have afterwards allowed Eden on his return to deceive the Governor-General and lead him to write to the Dhurma Raja that we had used violence. Our Bhotan custom is this, that an answer once given is given, and a bargain made is made, so we did not tell the Deb Raja of this. If the treaty made last year is not allowed, if another right dealing person will come, or if a representative is wanted from hence, write so, therefore we have sent this order to you, but if an attack made upon us is right or wrong, recollect that you are responsible as the go-between. We cannot make restitution of anything now. The low country is unhealthy also, and an envoy could not be sent; when the sickness is less send for one. The case as regards robbery and theft is as follows: In the Cooch Behar territory and ours, the faults are equal—besides the English Government has taken seven Talooks of the Dangsi Terai (the Assam Dooars), and the rent of Ambaree Fallacottah has been withheld for some years. These are causes for our declaring war, instead of which the British Government are doing it. Make them do right. If we can withstand them we will, if not we will remain passive. Now you are the originator of confusion, you are a Sikimese and we shall have something to say to you; remember this and say it to the English Authorities. Well, if there is no confusion between the British and the Dhurma Raja, there will be nothing to say between us. If you do make mischief it will not harm us. Having considered all this, send your answer through the Jungpen of Dhalimkote." Many no doubt will recognise the resemblance in tone which this communication bears to documents which have at times emanated from the Chinese, under circumstances somewhat analogous. The remark about faults being equal on both sides as regards aggressions against property, has very likely a fair amount of truth in it—at least such is my opinion, inasmuch as in compiling the narrative (contained chiefly in Appendix B) of the train of events which gradually brought matters to a climax, I formed the conviction that in the official sources from which my information was obtained, but one side of the case was prominently shown, and that as 'every medal has its reverse,' so, in all probability, had the Bhotanese a story of complaint also. Several occurrences which are casually alluded to in the documents referring to our troubles with Bhotan, tend to favour the impression that a series of raids and counter-raids have been going on for many years—the state of matters, in fact, on the north-eastern frontier, having been somewhat similar to that which was for so long characteristic of the English and Scotch borders.*

* Notwithstanding all that has been written against the Bhotanese, some grounds exist for entertaining the belief that at one time they were not so bad as it has become the custom of late to represent them, as well also as to give rise to a suspicion that defects of government on our part on the frontier may have had something to do with the insecurity to property and person which seems to have existed there for such a length of time. A correspondent of the "Calcutta Englishman" newspaper, writing from Darjeeling in the end of September 1864, in the course of some remarks expressive of the local opinion that mismanagement had brought about the necessity for military operations, stated—"In former years when the Bhooteahs were on friendly terms with our Government, they brought their ponies, musk, wax, dogs, &c. to Rungpore. Our Government to encourage the trade, provided suitable accommodation for these traders. Before however the Bhooteahs could bring their goods into our territory, they had to apply for a pass and Chuprassies (office messengers) were sent to accompany them. This they looked upon as degrading, let alone expensive, and once took the following humorous revenge. The then judge of Rungpore, Mr. N. Smith, and Dr. Morton simultaneously made a visit to Bhootan. The Doctor, a great favourite with the Bhooteahs, went on invitation; the judge under the idea that his position gave him free entry into a country, whose inhabitants, however, had not the same privilege of entering ours, went in without any notice to the Bhootan Government. The Doctor went off with his guides into the interior. The judge and his party pitched their tents in the Bhootan territory and went out shooting. One morning the Bhooteahs came down during the Judge's absence, and finished his breakfast, leaving their respects and a message for the Judge, saying that they found his cookery very good, that they would come down daily and partake of his meals. It was true they said, they were not invited by his Honour the judge, neither was the Judge invited by them to come into their district. This summary style of proceeding not suiting the Judge's views, the tents were immediately struck, and he and his party left Bhootan. On their arrival at Rungpore, 'the gross indignities' they had suffered from the Bhooteahs was made a very

Early in November 1864, the military preparations for the annexation of the Bengal Dooars and capture of the forts in the lower range of hills being completed, the following proclamation was issued by the Governor-General as the preliminary to the commencement of hostilities.

"Fort William, the 12th November 1864. *Proclamation.* For many years past outrages have been committed by subjects of the Bootan Government within British Territory, and the territories of the Rajahs of Sikhim and Cooch Behar. In these outrages property has been plundered and destroyed, lives have been taken, and many innocent persons have been carried into and are still held in captivity.

"The British Government, ever sincerely desirous of maintaining friendly relations with neighbouring

sensational story, by the additional information that poor Dr. Morton was cut off. A few weeks after, one fine morning, the Doctor was seen cantering into the station on his little pony 'Ginger,' looking as jovial and unconcerned as possible.—'Hallo Morton, we thought you had been killed, as the Judge's party was attacked.' 'Killed,' said he, 'well, so I have been almost, but it was with kindness; the more I grew in favour the greasier grew the bill of fare, and I should have been stuffed to death had I not managed to get away.' When, however, Lord William Bentinck visited Dinagepore and Rungpore, for the sake of economy he gave orders that no further allowance should be given to the headmen, and left the traders to find accommodation where and how they best could. The trade between Bhootan and Rungpore gradually fell off, and finally ceased altogether. Then Dr. Campbell, the superintendent of Darjeeling, established the Titalya fair, which was a great success while under his control. Titalya, however, was subsequently included within the Rungpore district, the fair then gradually languished, and is now one in name only." That there is reason for believing that the Bengalee subjects of the Bhotan Government—in other words, the inhabitants of the Bengal Dooars have had well-founded grounds of complaint with reference to aggressions from within the British and Cooch Behar frontiers will be shown at a future page.

states, and especially mindful of the obligations imposed on it by the treaty of 1774, has endeavoured from time to time by conciliatory remonstrance to induce the Government of Bootan to punish the perpetrators of these crimes, to restore the plundered property, and to liberate the captives. But such remonstrances have never been successful, and even when followed by serious warning, have failed to produce any satisfactory result. The British Government has been frequently deceived by vague assurances and promises for the future, but no property has ever been restored, no captives liberated, no offender punished and the outrages have continued.

"In 1863 the Government of India, being averse to the adoption of extreme measures for the protection of its subjects and dependent allies, despatched a special mission to the Bootan Court, charged with proposals of a conciliatory character, but instructed to demand the surrender of all captives, the restoration of plundered property and security, for the future peace of the Frontier.

"This pacific overture was insolently rejected by the Government of Bootan. Not only were restitution for the past and security for the future refused, but the British Envoy was insulted in open Durbar, and compelled, as the only means of ensuring the safe return of the mission, to sign a document which the Government of India could only instantly repudiate.

"For this insult the Governor-General in Council determined to withhold for ever the annual payments previously made to the Bootan Government on account of the Assam Dooars and Ambaree Fallacottah, which had long been in the occupation of the British Government, and annex those districts permanently to British Territory. At the same time still anxious to avoid an open rupture, the Governor-General in Council addressed a letter to the Deb and Dhurma Rajas, formally demanding that all captives detained in Bootan against their will should be released, and that all property carried off during the last five years should be restored.

"To this demand the Government of Bootan has returned an evasive reply, from which can be gathered no hope that the just requisitions of the Government of India will ever be complied with, or that the security of the Frontier can be provided for otherwise than by depriving the Government of Bootan and its subjects of the means and opportunity of future aggressions.

"The Governor-General in Council has therefore reluctantly resolved to occupy permanently and annex to British Territory the Bengal Dooars of Bootan, and so much of the Hill Territory, including the forts of Dallingkat, Passakha, and Dewangiri, as may be necessary to command the Passes, and to prevent hostile or predatory incursions of Bootanese into the Darjeeling District, or into the Plains below. A military force amply sufficient to occupy this tract and to overcome all resistance, has been assembled on the frontier, and will now proceed to carry out this resolve.

"All Chiefs, Zemindars, Munduls,* Ryots, and other inhabitants of the tract in question are hereby required to submit to the Authority of the British Government, to remain quietly in their homes, and to render assistance to the British Troops and to the

* In Hindoostanee "mundul" means "a headman of a village," also an "exciseman."

Commissioner who is charged with the administration of the tract. Protection of life and property and a guarantee of all private rights is offered to those who do not resist, and strict justice will be done to all. The lands will be moderately assessed, and all oppression and extortion will be absolutely prohibited.

"The future boundary between the Territories of the Queen of England and those of Bootan will be surveyed and marked off; and the Authority of the Government of Bootan within this boundary will cease for ever.

"By Order of the Governor-General in Council."

The following was the original composition of the force assembled to give effect to this Proclamation and the places which formed the base of operations of the columns prior to crossing the frontier and marching through the Dooars to the forts in the hills—the command of the force, generally, being given to Brigadier-General Mulcaster, at the time commanding in Assam, who was to operate on the right—the two columns on the left being under the command of Brigadier-General Dunsford, C.B.,

Right Column to start from Gowhatty against Dewangiri.

Three Mountain Train guns of the Eurasian (half caste) Company of Artillery.

One Squadron of the 5th Bengal Cavalry.

The 43rd Assam Light Infantry.

One Company of Sebundy Sappers and Miners.

Three Companies of the 12th Regiment Bengal Native Infantry and the Assam local Artillery, to occupy Gowhatty in support.

Right Centre Column to march from Goalpara against Bishensing.

Three Mountain Train Guns of the Eurasian Company of Artillery.

One Squadron 5th Bengal Cavalry.

Two Squadrons of the 14th Bengal Cavalry.

One Company of Sebundy Sappers and Miners.

A Wing of the 44th Regiment Native Infantry.

A Wing of the 12th Regiment Bengal Native Infantry.

Two Companies of the 12th Bengal Native Infantry to remain in support at Goalpara.

Left Centre Column to assemble at Cooch Behar, and march against Buxa and Balla.

Three Armstrong Mountain Train Guns (5th Battery, 25th Brigade Royal Artillery).

Two eight-inch Mortars (6th Battery, 25th Brigade Royal Artillery).

One Company of Sappers and Miners with three pontoon rafts for crossing rivers.

The 2nd Regiment of Ghoorkas.

A Wing of the 11th Native Infantry.

Left Column to move from Julpigorie against Dhalimkote and Chamoorchee.

Three Armstrong Mountain Train Guns (5–25 R.A.).

Two eight inch mortars (6–25 R.A.)

One Company of Sappers and Miners.

A Wing of the 11th Regiment Bengal Native Infantry.

A Wing of the 18th Regiment Bengal Native Infantry.

The 30th Punjaub Infantry.

Two Squadrons, 5th Bengal Cavalry.

In addition to the force detailed above, a Reserve consisting of three companies of Her Majesty's 48th and 80th Regiments, along with two companies of the

17th Native Infantry were placed at Darjeeling. The three companies of the 48th were subsequently withdrawn, their place being taken by two additional companies of the 80th. The only Europeans with the columns were the artillerymen on the left with the Armstrong guns and mortars.*

* The following is a translation of the evasive reply referred to in the Proclamation, which was in the form of a letter addressed to the Governor-General of India by the Dhurma Raja—"May you always remain well, and may God protect your power and authority. On the 21st Strabun (July) I received your letter, sent through the Jungpen of Dhalimkote, in which it is written that my subjects have committed robberies and other outrages on British subjects, and that you sent Mr. Eden to me to inquire into these matters. When Mr. Eden came to my court I was then only newly appointed Dhurma Raja; when he arrived I told my Council, 'See, these gentlemen have come a long journey, and are tired, therefore try and receive them well and do all they want.' After Mr. Eden had rested I met him and asked him for what purpose he had come, and he answered—'I have come to inquire into robberies and other outrages committed by your people on British subjects.' Regarding this I have given orders. You write that you have seized the revenue of the Assam Dooars and of Ambaree Fallacottah, and that you will not give it back unless I comply with your demands. You say that the Tongso Penlow has shown violence to Mr. Eden; this is true, but the Tongso Penlow has gone away to his country. To settle all, if this you wish, to send some officials again to me I can't object; but this will give them much trouble; if they come all this will be settled before them, and I will explain everything to them, and they will know the truth. If the officials do not come I will, if you want to inquire into the matter, send my secretaries in the winter season to any place where you may wish them to go, and then you can decide what is wrong and what is right, and do what is proper: do not send the officials or write on this matter to the other side (the Tongsow Penlow's residence). The Bhotan country belongs of old to the Dhurma Raja, and you may pay the revenue which you have seized or not as you please. You are master to give or not to give. Always write to me about your health." A reference to what Mr. Eden says of the Dhurma Raja, on the occasion of his seeing him at Poonakha, will show how improbable it is that he had anything whatever to do with the above communication, though it ostensibly emanated from him.

CHAPTER VIII.

Commencement of the Dooar War—Stockades of Mynagoorie and Dhamonee taken possession of—Advance of the Left Column from Julpigorie—Progress through the Dooars—Arrival at Dhalimkote—Communication with the Jungpen—Attack on the Fort—Catastrophe connected therewith—Capture of Dhalimkote—Remarks thereon—Occupation of Dhumsong—Proclamation by the Dhurma Raja—The Left Column descends to the Plains—Re-enters the Hills and captures Chamoorchee—Letter from the Deb Raja—Operations by the Left Centre Column—Capture of Buxa and Balla.

By the end of November 1864, all the preparations were completed, and the force was ready to take the field. The original intention was that the four columns should advance simultaneously. This, however, was not carried out; the movements of the right column being delayed some days, and the advance of the right centre column, some weeks, beyond the date that the columns on the left commenced operations. This delay was caused partly by some transport difficulties at Gowhatty—partly by Brigadier-General Mulcaster having ordered the right centre column, commanded by Colonel Richardson, C.B., of the 44th Native Infantry, to defer entering the hills until he had seen the work assigned to the right column completed at Dewangiri, and could himself join Colonel Richardson's force.

The annexation of the Dooars therefore was commenced by the two columns on the left, assembled at Julpigorie and Cooch Behar, under Brigadier-General Dunsford, C.B., who accompanied the left column, while Colonel Watson commanded the left centre one. In describing the operations, I shall commence with the movements of General Dunsford's force; the duty to be performed by which, was to capture the stockades of Mynagoorie and Dhamonee, situated near the Teesta, a few miles from Julpigorie, and then march across the Dooars into the hills, and take the fort of Dhalimkote. On this being done, the force was to return to the Dooars, and march along the foot of the hills in an easterly direction for about thirty miles, then re-enter the hills and secure the Chamoorchee Pass, and the Dooars in connexion with it.

On the 28th of November, an advanced party consisting of a detachment of the Royal Artillery, with two mortars, and detachments of Native Cavalry and Infantry, under the command of Major Gough, V.C., of the 5th Bengal Cavalry, accompanied also by a detachment of the Bengal Native Police Battalion under Major Pughe, crossed the Teesta near Julpigorie, and marched to Bakalee, in the vicinity of which a small Bhotan outpost, called Gopalgunge, was taken without resistance, by a few men of the police who had been sent ahead. The following morning at daybreak, the party marched to Mynagoorie. The stockade was empty, and exhibited no signs of any preparations having been made for resistance. The principal people of the village, which is one of some extent, waited on the Civil officer accompanying the party, and made their submission, the peasantry continuing at their agricultural operations with apparent confidence. The Proclamation was read and explained to the inhabitants—a few days prior to this however copies of it and invitations to tender submission had been sent to the Bhotan officials as far as Dhalimkote, and replies of a submissive nature had been received from those at Mynagoorie and Dhamonee. On the 30th November, Major Gough and his party proceeded to the latter place by a circuitous path, through a highly cultivated country, the inhabitants continuing their occupations undisturbed. The Dhamonee stockade, a small one at the junction of the Durlah River with the Teesta, had been abandoned two nights previously. Hereabouts no villages were seen, the peasantry being scattered about in detached huts. They came in however to the neighbourhood of the stockade, and attended their weekly market as usual.

On the 1st of December, a bridge of boats having been completed across the Teesta at Paharpore six miles to the north of Julpigorie, and nearly opposite Dhamonee, the column under Brigadier-General Dunsford marched from Julpigorie to that place, and crossed the Teesta, halting for a day at Dhamonee to enable the commissariat stores to come up.

On the 3rd of December, after a march of about three hours through a fine, level, open country, interspersed with patches of grass and jungle, the column reached Kyrantee, distant eight miles from Dhamonee. The chief cultivation noticed was rice, mustard, tobacco and hemp—indications were also seen of more extensive cultivation having formerly existed. On the 4th, the column moved on, and a few miles beyond Kyrantee, got into a country covered with thick jungle, the march being through a level path in the thicket. In about four and a half hours after starting, the foot of the hills was reached, and the force encamped at the Chayle river, near the entrance to the Pass leading to Dhalimkote. On the 5th, the country being found unsuited for cavalry, that portion of the force was sent back, and the remainder of the column, consisting of the artillery, with Armstrong guns and mortars, the 30th Punjaub Infantry, and a wing of the 18th Native Infantry, marched up the ascent to the valley of Ambiok, which was reached in four hours, the jungle being open and the path wider than on the previous day. The baggage and guns were conveyed on bullocks and elephants.

The village of Ambiok was found to consist at this time of about half a dozen bamboo huts, situated at the base of a densely wooded hill, immediately below the fort of Dhalimkote. All the inhabitants, with the exception of a man and his wife, fled on the approach of the troops. On the arrival of the column, a native was sent up to the fort with a message to the Jungpen, who sent down a Bengalee interpreter, in his employment, with a white scarf, as a mark of friendship, and intimating at the same time his intention to be pacific, and to submit to the directions of Lieutenant Colonel Haughton, the political agent accompanying the force. A written reply was sent him, referring him to the Proclamation he had received, and informing him that while possession would be taken of Dhalimkote and the Dooars attached to it, no injury would be done to either individuals or property, and that if the fort was quietly given up, all in it would be protected. The Jungpen was also requested to come down and conduct the troops up the steep ascent to the fort, the following morning at daybreak, but at the same time was told that in any case it would be taken possession of the next day. In the interval, however, the men in the fort were observed making hurried preparations for defence, by removing the roofs and woodwork from the towers at the angles of the fort; the idea of resisting, apparently having only then occurred to the Jungpen.

Next morning at sunrise, a little boy brought the following evasive letter from the Jungpen, in reply to the communication Colonel Haughton had addressed him the previous day—"Whereas your letter of Monday (the 5th), with the Pottrachin (Proclamation) has been received by me, I have acquainted myself with its contents. You have written requesting me to go to you this morning; but there is a large military force with you; how then can I go in the midst of them to see you? There is fear in my mind. If you are so inclined, come with three men to the road; I will also with three men go there and meet you and will inform you of everything: all will then be satisfactorily arranged; or else you may write to Cheeboo Lama at Darjeeling, and ask him to come. He knows everything. I will then consult with him and explain all to you. All then will be well. I am not in any way against you. But if after all matters have been explained to you, you still persist, right or wrong, to come here, then you may do as you like. I am quite well, and hope you are the same." A verbal answer was sent to this, informing the Jungpen that the force was about to advance and take possession of the fort.

Shortly after the Jungpen's messenger had left the camp, the troops commenced to ascend the hill, under the guidance of a native whose services had been procured by showing him a bag of rupees and allowing him to help himself. In the meantime, however, a bypath, better suited for the purpose than the one the troops were taking, was discovered by Colonel Haughton, and approved of by General Dunsford. The main column, therefore, retraced its steps and proceeded by it; this change involving a delay of about two hours. The Armstrong guns and eight inch mortars remained at Ambiok, and fired vertically on the fort. On the leading portion of the column reaching a ridge about two hundred feet below the fort, a fire of stones and arrows opened upon it, also a few matchlock shots from Bhotanese concealed in the neighbouring jungle—the latter fire being replied to by the advanced guard, consisting chiefly of men of the 30th Punjaubees. A short distance in front a barricade had been erected on the ridge, which was taken by the Punjaubees without either difficulty or opposition, and from thence they advanced to the foot of the ascent to the fort; here they were exposed to a volley of stones, thrown both by the hand and a catapult, also some arrows and matchlock shots, which killed two men and wounded several others. Here also Captain Macgregor* (the Brigade Major) and Lieutenant

* This officer when a subaltern of Fane's Horse, highly distinguished himself in the campaign of the Peiho in 1860. In a work by the writer of this narrative, styled "The British Arms in the North of China and Japan," the following mention is made of him at the action of Sinho: —"While this was going on (the advance of the cavalry brigade), Stirling's battery having been unable to follow the cavalry through the heavy ground, had been left behind with an escort of thirty men of Fane's Horse, under Lieutenant Macgregor, and just at the moment that the guns of the first division were heard on the left, a body of about seventy Tartars, to the surprise of every one, galloped from their front, and charging down on Stirling's battery attempted to take the guns in flank. The attack was so unexpected that Captain Stirling had but time to fire two rounds before the Tartars were within a hundred yards of the battery. There was no protection for the guns beyond the escort mentioned. Without a moment's hesitation Lieutenant Macgregor charged at the head of the Seiks and drove the Tartars back, in doing which he was severely wounded, also several of his men, one of whom was killed."

Loughman, of the 18th Native Infantry, were wounded, the former by a matchlock shot, the latter by an arrow. By this time two $5\frac{1}{2}$ inch mortars had been got up the hill to the ridge underneath the fort, and were placed in position. The charge of powder contained in the made up cartridges being too great for so short a range, it was necessary to weigh out charges specially suited for it, and a barrel of gunpowder was opened for this purpose. At the second round from the mortars one of the shells burst at the muzzle and exploded the powder cask. Major Griffin, who was at the time weighing the charges out, Lieutenants Anderson and Waller of the Royal Artillery, and four gunners of the same corps, were killed by the explosion, while Lieutenant Collins of the Royal Engineers, and several artillerymen, were severely mutilated. The cause of the premature bursting of the shell is supposed to have been some defect in the fuze; the result either of a crack in the woodwork or partial recession of the composition from the walls of the fuze, bringing the ignited composition prematurely in contact with the bursting charge in the shell. The supposition that there must have been want of caution displayed in exposing so large a quantity of powder to the risk of accidental ignition, is justified by the results—the more so, as the accident which led to it, though not a common occurrence, nevertheless is one that there must always be a risk of taking place, especially on active service in the East, where, from exposure to climate, fuzes are more likely to become defective.* Brigadier General Dunsford himself had

* In December 1851 Lieutenant Colonel Tomkins and Lieutenant Lugg, of the Royal Artillery, while superintending the arrangements for blowing up a house to arrest the progress of a fire in Hong Kong,

a narrow escape of being one of the victims of the explosion; having but a minute or two before it occurred left Major Griffin, with whom he had been conversing, to give some order to Captain Perkins of the Royal Engineers.

After the shock of the catastrophe had been recovered from, one of the Armstrong guns was brought up from Ambiok, the practice from which place, though apparently very good, was at the same time producing little or no effect. Towards evening the gun arrived, and after a few rounds had been fired from it at a tower, a breach was effected, through which the Punjaubees entered and took possession of the place, the Bhotanese having previously retired by a small exit on the opposite side, and descended the hill by a steep thickly-wooded bypath. By the time the main entrance to the fort had been blown open, the Jungpen's house, over the gateway, and several buildings inside the fort, including the monastery, were in flames, having been set fire to by the shells. In the course of the conflagration, a considerable quantity of rice and other grain was destroyed.

The capture of the place was thus effected after having been exposed to a fire which had ranged more or less over eight hours; namely, from 10 A.M. until 6 P.M., and notwithstanding the amount of munitions of war that had been expended, three wounded men only were found inside, one of whom, a Bengalee, afterwards died. Considering the precipitate manner in which the Bhotanese must have retired, and the nature of the ground they had to go over, it is very improbable

were killed by the premature explosion of the gunpowder from a cause analogous to that originating the accident referred to above; namely, a defect in the exploding composition (port fire) attributable to climate.

that any dead were removed. The loss of the British apart from those killed and wounded by the explosion, was two sepoys killed and about twenty wounded; the casualties having been chiefly caused by stones. The bodies of those killed by the explosion were found some distance down the hill from where it occurred, and most of them were so mutilated as to be hardly recognisable. Considering that Dhalimkote did not contain a single piece of artillery, and that with the exception of a few jingals and matchlocks, the means of defence consisted chiefly of stones and bows and arrows—also that the garrison did not exceed fifty men, at least so an officer who was present informed me, the capture of the place must be looked upon as a very poor affair, far from compensating for the melancholy loss by which it was attended; the more so as it is a place of no importance, not even commanding the Pass leading down to the Dooars—in fact it is only remarkable for the formidable nature of the position on which it is built. Mr. Eden, who visited it the previous year, thus describes it—"The fort is a miserable building; it consists of a large wall built of mud and stones; it has one large gateway to the north-east, in which the Jungpen resides; inside the wall are a number of houses and a garden; one house is assigned to the ryots of the Dooars, when they come up with their tribute, another is a monastery; there was a barrack, stables, storehouses and a residence for the women. . . . This fort was taken with great ease by Captain Jones and a few men in 1772; the people of the place, however, did not seem to be aware that we had ever sent a force there." A comparison of the circumstances attending its capture thus referred to and those attending its capture in

1864, do not seem to show that perfection of equipment and refined means of assault in operating against semi-civilized orientals are productive of results either more speedy or brilliant than those we have been in the habit of attaining by means, more simple, practicable, and infinitely less costly.

The only other operation to be carried out in this portion of the hills, was to take possession of the fort of Dhumsong, about twenty miles from the Darjeeling frontier. A letter was accordingly addressed by Colonel Haughton to the official in charge of it, a Neiboo, calling upon him to surrender. On the 10th of December, his reply was received tendering his submission. Mandates were also sent to the chiefs of the villages dependent on Dhalimkote, sixteen in number, calling on them to submit, and to send coolies in for employment with the force. In the meantime Captain Perkins, with a few Sebundy sappers, proceeded across the hills and took possession of Dhumsong fort, a small quadrangular building constructed of stone and mud; its beautiful situation being the only thing worthy of note connected with it. No attempt at resistance was made, the place being quietly given up. Colonel Haughton proceeded there and arranged that it was to be occupied by a detachment of fifty men of the 17th Native Infantry, who were accordingly sent from Darjeeling under the command of Lieutenant Dawes, and reached Dhumsong with their baggage, after a journey characterised by no ordinary difficulty and fatigue.

On the 16th of December, the following Proclamation, purporting to come from the Dhurma Raja, was given publicity to—"It is well known to the subjects of Bhotan that last year the Sikim man Cheeboo

Lama, without the consent of the Dhurma Rája, brought into Bhotan a band of Englishmen in spite of frequent warnings not to do so. Cheeboo has accepted the gold of the British Government and is their humble servant. The Sikim Raja was complained to on the subject of this conduct of Cheeboo Lama, but no reply was received. Now the Dhurma Raja has resolved on declaring war on the Sikim Government, who, it is well known, are the cause of all the evil. The Dhurma Raja has no desire to extend his territories; he addressed a letter to the Governor-General of India requesting him not to listen to Cheeboo or Eden, as both are dishonest. It is not the desire of the Dhurma Raja that innocent blood should be lightly shed, but the English do not cease attacking Bhotan, and the people must now prepare for the attack of the English. They will now try to take the Dooars, and after that they will attempt to proceed to take Poonakha, and deprive the inhabitants of Bhotan of the freedom they have enjoyed from time immemorial. It is the duty of the Penlows and Jungpens to be firm in their faithfulness and love of freedom to protect Bhotan." This manifesto, no doubt came from the Tongso Penlow, the Dhurma Raja being at the time an insignificant youth, and a mere puppet in his hands. The tone of the document clearly betokened that intention to continue resistance which subsequent occurrences sufficiently demonstrated.

On the 19th of December, Brigadier-General Dunsford having completed the military arrangements necessary for the annexation of the Dhalimkote and Mynagoorie Dooars, as well as for the hill territory between the fort of Dhalimkote and the Darjeeling, and portion of the Sikim frontiers of Bhotan, commenced to move his column by detachments down to the plains, for the purpose of proceeding along the foot of the hills to the Chamoorchee Pass, about thirty miles east of Dhalimkote. The day previous to the column moving, Colonel Haughton was attacked with fever, and the force was temporarily deprived of his services.

On the 22d of December the column reached Bullibaree, twelve miles south of Dahlimkote, the inhabitants of which had left the neighbourhood on the appearance of the troops in the Dooars; their sympathies seemingly being more Bhotanese than those nearer the British frontier. On the 23rd the column turned eastward, the route lying through level country containing but little jungle. Numerous patches of cultivation and Mechi villages were passed in the course of the day. A number of these Meechis, or inhabitants proper of the Dooars, had been employed as coolies, but many of them ran away on the march, having speedily imbibed that distaste for service with troops in the field which is entertained by coolies of every kind in the East, when they are made to carry things of a nature not admitting of being conveyed in the manner in which they are accustomed to carry loads. Great want of consideration also is frequently shown them, such as, on their arrival at an encamping ground, after having done their day's work carrying heavy loads and keeping up with the column, being made to collect fuel and do other work for the troops, without a thought being given as to whether their organisation is not similar to our own, and that physical exhaustion requires both rest and food. I have myself witnessed in China and India, an amount of cruelty thus exercised to both man and beast, which, but for the evidence of my own eyes, I could have hardly credited.

No signs were to be seen of a Bhotanese on the plains; in fact, as already stated, with the exception of a few officials and those connected with them, residing at the stockades near our frontier, they seldom visit the Dooars. The column having reached Tondoo, a spot at the foot of the hills about midway between the Dahlimkote and Chamoorchee Passes, a camp was formed there, and on the 29th December a reconnoitring party consisting of 150 men under Major Mayne of the 30th Punjaubees was sent on to examine the position of Chamoorchee, or Sumchee, as it is called by the Bhotanese; the former name like that of Zumerkote,* being obsolete in the country; in fact probably never known there, except perhaps to the frontier officials thrown into communication with the inhabitants of the plains with whom the present nomenclature of the Dooars generally seems for the most part to have originated: Dhalimkote for instance being a combination of the local Bhotanese word Dhalim, or Dalling, and the Hindostanee word *kote*, or fort. Major Maynes' instructions were to take possession of the place if no opposition was offered, but on no account to attack if the Bhotanese were found in any force. On the party reaching a flat piece of ground about 600 yards below the crest of the hill on which Chamoorchee is situated, the Bhotanese came down and attacked it, opening a fire of arrows, stones and matchlocks. The sepoys were restrained with difficulty from rushing up a narrow

* The name formerly given to the tract of land called the Mynagoorie Dooar.

and rugged winding path and engaging the enemy. Before they were withdrawn and placed in a position of security for the night, twelve men were wounded, one or two of them severely.

On the 31st December, Brigadier-General Dunsford came up with the main column, and finding the ground for the camp very confined and surrounded by dense jungle, sent the baggage animals down the hill to keep them out of harm's way, and placed them under the charge of a party of Bengal police that had just joined the column. A reconnaisance was then made of the position, which was much obscured by jungle, and a good site was found for the Armstrong guns, about 700 yards on the right of what was supposed to be the place that would be defended. An apparently unfrequented path also, was found leading direct to the village. Captain Perkins of the Engineers now volunteered to start early next morning with 100 men, and intercept the retreat of the Bhotanese by working to the rear of the village over the thickly wooded hills. This questionable proposition, in a humanitarian age, was acceded to, and the attack deferred until half-past eight o'clock the following morning, so as to give the party time to reach a position admitting of the Bhotanese being intercepted as they escaped to the rear. In the meantime Major Garstin, with 250 men of the 11th Native Infantry, one Armstrong gun, and one mortar, was detached to take up a position on the left; two Armstrong guns, covered by 50 men of the 11th, being posted on the right; while Major Mayne with 250 men of the 3rd Punjaubees, and one mortar, was detailed to ascend by the main road. At the appointed hour the attack commenced by the Armstrong gun on the right and the mortar in the centre opening fire. Owing to the nature of the ground on the left, the artillery could not be got into position, and after about a dozen rounds had been fired from the other guns, Major Garstin's party finding little or no semblance of opposition rushed into the village, which was immediately evacuated, and the Bhotanese seen flying over the hills, coincident with which Captain Perkins's party was heard firing upon them as they ran away. This was the whole affair—the total loss being two men killed and three wounded, the whole of them being men of Major Garstin's party. The Bhotanese had 13 killed, and are said to have carried off their wounded—a statement somewhat incompatible with the interception of their retreat by Captain Perkins's party, and calculated to excite the suspicion from no wounded being found, that they were either shot in attempting to escape or killed where they were found lying.

The village of Chamoorchee was found to consist of about twenty houses and a monastery, the latter being full of sacred books and manuscripts. On the top of the hill overlooking the village a stockade was found in an unfinished state, and to defend which no attempt had been made. One hundred men of the Bengal police were placed in it, with instructions to hold the post as a temporary arrangement. The column then descended to the plains, and returned to the camp at Tondoo, while Brigadier-General Dunsford went eastward, with an escort of 50 men, to inspect the posts at Balla and Buxa, which had been taken possession of by the left centre column under Colonel Watson, which had started from Cooch Behar simultaneously with the advance of the left column from Julpigorie.

The country in the neighbourhood of the Chamoorchee Pass was found to be in many places highly cultivated, and the Meechis had a healthy appearance as if the climate agreed with them, which is the contrary in the case of both the European and the native of Bengal Proper. The peasantry hereabouts made no complaints of oppression, and said that they seldom saw the Bhotanese except in the months of December and January, when they come down from the hills to collect the Dooar revenue. About this time, the following document, bearing date 27th December, is said to have been addressed by the Deb Raja to the Brigadiers-General commanding the force.

"The territory which the Deb Raja has long since governed, although very small, he is contented with, and is never desirous of taking possession of the neighbouring kingdoms of Chinese Tartary, China and English territory, nor ever put their peasantry into trouble. The Queen and the Deb Raja are like sister and brother. Last year when Mr. Eden came to me, I paid him such respect as was due to him, and introduced him to the Dhurma Raja, who settled the matter of captives with him. He, Mr. Eden, solemnly promised that he would never break the peace existing between us, or fight with us; but, in spite of this promise, you fight, which I do not like; you also never sent me any notice as to the reason of fighting, nor as to the time when you wish to do so, but at once began by taking possession of our country, and have driven out all our people, occupied all the forts, and have done great injury by burning them. I never thought you, who are friends, would do such acts, and I cannot believe that the Queen has ordered you to occupy my country. When two Rajas desire to fight, they send information as to when they will begin to fight. This is the custom of my country, and when any party is vanquished he loses his territory. But if you like robbers take possession of my country, it depends upon your will, and as you have done so, be satisfied yourselves; but I shall never consider that you occupied my country as I did not fight. As for the plains which you have occupied, you will not be able to hold them. I advise you to attend to this; but if you do not, I will not hear it afterwards. If you wish for peace and do not disturb our peasantry, it will be best for you to go back to your own country without doing any more harm to ours. But if you will take possession of my country, which is small, without fighting, and attach it to your own kingdom, which is large, I shall send the divine force of twelve gods, as per margin,* who are very ferocious ghosts. Of this force 7,000 stop at Chamoorchee, 5,000 at Doorma, 9,000 at Buxa, and 102,000 at Dhalim Dooar. You have done great injury to our country, and should not repeat it. For the present it is advisable for you to return to your own country and keep peace with me. I have never broken the ties of friendship and you should not do so, but if you do not like to withdraw your troops, you should write me in reply at once to Poonaka."

With respect to the proceedings of the left centre column, a reconnaisance was sent forward from the Cooch Behar frontier on the 28th of November, through which it was ascertained that Chickakotta, the Bhotanese frontier post in the Buxa Dooar, had

* In the original document the names are detailed, but as they are very unpronounceable, I shall not tax the reader with them.

been abandoned. The main column, under Colonel Watson then advanced across the Dooar, into the hills, and on the 7th December took possession of Passakha, or Buxa as it is more usually called. Two days afterwards, a sort of intrenchment being noticed on the opposite hill, the three Armstrong guns were placed on elephants and brought into a position within range of this work. After the firing had gone on for a short time, there being no signs of an enemy, it was brought to a conclusion and the guns removed. The so-called fort of Buxa was found to be a very poor specimen of military architecture, having neither a surrounding wall nor means of defence, except an old gun of Chinese manufacture, which was lying useless on the ground. The hill on which the fort stands is low and commanded on every side but one by other hills; all of them being thickly wooded. A few Goorkhas, who were sent out to explore, came upon a sort of enclosure in charge of some Bhotanese, who retired as soon as they saw the Goorkhas approaching. The country about here appeared to be well supplied with roads; one to the north leading to Poonakha being considered as the main entrance into the country. The portion of this road which came under the observation of the column, was very good and roughly paved with stone slabs. Amongst the trees in the neighbourhood the ash and the willow were very common.

The column now descended to the plains, and marched westward to the Balla Pass, commanding the Luckee Dooar, which was taken possession of, and a small force kept in a sort of stockade—thus completing the work assigned to this column. Colonel Watson established a camp at Santrabaree at the foot of the hills, between the entrance to the Buxa Pass and Chickakotta. The villagers in the Dooars passed through by this column professed to be well pleased at the change of government which was about to take place, and on some occasions displayed a desire to assist the troops, by burning the jungle in the neighbourhood of their villages. Near Santrabaree, in the dry bed of a mountain stream, a vein containing a small quantity of coal was found.

CHAPTER IX:

Operations on the Assam side—Advance of the Right Column from Gowhatty — Capture of Dewangiri — Garrison placed in it under Colonel Campbell--General Mulcaster joins the Right Centre Column —Advance on Bishensing—Capture of the Place—Nature of the Position and Country in its Vicinity—Return of the Column to the Plains— The Sidlee Raja — Apparent Termination of Hostilities — Orders issued for the break-up of the Dooar Field Force.

THE operations on the Assam frontier, by the two right columns, now require to be noticed. On the 2nd of December, the right column commanded by Colonel Campbell, 43rd Assam Light Infantry, and accompanied by Brigadier-General Mulcaster, crossed the Berhampooter at Gowatty, and encamped on its north bank preparatory to marching the following day for the frontier, where a standing camp was to be established at Koomrekatta, our advanced post in the Assam Dooars, forty-one miles from Gowhatty, and fifteen miles from the Bhotan hill post of Dewangiri at the top of the Darungah Pass. On the arrival of the force at Koomrekatta, Captain Macdonald was sent in advance with fifty men of the Bengal police. On the afternoon of the 9th, the column made a march of six miles, and halted for the night near the entrance to the Darungah Pass. Early in the morning of the 10th, it moved forward and entered the hills. The road wound up the bed of a mountain torrent, and proved very bad; half the day being occupied crossing and recrossing the stream. The advanced guard consisted of one company of the 43rd Assam Light Infantry, under the command of Lieutenant Peet. About six miles up the pass it came to what was supposed to be a stockade, from which a volley of stones and some jingals were fired, one man being wounded. The advanced guard returned the fire, and while this was going on some of the sepoys went into the jungle on the side of the pass, and ascertained that the obstruction, whatever it was, was open on both sides, and that there were about fifty Bhotanese behind it. General Mulcaster now came up, and as it was pretty well on in the afternoon, ordered the advanced guard to retire on the main column. The whole force now halted for the night, so as to enable the position to be reconnoitred. This was done the following morning, General Mulcaster proceeding through the jungle to the left, accompanied by a party of the 43rd. Shortly after he had left the camp, a Bhotanese arrived with a letter from Captain Macdonald, who had taken a different route from that followed by the column, to say that he had captured Dewangiri the previous night with his fifty native policemen. The letter was sent after the General, who on receiving it, ordered Captain Norman, the Depot Assistant-Quartermaster-General, to go forward and examine the stockade. This was done, and it was found to be only a sort of natural breastwork across the mouth of the pass, open, as the sepoys said, at each end, admitting of easy capture on either flank by going through the jungle. Not a Bhotanese was to be seen in its vicinity. Brigadier-General Mulcaster now pushed on with three companies of the 43rd to Dewangiri, and the remainder of the column reached it the following day :—a royal salute being fired on the arrival of the guns.

The capture of Dewangiri was effected by Captain Macdonald under the following circumstances. In the first place, when he reached the foot of the hills, the guide he had with him said that he did not know the road. A footpath, however, was pointed out to him by a villager, which he followed, and after a ten hours' march, found himself at Dewangiri. He stopped at a temple, and as he was civilly treated, thought the place was going to be given up without resistance. He then went on, and suddenly came to a small stone house, in front of which an extemporary breastwork had been thrown up. From this he was received by a volley of arrows and stones, and a single jingal shot, one of his men being mortally wounded by the latter. He immediately took up a position on a hill about thirty yards off, and while there a Bhotanese, a remarkably fine man, leapt over the breastwork, armed with a spear, and made a rush at him. As he advanced he was shot dead by one of the policemen, a native district superintendent. Shortly after this, Captain Macdonald and his party stormed the house, and the Bhotanese retired. They, however, returned on several occasions during the night, and harassed his men by firing at them. In addition to the man already mentioned, he had five wounded. A few Bhotanese were killed. They were fair complexioned, stout, and exceedingly well made men.

Dewangiri was found to consist of three temples and a number of huts. Dr. Griffiths, who visited it with Captain Pemberton in 1840, thus described it:— "Dewangiri, the temples of which are visible from the plains of Assam, is situated on a ridge elevated about 2,100 feet above the level of the sea, and 1950 feet above that of the plains. The village extends to some distance along the ridge as well as a little way down its northern face. The houses which are in most cases mere huts, amount to about a hundred; they are distributed in three or four scattered groups, amongst these a few stone-built houses of the ordinary size and construction occur, the only decent one being that occupied by the Soubah, who is of inferior rank, Along the ridge three or four temples of the ordinary Buddh mystical form occur. They are surrounded with banners, bearing inscriptions fixed longitudinally to bamboos, and attached to some monumental walls of poor construction; the faces of which bear slabs of slate on which sacred sentences are well carved.* The village abounds in filth. The centre of the ridge is kept as a sort of arena for manly exercises. About this space there occur some picturesque simool trees and a few fig trees, amongst which is the banyan. There is no watercourse or spring near the village; the supply is brought from a considerable distance by aqueducts formed of the hollowed trunks of small trees. . . . The Soubah we found to be a gentlemanly, unassuming man; he received us in a very friendly manner, and with some state; the room was decently ornamented, and set off in particular by some well-executed Chinese religious figures, the chief of which we were told, represented the Dhurma Raja, whose presence, even as a carved block, was supposed to give infallibility. We were, besides, regaled with blasts of music. His house

* Both to the east and west of Dewangiri there is a picturesque religious edifice with ornamented windows. Their effect is much heightened by the presence of the weeping cypress, which situated as it was here, gave an idea of extreme beauty.

was the most picturesque one that I saw, and had some resemblance, particularly at a distance, to the representations of some Swiss cottages. It was comparatively small, but, as he was of inferior rank, his house was of inferior size. The Soubah soon returned our call, and in all his actions evinced friendship and gentlemanly feeling. And we soon had reason to find that, among his superiors at least, we were not likely to meet with his like again. His followers were not numerous; nor, with the exception of one or two who had dresses of scarlet broad cloth, were they clothed better than ordinarily. The population of the place must be considerable; it was during our stay much increased by the Kampa (Thibetian) people, who were assembling there prior to proceeding to Hazoo. Most of the inhabitants are pure Bhoteahs. Many of these were fine specimens of human build, certainly the finest I saw in Bootan. They were, strange to say, in all cases civil and obliging. Cattle were tolerably abundant, principally of the species known in Assam by the name of mithan. They were taken tolerable care of, and were picketed in the village at night; some, particularly the bulls, were very fine and very gentle. Ponies and mules were not uncommon, but not of extraordinary merits. Pigs and fowls were abundant." This account may be taken as giving a very fair idea of what Dewangiri was, on our taking possession of it in 1864. General Mulcaster gave strict orders that the temples were not to be interfered with. This very proper injunction, however, was more honoured in the breach than in the observance, everything and place likely to contain anything of value being ransacked; the interiors of the deities themselves being subjected to close examination. One of the temples contained a large library, consisting of several thousand volumes of sacred writings. In the Jungpen's house, some manuscripts in the Thibetian language were found. A day or two after our arrival a former Jungpen and three Zinkaffs applied for permission to settle at Dewangiri, a deputation also of Bhotanese waited on Mr. Metcalf, the civil officer with the column, and requested to be allowed to bring their wives and children back to the village.

On the 17th of December the column at Dewangiri was broken up, and six companies of the 43rd Assam Light Infantry and two mountain howitzers of the Eurasian battery were left as a garrison under the command of Colonel Campbell of the 43rd. Instructions in the meantime having been sent by Brigadier General Mulcaster to Colonel Richardson, commanding the column starting from Goalpara, to halt at Sidlee until joined by him. Accordingly, on the above date, General Mulcaster left Dewangiri, accompanied by fourteen Eurasian gunners under Captain Cordner of the Royal Artillery, ond two companies of the 43rd under Lieutenant Wheler, as an escort for two mortars that the General had decided on taking with him from the camp at Koomrekatta. At this place the escort was strengthened by a squadron of the 5th Bengal Cavalry which had just arrived. The march from Koomrekatta to Sidlee occupied ten days. On the way several of the men, and four out of the nine European officers with the party, were attacked with the "Dooar fever." An excellent camp had been formed at Sidlee by Colonel Richardson, and the day after General Mulcaster's arrival, the right centre column marched for Bishensing, distant about forty-two miles; the approach to which was very difficult and tedious, sometimes not more than three or four miles' progress being made in a day, owing to the dense and tall jungle through which paths had frequently to be cut. To counteract as much as possible the effects of malaria, the troops had quinine given them every morning; on the principle of prevention being better than cure, but which, I am told, did not seem to be attended with any marked benefit. By the 5th of January the column had reached within three marches of Bishensing, which is situated a few miles in the hills, up a gentle slope thickly covered with jungle.

On the morning of the 8th of January, the force having reached a spot called Pakki Haga, on the bank of the Sooranbhanga River, within a short distance (about four miles) of the supposed fort of Bishensing, General Mulcaster went on ahead with three hundred men of the 12th and 44th regiments of Native Infantry, and on arriving in front of the position found it to consist of a single stone house, occupied by an old Lama Priest. This was the capture of Bhotan Hill Fort of Bishensing; for which duty a fully equipped column, about 2,000 strong, accompanied by 150 elephants, had been detailed, and had reached the place under circumstances of extreme difficulty and at great sacrifice of health. This place, it appears was used once in two or three years by the Angdu Forung Jungpen, as a temporary residence when he came down on a fishing excursion to the stream that flows near it. It would seem a matter of regret that before incurring the expense and trouble of moving a force through such a country, some idea of the nature and importance of the position had not been ascertained.

The force went into camp at Pakki Hagga, in the vicinity of the river, which is plentifully supplied with large fish, and some days were spent examining the country around. Bishensing was ascertained to be one edge of a lofty mountain, which runs first due east and then north, in the direction of Cherrung, the residence of a Jungpen, about thirty miles to the north-west. The country around Pakki Haga, and for some twenty-five miles to the south of it, is covered with timber; some of the forests containing very fine specimens of teak, saul, and oak trees. Others again, seemed stunted in their growth by the denseness of the brushwood and creepers about them. No signs of population were seen, nor indications of a human habitation ever having existed.

After a short stay at Pakki Hagga, the right centre column, with the exception of the two squadrons of the 5th Bengal Cavalry which were sent to Julpigorie, returned to the camp at Sidlee, leaving three companies of the 44th Native Infantry and fifty of the Bengal police as a garrison for Bishensing, General Mulcaster returning at the same time to Gowhatty.

While at Sidlee, on the way back, the civil officer with the force (Mr. Metcalf) received a visit from the so-called Raja of Sidlee, who turned out to be a Bengalee in the employment of the Bhotan Government. He told Mr. Metcalf, that though the Dooar was called Sidlee by the English, Cherrung was the only name the district was known by in Bhotan—also that he held his appointment by a warrant from the Deb Raja, and was allowed to collect the rents and make as much out of the Dooar as he could, on making an annual payment of money, as well as tribute in the form of dried fish, cloth, and some other produce. Of the amount of his revenue, the number and names of his villages, and their relative distances, he considered it prudent to affect ignorance. The people in the villages near, having been directed by some of his officials not to sell cattle to the troops, Mr. Metcalf referred to the matter. He pleaded ignorance of it, but at the same time said that the killing of cows was contrary to his caste. Between Sidlee and Bishensing there is no population whatever, the whole country being one vast forest, intersected with streams and forests of teak and saul. At a place called Bentook, seven miles to the north-west of Sidlee, there was the site of a deserted village, in the neighbourhood of which the jungle grass was so high as to conceal even the elephants accompanying the column.

The annexation of the Dooars of Bengal and Assam, as well as the hill posts by which they are erroneously supposed to be commanded, being completed, the Government of India issued orders for the breaking up of the Dooar field force early in February. The intention being to withdraw most of the regular regiments, and leave the occupation of the country chiefly to the Bengal Police Battalion (originally about 800 strong) that had accompanied the expedition. A few cavalry posts however were to be established between the advanced positions in the hills and the frontiers of Bengal, Cooch Behar, and Assam. Arrangements were also made for the civil government of the newly annexed territory, by dividing it into districts under Deputy Commissioners.

CHAPTER X.

Rumours of an Attack on Dewangiri—Warnings received by the Garrison —The Attack takes place by a Force under the Tongso Penlow and is repulsed—Death of Lieutenant Urquart—Thibetian Element in the Force.—The Attack resumed—The Garrison evacuates the Position and retreats to the Plains—Details connected with the Tongso Penlow's Force—The Bishensing Post attacked by the Bhotanese—Buxa threatened—Attack on Balla—The British Force repulsed and retires—Chamoorchee threatened—Reinforcements ordered to the Dooars—Change in the Commands—Disposition of the Reinforcements.

WHILE everything thus seemed over, and the force on the eve of breaking up, the Bhotanese were making preparations to attack the whole line of hill posts from Chamoorchee to Dewangiri; ample warnings of which were given at the latter place, but for some unaccountable reason, no attention seems to have been paid them. Amongst other information warranted to create suspicion, the following statement was made about the middle of January by a Bhotanese boy of fourteen years of age, named Bundoo, who had been employed by the Jungpen of the place, looking after the cattle which had been removed from Dewangiri on the approach of the force. The Jungpen it appeared retired to Saleeka, a village about two days' march from Dewangiri, and from there wrote to the Tongso Penlow, informing him of what had occurred, and asking for instructions. A reply to this letter was received about the end of December 1864, to the effect that the Penlow of Tongso would himself arrive at Saleeka with reinforcements within nine days, and that he would bring about six hundred men with him. This information the boy had gathered from conversations he had heard amonst the Jungpen's followers, shortly before he left Saleeka, which he did secretly; for the purpose of rejoining his relatives at Dewangiri, to which place they had returned. He also stated that the Jungpen had a picket of about a hundred men on the Tongso road, about half way between Saleeka and Dewangiri, and that there was a similar guard on one of the passes running to the north-east of the hill, from which the British garrison procured its water by a wooden aqueduct.

Warnings received from the local peasantry fully corroborated what this boy said with reference to there being indications of an impending attack. In addition to all, a letter was sent into the camp by the Tongso Penlow, but as it was in Thibetian, no one at Dewangiri could read it; no interpreter in that language being attached to the force. The letter consequently had to be sent on to Darjeeling, a distance of two hundred miles, for translation by Cheeboo Lama. It proved to be a caution to the officer commanding from the Tongso Pelow to evacuate Dewangiri within a week from the date of its receipt, otherwise that he would adopt compulsory measures.

On the night of the 29th January 1865, the Dewangiri garrison retired to rest entertaining no fears with reference to the proximity of danger. The camp faced the north, the following being its arrangement. On the extreme right the company of Roorkie Sappers (Seik's) was encamped, next to it the six companies of the 43rd Assam Light Infantry, and on the left, a little in front, was the Jungpen's house occupied by some officers and the Bengal Police; the artillery being encamped on a small mound about a hundred and fifty yards in front of the centre of the camp. About five o'clock on the morning of the 30th, it being still dark, a noise was suddenly heard in the camp as if cattle had got loose and were running about. Lieutenants Storey and Peet of the 43rd occupying the same tent were awoke by it, and almost immediately afterwards, they heard the ropes of their tent being cut. On looking out, they saw the Bhotanese cutting the tent ropes in the vicinity, and had just time to make their escape to the opposite side of the camp, when the attack upon it became general. The Eurasian Artillerymen stood to their guns and the troops fell in opening fire in the direction where they thought the Bhotanese were most exposed. They were thus kept in check until day dawned. As soon as their position could be made out, Colonel Campbell, who was at the time suffering from fever, charged them with the 43rd and the Sappers, and drove them off, though they held their ground for some time and fought with considerable obstinacy from behind rocks. They also attacked the Jungpen's house, but were driven off by the Police in charge of it commanded by Mr. Savi.

Early in the attack, Lieutenant Urquart of the Royal Engineers was killed by a large jingal bullet, which severed his femoral artery. He fell into the arms of one of his men and bled to death before he could be brought within the reach of surgical aid. Had the sapper known that tying a handkerchief or piece of calico round the leg immediately above the seat of the injury, and tightening it by passing his ramrod underneath it and turning it round once or twice, would have arrested the bleeding and given time for the surgeon to be found, the probabilities are that this officer's life might have been saved.* The other casualties were Lieutenant Storey, adjutant of the 43rd, wounded, four men killed and thirty-one wounded.

The attack was conducted by the Tongso Penlow in person. His Secretary, described as an exceedingly fine old man, was mortally wounded in the chest and taken prisoner. Before his death he was made to translate into Assamese some papers that were found upon him. They proved to be details connected with the distribution and provisioning of the force the Tongso Penlow had brought with him.

The loss of the Bhotanese was estimated at about sixty men, many of the wounded were remarkably fair complexioned men for orientals, and from inquiries made it was pretty well ascertained that a considerable proportion of the attacking force were Thibetians from the district called Kampa, stated by Captain Pemberton to be the only portion of Thibet that the Bhotanese have any intimate acquaintance with.† They are the class of Thibetians also, who for years have carried on trade at a certain period of the year with both Bengal and Assam—the great places of annual resort having been in former years Rungpore and Hazoo; the latter a village in Lower Assam

* A case of this kind is suggestive, that—as the minds of soldiers now-a-days are, in the course of the musketry instruction they undergo, called on to grapple with several facts in physical science, such for instance as recognising in the Enfield bullet they fire, "an elongated cylindro-conoidal expanding projectile"—the imparting of the knowledge to soldiers that constricting a limb in the manner referred to above will arrest hæmorrhage, might not prove an altogether useless task on their memories on active service.

† See note, p. 7.

about six miles from the northern bank of the Berhampooter.

Though the Bhotanese had been repulsed, they were by no means defeated inasmuch as they continued to hover about the camp harassing the garrison at intervals for the three following days. They succeeded also in cutting off the supply of water which was conducted into camp by a bamboo aqueduct from a spring about a mile and a half distant. On the 3rd of February, they threw up a stockade within jingal range (about six hundred yards) of the camp, and during the night succeeded in getting possession of the mouth of the Durungah Pass, cutting off communication by it with the plains. The troops were now getting very short of water, the only source of supply being a small and imperfectly fed spring which had become nearly dry, and it was deemed impracticable, with the force then available, to dislodge the Bhotanese from the position they had taken up commanding the water supplying the aqueduct, Colonel Campbell had written on the 30th of January to General Mulcaster, then at Gowhatty, asking for reinforcements. The latter wrote back to say that he considered the force at the time at Dewangiri, as ample for the defence of the place. Colonel Campbell continued to represent his position daily so long as the pass remained open, and as his ammunition was running short, a supply of 25,000 rounds was dispatched escorted by thirty-six men of the 12th Native Infantry. This party however on reaching the pass found it in possession of the enemy, and the officer commanding it (Captain Cunliffe) prudently determined not to risk so large a quantity of ammunition falling into the hands of the Bhotanese, and retired to Koomrekatta.

On the 4th of February, as the camp of the Dewangiri garrison was completely commanded by the stockade which had been thrown up, and as it was with the greatest difficulty that any water could be procured, Colonel Campbell made up his mind to evacuate the place that night and retreat to the plains by another opening in the hills known as the Libra Pass, and which communicated by by-paths with both the Durungah and another pass to the westward.* The following preparations were made for the retreat, 250 men of the 43rd were told off to carry and escort the sick and wounded, 50 to carry the guns (two twelve-pounder Howitzers), and the remainder of the force, about 200 men, to form the advanced and rear guards.

At one o'clock on the morning of the 5th of February, the place was silently evacuated, and the troops commenced their march covered by the pickets who kept up a fire to divert the enemy's attention. The main column unfortunately lost its way, and the extreme difficulty of the position in which the men were placed produced a sort of panic, which caused the retreat to become one of extreme disorder, in the course of which some of the wounded were left behind in the confusion, and the guns abandoned. With reference to the latter occurrence, it is but fair to state that when the men of the 43rd refused to carry the guns any longer, the Eurasian gunners, about twenty in number accompanying them, made an attempt to bring them on, but were unequal to doing so, and under the direction of their officer (Captain Cockburn, R.A.), threw them down a Khud, as the ravines in the Himalayas are called, to prevent

* Dewangiri is the terminus of five passes; the Durungah being the centre one.

them falling into the enemy's hands. This mode of disposing of them, however, was not successful, as the guns were found by the Bhotanese and they are now in the possession of the Tongso Penlow at his seat of government in the interior.

The troops succeeded, after many difficulties and dangers encountered in the dark, in getting clear of the hills and finding their way to the camp at Koomrekatta, officers and men having lost everything they possessed except what they marched in. A few men fell into the hands of the Bhotanese, two of whom had been severely wounded in the attack on the 30th of January. The immunity from pursuit which the garrison enjoyed is attributable to the Bhotanese having, on discovering the evacuation of the place which they did two hours afterwards, devoted themselves in the first instance to appropriating the property which had been left behind.

Shortly after the evacuation, the Tongso Penlow sent a letter down to the camp at Koomrekatta, inquiring after the health of the Bhotanese prisoners that were with the force, and informing the British that the prisoners belonging to them, which he had, were in a satisfactory state. He also enclosed some money to cover any expenses which might be incurred in sending him a reply.

The impression formed of the Tongso Penlow by officers who served at Dewangiri, I find to be by no means of an unfavourable nature, notwithstanding his unseemly behaviour to Mr. Eden. He appears in the moment of victory to have behaved with considerable forbearance, and there is no proof of any of the prisoners having been badly used. He also invariably treated the messengers who were sent up from the camp at Koomrekatta with kindness, fed them well and generally gave them a small present, though he would not allow them to come into the stockade.

The evacuation of Dewangiri has been somewhat harshly criticised, and the conduct of the 43rd Assam Light Infantry censured with more asperity perhaps than fairness. The men behaved well enough on every occasion that they were brought face to face with the enemy, but considering the peculiar circumstances under which they were placed, retreating in the dark through a wild and mountainous country, by pathways that they were ignorant of, with a numerous enemy in their immediate rear, that they should have become panic-stricken, admits of much extenuation—and it must be borne in mind, that panics are occurrences that no bodies of men, however good their antecedents may have been, can be altogether warranted as free from the liability to—and of which an illustration so recently occurred in New Zealand. The 43rd Assam Light Infantry moreover, until the Bhotan expedition, never previously had the advantage of acting as a regiment; the corps having been broken up ever since its formation into small detachments scattered over Lower Assam, and which were hurriedly collected at Gowhatty to form a portion of the field force.

The suspicion that the Tongso Penlow had procured assistance from beyond the frontiers of Bhotan was fully confirmed by facts subsequently ascertained, and the following information having reference thereto appeared in the "Calcutta Englishman." "Our late encounter with the Bhooteas has shown us—1st, that they can collect a far stronger force of men than we ever gave them credit for; 2nd, that they have a good system of military organization; 3rd, that they have larger resources in the shape of food in the interior than we were led to believe; 4th, that they are as soldiers cool under fire, but they cannot stand close quarters or hand to hand fighting; 5th, that they are admirable marksmen, both with fire-arms and bows, and that the former have a longer range than the plain firelocks of our infantry. It is probable that no small portion of the Tongso Penlow's territory has been indented on for the supply of this force. All those concerned in the fighting of the 30th January and the 3rd of February at Dewangiri, agree in stating that the enemy aggregated about 5,000 men. This large number was composed; 1st, of fighting men; 2nd. Oubas or Porters; 3rd, Lopas or coolies; 4th, Musicians or Servants. The men of the first class were fair and large limbed, from that division of Bhootan (Thibet) called Kampa. Of these there were probably not more than 1500 men. They were armed with jingals. The Porters were employed in carrying away the wounded which they do on their backs. The 3rd class carry the provisions which are tied up in cloth on their backs. These two divisions also build stockades and carry up timber. The last division plant standards and blow horns to excite the combatants. Each fighting man carries, in the fold of his dress, a circular powder flask containing from 100 to 150 bullets, about three seers (six pounds) of rice and dried meat, and in addition to this from ten to twenty stones of a size sufficient to stun a man. Their plan of attack is this. First to choose a crest overlooking the position to be attacked. The conformation of the Bhootan mountains appears to be one hump above another joined by narrow ridges covered with dense jungle. The crest which is generally ascended in perfect silence during the night, is at once stockaded by felling trees and closing up the spaces with branches. The stockade is about twelve feet square and six feet feet four inches in height. Starting from this stockade, they descend the ridge, cutting a pathway and closing up the sides. On another crest a second stockade is established till the position to be attacked is completely surrounded. The besieged are then harassed till they give in, it may be a matter of days or weeks. But this appears to be their plan of action. Their Rajas (Chiefs) also take part in the contest. During the fighting at Dewangiri, there were frequent duels between our officers and the Bhootan Chiefs in which the former were not always victorious, although armed with rifles against arrows. Some of the men who were killed, had circular pieces of bamboo on the top of their helmets. These were covered with cloth and gave the men the appearance of being gigantic." The writer of these remarks, it will have been observed, is unaware that Kampa is in Thibet, and not a portion of the Tongso Penlow's territory. If as asserted, these men came from Kampa, the aid must have been given by some Thibetian local authority on friendly terms with the Tongso Penlow. There is no doubt that the men had come a considerable distance, according to what could be ascertained from those who fell into our hands, upwards of a month's march.

The attack on Dewangiri was but one of a series of demonstrations made about the same time along the whole line of hill posts to Chamoorchee. On the 25th of January Bishensing was attacked by several hundred men, whose approach, owing to the denseness of the jungle, was not noticed until they appeared in front of the stockade that was in course of construction for our troops. They were however beaten off by the three companies of the 44th Sylet Light Infantry stationed there, with trifling loss; two men only being wounded, and both of them with arrows. The Bhotanese are believed to have lost several men.

On the 26th of January at three o'clock in the morning, the post at Buxa was threatened, but the Ghoorkas stationed there, discovered the advance of the Bhotanese in time to save their pickets from being cut off. They then came down to the vicinity of the position but retired on the Ghoorka detachment opening fire. At day-break they were discovered on the summit of a neighbouring hill, commanding the road leading into the interior. They were immediately attacked and driven from their position, where they had commenced to construct a stone breastwork across the road.

Early on the morning of the 27th January, Tazagong, the stockaded post in the Balla Pass, occupied by a detachment of 50 men of the 11th Native Infantry under Lieutenant Millett was attacked. The Bhotanese advanced with great determination, and endeavoured to force their way into the stockade. The detachment of the 11th behaved with great steadiness and repulsed them, losing one sepoy killed and six wounded. The loss of the Bhotanese was not known. With the exception of one man found dead underneath one of the loop-holes of the stockade, no indications of casualties were seen, and it was consequently inferred that they had removed their killed and wounded.

As at Dewangiri, the Bhotanese however were not

discouraged by their repulse, but proceeded to construct a stockade commanding the one occupied by the troops at Tazagong, and soon made it so hot for them that Colonel Watson who had arrived with reinforcements from the plains determined to dislodge them. Accordingly on the 4th of February he advanced against the stockade with a force of infantry, two Armstrong guns and a mortar, and after engaging the enemy for a couple of hours found it impracticable to dislodge them, and retired with a loss of Lieutenant Millett killed, Lieutenant Cameron Royal Artillery mortally wounded and several men of the 11th Native Infantry killed and wounded.

At the same time that these attacks were occurring Chamoorchee was also threatened. The pass was held by a detachment of 150 of the Bengal Police, one of the sentries of which was attacked at night and cut down. Major Pughe commanding the Police force proceeded to Chamoorchee and finding the Bhotanese to be in a strong position behind stone entrenchments, considered the force at his disposal unequal to driving them out, and applied to Brigadier-General Dunsford for a small reinforcement. Accordingly 150 of the 30th Punjaubees and two mortars under the command of Captain Huxham 30th Punjaubees was sent off to co-operate with the Police. The place was at once attacked and the Bhotanese driven out. They returned however, as soon as the troops retired to the plains, and re-occupied the entrenchment, which was so situated as not to admit of being held by us. The Bengal Police detachment however continued to hold the original position in which it had been placed, and the Bhotanese confined themselves to their own entrenchment.

On the news of the unexpected change matters had

taken in Bhotan reaching Calcutta, immediate preparations were made for recovering our *prestige* which had been tarnished at Dewangiri and Balla, as well as for strengthening the posts remaining in our hands. Two Batteries of Royal Artillery—the one from Meerut, the other from Calcutta, the 55th Regiment from Lucknow and the Head Quarters of the 80th Regiment from Dum Dum were ordered to the north-eastern frontier without delay—also the 19th, 29th and 31st Regiments of Punjaub Infantry. Being an addition to the large force already in the Dooars, of about 1300 British Infantry, 160 Royal Artillerymen and 2,000 Native Infantry.

A change in the command was at the same time made, Brigadier-General Tombs C.B., V.C., commanding at Gwalior was appointed to the command on the right in place of Brigadier-General Mulcaster, who reverted to his former command in Assam, and Brigadier-General Frazer Tytler, C.B., was nominated to succeed Brigadier-General Dunsford, C.B., on the left; ill health compelling that officer to resign and leave the Dooars.

During the latter portion of February 1865, great activity prevailed at Calcutta in getting the necessary arrangements made for the conveyance of munitions of war and for the transport of the troops to the two Brigades of the Dooar field force. The 3rd Battery of the 25th Brigade Royal Artillery, the Head-Quarters of the 55th Regiment and the 29th Punjaub Infantry were ordered to Gowhatty to operate against Dewangiri, while the 7th Battery 22nd Brigade Royal Artillery, the left wing of the 55th Regiment, the Head-Quarters of the 80th Regiment, with the 19th and 31st Regiments of Punjaub Infantry were detailed to join the Brigade on the Left.

CHAPTER XI.

The Author starts with the 80th Regiment for the north-eastern Frontier—Journey from Calcutta to Colgong—Difficulties encountered on the Ganges—Arrival at Carragola—Grooming an Elephant in the Ganges—Thibetian Traders—The Dawk Bungalow—The Snowy Range of the Himalayas—Method of tracking Boats—Arrival of the 12th Punjaubees and Left Wing of the 55th Regiment—Nature of the Land Transport provided for the Troops—The Village of Carragolee—Unhygienic mode of preventing Milk souring.

At noon on the 23rd of February I received a copy of a General Order by the Commander-in-Chief, directing my transfer from the medical charge of the 54th Regiment, then in Fort William, to that of the 80th Regiment; the completion of the equipment of which for field service, requiring that it should be in medical charge of an officer of the rank of staff-surgeon: the surgeon of the corps being at the time abseut on sick leave in England. The same day the 80th Regiment marched into Calcutta from Dum Dum, and at half-past seven in the evening I joined it at the terminus of the East Indian Railway at Howrah, on the bank of the Hooghly opposite Calcutta. A scene of great confusion prevailed inside the station where the men of the regiment were working in fatigue parties, getting the field equipage stowed away in the railway waggons, in the course of which, making free use of very expressive language towards the native servants connected with the railway: their colour admitting of an additional expletive being added to the combination most approved of by the British soldier.

The train, a special one, was to have started at half-past eight for Colgong on the Ganges, 245 miles from Calcutta. It did not however get away until half-past eleven. At seven o'clock the following morning, it reached Lynthea, a fine open plain 120 miles from Calcutta, which had been lately used as an encamping ground for time-expired soldiers, waiting for their passages to England. At nine A.M., the train reached Nal Hattie station, where it halted twenty minutes, to allow the officers time to breakfast at a small refreshment establishment attached to the station. The men had cooked provisions in their haversacks, and breakfasted in the carriages. The next halt was made at Sahibgunge 220 miles from Calcutta, where the railway meets the Ganges. Here there is a standing camp, where drafts coming out from England halt for the day, after their first night's journey up country by railway. Some miles beyond Sahibgunge the train passed underneath the remains of the fort of Tileagunge, situated near the Rajmahal hills. In former years it was close to the banks of the Ganges, but is now some distance off; owing to recession of the river. The Rajas to whom it belonged, used to levy a sort of black mail on boats as they passed up and down the Ganges. It fell about the same time that the battle of Plassy was fought, and exists now only as a ruin.

At four o'clock in the afternoon, the train reached Colgong, a large village close to the Ganges. Here the regiment was transferred to native boats for conveyance to Carragola, a landing-place on the opposite bank of the Ganges, twenty miles down, in the direction of Sahibgunge. This somewhat roundabout route having been adopted owing to the difficulty of getting a large number of men with baggage across from the latter place against a strong running tide. From Carragola the regiment was to march 105 miles due north through Purneah as far as Titalyah, in the Rungpore district, on the north-eastern frontier. Here the five companies constituting the head-quarters were to become a Wing, and proceed to Mynagoorie in the Dooars; Colonel Hawkes, the regimental staff, colours and band going on fifty-five miles further, to Darjeeling in the Himalayas; the left wing already at that station becoming the head-quarter one, and the officer at the time commanding it (Major Hardinge) being transferred to the command of the Wing detailed for the Dooars. The 7th Battery of the 22nd Brigade Royal Artillery was also ordered to Darjeeling.

By midnight on the 24th of February the 80th Regiment and its baggage was on the Ganges. Shortly afterwards heavy rain set in, against which the matting coverings of the boats proved but an indifferent protection, both men and baggage getting soaked. Towards morning a strong breeze set in right ahead, which prevented the boats keeping together, and ultimately resulted in several of them getting fast in the mud near the banks of the river, while the remainder had to anchor. The boat I was in got aground about eight miles above Carragola. The colonel and officers who were in it got out and followed the course of the river until we reached Carragola. On the way two or three of the boats were passed stuck fast in the sand; the soldiers out of them endeavouring to draw them along.

The men being without provisions, and there being but a poor chance of their getting into Carragola that day, Colonel Hawkes made arrangements with the commissariat officer at the place, for the dispatch up the river of such food as it was practicable, under the circumstances, to supply the men with, and which had to be confined to bread and rum. A sufficiency for each man was accordingly put on board a light boat, under the charge of some of the officers, with orders to communicate with each of the stranded and weather-bound boats.

Towards sundown a few of the boats most in advance succeeded in reaching Carragola, and as I was standing on the bank of the river, looking at the men tracking them against the strong wind still blowing, I had the opportunity of watching the grooming of an elephant in the Ganges, which is effected much after the manner in which ships' decks are scrubbed by the process called holy-stoning, the animal being partially immersed in the water, and his hide vigorously rubbed by a piece of brick. His docility was remarkable, every order of the mahout being obeyed with alacrity; and it was curious to observe the variety of positions he assumed, so as to bring the different aspects of his body within convenient distance of the water to admit of the holystoning process being efficiently carried out.

Near the landing-place a small party of the Kampa traders from Thibet had their tent pitched, and their goods collected under it. They had come down thus far to the plains in hopes of bartering their wares for arms and ammunition, but found that trading in these commodities was at the time interdicted; consequent on the hostilities going on with Bhotan. One of the party was a woman, the picture of happiness and good nature. Her features were comely, and she would not have been bad-looking but for some rouge with which she had disfigured herself by smearing it over her cheeks and forehead. Her hair was plaited into two tails, which hung down her back in the same manner as was the fashion some twenty years ago amongst the young ladies of the West. Her outer clothing consisted of a robe made of purple-coloured woollen stuff, and her shoes resembled those of the Chinese in shape, but were continuous, with a sort of stockings or leggings made of woollen material, similar to her outer garment. On one arm she wore a portion of a large shell as a bracelet, and round her head a double row of red coral beads, arranged alternately with rounded pieces of malachite. The men, with the exception of wearing woollen clothing, and having their shoes and stockings in one, reminded me much of the Chinese.* Their features were very similar, and they wore the same small round-topped felt hat, turned up at the brim, which is worn by the peasantry all over the north of China.

It rained heavily at intervals all day, and in the evening we dined at the dawk bungalow—the first of a series of resting-houses for travellers, established by the Government, at distances averaging about twenty-five miles from each other along the road to Darjeeling. They are placed in charge of native servants, and usually contain four small rooms, two

* Calico thickly quilted with wadding is the cold-weather dress of the lower orders of the Chinese. Their shoes and stockings also, are distinct: the latter being likewise of calico.

being set apart for female and two for male travellers. Any person travelling can claim shelter in one of these houses for twenty-four hours, but not longer, paying for the same one rupee. The servants attached to the bungalow can be required to cook such provisions as travellers may bring with them—they paying for the cost of the firewood, or they can be furnished by the head servant, known as the Khansamah, with such food as the place supplies; in which case, according to the rule laid down in the Government regulations hung up in each bungalow, the traveller is supposed to submit to whatever charge is made. This is the theory, but the practice is, as a general rule, that the traveller pays whatever he likes, and sometimes not at all, but in lieu gives the Khansamah a beating for making an overcharge. These dawk bungalows are Government institutions along all the main routes in India, and are, notwithstanding the many defects and inconveniences connected with them, such as want of repair, absence of supplies, presence of snakes, &c., a source of great convenience to the traveller, and the want of which would be much missed, though, as a general rule, abuse is pretty freely lavished upon them, judging from the remarks in the books in which travellers enter their names, date of arrival and departure, and the amount paid the Khansamah for lodging, appending in a column for remarks any expressions of satisfaction, or the contrary, that it is wished to place on record. Advantage, it is to be regretted, is frequently taken of this to append indecent observations and offensive personalities to names appearing in the books, and upon which there is no check, as they are at the command of whoever comes to the bungalows, and the native servants are in ignorance of what is entered in them.

After dinner I went down to the river and slept in one of the boats, so as to be at hand in the event of troop-boats coming in during the night, in which there might be sick men; the dawk bungalows being about half a mile from where the boats were arriving and the men going into camp. The rain fell in torrents, the boat leaked both above and below, and I, in common with others, was glad when morning came to again find shelter in the dawk bungalow, numerous as its shortcomings were. Heavy rain fell the greater portion of the 26th of February, accompanied by thunder and vivid lightning.

At two o'clock the horizon cleared for a short time to the northward, and disclosed the top of the snowy range of the Himalaya mountains, distant upwards of 200 miles, a sight rarely seen from so far down in the plains, except immediately after heavy rains, when the atmosphere suddenly assumes for a short time a character of unusual clearness. Considering the vastness of the distance, and the perfect distinctness with which the snow-covered peaks were seen, one could not but be struck with more than usual wonder at the power and perfection of the human eye. These snowy peaks can occasionally be seen from even a greater distance than Carragola, being now and then visible from the plains of Bengal, on the opposite side of the Ganges, as far as Bhaugulpore, a distance, as the crow flies, of 220 miles. One of the peaks seen was that of Kenchinjunga, in Sikim, 28,177 feet, now recognized as the highest mountain in the world.

During the day troop-boats arrived from time to time, the men wet, cold, and hungry—their tents and bedding saturated from the heavy rain to which they had been exposed in the badly-covered boats. As several of the boats were still missing, a further supply of bread and rum was sent up the river for the relief of the men in them, and the 26th of February closed with the unsatisfactory intelligence that the whole of No. 6 Company, the boat with the officers' baggage, and the greater portion of the hospital equipment, were still out in the river, the wind continuing to blow with such strength as to render the tracking of the boats down impracticable.

The mode of tracking boats on the Ganges is much the same as that followed on the banks of the Peiho. A rope is attached to the top of the mast, and two or three men harness themselves to it, each man making fast two smaller ropes to the main one, the end of the one being secured to a piece of thick bamboo, which is held perpendicularly against the right shoulder, and traction applied in that way, while the end of the other rope is held in the left hand, and additional force thus brought to bear. In China the boatmen harness themselves on to the main rope passed from the mast-head to the river bank, also by two smaller ropes, but they attach the ends to a piece of flat wood, which they place across their chests, and consequently bring a greater and more steady force into play than can be attained by the method under description.

In the course of the day a portion of the 19th Punjaub Infantry arrived from Colgong, their boats having been fortunate enough to avoid getting aground. Owing to the wet rendering it difficult for the men to pitch their tents they were kept in their boats for the day. This regiment was on its way to join the column in course of formation to attack Balla, from which the Bhotanese had succeeded in expelling our troops as effectually as they did at Dewangiri.

By degrees the men of the 80th were got under cover, the tents being pitched on a sandy patch on the bank of the river as they arrived; such of them as were unprovided with covering were sheltered during the heavy showers that fell in the course of the day in some native sheds in the neighbourhood of the encamping ground.

After a very stormy night, the morning of the 27th of February promised something better, and cleared up into a fine day, bringing with it a definite prospect of the regiment getting out of Carragola; as the missing company arrived in the forenoon, the Left Wing of the 55th Regiment arriving at the same time *en route* to Cooch Behar, the portion of the frontier for which it had been detailed.

The day was occupied drying bedding and clothing, cleaning arms, &c., and in the afternoon a portion of the baggage was packed in hackeries, or small country carts, formed of a light bamboo frame, drawn by two little bullocks. Several hundred of these carts were at the time collected at Carragola for the land transport of the troops proceeding to the seat of war. They were not well suited for the purpose, being too small, and otherwise unadapted for the conveyance of field equipment. In addition the service was one of compulsion to their owners, and particularly distasteful, notwithstanding that a fair rate of daily remuneration was allowed them.

and steady employment secured for the greater portion of a month. The exigencies of the Government, however, required transport, and the duty of the district officials was to collect it from all the surrounding villages, irrespective of the extent of inconvenience to which the agricultural population might be exposed by being deprived of their means of local conveyance at a season of the year when it was much wanted by them. These hackeries were to go as far as the nature of the country admitted of their travelling over, namely, about 140 miles, receiving eight annas (one shilling) per diem, and return hire at the rate of four annas per diem, each day's journey being calculated at sixteen miles. About 3,000 of these hackeries were collected and made available at different times for the purposes of the Bhotan expedition, consequent on the Dewangiri and Balla disasters. How far the owners had reasonable grounds for objecting to the kind of service their carts and bullocks were pressed into will shortly be made apparent.

In the afternoon of the 27th of February the orders were issued for the regiment marching at five o'clock the following morning, and such of the baggage carts as were packed were started off ahead for the first encamping ground along with the camp colour-men.* As soon as they began to move, the

* The camp colour-men are soldiers, usually the pioneers, who go on ahead to the next encamping ground, when a regiment is on the march, and indicate by flags the positions on which the tents are to be pitched, when they arrive on the ground. This would seem a very old practice, inasmuch as in Adams's "Roman Antiquities," describing soldiers on the march, it is stated, "When they came near the place of encampment, some tribunes and centurions with proper persons appointed for that

road leading north assumed a bustling appearance—the long line of loaded hackeries varied by native followers attached to the regiment, many of them attired in old military uniforms, commissariat cattle, and motley groups of women and children belonging to the native followers.

Carragola, as the river port of the Purneah, Darjeeling, and the Rungpore districts, is a place of some little importance, and consists of a native village and bazaar, the houses being mere huts, however, with thatch and matting roofs. The presiding genius of the place is a native called Moonshee Kyrat Alli, who takes all the ordinary Government contracts for transport to Darjeeling, &c. The conveyance, for instance, of the reserve ammunition of the 80th Regiment, amounting to 500,000 rounds of Enfield cartridges, having been entrusted to him. There is a considerable population in the village, and on walking through it and observing the filth, foul odours, and defiance generally of all those hygienic principles which we consider essential to physical integrity, and yet seeing large and healthy-looking families being reared there, one cannot but feel that nature unadorned is not that malignant enemy to vitality that it has become the fashion of the day in our part of the world to depict her.

Noticing the milk at Carragola to have a peculiar odour and taste I inquired as to the cause, and found that it results from a custom which prevails amongst the natives in this part of the country of impregnating the vessels in which the milk is kept with the

service were sent before to mark out the ground, and assign to each his proper quarters; which they did by erecting flags of different colours in the several parts."

fumes of burnt cow manure, the object being to counteract the tendency which the milk has to curdle from acidity acquired by the vessels from absorption of some of the milk they previously contained.

CHAPTER XII.

March from Carragola — Camp at Luchmeepoor — Cholera — Burial at Chitreepeer — Purneah Station — March to Balgatchie — Sanitary Paradoxes — Hackery Men take their Bullocks away — Dingra Ghaut — Transport Difficulties increase — Cross the Mahanuddy — Affray at Assooraghur — Early Marching — Objections to it — Remarks on Sunstroke — Raja of Kishengunge — Tigers in the Vicinity — Elephants and their Mahouts — Narrow escape from Drowning — Arrival at Chopra — Examination of the Soldiers' Rifles — Necessity for Water-proof Covers.

At five on the morning of the 28th of February, the 80th Regiment marched from Carragola for Luchmeepoor, an encamping ground nine miles distant. On the way one of the soldiers was attacked with cholera, and the sanitarian may feel inclined to say, "here are the effects of exposure, want of proper food, &c., already beginning to show themselves;" this man however was one of those who had suffered no undue climate exposure, nor any inconvenience from want of food, as he belonged to a company, the boats of which had started from Colgong several hours before the others, and got to Carragola the next day.

The country passed through on the line of march was similar to that at Carragola; namely, low swampy grazing land, intersected by a single causeway road raised several feet above the level of the plain, owing to the country becoming flooded during the rains.

On arriving at Luchmeepoor, a small piece of ground tolerably well drained, in the neighbourhood of a few native huts, the men pitched their tents according to the following system of castramentation. The front of the camp was made to face the road, the "main street" of the former being at right angles with the latter. The mess tent of the officers was pitched at the foot of the main street, while the main guard tent, with the colours and drums in front, was pitched at the head of it; the companies' tents being pitched one behind the other on each side of the street in lines parallel with it; the officers' tents being in the rear of their respective companies. On the flanks again of the mess tent were the tents of the colonel and regimental staff, with the quarter guard tent in the rear, and those belonging to the hospital establishment on the extreme flank, the tents of the staff sergeants being on the right of the companies' ones and parallel with them.

The tents used in ordinary marching in India contain sixteen men, their dimensions allowing each man about 340 cubic feet of air. They are vastly superior to the bell tent in general use elsewhere; a similar number of men in them (as I have frequently seen in China) having but one sixth of the cubic space afforded by the Indian tent.

We marched at half-past four the following morning for Chitreepeer, eleven miles from Luchmeepoor. The man seized the previous day with cholera, died just as we were on the eve of starting, and there being no time to bury him, his corpse, in a dhoolie, followed in the rear of the column. About an hour before marching a second case of the same disease occurred, and while the man just dead had undergone the minimum of exposure, the one now attacked had undergone the maximum, as he belonged to the company longest out on the river. I interrogated him closely and failed to elicit any information rendering it probable that he had committed any dietetic irregularity either on the way down to the river or at Carragola; the only thing he had purchased at the latter place having been a little wheaten flour. At the same time that this man was brought to hospital another soldier reported himself sick, complaining of some slight derangement: he again readily admitted having eaten raw pumpkins and green peas, in the fields near where the boat he belonged to was aground, to stay his hunger, and his symptoms were of the most trivial nature, showing how difficult it is to connect the occurrence of cholera—especially the now epidemic form—with any single cognisable cause.

The halting ground at Chitreepeer was very similar to that we had just left, and as soon as arrangements could be made a grave was dug for the corpse we had brought with us, alongside of the grave of a former comrade named McGuire, which was discovered by a piece of tin nailed on a tree, with his name scratched on it and the date of his death. He had died at Chitreepeer on the 18th December 1864, while proceeding to Darjeeling with the Left Wing and those who left him in so lonely a spot little thought that another of the regiment was destined there to join him.

On the 2d March, the camp was struck at 3 A.M., and an hour afterwards the regiment marched for the civil station of Purneah, distant ten miles. Just as day was dawning we crossed a rather wide river, usually called the Purneah river, bridged over by two causeways, united by a bridge supported on piles. At seven o'clock we reached Purneah, and encamped on a clear space in the centre of the station, near the dawk bungalow.

Purneah affords but little scope for description. It is the civil station of the district of that name, and the country about it is perfectly level and very moist; its products being chiefly indigo and rice. The station consists of a few detached residences, occupied by the Government servants, a post-office, jail, billiard room, and two stores, or "Europe shops," as they are called in India. In the afternoon the band of the 80th played for an hour, and most of the residents in the neighbourhood were present. Some Eurasian families also were on the ground in bullock carriages, and several natives in curious looking private vehicles, in the form of chair-hackeries, in which they sat cross-legged.

On the morning of the 3rd of March, the camp was struck just as drizzling rain commenced, and at four o'clock the regiment marched along a bypath for the purpose of avoiding a portion of the main road, intersected by a river not yet properly bridged over. The morning was very dark and it was with the utmost difficulty that the way could be made out, several of the men getting into ditches on the side of the pathway. After no small trouble the detour was effected, and the main road reached, which, owing to the heavy rain now falling, was soon converted into a quagmire that it was no easy matter to keep footing on. At ten A.M., exactly six hours after starting, I reached the encamping ground at Balgatchie, thirteen miles by the road from Purneah, but somewhat longer the way we had come. The regiment had arrived about three quarters of an hour sooner than the dhoolies containing the sick did. The ground had become nearly a swamp; the rain still falling heavily, and the men were standing in the open, saturated, and without any prospect of their tents arriving for some time, the hackeries being miles behind. I was able however to provide shelter for the sick, having fortunately sent on the previous evening the hospital tents that were not in use, with a portion of the establishment, so as to have tents ready pitched on the arrival of the sick. Towards the afternoon the hackeries began to arrive, and the men got their tents pitched: the ground at the time being literally a swamp, but there was no help for it as it was the best for miles around, and the men worked away with good will and did their best to make themselves comfortable by flooring their tents with straw procured from a neighbouring hamlet. At the close of the day eighty men were without tents and sixty without bedding, the hackeries containing them having been unable to come on, owing to the weight of their burdens and the badness of the road.

The following morning some of the baggage carts being still missing, and heavy rain falling, rendered moving from Balgatchie neither desirable nor practicable. Notwithstanding the great exposure to wet from above and damp from below, which the men had recently undergone, paradoxical as it may seem to the modern sanitarian, their general health at this period was excellent, and there was less than the ordinary amount of sickness complained of. The cholera case also, which occurred three days previously, unfavourably placed as it had been for recovery, nevertheless was rapidly convalescing—at the same time, however, one of the Gharrywans, as the hackery drivers are called, died of cholera during the night, showing that frequently in the causation of this disease, the systemic state of the individual plays a more important part than the external influences which he may be casually exposed: no epidemic of it at the time in question existing, and only three cases having occurred out of a moving body of men, European and native, numbering about a thousand.

In my own case the following sanitary paradox was apparent. When I left Purneah I was suffering from what is familiarly known as a "cold in the head," and after getting wet through and through on the march went about the camp the greater portion of the day in saturated clothing. On the morning of the 4th March, after having passed the night in a tent on ground in a state of swamp, far from feeling the cold aggravated I got up perfectly free from it. I have frequently observed both in India and China a sudden change for the better takes place in men suffering from malarious fevers, at the time resisting the ordinary remedies, immediately on heavy rain setting in—while again, I have as frequently seen persons in whom the tendency to ague was at the time dormant, display active manifestations of it as well as the ailments allied to it, coincident with the occurrence of rain, and other marked atmospheric changes, irrespective altogether of locality or elevation, and particularly so of exposure to what is generally believed to be the special exciting cause of malarious disease, namely, marsh miasma. Facts such as these, demonstrating as they do how similar atmospheric changes will bring sudden restoration to health to some, while others they prostrate on the sick bed, convey the hint also that the practice of the healing art, the study of the individual constitution and idiocyncrasy, should become a point more salient than the routine application of what are termed general principles.

March 5th. Rained the whole of yesterday and the greater portion of the night. The carts containing the remainder of the tents and bedding did not get into camp until ten o'clock last night. The work has been so severe on the bullocks that several of them are in a dying state, and some are already lying dead on the ground. The hackery drivers seem to feel this so much, and dislike the work to such a degree, owing to the great weights their animals have to support and drag, and the unusually quick pace they are made to travel at (stimulated by having their tails nearly twisted off,) that a considerable number of them have fled during the night, taking their bullocks with them and leaving their hackeries behind; hoping to recover them when the regiment leaves the encamping ground. In consequence of this the soldiers were authorised to seize bullocks wherever they could find them, whether loose in the fields or in hackeries on the road; as it was imperative that the regiment should now move on, so as to make room for the 55th Wing: the ground not affording space for the tents of both corps, and there being no other anywhere near, at all suited for the purpose.

The camp was therefore struck at half-past eleven, the weather being still unsettled, and the column marched at noon, thirty men per company however being left on the ground to bring on the hackeries, about forty in number, that were unprovided with bullocks, and for which it was at the time presumed animals could be procured by seizing one or two herds that were grazing in the neighbourhood. Just as the regiment moved off the rain re-commenced, and I remained a short time behind; having a suspicion that the transport difficulties would not be so easily got over, and that the evacuation of the camp that day was a matter of considerable doubt. The men who had been left with the hackeries were out in the vicinity capturing bullocks wherever they could find them, much the same as would be done in an enemy's country, and while I was there thirty in a herd were driven in. They were quite unbroken however and useless for draft purposes. Some forty hackeries laden with tents, bedding, and stores, were standing on the ground without an available bullock. Some of the men were amusing themselves firing the straw on which they had been sleeping the previous night, while others were burning two hackeries the bullocks of which had been taken away, as well as portions of the wheels that rendered them unfit for use at the time. Having satisfied myself that a considerable portion of the baggage guard would have to remain at Balgatchie for the night, I sent back a portion of the medical establishment, in case any sickness should occur.

The encamping ground the regiment was marching for, was on the bank of the Mahanuddy River, at a place called Dingra Ghaut. The road leading to it was bad in the extreme, for the most part being ankle-deep in mud, and proving extremely trying for the bullocks in the hackeries; their progress being very slow through it. The ground was reached at four o'clock, and the men bivouacked; none of the baggage having come up. In the course of the evening a few tents arrived, and as many men as they would hold went into them, while the remainder, with the exception of one Company that got under some native sheds, slept on straw in the open air.

Late in the evening we heard that thirty carts were still on the ground at Balgatchie unprovided with bullocks, and that the soldiers remaining with them had re-pitched some of the tents—also that all along the line of road loaded hackeries were fast in the mud, some with bullocks lying down exhausted, others without bullocks at all; the drivers having removed them, and abandoned their carts; consideration apparently for their animals' sufferings outweighing the loss of property thus sustained by them. The men at Balgatchie being without provisions, a supply of bread and rum was sent off to them about midnight, the distance being between nine and ten miles, but from the badness of the road equal to half as much more.

The Mahanuddy is a good-sized non-tidal river, a steady current running constantly down. It is not safe to bathe in, owing to the number of muggers or round-headed alligators it contains. The banks are very sandy, the right one sloping, while the left one is nearly perpendicular, reminding me of some parts of the Peiho. In its neighbourhood, that is to say, Dingra Ghaut, the point that it is crossed by a ferry, there are a few villages, and the country on both sides is well under cultivation, the ground having been recently ploughed. The electric telegraph from Calcutta to Darjeeling is carried across the river where the ferry is.

March 6th.—This morning a number of our bullocks, exhausted as they were with their work of yesterday, had to be sent out to bring in the hackeries abandoned on the road, and those also still unprovided with the means of moving from Balgatchie. The day being fine the saturated tents and bedding were partially dried, and during the latter portion of the day the hospital establishment carts, thirty in number, and two Companies, were got across the river in ferry-boats. After this had been effected the remainder of the regiment crossed, and the camp was re-established on the left bank of the river on a piece of ground much better suited for the purpose than that on which it had just been struck. In crossing the river the hackeries were taken over in boats three at a time; the bullocks going separately.

Another day's halt had to be made on the Mahanuddy waiting for the baggage to come up, the last of which arrived in the evening, and on the morning of the 8th of March the regiment was enabled to move on to Assooraghur, a short march of seven miles: a supply of bullocks and hackeries having been procured by taking them wherever they were to be found. The loss to the unfortunate villagers must have been considerable, hackeries being seized indiscriminately, while droves of cattle were driven in from the fields, and bullocks appropriated for transport purposes by whoever was active enough to catch them. Before leaving Dingra Ghaut a complaint was received from a European connected with the Purneah and Darjeeling Conveyance Company, demanding seven bullocks belonging to it that had been seized on the road, and threatening an action of compensation for loss. The bullocks were accordingly surrendered, but on what grounds of equity I am at a loss to say, considering the manner in which necessity compelled their being taken from the natives.

In making these remarks I must eschew any intention of reflecting personally on any one; I believe that the transport arrangements were made by the Bengal Government with as much care as it was practicable, under the circumstances, to exercise, and with a due regard also that fair dealing in the way of remuneration should be extended to the people whose carts were required for the public service—the failure resulting from a misconception of their fitness for the conveyance of the equipment of European troops proceeding hurriedly on field service. It may perhaps be supposed that the case of the 80th Regiment was exceptional, but I have it from the best authority, namely, Mr. Beames, the collector of the Purneah district, that the progress of the 80th had occasioned but few grounds for complaint as compared with what resulted from that of the Wing of the 55th Regiment; the baggage difficulties connected with which, and the means adopted by the men of remedying them having fallen so severely on the district as to have required official representation. Having thus plainly stated facts, I may now point out that in the event of similar transport being again employed under similar circumstances, the probabilities are that consequences of a like untoward nature will result so long as soldiers are allowed in any way to interfere in the management of the carts, either as regards estimating what they are fit to carry, or the pace the bullocks should travel at.

On arriving at Assooraghur we found that the camp colour-men, who had gone ahead the night before to select the ground, had had an affray with some villagers in the neighbourhood, and had been severely beaten: the facts of the case being the following. An arrangement had been made by the commissariat agent accompanying the regiment that this village was to supply a certain number of hackeries to aid in bringing on the baggage at Dingra Ghaut that there was no transport for, and on the hackeries being collected, two of the byles, as the bullocks are called, were wanting for one of them. The soldiers went to the village, and finding where the byles were demanded them through the interpretorial aid of a native policeman. They were told if they wanted the bullocks to wait, and they would be brought out. This they declined doing, and forced their way into the private domain of the native, and into that portion of it where foreign intrusion is most objectionable. Immediately on this occurring the villagers turned out in a body to resent a violation of one of their cherished prejudices, and administered a sound thrashing to the soldiers, who seemed to think themselves fortunate in having escaped with their lives.

At Assooraghur the camp was pitched within the lines of an old Nepaulese fort; this part of the country having once been in the possession of Nepaul. The only indications of the fort now remaining are a few earthen mounds concealing some brickwork. At no great distance from it the Mahanuddy flows past, and the country around is under rice and indigo cultivation.

A telegram having been received from Calcutta, conveying the "most positive orders" of the Commander-in-Chief that the marching of the regiment was to be so arranged that the tents should be pitched before sunrise, an endeavour was made on the morning of the 9th of March to give effect to it, by striking the camp at two A.M., and marching the column at five minutes to three. Daylight broke about half-past five, and revealed to us that we were marching through a perfectly level lightly-wooded country, presenting no perceptible difference from that we had been passing through since leaving Carragola, with the exception that since crossing the Mahanuddy at Dingra Ghaut hamlets seemed to occur at shorter intervals from each other. At half-past seven the encamping ground at Kishengunge, the seat of the Raja of that name, was reached. The sun was then very strong and the ground very damp from the heavy dew which falls regularly during the night in this part of India, and the practical result of the endeavour to carry out the order of the Commander-in-Chief was that the men had to stand on the damp ground for betweeen two and three hours exposed to the full force of the sun before their tents arrived; the hackeries being unequal in the dark to coming at anything like the same pace the men marched at, and which was only three miles an hour: the regiment also having been several times halted to give them time to come up. The carrying out of the order was simply impracticable, situated as the regiment was—unless, that is to say, the men were deprived of a portion of their rest under canvas and made to sleep in the open air for two or three hours after midnight, so as to enable the tents to precede them and be pitched on the next encamping ground before sunrise, and then again the ground would be too wet at that period of the morning to put bedding on. While this order was issued from a feeling of solicitude that the men should be saved as much as possible from solar exposure in the early day, the circumstances attending the endeavour to carry it out, practically demonstrated how necessary it is that orders issued at a distance should be qualified by discretionary power on the part of those entrusted with the giving effect to them.

As far as my experience warrants an expression of opinion, there are circumstances when extreme early marching in India appears to be open to several objections, and I am inclined to think in such cases that so long as a prejudice exists, which may or may not be well founded, against exposing men on the march to the morning's sun, it would be better to march them in the afternoon and have their tents re-pitched in the evening (which could be easily done in the dark at night as in the dark in the morning)—an arrangement which would enable the men to enjoy a proper night's rest during natural hours, and get up each day refreshed in place of having to do so, shortly after midnight, feeling drowsy and unwilling to move. For instance, on the occasion in question I find the difference thus noted by me—"Yesterday (8th March) we marched at six A.M. Everything went off very well; having the advantage of daylight. The baggage came in steadily without mishap, whereas this morning in the dark two of the hackeries went over the causeway embankment, and some six or eight others became unpacked on the road, and their contents tumbled off from hurried packing in the dark. Yesterday, again, the men were active and lively, moving about the camp amusing themselves, sorting their kits, cleaning their accoutrements, &c., while to-day they are lying sleeping and sweltering in their tents, until, comparatively unrefreshed, they have to get up towards sundown and dress for afternoon's parade." Apart altogether from the question of marching, I think that the system of early rising is carried to an extreme extent in the army in India, and consequently the propensity to sleep during the hours that nature intends the mental and physical powers to be active, encouraged to a degree that cannot be beneficial, and more than likely is injurious.

The objections to exposing the men to the sun, it is almost unnecessary to remark, are based on the supposed liability they have when so situated to suffer from the very fatal disease usually known as *coup de soleil.* Now, without attempting to say that the disease cannot be caused by solar exposure, there can be no doubt that whatever influence heat exercises in developing it, solar exposure is not its essential cause, inasmuch as the worst forms of the disease that are met with occur in sultry, cloudy weather, and in barrack-rooms at night. I have frequently seen it occur in hospitals, both in China and India, where the patients attacked had been completely removed from the direct influence of the sun for weeks previously. It is clear therefore that we have not arrived at the true nature of *coup de soleil,* which is altogether a misnomer; heat apoplexy being the designation conveying a more correct idea both of the symptoms themselves and the circumstances under which they occur. Having during three consecutive summers in China, on one occasion in Japan and several times in India, seen cholera and heat apoplexy occur coincidently, I have formed the opinion that, under certain circumstances, the two diseases occur from analogous causes. In making this statement, what I mean to convey is, that certain abnormal conditions of the atmosphere during warm weather, will in some persons develop symptoms the same as those to which the term heat apoplexy is commonly applied —while in others it will produce those to which it is customary to give the name of cholera—both of them generally equally fatal in result—and their causes, I believe, the operation on the nervous system of electro-chemical agency originating in the atmosphere; devitalisation of the blood occurring as the consequence: in both diseases its appearance after death being the same as is observed in cases of death from lightning, namely, unusual fluidity.

This view of the existence of an analogy between one form of cholera and heat apoplexy derives some support from the fact, that, while Mooltan is the only station in India, which, as far as we have any statistical knowledge, has enjoyed perfect immunity from cholera, it nevertheless has suffered severely from heat apoplexy, occurring under circumstances resembling those of an epidemic character—a number of cases taking place about the same time during a period of extreme heat, and without any reference to direct solar exposure—cases for instance having occurred at night in the hospital of the 89th Regiment in the summer of 1863. It would therefore seem, from some cause which cannot even be guessed at, that at Mooltan epidemic constitutions of the atmosphere occurring in connection with peculiar heat display their effects on the human system by a group of symptoms to which we give the name of heat apoplexy—in other places the same influences developing those we call cholera—both of them being groups of symptoms respecting the precise nature of which our ignorance is equally complete—any explanation we can offer being but little better than loose conjecture.

Having thus stated that the so-called *coup de soleil*, or heat apoplexy, is not caused by the sun, I would wish it to be understood that I by no means say that the sun cannot cause insensibility; I believe it can, and that there is a disease to which the name sunstroke is fully admissible—the latter however being a much less serious ailment, and one as commonly terminating in recovery as the other does in death—a distinction which, combined with the fact of the sun's direct influence being in no way essential for the production of the former, indicates the necessity for recognising in sunstroke and heat apoplexy, two diseases, and not amalgamating them as is now done; thereby investing the minor affection with a much greater degree of gravity than actually belongs to it. In other words, what is required is to distinguish effects due purely to the action of the sun from those due to a sultry and abnormal condition of the atmosphere. The necessity for what I now point out will perhaps be the more readily understood when I mention the fact that at the present time the military medical officer has no option but to return all cases of insensibility the effect of heat—whether of a partial and evanescent character resulting from pure solar exposure, or from the death-sleep of heat apoplexy occurring under a punkah in a barrack room or hospital at midnight or on the march before daylight—under the one head of "Insolatio," a Latin substitute for *coup de soleil*, or sunstroke, which has been adopted in the classification of diseases now in use in the army, based upon the Nosology of Dr. Farr, the Registrar-General, which was introduced into that branch of the service in 1859, and from which no deviation is permitted; in plainer terms, whatever the symptoms may be which necessitate the admission of a soldier into hospital, in whatever part of the world he may be serving, a name must be found for them in this nosology or catalogue of diseases; no other names being admissible in the military medical returns—hence, heat apoplexy must continue to be sunstroke, because Dr. Farr has willed it so.

While fully admitting that the sun exercises in India, an unquestionably injurious effect on some, I have at the same time considerable doubt that it is so inimical to life as it is the custom to represent it; inclining to the belief that this is an impression which has taken root as the direct result of the wholesale misapplication of the word sunstroke. It seems to me also open to question as to whether the artificial life soldiers are compelled to follow in India, does not, by lowering their vital power, render them more predisposed to suffer from the sun when casually, or from necessity, exposed to it, than if they were more habituated to it than they now are, which I think they might be without risk to their health; especially so, as every precaution is now-a-days taken to protect their heads by solar helmets. I would go a step farther and protect their spines also, because there are many who feel the effect of the Indian sun as much on their backs as on their heads. This could be easily done either by padding and quilting that portion of the soldiers' warm weather clothing which is immediately over the spinal column, or by a piece of quilting about eighteen inches long and three inches wide, which could be kept *in sitû* over the spine by strings round the neck and waist respectively, and worn either over or under their coats. The importance of protecting the heads of soldiers against direct solar influence is fully recognised and carefully enforced, and I therefore submit that a similar necessity exists for the protection of their spinal cords as one of the great centres of the nervous system,—a necessity certainly greater than there is for the protection of the abdomen by the broad flannel bands, called "cholera belts," which the soldiers in India are made to wear as a protection against that disease. I question much, if the present system of extreme early rising and parades does not tell more on the men than if they had a longer period in bed during natural sleeping hours, and more solar exposure during those that nature intends they should be awake and employed.

The residence of the Raja of Kishengunge was at a short distance from where we encamped, and some of the officers called on him for the purpose of borrowing elephants to go after three tigers reported by the natives to be in the jungle two miles distant from the next encamping ground. Most of the Raja's elephants had been required to aid in conveying the baggage of the 19th Punjaubees, and were at the time absent, but he undertook to send one on to the place next day. On leaving, he presented them with a quantity of fruit, consisting of small stoneless raisins, walnuts, almonds and pistachio nuts; also a large piece of a slightly acidulated fruity paste, like vegetable casein.

At Kishengunge there is a native town of some size, and also a dawk bungalow. Hanging up in the latter, I observed a notice signed by one of the district officials, the tenor of which was not favourable to the supposition that travellers invariably behave fairly to the natives in charge of these establishments, in the matter of remuneration for supplies furnished.

On the 10th of March the camp was again struck at 2 A.M., and at daybreak the Himalayas were very distinctly seen: the first time they had been visible since leaving Carragola. On reaching the encamping ground at Gozal, ten miles from Kishengunge, the three tigers of which we had heard the previous day were still in the vicinity, and had two nights before carried off two men. The villagers were very anxious to have them destroyed, and as the Raja of Kishengunge had sent on an elephant, one of the officers, (Captain Tucker) started on it for the jungle, but had to return shortly afterwards; owing to an attack of fever. It was interesting to notice how promptly the elephant obeyed the mandate of the mahout sitting across his neck, and brought his under surface in contact with the ground to enable himself to be mounted. These mahouts also are notable in their way. Their occupation is one of considerable risk, as they not unfrequently meet their deaths in course of attempting to manage imperfectly tamed and vicious elephants. The danger likewise to which they are exposed in the course of tiger shooting is necessarily great,—still they are represented as being exceedingly cool, and as having, as a general rule, implicit confidence in the skill of the European sportsman. The moral control they acquire over the elephants is remarkable, and equally so, is the appreciation of the meaning of words which the elephant seems to be capable of acquiring—at the word *bite*, for instance, he immediately brings his body near the ground. At the word of command also he will knock down any obstruction in the pathway, such as a small tree, and I am told that he appears to appreciate the meaning of directions which in English would be to the following effect,—"take care where you are going—stick your toes well into the ground," and which are usually given him when ascending bad pathways at the foot of the hills. Apropos of elephants we heard at Gozal that in the Nepaul jungle about sixteen miles west of where we were encamped, Jung Bahadour was, at the time, with a large body of men, seeking for a valuable elephant he had lost.

The encamping ground next day was at Illiobarree, the country about which was very open and less wooded than at the last two places we had halted at. Notwithstanding the many vicissitudes the men had been exposed to since leaving Colgong, their general health continued excellent; only one case of serious sickness having occurred since marching from Chitreepeer, and in connection with it, a somewhat singular verification of what may be termed an unconscious presentiment occurred. The soldier was suffering from what is usually called jungle fever, and on visiting him in the evening I found him slightly delirious. I therefore directed that an orderly should be placed over him during the night, and as there were several open wells in the neighbourhood, gave particular orders that a constant watch was to be kept upon him in case he might get up and run out of the tent and tumble down one of the wells. The very accident I was guarding against occurred at midnight. The orderly on duty had been taking "forty winks," and on his drowsiness passing off he saw the dhoolie he had been watching empty and the patient gone. He went outside and asked a sentry who was near, if he had seen any one leave the hospital tents. He said yes, and pointed to a man going across an adjoining field. He was seen quite distinctly in the moonlight and the next moment disappeared. The alarm being given the hospital sergeant went in search, and found the man down a well, fortunately not containing water sufficient to immerse him. One of the natives attached to the hospital was lowered by a rope, and passed another one under the patient's arms by which means he was extricated,—apparently uninjured by the accident; as far as could be judged by external indications.

On the 12th of March we encamped at Chopra, on the bank of the Doank River, a very pretty stream, the banks of which were covered with white sand. Its breadth when in full stream is about 120 feet, and it is crossed by a good wooden bridge. Here the men enjoyed the luxury of bathing, the first general ablution that they had had an opportunity of having during their long and fatiguing march through Purneah. At this place a change in the aspect of the country was becoming apparent; it was losing its perfectly level character and becoming somewhat undulating as well as more thickly wooded.

As our next encamping ground (Titalyah) was the place where the five companies branched off for the Dooars, the men had their rifles examined by the armourer sergeant, owing to the successive wettings to which they had been exposed. I looked on while some of them were being overhauled, and the damage the woodwork of many of them sustained from alternate exposure to heavy rain and strong sun, as well as the rusty state of the locks, seemed to indicate a necessity for furnishing soldiers going on service with waterproof covers for their rifles. This precaution I may remark was adopted by a regiment of Beloochees, armed with the Enfield rifle, that formed a portion of the North of China field force in 1862-63. The covers were brought by the men from Scinde, where they are regularly used, owing to the sand storms which prevail there, and the consequent liability there is to injury being done to the finer mechanism of the locks. In the event of the army being supplied with breech-loading rifles, covers will probably be even more necessary. Some of the men had ammunition boxes of Indian manufacture, and the experience of this march proved that they are not waterproof—at least not invariably so, as there could be no question as to the unsatisfactory state they were in as compared with those which had been made in England.

CHAPTER XIII.

Arrival at Titalyah—The Fair of that Name—Primitive Post Office—The Wing of the 80th marches for Mynagoorie and the Head Quarters for Darjeeling—Arrival of the latter at Silligoorie—The Terai—The Foot of the Himalayas—Punkabarree—Snake in the Dawk Bungalow—Effects of Chloroform on Snakes—Native Antidote for Hydrophobia—Hill Coolies, their Mode of carrying Baggage to Darjeeling and marking Weights thereon—Ascent to Kursiong—Sudden Transition of Temperature—Signs of the Mongolian Race—Pacheem—Hope Town—Arrival at Julla Pahar overlooking Darjeeling.

On the 13th of March we reached Titalyah, where the Purneah district terminates and that of Rungpore commences. The road was very hard and full of deep ruts, reminding one of walking over a ploughed field after a strong frost. Within two miles of the place we passed a telegraphic station, situated where a pathway leading to Cooch Behar turns at right angles off the main road, and along which the electric telegraph is carried to Dinagepore and Gowhatty. Two telegrams from the Commander-in-Chief were waiting the arrival of the regiment—one of them repeating the order about marching so as to have the tents pitched before sunrise, and the other inquiring as to whether, when the cases of cholera occurred (notice of which in accordance with standing orders had been telegraphed) the men had arrived on the encamping ground before sunrise. The commanding officer however was able to reply that no data existed for identifying the occurrence of this disease with solar exposure, as both the men had been attacked in the early morning some time before daylight. At Titalyah we found forty-two men of the Darjeeling Wing of the regiment under Lieutenant O'Connor, waiting to join the Companies going to Mynagoorie in the Dooars. They had been ordered down to take the place of a like number of weak and sickly men who had been left behind, with the women and children, as a depot at Dum Dum.

Titalyah consists, under ordinary circumstances, of a few native huts, annually however, an extensive fair is held there, the goods being brought up chiefly from Lower Bengal. This annual fair had just commenced as we arrived, and there was a regular little town extemporised out of calico-covered booths arranged in streets parallel with each other, with cross streets intersecting. A great variety of goods, both European and native, were exposed for sale, and it was astonishing to see how judiciously the selection had been made. This fair, which was originally established by Dr. Campbell, the Superintendent of Darjeeling, is usually numerously attended by natives, who however on this occasion were not present in any number, the result probably of the hostilities going on on the frontier. A good many purchases were made by the officers and men, but the venders seemed indifferent at so early a stage of the proceedings about forcing the sale of their wares, and held on to first prices with a tenacity quite foreign to the native commercial character, and especially to that phase of it witnessed in the "China Bazaar," the great outfitting emporium of Calcutta, where the natives will almost rather sell below prime cost than allow a customer to depart, however great the difference may be between that and the sum originally asked.

We halted two days at Titalyah, so as to enable the inspection of the arms to be completed as well as other arrangements regarding the field equipment of the Wing, such as the division of the hospital establishment, &c., the senior assistant surgeon, Dr. Inkson, going in medical charge of it. The post-office at this place, in which we had to leave our letters for the overland mail, was of a very primitive nature, consisting of a tin box suspended by a chain on the outside of a hut near the dawk bungalow.

At three o'clock on the morning of the 15th of March, the head-quarters and the Wing separated, the former marching for Sunnasakota on the way to Darjeeling, the latter for Julpigorie on the Teesta River *en route* to Mynagoorie. I accompanied the former, which reached its encamping ground at five A.M. It was then quite dark, a heavy dew was falling and the ground was very wet. We had to stand waiting until the tents came up, which they did not do for upwards of an hour after daylight, having as usual had difficulty in coming along in the dark.

During the night our rest was disturbed a good deal by jackals in large numbers screeching about the entrances to the tents, and next morning at three o'clock we marched to Silligoorie, the road to which was very bad, in many places resembling an Australian bush track. Silligoorie is 122 miles from Carragola and 40 from Darjeeling. The Mahanuddy flows past it, and about three miles on the other side of the river the portion of the Terai commences which has to be passed through before the ascent of the hills commences. It was in this Terai, returning from Darjeeling, that Lady Canning contracted the fever of which she died. As local experience has demonstrated that it is during the hours immediately preceding daylight that the malarious influence is most active there, I pointed out to the commanding officer the possible risk which would be run of exposing the men to fever if the march was made at as early a period in the morning as it had been for some days previously, and recommended that it should be deferred until the sun had risen well and the morning's malaria dissipated.

This suggestion was carried out and at ten A.M. on the 17th of March we left Silligoorie, which is represented by a dawk bungalow and a few native huts, and crossed the Mahanuddy by a rickety wooden bridge about 600 feet long. Shortly after eleven o'clock we entered the Terai, which at its commencement consists of a thick jungle of light trees about twenty feet high. In a few minutes we came upon a bend of the Mahanuddy where the country was partially cleared and some cattle grazing. At noon the mist which hitherto had obscured the view ahead, cleared off and disclosed to us the lower range of hills to which we seemed to be quite close. As the sun was now rather strong we halted for an hour at a small wooden house amongst a clump of bamboo trees, which afforded shade for the whole party. The house was surrounded by a ditch and a strong fence as a protection against tigers. The occupants were Mechis,* who have already been referred to as the only people who seem to be so constituted as to be able to reside permanently in the Terai.

From where we halted until the ascent of the hills

* Pronounced Metchees.

commenced, the road lay through dense jungle; many of the trees having matting huts constructed in their branches. They are used by the natives as sleeping places out of the reach of tigers. In the afternoon we reached Parseebutty, the first resting-place at the foot of the hills where there is a shed for storing goods, and a few huts. We went on about two miles further to Punkabaree, which is the highest point that hackeries can go to. The ascent in some places is very steep, so much so that the carts we had with us had considerable difficulty in reaching the place, some of them requiring to be pushed up by hill coolies,—fine sturdy specimens of the Mongolian race, chiefly natives of Sikim, who were waiting to aid in the conveyance of the baggage to Darjeeling.

Punkabaree is upwards of a thousand feet above the plain, and is the portion of the Darjeeling district where the culture of the tea plant commences, several tea gardens being in course of formation on the slopes of the hills near where we halted for the night—namely, on a small piece of ground artificially levelled, near the dawk bungalow. The tents were here handed over to a commissariat agent and placed in store; as it was impracticable to take them further up the hill, there being neither ground suited for pitching them on nor means of conveying them so as to be available for the men on the three days' march they had still to make. As a substitute for tents road-side barracks have been built by the Government at two places between Punkabaree and Darjeeling, namely, Kursiong and Pacheem.

We slept at the dawk bungalow, and the following day had an illustration of one of the disagreeables connected with them. The only lady who had ac-

THE DAWK BUNGALOW AT PUNKABAREE, AND VIEW OF THE TERAI AT THE BASE OF THE SIKIM HIMALAYAS.

companied the head-quarters from Dum Dum was with her husband, the Musketry Instructor (Lieutenant Ridout) occupying the division of the bungalow set apart for families, and in the forenoon her Ayah or native nurse gave the alarm that there was a snake in the room where she was with the baby. On going into it we found a long thin and very poisonous snake slowly creeping through a crevice in the floor on to a mattress on the ground, on which the child was lying at the moment that the Ayah noticed the snake appear. Its head was immediately crushed by a blow from a heavy piece of wood, and though virtually dead, the body continued to move for a long time after cerebral life was extinct—hence I conclude, the popular belief that a snake will never die, however much it may be injured, until sunset.

Talking at this time to Mr. Hart, the hospital steward of the regiment, about Indian snakes, he mentioned that the results of experiments with chloroform show them to be remarkably susceptible of its vapour, so much so that they never recover its effects. As an illustration of the rapidity of its action, he cited the following, which occurred when he was stationed at Benares. A cobra got into a part of the bungalow he was occupying, where there was some oil, which snakes are said to be very partial to. When the door was opened and its dislodgment attempted, it displayed an unusual determination to resist by placing itself in a springing attitude and hissing loudly. As it was not safe to approach, a long piece of bamboo with some cotton on the end saturated with chloroform was passed to the place it had retired to. The cobra seeing the cotton approaching sprang at it, bit it and instantaneously became senseless, in which state it was killed.*

From the same source I learned that when bitten by mad dogs the natives of some parts of Bengal adopt preventive treatment by taking about three grains of muriate of ammonia (sal ammoniac) every hour for

* An officer of the Indian Army lately mentioned to me a curious case of recovery from snake-bite which occurred at Agra three years ago. One of the native servants belonging to the bungalow where he was residing, was bitten by a snake, stated to be a cobra, and was immediately seized with the usual symptoms of poisoning, amongst others restless drowsiness. Attempts were made to keep him awake by the Europeans in whose service he was—an old native, however, living near, came up and requested that the management of the case might be left to him, which was done. He then went out and got a branch of the neem tree, and waving it slowly up and down before the man's face, it seemed to produce a mesmeric influence, as he became quite tranquil and fell into a natural sleep, and awoke some hours afterwards quite well. Of course in a case of this kind it is impossible to say what influence the imagination had, either in leading the man to believe that the snake which had bitten him was a cobra, or in leading him to believe that the mystic remedy employed was certain to secure him immunity from the effects of the bite. Be this as it may, the same officer mentioned another illustration of a similar application of the neem branch, which, to say the least of it, is worthy of note. A Scotch terrier was bitten by a scorpion and was howling from the pain, when a native servant went and got a branch and waved it before the animal in the manner already described. The dog almost immediately ceased howling, and like the man who was snake-bitten, became perfectly tranquil. Those who are inclined to ridicule matters they do not understand, will probably say that the dog's becoming quiet admits of easy explanation by reference to the fact that he was induced to do so from the fear of receiving chastisement from the branch, which was kept for a prolonged time before his eyes. Individually I am disposed to take a wider view of the question, and entertain the possibility that there may be some influence developed on the nervous system by the means described. The neem tree is held in high esteem by the natives of India, on account of its medicinal virtues which are numerous, and they have a proverb,—"that he who lives under the neem tree has no need of the physician." The tree is a very common one, is of small size, and bears a flower very similar to the lilac of England.

several days successively after the injury—also that they employ it in similar doses as a curative agent after the symptoms of hydrophobia have actually appeared, and occasionally with apparent success.

From Punkabaree to Darjeeling, which is twenty-five miles of ascent by a zigzag road made on the mountain slopes, goods and baggage are conveyed on the backs of coolies, who for the most part are natives of Sikim and Bhotan—the former known under the local name of Lepchas, a word I believe of Nepaulese origin. These people (women included) carry enormous weights, especially so when the fatiguing nature of a good deal of the ground they go over is considered—250 lbs. for instance being an ordinary load, and nearly double that not being an uncommon one for them to start with. The time they take to perform the journey of course depends upon the weight of their burdens, but as a general rule with an average load, say two maunds and a half, three days is about the period. They are very independent, declining to work unless they are paid in advance, and as their services are indispensable the European has no resource but to conform—a proceeding contrasting as it does strongly with the manner in which the meek Hindoo usually allows himself to be overawed, that is not by any means congenial to him—necessity however begets compliance, and the sturdy Mongolian gets his rupees into his hand before shouldering his load. The women are as stoutly built as the men, and seem able to carry nearly equally great weights.

A large number of these coolies, a considerable proportion of them being women, were collected at Punkabaree under a sirdar, or headman, to convey the regimental baggage to Darjeeling. A curious method they have of marking the weights on the things to be carried was noticed. In this work they adopt the Indian maund of forty seers (80 lbs.) as their standard, which they represent by a circle made with a piece of chalk thus ○ and should the weight be under a maund the number of seers that it is short is shown by strokes from within the circle outwards in this manner  indicating that the weight is six seers less than a maund. In the event again of the weight exceeding one but not amounting to two maunds, it is shown by a circle with the strokes outside thus ○ IIII being one maund four seers.

On the afternoon of the 18th of March, after a great deal of trouble in getting the lighter portions of our baggage dispatched by pre-paid coolies, we started for Kursiong, which, though only six miles distant, proved a fatiguing march, occupying nearly four hours, owing to the steepness of the ascent. At short intervals along the sides of the winding pathway we saw baggage, which had preceded us, standing unprotected: the coolies having gone to rest and refresh themselves in some of the neighbouring huts on the hill sides. Though valuable property is left standing in this way all night it is very rarely interfered with, and the coolies are stated to be strictly honest in acting up to their engagements, and never to desert their loads otherwise than for the purposes of rest and food.

At Kursiong, which is about 4,000 feet above the level of the sea, several tea-planters' houses are dotted about, and considerable tracts of hill land have been converted into tea-gardens. The soldiers went for the night into the road-side barracks referred to, which are situated about half a mile from the dawk bungalow. They were built originally for the accommodation of invalids on their way to and from the convalescent depot at Darjeeling. They are merely stone substitutes for tents, having earthen floors and a row of planking down each side of the rooms, raised three feet from the ground, for the men to sleep upon. With the exception of a fireplace at the end of the rooms, they have no pretensions to comfort.

We were now very sensible of the change of temperature from that experienced in the plains, especially the phase of it we had in passing through the Terai, exposed to the full force of the sun during the hottest period of the day, and which, I may remark, was productive of no ill consequences whatever; the men's heads having been well protected by wicker-work helmets, covered with white quilted calico, and having the additional protection of the puggery or roll of muslin round the outside of the part in contact with the head. The pattern was a new one that had recently been made the regulation one for the army by orders of the Commander-in-Chief (Sir Hugh Rose), and is a decided improvement on the unsightly and cumbrous wicker-work head-dress formerly worn. On the march to Kursiong the sun also was very strong, and the heat consequently considerable—especially so, under the circumstances attending the steep ascent we had to make, but no sooner did sundown approach than the air became chilly, and by the evening it was so cold that we were glad to avail ourselves of wood fires, and of about the same amount of bed-clothes as would be required at the same period of the year in England.

Our next and last halting-place before arriving at Darjeeling was Pacheem, for which we marched on the morning of the 19th. Just beyond the dawk bungalow at Kursiong we passed through a village, the houses of which were built with wood and the roofs formed of matting. Here I saw much that reminded me of China, amongst other things a pony with the same kind of saddle and bridle on, that is in ordinary use in that country. The population was a mixed one, partly Hindoo, partly Lepcha—the latter were jolly, good humoured and dirty looking, recalling forcibly to mind the Mongolians I had been accustomed to see in Peking. There appeared to be a great absence of poverty in the place, judging from the strings of rupees which the women had on as neck ornaments. Some of the men were dressed in pretty coloured garments reaching to the knee, and were armed with a short sword similar to what is sometimes worn by Chinese soldiers. The ordinary weapon however carried by the Lepchas, is a long knife in a wooden sheath, one side of which is open, the blade being kept in position by two cross bands of tin.

The road to Pacheem was very good; the slope so gentle as hardly to be felt; the incline being one foot in thirty. The road is about twenty feet wide, and its outer side is provided with a parapet two feet high. The electric telegraph runs along it except at its bends. The wire is then carried across the mountain sides to shorten the distance. Here and there amongst the hills, planters' bungalows and sheds are seen—the latter used in preparing the tea, a good deal of which is under cultivation in the neighbourhood. The soil here seems to be light, sandy and stony—it also contains a good deal of mica, which, in places where it is exposed on the surface, gives the ground a glistening appearance in the sun.

On the way I had several opportunities of observing how the coolies progressed with their heavy loads brought up from Punkabaree. The weight is divided between the head and the shoulders—a band of plaited cane-work passes across the forehead while two others pass round their shoulders like the straps of a knapsack, and support a bamboo framework resting on their backs, on which their burdens are secured. Each coolie carries a thick tube of bamboo, by means of which, when fatigued, he relieves himself from the weight of his load without putting it on the ground—simply resting it on the end of the bamboo. In this tube or choonga, as it is called, he also carries a supply of water, and when two coolies meet they refresh each other by pouring a little of it over their hands, wrists and feet. One man in particular, I noticed, carrying two large iron pipes for water-works about to be introduced into Darjeeling—each pipe weighing two maunds, making his total weight 320 pounds. He went along at a slow and steady pace, and his muscular powers did not seem to be overtaxed. I have seen a mode of carriage similar to this in the streets of Peking, but confined to light substances, such as baskets of charcoal.

The trees in this part of the Himalayas have but little foliage upon them, and their trunks are of unusual length and remarkably straight. For the most part they have creepers devoid of foliage twisted spirally round them, which ascend to the branches and from hence hang down frequently to the ground. These creepers, from interfering with the circulation in the bark, are said to be injurious to the trees.

After a march of nearly twelve miles along an excellent road, having, as already stated, an incline of only one foot in thirty, we reached the village of Pacheem, and here had to turn off the road and take a steep pathway leading up to the barracks which are about a mile up the ascent on the side of a track known as the old road—now in disuse. The barracks are similar to those at Kursiong, and only suited for resting-places for the night. The path by which they are reached from the new road is both rugged and steep, and proved the most trying portion of our mountain march, especially so, coming in as it did at the end of the day's journey.

In the neighbourhood of Pacheem, there is a small tea growing settlement, which has been recently established on a spur in the centre of an amphitheatre of hills, to which the name of Hope Town has been given. The soil consists of yellow clay mixed with disentegrated gneis covered with a layer of black vegetable mould here and there washed away by the rains—the timber in its vicinity being chiefly the oak, chestnut, and magnolia. The elevation of Hope Town is about six thousand feet, and viewed, as approached by the new road from Kursiong, it has the appearance of being built on a very abrupt ascent, which however is not the case, the slope being moderate. The settlement does not promise to prove a success.

After halting the night of 19th of March at Pacheem, the following morning we descended by the same path to the new road, and proceeding along it for about six miles came to a part of it known as the "saddle," where a winding pathway ascends the mountain of Senchal, on a ridge near the top of which the cantonment or ordinary military station of Darjeeling is established. Senchal, which is 8,600 feet high, overlooks the hill of Julla Pahar, distant from it three and a half miles, on which the convalescent depot stands, while Julla Pahar again overlooks the civil station and Darjeeling, about a mile and a half lower down. Crossing the "saddle," which is a ridge connecting Senchal and Julla Pahar, we ascended the latter mountain by a somewhat steep path and reached the convalescent depot, consisting of several small buildings perched one above the other on sites cut for them on the abrupt slopes of the hill at an elevation of 7,800 feet—the communication between them being by zigzags, protected on the outside by wooden railings. The view as we ascended was very fine, the khuds (ravines) being of great depth and extent. From the brow of Julla Pahar a number of detached houses built on slopes of a mountain, about a thousand feet lower down came in view; this was the civil station and settlement of Darjeeling, the height of the hill from which it takes its name being 7,166 feet above the level of the sea.

Before proceeding further with the narrative of events, a notice of the circumstances under which Darjeeling came into our possession may not be without interest to the reader. To this subject therefore I shall devote the following chapter.

CHAPTER XIV.

British Intercourse with Sikim—Circumstances under which Darjeeling became British Territory—Progress of the Settlement—Dr. Hooker's Visit to it—Troubles with Sikim—Dr. Campbell's Expedition and its Disaster—A Force sent into Sikim—A Treaty concluded—Details connected with the Origin of the Sikimese or Lepchas—Contradictory Character of the Information—The Author's Views—Limitation of the term Mongolian necessary for the right understanding of the Question — Meaning of the words Lepcha and Sikim — Confusion caused by the Use of the former—Improvement of Terms suggested —Unreliable Nature of the Lepcha Traditions.

THE portion of Sikim, now known as the Darjeeling district, in the year 1816 belonged to Nepaul; having been won by conquest from the Sikimese. At the end of the war we had with Nepaul it was ceded to the British Government, and by it given back to the Raja of Sikim, with whom a treaty was executed at Titalyah in February 1817. The object which the Governor-General (the Marquis of Hastings) had in view in so doing being to wedge in Nepaul as it were by territory belonging to an ally, and thus prevent her encroaching eastward.

Early in 1828 Mr. Grant of the Bengal Civil Service, the Resident at Malda, and Captain Lloyd,* who was employed settling the boundary between Sikim and Nepaul, made an excursion from Titalyah

* This officer, then Lieutenant General Lloyd, C.B., died at Darjeeling on the 4th June 1865, aged 76 years, and was buried with military honours by the 80th Regiment, and 7th Battery, 22nd Brigade, Royal Artillery.

into the mountains of Sikim, and when at a spot a few miles from what is now called Darjeeling formed the idea that the place was well adapted for a sanitarium. They brought the subject under the notice of Lord William Bentinck, the Governor-General, and in 1829 Major Herbert, the Deputy Surveyor-General, was instructed to visit the part of Sikim referred to, which he did along with Mr. Grant in 1830. The reports prepared by these gentlemen were submitted to the Court of Directors of the East India Company, who approved of them, and recommended the local Government, if practicable, to establish a sanitarium at Darjeeling, which had been particularly noted as suited for the purpose.

Negotiations were accordingly entered into with the Raja of Sikim for the transfer to the British Government of a track of hill land sufficient for the proposed sanitarium, and in the year 1835 they were concluded: the Sikim Raja receiving a compensation of three thousand rupees per annum in consideration of signing the following agreement:—

"The Governor-General of India having expressed his desire for the possession of the hill of Darjeeling, on account of its cool climate, for the purpose of enabling the servants of his Government suffering from sickness to avail themselves of its advantages, I the Sikim Raja, out of friendship to the said Governor-General, hereby present Darjeeling to the East India Company, that is, all the land south of the Great Rungeet River, east of the Balasun, Kahail, and Little Rungeet Rivers, and west of the Rungnoo and Mahanuddy Rivers."

British Sikim being thus established in 1835, Captain Lloyd came up the same year and resided at

Darjeeling, the spelling of which originally was Dorjiling, being a nearer approximation to the native pronunciation of the word; the meaning of which, according to Csoma de Korosi, is the "Holy Spot." Some however allege that it is the "bright and sunny spot," which would certainly be a misnomer, as during a considerable portion of the year the place is exceedingly cloudy. The former conjecture is the more probable one, as the remains of a Lama monastery may still be seen on the highest part of the mountain.

Captain Lloyd having inaugurated the sanitarium remained there until 1839, when he made over charge to Dr. Campbell, under whose able superintendence the district gradually progressed, roads being made, mountain torrents bridged over, a church erected, a bazaar organised, a convalescent depôt for 200 soldiers constructed, a municipality formed, a revenue created, a corps of Sebundy Sappers (native local militia) raised for keeping the roads in order, and other indications of progress developed.

For the first ten out of the twenty-two years that Dr. Campbell presided over the fortunes of the new settlement, no event of note occurred. In 1849, however, Dr. Hooker, the distinguished botanist, visited the Sikim Himalayas, and the Governor-General (Lord Dalhousie) made a special request to the Raja of Sikim, through Dr. Campbell, that every facility should be given him of prosecuting his researches. Far from this request being attended to, the contrary course was pursued by the Sikim authorities. Dr. Campbell in consequence thereof obtained the permission of Government to visit the country, which he did, and joining Dr. Hooker accompanied him to

Toomloong, the capital, for the purpose of having an interview with the Raja. They arrived there on the 3rd November 1849, but the Raja declined to see them, and left the following day for the Cholah Pass. Four days afterwards, as they were returning to Darjeeling, they were attacked by about fifty Sikimese, headed by an official called the Singtam Soubah, who seized Dr. Campbell, bound his hands and feet, knocked him down, kicked him, and otherwise ill-treated him. This assault, it appeared, was perpetrated at the instigation of the Dewan, or prime minister of the Sikim Raja, who owed Dr. Campbell a grudge, in consequence of his having interfered to procure the release of a Nepaulese girl that had been kidnapped and taken into Sikim.

Doctors Campbell and Hooker were marched back to Toomloong, where they were detained until the 25th of December 1849, the former having been confined in a room twelve feet by four. On that date, however, they were released, and allowed to return to Darjeeling, indications by this time being apparent of the intention of the British Government to effect their release by force; a Company of the 80th Regiment, under Captain—now Colonel Hawkes, being sent up from Dinapore to Darjeeling for the purpose.

As a punishment for this outrage the Indian Government resumed the whole of the land that had been presented to the Raja of Sikim, on its cession by Nepaul in 1817; and thus British Sikim assumed the proportions by which it is now represented—namely, a small tract of country extending for some miles on each side of the 27th degree of north latitude, and 88th of east longitude: its length as the crow flies being about thirty-five miles, and its breadth about eighteen miles. These dimensions include the plains land by which it is approached, from what was formerly our frontier, and admit of its being divided into a northern and southern portion: the former, from being mountain land, containing about half as much more surface as the latter. British Sikim, on the north, is bounded by the Great Rungeet and the Rummun Rivers; on the south by a boundary line about seven miles north of Titalyah, running from the Mahanuddy to the Mechi River; on the east by the Teesta and Mahanuddy, and on the west by the Mechi River and the Singalelah range of mountains; some of the peaks of which rise to elevations of ten and twelve thousand feet, and look down on the valleys of Nepaul.

No other event of importance occurred until towards the end of 1860, when Dr. Campbell, having represented to the Government that for some time the Sikimese had been misconducting themselves, closing roads, prohibiting trade, kidnapping people, &c., and treating remonstrances with contempt, was directed to proceed in person with a detachment of Sebundy Sappers and occupy a portion of Sikim, to the north of the Rummun and west of the Rungeet Rivers, pending compliance with the demands for redress. Dr. Campbell's force of occupation consisted of one three-pounder gun, four Europeans, and one hundred Sebundy Sappers. With this he started in November 1860, and took possession of the village of Rinchinpoong, about forty miles from Darjeeling. No signs of opposition were met with for a month; at the expiry of this time, however, Cheeboo Lama, who has always been friendly disposed towards us, gave information that an attack was intended, and which occurred the day afterwards. A fire of matchlocks and arrows was opened on the party in the dark, and some of the sentries were cut off; possession being obtained of their arms and ammunition. The attack was renewed several times during the two following days, and as the ammunition of the party was nearly exhausted, and reports were current that Darjeeling was about to be attacked, it was determined to retire at once on that station. The gun was spiked and abandoned along with the baggage. The retreat commenced in an orderly manner, and continued so for the first six miles, when the Sikimese took advantage of a rocky pass, and recommenced the attack, firing from above, and rolling stones down on the party, which threw it into confusion, and compelled it to take flight. The party succeeded in getting back to Darjeeling, having lost in this unfortunate affair about one-fifth of its original number.

The Sikimese now marched to our frontier, and occasioned considerable alarm in Darjeeling for some time, daily apprehension existing of an attack being made on the station. In the meantime the Government ordered a small expedition to be organized against Sikim, which was placed under the command of Colonel Gawler, of the 73rd Regiment, and consisted of two mountain howitzers, with a detachment of Royal Artillery, 300 men of the 6th Regiment, 200 men of Rattrays Seiks, and the Sebundy Sappers. This force reached the Rungeet River on the 2nd February 1861, and found the Sikimese in position on a stockade on the opposite bank; a few shells from the howitzers dislodged them, and enabled the Sappers to throw a bridge over the river, by which the force crossed into Sikim. After this little or no attempt at resistance was made, the chief difficulties encountered by the force being those connected with transport. It succeeded, however, in reaching Toomloong on the 9th of March, and shortly afterwards the Raja arrived from Choombi, in Thibet, where the Sikim court usually resides. On the 28th of the month he concluded a treaty with the Honourable Ashley Eden, who accompanied the force as Envoy and Special Commissioner. In this treaty it was agreed that a representative, accredited by the Sikim Government, should reside permanently at Darjeeling. Cheeboo Lama was selected for the post, and under his judicious management our diplomatic relations with Sikim have been carried on harmoniously ever since, and may be now considered as fixed on a secure basis.

There are few countries that less has been written about than Sikim; attributable, I presume, to the limited opportunities which have existed until recently of procuring information about it, and having given this general sketch of the circumstances under which a portion of it became British territory, I may be expected to say something about its people. The conclusions I have arrived at regarding them, are based partly on personal observation, partly on information locally acquired, and as their result inclines me to question the accuracy of the few opinions which have been given expression to in print concerning the source from which the present inhabitants of Sikim have sprung, I shall commence by placing these opinions before the reader prior to stating my grounds of dissent. Dr. Hooker in his account of a visit to the Sikim Mountains, contained in his "Himalayan Journals," states:—

"The Lepcha is the aboriginal inhabitant of the country, and the prominent character in Dorjiling (Darjeeling) where he undertakes all sorts of out-door employment. The race to which he belongs is a very singular one: markedly Mongolian in features, and a good deal too in habit; still he differs from his Tibetian prototype, though not so decidedly as from the Nepaulese and Bhotanese, between whom he is hemmed into a tract of country, barely sixty miles in breadth. The Lepchas possess a tradition of the flood, during which a couple escaped to the top of a mountain (Tendong) near Dorjiling. The earliest traditions which they have of their history date no further back than some three hundred years, when they describe themselves as having been long-haired half-clad savages. At about that period they were visited by Tibetians, who introduced Bood worship, the plaiting of their hair into pigtails, and many of their own customs. Their physiognomy is however so Tibetian in its character, that it cannot be supposed that this was their earliest intercourse with the trans-nivean races: whether they may have wandered beyond the snows before the spread of Boodism, or whether they are a cross between the Tamulian of India and the Tibetian, has not been discovered. Their language, though radically identical with Tibetian, differs from it in many important particulars. They, or at least some of their tribes, call themselves Rong and Arrat, and their country Dijong: they once possessed a great part of East Nepaul, as far west as the Tambur River, and at a still later period they penetrated as far west as Arum."

This ethnological notice of the Lepchas, or so-called aboriginal Sikimese appears to me so very vague, and in one or two respects so markedly contradictory, as to give rise to the impression that the subject must have received but a superficial share of attention from the high authority from which the notice emanates. The only other account of the Sikimese I have met with is the following, compiled by Captain Hathorn, of the Royal Artillery, and introduced into his "Handbook of Darjeeling," published at Calcutta in 1863.

"The Lepchas have a written language, but no recorded history of themselves or others. They are divided into two races, 'Rong' and 'Khamba.' Rong, is a generic term and equivalent to 'Lepcha' with us, but a man who calls himself a Lepcha in speaking to a European, may turn out to be a Khamba. The real Lepcha or Rong proper has no tradition of his tribe having immigrated from some other part of the world. His 'habitat' extends 120 miles from the north-west to south-east along the southern face of the Himalayas, and here he has always been, according to the best of his knowledge and belief, and this is corroborated by his neighbours. It extends to the west as far as the Tambur branch of the river Koosee, and its eastern limit is undefined somewhere in Bhotan, probably some fifty miles east of the Teesta, although a few of them are said to be located as far east as Punnaka and Tasgong. The Khambas, though now the same in all essentials of language, customs, and habits as the Rong, are immigrants from beyond the Himalaya. They appear to have come from Kham, a province of Thibet, lying next to

China and under Chinese rule. They reckon seven generations (or say 200 years) since their arrival on this side of the snows. They were headed by the first ancestor of the present Sikim Raja, who is himself a Khamba. This ancestor was invited from Thibet to accept the throne of Sikim, on account of the incessant struggles for supremacy which had previously convulsed the latter country. The first Raja did not exercise any spiritual authority. But the chief priestly power is now generally vested in a member of the Royal family. The Lepchas, both Rong and Khamba, are Boodhists."

This account of the Sikimese, though more precise than that given by Dr. Hooker, is nevertheless also somewhat contradictory: inasmuch as we are left to infer that the class of Lepchas who call themselves Rongs, are really aboriginal to the part of the Himalayas where they are now found—and at the same time are told that another class of Lepchas who call themselves Khambas, and between whom and the Rong there is no essential distinction, moral or physical, are of comparatively recent Thibetian origin—evidence to my mind conclusive that they must have sprung from a common source, and that any difference which may exist between them must be merely of name and not of race: in all probability not greater than the county distinctions existing in our own country.

Having thus ventured to question the accuracy of the only published information I have been able to find, with reference to the origin of the Sikimese, I shall now endeavour to show that the subject is not one of much ethnological obscurity. Before proceeding however further in the inquiry, it is necessary to come to an understanding as to the interpretation to be put on the word Mongolian, which, as generally used, has a very wide signification, indicative of a vast and widely-spread race, constituting over one half of the whole human species. In using the term in the following remarks, I mean it to be restricted to the inhabitants—or their descendants—of that portion of the Chinese Empire called Mongolia, which stands in a relation to China similar to that in which our colonies stand to their mother country; its affairs in common with those of other out-lying possessions, being presided over at Peking, by a Board called the Ly Fan Yuen, or Colonial office. Mongolia consists of four great divisions and between its people and the Chinese there is as wide a distinction as there is between the Saxon tobacconist and the kilted Celt, of whom he usually has a representation in wood at his door. The divisions of Mongolia are: 1st. Inner Mongolia, lying between the Great Wall and the desert of Gobi. 2nd. Outer Mongolia, between the latter and the Altai Mountains. 3rd. The Koko-nor country, between Kansah, Sz'chuen, and Thibet; and 4th, the dependencies of Aliasutai, lying north-westward of the Kalkas Khanates. Mongolia consequently borders on Thibet, and several of its nomadic tribes have settled there: chiefly in, what is called by the Chinese, Anterior Thibet,—the country to the north of Lassa and Kham.

When I first saw the Lepchas at Punkabaree, their features appeared so familiar that it almost seemed to me as if I had again reached the confines of China, and I was not long in recognising points of resemblance between them and the Mongols I had been accustomed to see in Peking, sufficiently marked as to satisfy me that Mongolia was the country from which they had originally come—and that an easy solution was afforded of how—owing to the difference existing between them and the Thibetians (including the Bhotanese) the belief had arisen that they were aboriginal to the parts of the Himalayas they now inhabit.

In the first chapter of this narrative, I have shown that the word Bhoteah is generic for Thibetian, and that at Darjeeling there is a mixed population of Sikim, Nepaul, and Dhurma Bhoteahs—also, Lepchas and Paharees; the latter being in all probability the descendants of the true Himalayan aborigines; their name meaning "hill men." The population of Sikim is of the same mixed character, but I have been as yet unable to ascertain whether the Mongolian or Thibetian element predominates. That there is a close relation at the present day between Sikim and Thibet is manifest from the fact that one of the clauses of the treaty executed by Mr. Eden, in 1861, is to the following effect: "With a view to the establishment of an efficient government in Sikim, and to the better maintenance of friendly relations with the British Government, the Raja of Sikhim agrees to remove the seat of his government from Thibet to Sikhim, and reside there for nine months in the year"—than which stronger evidence, it would be difficult to adduce. That there is also a close relationship between the Thibetians and Mongolians, is equally manifest from a glance at the geographical position of their countries, a comparison of their religion, their appearance, manners and customs—to say nothing of the fact that the two countries, along with the province of Ili, constitute the three great colonial divisions of China, supervised by the Ly Fan Yuen at Peking.

Of the meaning of the word Lepcha I have been unable to procure any information, further than that it is believed to be of Nepaulese origin; even those who have been longest resident at Darjeeling, and most versed with the natural history of the people, know nothing more about it. The people, however, to whom we apply it do not use it amongst themselves; it is consequently a term of purely local signification, and I am inclined to think that as the word Lepcha is locally applied to the sacred cairns or piles of stones on which flags, written prayers, and other emblems of Lama Buddhism are placed, that the name was originally given by the aborigines of the hills to the Mongol intruders, whose presence amongst them these rude votive altars became indicative of. This supposition is the more probable from the fact that the word we call Lepcha is pronounced by the Nepaulese Lapcha, and is employed by them to distinguish the same class of people that it is by us.

The word Sikim, like Lepcha, is a purely local one, and only used by its inhabitants in conversation with Europeans or natives from the plains, or the neighbouring hills. It is of Hindoostanee origin, and by the Nepaulese is pronounced See-i—what it means I have been unable to ascertain. By the Sikimese their country is called Dee-jon, or the "rice-growing place"—so at least I have been informed by Cheeboo Lama.

There is no doubt that the Lepchas proper, though as pure a specimen of the Mongolian race as the Thibetians, still differ from them, inasmuch as their language is different, which is in accordance with what might be expected; the dialect of Mongolia differing from the dialect of Thibet.* Their dress also differs somewhat, though both wear the tail. The Lepcha frequently wears a small "pork pie" shaped hat, made of yellow silk, with a red silk knob on the top of it, the turned up part being lined with a coarse kind of black velvet. This hat bears a close resemblance to that which is commonly worn by the Mongolians from the neighbourhood of the Great Wall and the desert of Gobi, who bring their commodities for sale to Peking—the difference being that in the case of the latter the turned-up part is covered with fur, and has a slit behind, from which two pieces of ribbon hang down the back.

To sum up in a few words what has been said about the Sikimese, they consist of two classes of people, the one being of Mongolian, the other of Thibetian descent; neither of them consequently aboriginal to the country, any more than the Bhotanese are to the hill tract and portion of the plains of Bengal that they have effected possession of.

It may seem to some that I have just arrived at a conclusion differing but little from that contained in the account given in the "Darjeeling Handbook," to which I commenced by taking exception. A re-perusal, however, of the quotation referred to will show that this is not the case; the alleged aboriginal Lepchas or Rongs, and Thibetian Lepchas or Khambas, being there represented as "now the same in all essentials of language, custom, and habit;"

* Even the dialects of Thibet differ, the inhabitants of the Eastern parts of the country not understanding those of the Western.

whereas I do not admit that any essential difference can ever have existed between them; believing them to be both of Mongolian origin, and therefore distinct from the Thibetian element in Sikim—in other words, from the Sikim Bhoteahs; Lepcha being a sort of collective synonym for the whole, whether Thibetian or Mongolian, which has proved very misleading. The absence of clear views on this subject, as well as the general confusion of terms which exists, I believe to be solely attributable to the fact that the admixture of the Mongolian element with that of the Thibetian in the Himalayas of Sikim has hitherto been overlooked. The traditional distinction between the Rongs and the Khambas, referred to by Captain Hathorn, may be, that, though of the same people, they are sprung from separate clans or tribes, one of which may have established itself at an earlier date than the other in the country of their adoption.

At a future page, when I come to narrate a conversation I had on this subject with Cheeboo Lama, who is himself a Lepcha proper (Mongolian), I shall be able to show how exceedingly difficult it is to obtain information regarding it, however favourably one may be locally situated, even he who, according to Mr. Eden, "has studied the histories of Thibet and the countries adjoining it more than any living man," being singularly inaccurately informed with reference to the circumstances under which his race became settled in Sikim, and also with respect to its philology.

As the term Lepcha is now so identified with the word Sikimese, and two really distinct people included under it, the simplest mode of distinguishing them will be by adopting the terms Mongolian, Lepcha, and Thibetian Lepcha; Sikim Bhoteah being synonymous with the latter amongst the people themselves, when interrogated concerning their descent.

From what has been said the reader will probably be better able to understand such casual observations as occur in the course of my jottings at Darjeeling, respecting the types of the great Mongolian race which are met with in this part of the Himalayas, and in thus differing from the authorities I have quoted it is only fair to state that, but for the advantages I had while residing at Peking of becoming familiar with the characteristic of the Mongolian tribes, I should not have been in a position to do otherwise than they have done, namely, trust to local tradition, which amongst the people in question there is reason to believe is by no means a reliable source of information.

I may add that I brought the view now propounded of the descent of these so-called Lepchas, under the notice of Lieutenant-Colonel Shelton, of the Bengal Staff Corps, Station Interpreter at Darjeeling, and the Reverend Mr. Niebel, who has resided there twenty-two years, both of whom have devoted considerable attention to the question of race, and are well acquainted with the Lepcha character, and I had the satisfaction of finding that it was favourably entertained by them; as it seemed to be a reasonable explanation of a distinction between the two Mongolian elements of Sikim, which hitherto had been so obscure as to countenance the idea of one of them being aboriginal.

CHAPTER XV.

Military Arrangements at Darjeeling—Formation of a movable Column —Protective Measures—The Soubah of Dhumsong a State Prisoner —The Cantonment of Senchal—Relation between the suicidal Mania and foggy Weather—Route to the Rungeet—Cane Suspension Bridge —Sikim—Venomous Insects—The Teesta and the Bhotan Frontier— Heat of the Valley—Our advanced Picket — Cross the Teesta — Nature of the Suspension Bridge — Bhotanese Peasants — Their Arrows—Track over Pushok Mountain—Return to Darjeeling.

On arriving at the Convalescent Depot at Julla Pahar, the headquarters of the 80th was temporarily established there, until accommodation could be found for it in the station of Darjeeling, where two companies from the cantonment at Senchal were at the time quartered, while a third company was at Julla Pahar. These arrangements had been made consequent on the apprehensions entertained that the Bhotanese would attack the Civil Station, and coincident with our arrival, instructions had been received from the Government that as soon as practicable accommodation for the whole of the 80th Regiment (less three companies at Senchal) was to be provided in Darjeeling—the Wing detached to Mynagoorie having been stopped at Julpigorie and ordered to join headquarters at Darjeeling. Orders were at the same time issued for the formation of a movable column, to consist of a battery of artillery with two mountain howitzers and two 5½ inch mortars, 300 men of the 80th Regiment, 200 of the 17th Native Infantry, and a company of Sebundy Sappers. The baggage of the column to be conveyed by ponies; owing to the uncertainty connected with coolie transport, especially during military operations.

The battery of Royal Artillery being then on the march up, and as the most suitable accommodation for it was at the convalescent depot, it was decided to quarter it there, which necessitated arrangements being at once made for removing the head-quarters of the 80th to Darjeeling. Accordingly, on the 21st of March, Colonel Hawkes, Captain Staunton of the Royal Engineers, and myself, went down to Darjeeling to select such vacant houses as could be converted into temporary barracks. A good but rather steep road, protected on the outside by a wooden fence, communicates between Julla Pahar and Darjeeling: connecting as it were the two stations—the hill of the one joining on to that of the other by a ridge about midway down the road. On the slopes of both hills, houses are built at intervals the whole way along. Some of them belong to permanent residents, while others have been built with a view to their being let to invalids from the plains of Bengal.

The unsettled state of matters on the frontier at this period had operated against the interests of the place as a sanitarium, and several vacant houses were found tolerably well adapted for the purpose wanted—that is to say, the accommodation was much superior to that afforded by tents, but by no means up to the modern sanitary standard, which, with every feeling of respect for what has as its basis the maintenance and improvement of the health of soldiers, I must say aims at a degree of uniformity of perfection which it is simply impracticable to carry out otherwise than in model barracks—a form of accommodation which can only be extended to soldiers in connection with one phase of their military career—namely, peace; and even then it is far from that easy matter that sanitarians, especially those of the amateur class, seem to think. All the houses we looked at were fully furnished, and the chief difficulty the owners seemed to have in letting them for barracks referred to the disposal of the furniture, storage being both scarce and expensive in Darjeeling.

Of the two companies then in the station, one commanded by Captain Amiel was quartered partly in a house called the Dell, partly in the old native hospital, while the other company under Captain Sullivan was lower down the hill in the station theatre. Double sentries and a guard were posted at a point called the Chow Rusta, overlooking the valley of the Rungeet; the quarter from which the Bhotanese were expected to attack. Two mountain howitzers were also in readiness at the Dell, and signals of communication had been arranged by guns and rockets, so that in the event of an attack the companies from Julla Pahar and Senchal would come down in support. Advanced pickets of the 17th Native Infantry were some miles in front on the banks of the Rungeet and the Teesta.

The following day in the course of visiting the rooms in occupation as barracks in Darjeeling along with the Adjutant (Lieutenant Huskisson) we found that one of them in the old native hospital was used as a place of confinement for a Bhotanese official, the Soubah of Dhumsong, who had been made prisoner under the following circumstances. In the first instance he had submitted to the authority of the British, and having given up his fort without resistance, was allowed to reside at Dhumsong. He was afterwards, through the interception of a letter, detected corresponding with his own Government, and detailing a plan by which, if authorised, he would undertake with a small body of men to cut off the detachment of the 17th Native Infantry at the time stationed there. In consequence of this he was arrested, and it was thought the best course to destroy the fort and withdraw the detachment, which was done. The Soubah was a fine looking old man, very thick set and muscular, with a round face, open countenance, and thick head of black curly hair.* He was dressed in a blue cloth robe thickly lined, and had a countryman of his own attending him as servant. He seemed in very good spirits and was sitting outside in the verandah, playing at a kind of native draughts with the Havildar of Police in whose charge he was, and appeared to be getting the best of the game. There did not seem to be any intention of adopting more severe measures towards him than deprivation of liberty for the time being—nor could any other course well be pursued, as the proposal he made to his Government was only what might have been expected under the circumstances.

Orders having been received from the Government to the effect that a Board, composed of the Officer commanding the Station, the Executive Royal Engineer, and the Senior Medical officer, should examine and report on the nature and amount of the accommotion for European troops in the barracks at Julla Pahar and Senchal, Colonel Hawkes, Captain Staun-

* The Bhotanese neither shave the front of the head nor wear tails, though in other respects they are like the Thibetians.

ton, and myself were occupied the greater portion of the first week after our arrival at this duty. On the 24th of March we visited Senchal; proceeding to it by descending the Julla Pahar hill to the narrow and short ridge called the "saddle," connecting the two mountains. Crossing this we ascended Senchal from a point about 5,000 feet above the sea, by a zigzag path. The barracks, which though commenced in 1857 were not completed or occupied until 1860, we found to be in a very tumble-down condition: their walls being of the flimsy structure known as "wattle and dab," supported on stone foundations. Altogether there were about thirty small single-storied buildings, arranged in various ways on a long ridge about a hundred feet from the top of the mountain; some of them being parallel to each other, others longitudinally on elevations on the ridge. The roofs were originally of sheet-iron, and were found to leak, they were then covered with thatch which proved combustible from the sparks from the wood fires, and had to be re-covered with a layer of sheet-iron in the neighbourhood of the chimneys. The hospital, from having a glass verandah round it, was the best building out of a very bad lot. The barracks generally were at the time under repair, and upwards of thirty men of the 80th stationed there, were receiving twelve annas (eighteen pence) per diem working pay as labourers, while four men who were tradesmen were getting a rupee per diem in addition to their military pay; which in India is ninepence a day and a complete ration. There can be no doubt that the selection of Senchal as a military station was a mistake on the part of Dr. Campbell; as, from its great height it is enveloped by clouds the greater portion of the year, besides coming in for an amount of rain much in excess of what is experienced at Darjeeling. The only grounds on which the place could have been selected must have been from a desire to keep the military and civil elements of the settlement at as great a distance from each other as practicable. A more dreary residence for the British soldier than the cantonment of Mount Senchal could not well be found, or one more likely to develop the suicidal mania where a predisposition to it exists.* It is to be hoped as soon as the Bhotan difficulties are terminated, that the Government in place of rebuilding these barracks will direct their being pulled down, and such materials as may be available applied to the construction of new ones in a more suitable and cheerful locality.

On Sunday, the 26th of March, the head-quarters of the 80th Regiment marched to church at Darjeeling with the band playing, which caused extraordinary excitement amongst the Lepchas, who flocked up the mountain sides in all directions, and crowded round the musicians; the present being the first time the head-quarters of a European regiment had ever been to Darjeeling. The same afternoon a portion of the detachment temporarily located at Julla Puhar moved down to the civil station, and the following day the 7th Battery of the 22nd Brigade Royal Artillery, under the command of Captain Taylor, arrived and went into the quarters thus vacated at the Convalescent Depot.

At six o'clock on the morning of the 29th of

* An illustration will be found at a future page (under date May the 6th), supporting the belief which is entertained by many, that a relation exists between suicidal insanity and meteorological influences.

March, along with Lieutenants Ridout and Howard of the 80th, I started from Julla Pahar for the valleys of the Rungeet and the Teesta for the purpose of visiting the frontiers of Sikim and Bhotan. The sun was just rising, and the snow-covered peaks of the distant ranges were seen with remarkable distinctness. From Darjeeling we descended by a steep and rugged path to the Lepcha village of Leebong, situated at the commencement of a spur on the opposite side of the Darjeeling Hill, from where the station is. It consists of a number of bamboo framework huts, raised about four feet from the ground, and roofed with split bamboo. This village has been long a place of rendezvous for the Thibetian and Bhotanese traders, and on the slope of the Darjeeling hill, immediately above it, Cheeboo Lama resides in a small European-built house, roofed with shingles. This form of roofing is in general use for English residences in British Sikim—as it is in Australia. The split wood is put on in the same manner as slates, and after it has been exposed for a short time to the sun it acquires a grey colour, which to the eye of a stranger gives the houses the appearance of being roofed with light-coloured slates. The roofs of the Convalescent Depot are of this material, and why those of the Senchal Barracks were not originally made so, I am unable to say.

From Darjeeling to the Rungeet the distance is twelve miles; and from Leebong the course to it was one of continuous descent by a winding path for upwards of 6,000 feet: the bed of the river being 1,000 feet above the level of the sea. After we had descended about half-way we came amongst some tea-gardens, the plant not thriving well at altitudes exceeding 4,000 feet. The bushes in the plantations we passed were about a foot and a half high, and four feet apart; their leaves being about the size of small laurel ones, but differing from them by having serrated edges. Leaves of that size, however, are not used for tea-making, only the young ones in their early stage of growth.

After we had descended continuously for nearly three hours, at the rate of about four miles an hour, the rustling of water was heard, which proved to be a stream called the Rungnoo, which flows down the valley and joins the Rungeet. Near where it takes its origin in one of the spurs of Senchal, there is a mineral spring, to which invalids are occasionally sent from the Convalescent Depot, a hut having been erected for their accommodation.

Shortly after the waters of the Rungnoo were heard, the Rungeet River came into view, several hundred feet underneath where we then were, its stream having a singularly black appearance in the distance, from the dark shadows of the lofty and almost perpendicular jungle on each side of its banks. Continuing to descend we reached the Rungnoo, near where it joins the Rungeet, and crossing it by a rustic bridge we found ourselves on the right bank of the latter river, near where a cane suspension bridge of singular construction has been thrown across it into the territory of the Sikim Raja. In a rude stockade commanding this bridge a Company of the 17th Native Infantry was posted as an advanced picquet, in case the Bhotanese might attempt to enter Darjeeling from the Sikim frontier.

Having brought some breakfast with us, carried by a coolie, we crossed the Rungeet by the cane suspension bridge, which, as it swung about over the rushing torrent underneath, was calculated to try the nerves of any one not having implicit confidence in the integrity of native engineering. Near the bridge a family of Sikimese were residing in a raised bamboo hut, similar to those at Leebong.

HIMALAYAN CANE SUSPENSION BRIDGE.

The owner of the house was very civil, and allowed us to come in and take our breakfast on the floor, the house being without furniture of any kind beyond a cooking hearth, which is one of the characteristics of the residences of the Lepcha and Bhotanese peasants. The Sikimese family were altogether above anything like caste prejudices, and were delighted to partake of the remains of our meal. The coolie again who had carried it was a Nepaulese, and who consequently was a Hindoo, would not touch it, though no doubt hungry and tired after his twelve miles' walk. Neither would he take some sherry that was offered to him. The Sikimese however did so without hesitation, and asked for more.

While at breakfast we were repeatedly bitten by "pipsees," venomous insects resembling small flies, and one of the chief plagues of the banks of the Rungeet. Their bite draws blood, and leaves a dark raised stain, which remains for some time, and very frequently occasions troublesome sores. The sepoys of the 17th were at the time suffering severely from them, several of the men having been rendered incabable of duty owing to the large sores the bites had occasioned.

The country in the neighbourhood of the hut presented no diversity of appearance; all that was to be seen being a dense jungle of bamboo trees, traversed by two narrow paths, the one to the eastward communicating with a road leading to Toomloong, the capital.

After breakfast we returned to the British side of the Rungeet, and called on Lieutenant Dawes commanding the detachment. He had lately returned with it from Dhumsong; the position having been abandoned on the fort being destroyed. The sun was now very strong, and the heat in the valley oppressive. Up to this period we had not used our ponies, so as to keep them as fresh as possible for the more fatiguing journey homewards in the afternoon, involving 6,000 feet of steep ascent. Having got thus far, notwithstanding the heat, I determined to go on and take a look at Bhotan, which I was able to do easily through the kindness of Mr. Dawes, who lent me his pony, and thus escaped the fatigue of walking the whole distance, which otherwise I should have experienced.

Following the course of the Rungeet in an easterly direction for six miles along a very bad path, which had been recently cut on the steep bank of the river, and which a number of Nepaulese coolies were endeavouring to convert into a narrow road, I came to where the Rungeet joins the Teesta. The opposite bank of the latter river was formed by the abrupt slope of mountains about 4,000 feet high, and covered with jungle from the water's edge to their summits—this was Bhotan. High up the mountain sides here and there a solitary hut and little patch of cultivation could be seen—the latter appearing as bright green spots, at distant intervals, contrasting strongly with the dark hue of the large surface of forest jungle surrounding them. The Teesta hereabouts is a swift and deep rolling stream, between two and three hundred feet wide; its current running down towards the plains at the rate of about ten miles an hour. I turned to the right, and following its downward course for a mile, came to a suspension bridge similar to the one over the Rungeet, but in a much more shaky and doubtful condition. Here, another picquet of the 17th Native Infantry was stationed, and on the bank 500 feet above, a company of the same regiment under Lieutenant Barlow was quartered in bamboo huts; the ascent to which being very steep.

The heat was now intense, the Teesta here flowing

between mountain banks, the heights of which average from four to six thousand feet. I have rarely felt heat more oppressive, and certainly never felt anything more grateful, than a draught of the cool water from the river, drank from the hands of one of the Sepoys, joined together to form a cup: the only mode of getting water at the time available.

Having thus refreshed myself and left my pony in charge of the guard, I crossed over into Bhotan by the suspension bridge, which proved to be in a very rickety state compared with the one at Rungeet, which was of more recent construction, and found myself upon a steep, narrow and rugged path, resembling a sheep track, and surrounded by jungle—this was the high road to Dhumsong and Dhalimkote, by which Mr. Eden's mission entered Bhotan. I ascended it for about two hundred feet, but seeing no prospect of a change of scenery for an indefinite period, I returned to the bridge, and on the way down the hill I met two friendly Bhotanese, who came out of the jungle by a side path. They were armed with bows and arrows, the latter carried in a bamboo quiver slung across the shoulder, and fitted with large barbed iron heads, apparently poisoned. These arrows, I am told, are used for hunting purposes, and that as a general rule they do not poison them in warfare. The men were dressed in loose short robes, coming down to the knee, made of dusky-red woollen material, and on their heads they had the small felt hat usually worn by peasants in the north of China. They were civil, and allowed me to examine their weapons. They followed me down to the bridge, but did not venture on it till I had crossed, and then came over themselves, one at a time; showing that their confidence was not great in the bridge at that period, and with good reason, as a few weeks afterwards it became unserviceable, and a new one had to be constructed. The dimensions of this primitive suspension bridge, I may state, were seven paces of gentle incline to where the chief wooden supports were secured, at the water's edge on the right bank, seventy-six paces of suspended portion to the supports on the Bhotan side, and five paces of descent to the bank; making its total length about 270 feet. With the exception of the wooden supports on each bank, the whole structure was composed of cane-creepers and bamboo; not a nail, peg, or particle of rope-work entering into its composition.

The mountain on the British side overlooking the suspension bridge, is called Pushok, and until the recent attempt at road-making along the banks of the Rungeet and Teesta, the only means of reaching this part of the latter river, where the communication existed with Bhotan, was by a path across Pushok hill, from a point on the Rungeet about midway between the cane bridge and the junction of the river with the Teesta. It was this track that Mr. Eden's mission had to take, and it very probably will have to be resumed; as the road in course of formation is almost certain to be swept away during the rainy season.

I got back to the post on the Rungeet at half-past four, and by five o'clock the force of the sun was on the decline, and we started homewards, reaching Julla Pahar the same evening a little after nine o'clock, having found the ascent in the dark rather trying and tedious.

CHAPTER XVI.

Recommencement of Hostilities by the Left Brigade under Brigadier-General Tytler—Recapture of Balla—Translation of a Bhotanese Document found in the Stockade—Dislodgement of the Bhotanese from Buxa and Chamoorchee—Evacuation of Bishensing—Operations on the Right under Brigadier-General Tombs—Examination of the Passes leading to Dewangiri—Communication from the Tongso Penlow—Advance on Dewangiri—Attack on the Position—Its Capture and Slaughter of the Enemy—Firing of the 55th Regiment—Destruction and Evacuation of Dewangiri — Termination of Field Operations and Distribution of the Force of Occupation and Defence.

THE Bhotan Field Force, in place of being as formerly one command, was now divided into two independent ones, under Brigadier Generals Tombs and Frazer Tytler respectively, and designated Right and Left Brigades. To the latter the Darjeeling force belonged, and formed its extreme left. On the 15th of March General Tytler commenced operations, and recaptured Balla without difficulty. The attacking force consisted of a Wing of the 18th Regiment of Native Infantry, the 19th and 30th Punjaubees, with the Armstrong guns and mortars attached to the brigade. The stockade (Tazagong) was exposed to a heavy fire from the artillery and set in flames. The infantry then advanced from two directions and drove the enemy out. The Bhotanese lost 44 men, and requested permission to bury their dead, which was granted. The British loss was three men killed and sixteen wounded, these casualties being confined to the 18th, 19th, and 30th Regiments. Captain Magregor, the Brigade Major, referred to as having been wounded at Dhalimkote, was again wounded at this place; being shot through the hand.

A document addressed by the Angdu Forung Jungpen to the Bhotanese official at Balla, of which the following is a translation, was found in the stockade: "I have heard that you are prudently acting, by building a strong stockade at Tazagong, for the protection of our country from the attacks of the ambitious and all-country-destroying English. As the hot season is at hand, you have requested permission to leave the position. I am aware that the place is getting warm, but if you return without gaining a decided victory, the great Chiefs and Lamas will surely hold you in great disgrace. So resolve never to come back but die in war. If you now come back, then what avail the hardship you have undergone so long in fortifying the position? What was the good of your undergoing labour so hard that you have reckoned one day as ten? What is the consequence of your lying in the open air whole nights, and sleeping upon the grass, having only a stone for your pillow? Certainly the old Penlow of Paro will be highly displeased with your conduct, in spite of all the troubles you have undergone. In fact, in that case you will have no excuse to offer to the same. I am informed that the old Zimpen, instead of accompanying you, went to the Lama. I am also informed that four men were killed in a battle. Do not be afraid on account of it, but remember that they were killed for the sake of their country. Resolve that we must take vengeance for it, by punishing the ambitious English, at the expense of our own lives. It is better to have our bodies cut into pieces than to come back without punishing the enemy. He who is the most prudent and careful can never be defeated. The Paro Penlow is determined to fight at all hazards, and retain one side of the country. Resolve that we should work hard, so as to cut the hardest stones and iron to pieces. Balla cannot be very hot this season, so do not fear sickness; and in the hot season there is a cool place for you at Tazagong. In the hot season the troops will fight, and if they get sick we cannot help it. Buxa, Chamoorchee, and Tazagong, are cool places; we shall therefore be able to fight from there. I alone have considered the propositions from head to foot. You make a committee and consider the ways of keeping our country. I am ready to accompany you, but as there is a festival held by our Lamas, I am obliged to remain with them. It will be finished on the 10th. I shall answer the letters from the East and the West on the 11th or 12th.—come home on the 13th, and start to join you on the 15th. Most probably I shall arrive at your place on the 18th or 19th; but do not be sorry if I do not join you at the time I mention." This document is of some interest, as it shows that, however much the Bhotanese may fight amongst themselves, and however chronic the state of warfare may be between the Penlows of Eastern and Western Bhotan, they nevertheless seem to act in unison in resisting foreign invasion.

The force under General Tytler now moved towards Buxa, where the Bhotanese had established themselves in stockades in the neighbourhood of the position held by us at that place. They were taken possession of without opposition on the 23rd of March, the Bhotanese having abandoned them on the approach of the troops. After this, a movement was made towards Chamoorchee, and on the 24th of March the stockades there were evacuated, immediately on the artillery opening fire, and before the infantry had approached within storming distance.

As regards the operations of the Right Brigade, it will be remembered that about the same time that Dewangiri was attacked, and captured by the Bhotanese, an attempt was made to dislodge three companies of the 44th Native Infantry, stationed at Bishensing, which was successfully resisted. In consequence, however, of the distance of this position and the difficulty of keeping up communication and supplies, it was decided to withdraw the garrison and destroy such defences as had been constructed during our brief occupation of the place. Accordingly Colonel Richardson proceeded there a second time, with a portion of his column from Sidlee, and on the 25th of February destroyed the position and withdrew the detachment of his regiment from it. How this post ever was included amongst those, the occupation of which were considered necessary, is not easy of comprehension.

On the 7th of March, Brigadier General Tombs arrived at Gowhatty, and from thence went on to the camp at Koomrekatta, where preliminary arrangements were commenced for the recapture of Dewangiri: active operations being deferred until the arrival of the battery of Royal Artillery and the headquarters of the 55th Regiment.

Koomrekatta Fort is on an extensive plain forty-one miles from Gowhatty, and between five and six in a straight line from the foot of the Bhotan hills. At the time in question it was a mere earthwork, which had been constructed by us in 1856. This fort was the site of the camp, where the troops were collecting for an advance on Dewangiri.

In a note at page 199, I have stated that Dewangiri is the terminus where five passes communicating with the plains meet. The names of these, commencing with the one most to the eastward, are the Baladee, Gooroogaon, Durunghah, Libra, and Soobhankhatta Passes. In the whole of them the Bhotanese threw up works to oppose our advance on Dewangiri; the place admitting of being approached by any one of the five.

Reconnoitering parties were sent out from Koomreekatta to examine these defences. On the 13th of March a reconnaisance was made of the Baladee Pass, the most eastern of them, by Captain Norman, with two companies of native infantry, which resulted in the capture of the stockades; the Bhotanese evacuating them with a loss of twenty-four men. On the 17th of the same month, a force of 800 infantry with four guns went up to a stockade in the Durungah Pass, from which the Bhotanese fired a few shots at the column as it approached, and then evacuated the position. The following day, the Soobhankhatta Pass was examined by two hundred men, who proceeded up it to within about three miles of Dewangiri. The pass was there found to be strongly stockaded, and the officer in command of the party having instructions not to attack any defences that he might meet with, withdrew his men and returned to Koomreekatta. On the 21st of March the Libra and Gooroogaon Passes were similarly examined; Brigadier-General Tombs accompanying the reconnaissances.

While the force was thus occupied until the European artillery and infantry arrived, two messengers who had been sent to Dewangiri to make inquiries after the prisoners in the hands of the Bhotanese, returned to Koomrekatta, and from what they said a favourable impression was formed of the Tongso Penlow; who it appeared treated them kindly, gave them a good dinner, and safe convoy clear of the hills. He had also treated the prisoners well, and altogether seemed to be by no means such an objectionable character as he had made himself to Mr. Eden. He sent his compliments to the officials in camp, stating that he was quite well, and hoped that they were so likewise. At a subsequent period a communication was received from him to the following effect—"You are wanting Dewangiri again, but from whom did you receive permission to take possession of it, when you first captured it? You will either have to fight with us or write a letter to the Dhurma Raja, if you are desirous to recover Dewangiri. If he gives it to you, then we must yield. Apart from the question of Dewangiri, it is our desire to obtain possession of the lands formerly held by us. You used to give one part to us and keep the rest. This not having been given, we are not so angry, because when we were powerless, you took possession of Dewangiri, but when we were really angry, you were driven out of it. There is no quarrel at all between us, if you will allow us to possess the lands on the former boundaries. We have stated to you the order of the Dhurma Raja, do as you like now." There would seem to be no doubt that when we first commenced operations in December 1864, the Bhotanese had made no preparations to resist us, probably looking upon the ultimatum of the Government as a mere threat that would not be enforced.

By the end of March, the 3rd Battery of the 25th Brigade Royal Artillery and the headquarters of the 55th Regiment had reached Koomrekatta. The rains being now close at hand, an immediate advance on Dewangiri was imperative. Accordingly, at two o'clock on the morning of the 1st of April, an advanced guard of 1,000 men, consisting of one company of the 55th Regiment, the Eurasian battery of Artillery, and detachments of the 12th, 29th, and 44th Regiments of Native Infantry, marched from Koomrekatta and entered the Durungah Pass; which was the one that it had ultimately been decided to approach Dewangiri by. Passing an abandoned stockade about two and a half miles from the mouth of the pass, the advanced guard, some distance further on, came to a second stockade from which a fire was opened. A gun was brought to bear upon it, after a few rounds from which, the fire ceased, and the troops advancing on the stockade found it empty, with the exception of the remains of a man killed by a shell. The defences consisted of two rows of trees with stones between them, and some time was occupied in clearing the obstructions away. After this was done, the column advanced to the extremity of the pass, and halted in the jungle at the foot of the hill leading to Dewangiri. Here, the main body of the force, consisting of the Battery of Royal Artillery, head-quarters of the 55th Regiment, the 12th, 29th, and 44th Native Infantry, also part of the 43rd, arrived in the course of the evening.

The following morning at seven o'clock, the troops

advanced up the hill towards Dewangiri, the Bhotanese position now consisting of a centre stockade flanked by one on each side, distant respectively from the centre one 120 and 250 yards—the latter being on the right. A company of the 55th, in skirmishing order, covered the advance. The artillery were now got into position at a range of about 600 yards, the howitzers on the right and the mortars on the left. After a few rounds, the guns were advanced nearer and fire reopened. Shortly afterwards a third advance was made, which brought the guns to within 300 yards of the centre stockade. The ground was not at all suited for artillery, and but little damage appeared to be done by the fire. The skirmishers of the 55th now crept up the spur of the hill to within a hundred yards of the stockade and fired at the loopholes.

The fire from the stockades having been pretty well silenced, orders were given for the storming parties of native troops to advance. One party attempted to storm the stockade on the right but was driven off. Another party advanced against the centre stockade, and, on getting up to it, found it difficult of entrance, and the following officers showed the men the way in by climbing over the works, namely, Captain Trevor and Lieutenant Dundas, Royal Engineers, and Lieutenant Griffiths, 43rd Native Infantry. The Bhotanese inside the stockade by this time appeared to have become panic stricken, and made no resistance. The native troops now poured into the stockade, and an indiscriminate slaughter of its inmates commenced; in which, the storming party that had been discomfited on the right, joined. The British officers did what they could to arrest the wholesale butchery going on, but their efforts were not attended with much success; as nearly the whole of the Bhotanese within the stockade, about 120 in number, were put to death: many of those who were lying on the ground wounded, being included in the massacre. The troops who behaved in this merciless manner were Seiks and Pathans. Their conduct on this occasion was not exceptional—it is their character when ever they get an opportunity of so dealing with a beaten foe. To them the word "quarter" is unknown, and it appears to me questionable how far it is consistent with advancing civilization to employ at work of this kind a class of ruthless auxiliaries, whose thirst for blood military discipline would seem to be unequal to controlling. Very different is represented to have been the conduct of the men of the 55th Regiment, to such of the wounded, as escaped the bayonets of the native soldiery. They were seen supplying them with water, and doing what they could to relieve their sufferings by placing them in more comfortable positions.

The Bhotanese in the two other stockades, seeing that the centre one, which was the key of their position, had fallen, evacuated them and made their escape—such was the recapture of Dewangiri, the casualties on our side being trifling. One officer, (Mr. Weldon, of the police) being shot in the groin, and three officers struck on their heads with stones, namely, Captain Trevor and Lieutenant Dundas, R. E., and Ensign Chatterton, 29th Punjaubees. The other casualties were confined to the native troops, and amounted to about thirty in all.

The company of skirmishers of the 55th, which

was the only portion of the regiment engaged, did very good service, and their fire is represented as having been more effective against the central stockade than that of the artillery was—that is to say, that its effect was greater on those inside. The battery of Royal Artillery was present but hardly engaged—the firing having been chiefly carried on by the Eurasian gunners. The non-effectiveness of their fire was attributed to the very bad ground on which the guns were placed, and for which there was no remedy.

Dewangiri being thus retaken, and the prestige of the British name restored in this part of the world, it was decided that as the place was untenable during the rains, it should be at once evacuated, and the buildings destroyed. The European troops got the route for Calcutta the following day, and the work of destruction having been completed by the 6th of April, all the troops were withdrawn and the place abandoned. Such having been the result of the re-capture, the query naturally suggests itself as to whether it would not have been the better course to have deferred making any fresh movement against the place until after the rainy season, when it would have been practicable for six months to have kept up communication with it, and to have furnished it with adequate supplies in the event of its being decided to keep a garrison there. Whatever may be ultimately done in reference to this hill post, it is clear that the position originally taken up is an objectionable one; owing to the water supply being completely at the command of the Bhotanese, and in the event of its future occupation, it will be necessary to advance a mile and a half further into the country, and select such a position as will secure the water being cut off as it was in February 1865.

The operations in the Dooars and the adjoining hills being now completed as far as it was practicable to do anything more than act on the defensive until the ensuing year—should it then be the intention to prosecute hostilities further—Brigadier-General Tombs returned to his command at Gwalior, and the two brigades of the Dooar Field Force were consolidated into one, under Brigadier-General Frazer Tytler; Gowhatty being fixed as the headquarters.

On the termination of active operations, the following became the distribution of the force, commencing from the eastern or Lower Assam side.

TEZPORE. Wing and headquarters of the 12th Bengal Native Infantry.

KOOMREKATTA. Two companies 44th Assam Light Infantry; Troop 14th Bengal Cavalry.

RUNGEAR. Headquarters 29th Punjaub Infantry, headquarters 14th Bengal Cavalry, headquarters 44th Assam Light Infantry.

GOWHATTY. Left Wing 12th Native Infantry, 43rd Assam Light Infantry, the Eurasian Battery of Artillery.

DUTMAH. Left Wing 44th Assam Light Infantry, Squadron of the 14th Bengal Cavalry.

In addition to the above, which constituted the distribution of the field force in the Assam Dooars—The 42nd Assam Light Infantry and Local Artillery were stationed at Debroghur and neighbouring posts in Upper Assam, to the eastward of the Bhotan frontier.

BUXA. One division (two guns) Armstrong Battery (6–25, R.A); one division 5th Battery 25th Brigade, Royal Artillery, the 3rd Ghoorkha Regiment, and three companies of the 30th Punjaub Infantry.

BALLA. The 19th Punjaub Infantry.

PUTLA KOWA (in the Dooars). Detachment of Sappers and the 11th Native Infantry.

CHAMOORCHEE. One Company of the 30th Punjaubees, and Bengal Police Battalion.

DHALIMKOTE. One Division of the Armstrong Battery, and one of the 5–25th Royal Artillery; Wing 30th Punjaub Infantry, and company of Sebundy Sappers.

JULPESH (in the Dooars). Headquarters 5–25, and 6–25 Royal Artillery, 5th Bengal Cavalry, and 31st Punjaub Infantry.

DARJEELING. 7th Battery 22nd Brigade Royal Artillery; Detachment Sebundy Sappers, the 80th Regiment, and two companies of the 17th Native Infantry.*

* The following changes in the distribution of the force as here given occurred in the course of the ensuing month (May). The 29th and 30th Punjaubees were withdrawn from the Dooars. A Wing of the 31st went to Dhalimkote, and the head-quarters of the two batteries of artillery at Julpesh were removed to Darjeeling. Chamoorchee also ceased to be occupied by a British force, and was placed in charge of some native troops belonging to the Raja of Cooch Behar.

CHAPTER XVII.

General Tytler visits Darjeeling—Tea Planting and Mode of preparing the Tea in the Sikim Himalayas—View from the 80th's Mess-House—Change in the Weather and coincident appearance of Ague—Proofs of the Atmospheric Origin of the outbreak of the Disease—Goitre in the Himalayas, and its Cure—Lepcha propitiatory Sacrifice—A Native Group—Cholera appears in the Dooars—Removal of the Royal Artillery to Darjeeling.

ON the 6th of April, Brigadier-General Tytler visited Darjeeling and inspected the mode of location of the troops. The arrangements for the accommodation of the 80th Regiment were now complete; private houses for five companies had been found in Darjeeling, and for two companies on the slope of Julla Pahar, near the Convalescent Depot (occupied by artillery and about fifty invalids). Senchal supplied quarters for the three remaining companies, also for the women and children: those left behind at Dum Dum having arrived the previous day. Two days afterwards the Wing from Julpigorie rejoined headquarters, and all the married men were sent up to Senchal; there being no means of accommodating families in the temporary quarters taken up lower down.

At this period (8th April) through the kindness of Mr. Crossman, Manager of the Darjeeling property belonging to the well known Mr. David Wilson of Calcutta, I had an opportunity of visiting the tea plantation belonging to the latter, which is situated on the slopes underneath the collection of houses at the northern end of Darjeeling Station, known as "Wilson's Bustee."* The plantation ranges over an altitude varying from two to four thousand feet, and we descended through it to a distance of about four miles below Darjeeling, as far as a ravine with a mountain-stream flowing through it, near which red coloured monkeys were seen sporting about in the trees. The plantation was not at the time productive; an interval of three years being required in British Sikim, from the period of sowing the seed until the bushes are fit for plucking. The soil of this plantation was light and stony, very similar to that in which the vine grows with great luxuriance in Western Australia.

At Darjeeling and vicinity, the tea seed is sown about the beginning of the year, each seed being placed in the ground about two inches apart. The young plant is not interfered with for about eighteen months. It is then transplanted at the commencement of the rainy season, in June; being placed in a hole two feet deep, having a clear space of four feet on each side. This hole, in the first instance, is only half filled with earth; the remainder being filled in as the plant gradually becomes rooted.

While moisture is indispensable for the growth of the tea-plant, it is also necessary for its well-doing that water should not remain for any length of time in contact with it. Hill-land, as being antagonistic to this occurring, is thus so far favourable to tea-planting, but elevation appears to be a matter of much importance, and the candid opinion of a considerable

* "Bustee" is the Hindoostanee name for "village," or collection of houses.

portion of the tea-growing community in British Sikim is, that the attempt has hitherto been made at so great an elevation as to render the ultimate success of the existing plantations very doubtful. Large sums of money have unquestionably been made in connection with tea speculation in the Darjeeling district, but not as the produce of tea-growing, but of land-jobbing, and the formation of tea-growing Companies, promising handsome dividends—the realisation of which, however, has not, as far as I have been able to learn, yet commenced.

Two kinds of tea are grown in the Darjeeling plantations, the one from China seed, the other from the seed of the tea-plant that is indigenous to Assam. The former is more bushy in shape, and throws its branches out nearer to the ground. It attains a height of from six to eight feet. The latter is longer in the stem, and grows to much greater height; being in shape not unlike a small poplar tree.

The operation of picking the leaves commences in the third year, and is carried on from April to October. The labourers, who for the most part are Nepaulese, pick from six to sixteen pounds of leaves daily, according to the size and productiveness of the ground. Four pounds of the soft young leaves usually yield one pound of manufactured tea. The amount yielded per acre of course varies according to the age of the plantation, but it may be stated as averaging from one to four maunds—in other words from 80 to 320 pounds.

The following account of the process adopted of preparing black tea is given by Captain Hathorn—"In large plantations there is generally a spacious brick building erected on purpose for the manufacture. In small plantations, such as we advocate, as soon as 100 acres are under cultivation, a factory, 160 feet by 45, of ruder structure would probably suffice. Furnaces built of ordinary, or we believe sometimes of cutcha (unburned) bricks must be erected at one end, with a chimney to carry off the smoke. Over brisk wood fires in the furnace are placed iron pans with two handles, such as are used by the native sweetmeat sellers in the bazaars in the plains. They are made of cast iron ⅜-inch thick. Two or more strong tables, like English kitchen tables, are also required in the factory, These are generally covered with fine bamboo matting.

"The young leaves of the tea-plant having been picked in the afternoon, the manufacture begins the following morning. They are left all night in the factory spread out on round trays made of flat strips of bamboo. In the morning the trays, which are about three feet in diameter, are placed on a muchan, or platform, of bamboos in the sun. On each tray are spread about three seers (six pounds) of leaves, forming a thin layer, half an inch over the entire surface of the tray. In about two hours, when the leaves are limp, they are brought into the factory and placed on sieves, made of narrow slips of bamboo. Basket-work frames, three feet high, something like immense dice-boxes with the bottoms out, are then ranged along the floor, in the centre of each of which is placed an iron vessel of red hot charcoal. The sieves, covered thinly with leaves, are then placed in the upper part of the basket-work, and the leaves thus warmed and 'withered' as it is called. They are then thrown upon the bamboo matting on the table, spread out and well beaten with the palm of the hand. They are tossed about a little, and again beaten once or twice. The men then take, each as many leaves as can be held easily in two hands, squeeze them up into a ball, and roll and pass it about on the table, taking it to pieces and again rolling it about until the leaves are considerably crushed and twisted. The mass is by this time very damp from the crushing out of the moisture of the leaves. This may be considered the end of the first process. The crushed and half-rolled leaves are then put into small deep bamboo baskets, which are closed up and kept in the sun or other warm place for two hours.

"The next or second process is the roasting. The furnaces are made so hot that the hand cannot touch the pans. The precise heat must be gathered by experience. Two or three seers of the crushed and half-rolled leaves are then thrown into the pan. They are instantly tossed about the pan by two men, each of whom has a stick in each hand, with two prongs like a pitchfork. These men keep the leaves in constant motion, not a leaf being allowed to remain many seconds unmoved. After five minutes roasting, at a signal the leaves are suddenly swept out of the pan and thrown out of the matting on to the table, and rolled again finally for about a quarter of an hour. They are then spread out exceedingly thinly on the bamboo trays in the sun for another two hours. This concludes the roasting process.

"The third and last, or drying process, now begins. This is a sort of repetition of the withering process. The leaves are spread out thinly on open bamboo sieve trays, which are placed again over clear charcoal fires in the basket-work frames before mentioned. The leaves are some two feet or more above the fires, and are very carefully dried. The sieves are taken off once or twice, the leaves mixed and moved about gently with the hand, and then again placed over the red hot charcoal until the leaves are perfectly dry, crisp, and brittle. The tea is then ready, and should be nearly black in colour. The different names of Pekoe, Pouchong, Souchong, Congou, &c. are applied to the same teas, and merely distinguish those that pass through sieves of a certain finenesss. Still, as the younger and smaller leaves make the best tea, and these also will, as a general rule, pass through the finer sieves, there is a real difference in flavour between the finer and coarser teas."

In the preparation of green tea, which is made from the same plant, the only difference is that the leaves are thrown at once into the roasting-pan without being withered, beaten, or rolled. After it has undergone the roasting process the remaining operations are the same as for making black tea.

On the 15th of April, a house overlooking the villlage of Leebong, immediately above the residence of Cheeboo Lama, was taken into occupation by the officers of the 80th, as a mess-house. From the front of it four countries were distinctly seen, namely, Nepaul, Sikim, Bhotan, and Thibet—in clear weather the snowy range towering in the distance from east to west as far as the eye could reach: the lofty snowclad peak of Kenchinjunga overlooking the whole.

At this period, the weather, which, since our arrival, had been usually fine and clear, now became damp and foggy. Coincident with this atmospheric change, the health of the soldiers underwent a marked deterioration. Since leaving Calcutta, little or no sickness had occurred, with the exception of what took place on the march—now however the men began to suffer in considerable numbers from the forms of periodic fever, chiefly ague, which it has been the custom heretofore to identify with exposure to marsh malaria. Now, in the instance in question, the men were as far removed from such an influence as it was practicable for them to be: clearly showing that whatever part residence in malarious districts may play in conferring a predisposition to fever, what is ordinarily called malaria, is not the actual exciting cause of ague fits. The fact, as here observed, was by no means novel to me, it was only confirmatory of what I have several times noticed before. At the time in question, ague became more prevalent in the regiment than it had been for three years previously, notwithstanding that the stations it had been in were of the nature much more likely than Darjeeling to give origin to active malarious disease.

It must not be supposed that there was anything connected with the circumstances under which the soldiers were either placed at the time, or had been shortly before, which rendered them exceptionally susceptible of the atmospheric influence at the time prevailing; because the civil community were similarly affected. The morbific agent, therefore, was purely atmospheric, and altogether unconnected with local causes such as those that modern sanitarians endeavour to identify almost every deviation from health with, that suffering humanity is heir to.

On inspecting the detachment at Senchal, I found

the same prevalence of ague existing there, notwithstanding that the station is nearly 1,500 feet higher than that of Darjeeling. On the 21st of April there was an improvement in the weather; the fogs disappeared, as did also the showery tendency which had accompanied them. With this change, there was a corresponding disappearance of ague. On the 24th of the month, however, the fog returned, and with it the disease became as prevalent as formerly. No abatement took place until the weather again became fine, which was not for some twelve days afterwards, and then its disappearance was complete: to my mind, demonstrating the very important part played by the nervous system, as subordinate to altered states of the atmospheric electricity, in the causation of trains of symptoms presenting no cognisable difference from those commonly attributed to specific emanations from marshy soil and rank vegetation.

While thus alluding to atmospheric influences, I may mention that one of the diseases that the natives of the hills about Darjeeling are subject to, is the unsightly enlargement of the throat, so common in Switzerland, under the name of goitre. The remedy which has proved of the greatest service in causing its removal is an ointment composed of fifteen grains of the bin-iodide of mercury and one ounce of lard. This is smeared over the goitre and its efficacy appears to be much increased if the part is exposed immediately afterwards to the sun. Dr. Simpson, the civil surgeon of the station, tells me that the curative effects of this external application are very striking.

Altitude appears to confer no immunity from

cholera; as it was but in 1864 that Darjeeling was severely visited by it, and, strange to say, the part of the settlement where its effects were most lightly felt, was in its dirtiest portion, namely, the native bazaar.

On the 25th of April, while looking at "Rockville," one of the houses in occupation by the 80th Regiment, Captain Wilkinson pointed out to me a rude altar amongst a clump of trees near it, on which a few days previously he had seen several male Lepchas performing a sacrifice in the following manner. Fires were lit on the altar, which consisted of a few stones placed on a hillock. A kid was tethered near the altar, and was quietly grazing. Some fatty substance was thrown on the fires, the fumes of which rose into the air. One of the men, apparently a priest, was muttering prayers over the fire, and scattering rice about—near the altar, another priest was sitting near a larger fire. The former having ceased throwing the rice about, took an egg, broke it, and caught the yolk on a leaf. He then carefully examined it, and apparently endeavoured to decipher some meaning from its appearance. It was then handed to the priest at the other fire, who cooked it. The kid was now brought near the altar, and the priest seized it, cut its throat and then severed the head, sprinkling the blood over the altar. More prayers were now said, and the ceremony concluded by the liver of the kid being cooked at the larger fire in the same manner as the egg was. No women were present, and the Lepchas said that the object of the sacrifice was to propitiate; in consequence of sickness being prevalent in the village—most likely an outbreak of fever similar to that at the time prevailing amongst the troops and civilians of the station, and which it is probable was occasioning considerable alarm; owing to a bad form of fever having been common amongst them the previous year. Though the climate of Darjeeling is no doubt a great improvement on that of the plains of Bengal, the facts nevertheless to which reference have lately been made, tend to show that it is by no means a perfect one.

Two mornings after the sacrificial ceremony was mentioned to me, I happened to pass the Chow Rusta as an unusually large group of natives were standing in conversation, and interrogated them as to their nationalities. The most of them were either Dhurma, Sikim, or Nepaul Bhoteahs, a few were Paharees. Two denied belonging to any of these tribes, but said "Bot," adding in Hindoostanee, "Cheen Ka Mullick;" meaning that they were Bhoteahs of the country of China, *i. e.* Thibetians. In this group there were no Lepchas, according to the native rendering of the word; though, with the exception of the Paharees and the Thibetians, the whole were Lepchas, according to the undefined way in which the word is ordinarily useed by us.

On the 29th of April, cholera appeared amongst the European artillerymen stationed at Julpesh in the Dooars, where a cantonment had recently been established as a substitute for that which had previously existed at Julpigorie, and also to act as a support, if necessary, for the garrison holding Dhalimkote. General Tytler immediately telegraphed to Darjeeling for additional medical aid, and also to know if it would be practicable to find accommodation there for the men in question; namely, the headquarters of the Armstrong, and the Mountain Train Batteries. A reply was sent to the effect that it was impracticable to find quarters for them either at Darjeeling or Senchal, but that the accommodation required could be provided in the roadside barracks at Pacheem, or Kursiong—the latter being recommended as the preferable. The artillerymen were accordingly moved at once from Julpesh, and a few days afterwards arrived at Kursiong. New military stations in connection with the annexation of the Dooars appear to be a dangerous experiment, inasmuch as the one further east, called Putla Kowa, which stands in the same relation to Balla and Buxa that Julpesh does to Dhalimkote and Chamoorchee, was about the same time severely visited by cholera, and also became generally unhealthy.*

* Since the above was written, the following remarks, having reference to Putla Kowa, have come under my notice. In the "Calcutta Englishman" of the 9th August 1865, it is stated—"The accounts from Pulta Kowa are sad indeed. Another poor officer—Knatchbull of the 11th—has died; making the fourth officer the corps has lost by death in a few weeks. Seven officers have been sent away sick. There is, I believe, only one officer now left with the regiment. . . . It cannot, I hear, turn out, fit for duty, twenty-five men, irrespective of guards. The squadron of the 5th Bengal Cavalry can hardly turn out a duffadar's (troop sergeant's) party. At Putla Kowa, there are now only five officers left, including staff, cavalry, and infantry. The Calcutta correspondent of the "Times," again, writing under date 8th October following, states—"Scurvy has been laying low the force on the Bhotan frontier; more than half have been affected, and nearly all have been tainted. . . . The almost extinct 11th Native Infantry has been sent to the plains, and that pest house Putla Kowa has been abandoned." The outbreak of scurvy, here referred to, appears to be attributed to defective dieting of the native troops, but I may observe, when I was surgeon of the 31st Regiment in China, a number of cases of scorbutic dysentery, as well as several well marked cases of ordinary scurvy, occurred in that corps, under circumstances where the soldier's diet was open to no objection whatever; fresh meat having been issued daily, and the supply of vegetables, including excellent potatoes, abundant. I could account for it in no other way than by referring it to the depressing influence of malaria, which was very prevalent at the place (Fa-wah near Shanghai), where the most marked cases of scurvy occurred.

CHAPTER XVIII.

The Chota Bursawt—A Thibetian Trader—Prepare to visit Dhalimkote—Interview with Cheeboo Lama—His Character—He undertakes to make arrangements for our Party crossing the Teesta—His Views on the Language and Country of the Lepchas—Lama Priests—The Kowtow, a Custom in the Himalayas—Cheeboo's News from Bhotan—Suicide of an Artilleryman at Julla Pahar.

THE month of May at Darjeeling opened with a continuation of the rains which had been more or less prevalent for the previous fortnight; constituting what are called the "Chota Bursawt," or little rains, in contradistinction to the "Burra Bursawt," or great rains, which commence about June and terminate in the end of September.

During an interval of fine weather on the 4th of May, as I was passing through the bazaar, I observed a man standing amongst the crowd having a remarkably Chinese look about him. His headdress was the felt hat, the pattern being one that is a favourite with the peasants in the north of China; namely, fawn colour, with a black border round the margin of the turned-up part. Over a robe of reddish brown woollen material he wore a Tartar-looking overcoat, made waistcoat fashion, without sleeves. The buttons were the small, round, embossed, brass ones, common to all Chinese dresses. The front part of his head was cleanly shaved, and his tail was as neatly plaited as if it had been done in the celestial capital. His purse was suspended from his girdle—also a case, similar to that in which the Chinese carry their chop-sticks. It contained however only a knife. He wore loose Tartar trousers, stuck into a sort of half-gaiter, half-boot, coming up to the knee, and made of woollen fabric like his under robe, but ornamented with variegated stripes. The shoes were attached to the leggings, and were of the same shape and make as those of the Chinese. I asked him what his country was, he answered "Cheen Ka Bot." As to the part of Thibet he came from, I could not make out, but judging from his resemblance to the traders I saw at Carragola, the probabilities are that he was from the Kampa district, which appears to be a geographical distinction not recognised in European maps.

Early in May a party of officers of the 80th Regiment, of which I was one, obtained ten days' leave of absence, to take a ramble amongst the neighbouring hills, and decided on visiting the fort of Dhalimkote—distant from Darjeeling between sixty and seventy miles. The route we determined to take was that followed by Mr. Eden's mission, namely, across the Bhotan Mountains, on the left bank of the Teesta. We were ready to start on the 6th of May, and had coolies engaged to carry provisions, bedding, &c. The previous evening however I received information from Dr. Simpson (who had been the route with Mr. Eden) that the cane bridge over the Teesta at Pushok had been carried away two days before by the torrent, and that it would be impossible to get across the river until either a new bridge was constructed or a bamboo raft got into operation. Dr. Simpson kindly offered to go with me the following day to Cheeboo Lama, and ascertain from him the actual state of matters, at the

Teesta; as he had always good information; having property in the neighbourhood.

With the break of day on the 6th of May heavy and steady rain set in. Some of the coolies we had engaged made their appearance at the mess-house, which had been fixed as the rendezvous. In a short time they showed an indisposition to remain, and went off to their homes, evidently having made up their minds not to undertake the journey until the weather cleared up.

It rained steadily until noon, and during a slight break in the weather I went with Dr. Simpson to Cheeboo Lama's house, the position of which overlooking the village of Leebong has already been described. Cheeboo's style of living is not strictly ambassadorial. The house, which is a small single-storied one, built in the European style, was dirty and devoid of furniture, with the exception of a few shelves, a cupboard, and two old arm-chairs. Cheeboo received us cordially, and handed us the chairs, he himself taking a seat on his bed; a sort of couch raised about a foot from the ground, and, like Cheeboo's own attire, very dirty and greasy-looking. In plain terms Cheeboo looked an old gentleman with whom water was on the most distant of terms. His appearance was particularly Mongolian, with the exception, that though wearing the tail, the front of the head was unshorn; also that he allowed his whiskers, such as they were, to grow, in place of adopting the close shaving of the cheeks universal in China. He wore a very dirty, greasy, yellow silk robe, without sleeves, over an inner robe of woollen material. On his head he had the yellow silk pork-pie hat, turned up with velvet, already described as worn by the Mongolian Lepchas.

Cheeboo, though a priest, has been allowed to marry, in consideration of his being diplomatically employed. He was educated at Lassa, and is reputed to be a very clear-headed, intelligent man. One way and another he has made himself so useful to the British Government that he has been presented by it with an extensive and valuable tract of land within our territory—the whole of a spur, in fact, of one of the mountains. This land he could readily convert into a large sum of money by selling it to Europeans engaged in tea company speculations. He prefers however, in accordance with the custom of his country, to sub-let it to peasants for agricultural purposes, rather than adopting the more directly lucrative course.

On Dr. Simpson stating in Hindoostanee to Cheeboo, the circumstance of a party of officers being anxious to go to Dhalimkote, but that the bridge at the Teesta having been carried away was an obstacle to their so doing, he at once undertook to make arrangements for getting the party across the river, and brought out a roll of paper, native made, from the daphne, on which he wrote a letter to some friends near the ferry at Pushok, requesting them to have a raft constructed at once, and men in attendance to work it within three days of the date of his letter, which was about the time he calculated the weather would allow the party to start; there being then a change in the moon, until which took place, he prognosticated a continuance of rain, and on this point he proved quite correct. He wrote his letter from right to left in the Thibetian character, which is an alphabetical one, and judging from the rapidity with which he wrote he seemed to be a thorough master of the pen.

Interrogating him with reference to the Mongolian Lepchas, of which he is one, he stated that they have a language and writing of their own, quite different from that of the Thibetian, and which was given them by a former Sikim Raja. He gave us an illustration of the writing in his own hand, and stated that the Lepcha language does not contain a single word of Thibetian—a statement which, at a future page, I shall show very good grounds exist for doubting the strict accuracy of.

With reference to the origin of the Lepchas (Mongol) Cheeboo's opinion is that they have always existed where they are now found—in other words that they are the aborigines of Sikim, which, according to him, was once a much larger country than it now is ; a considerable portion of it having been taken by the Bhotanese on the one side and the Nepaulese on the other. He, however, volunteered the information that the Lepchas in question are particularly numerous at the Donkia Pass, one of the communications with Thibet—which appears to me to support the view I have expressed with reference to their having originally come from the latter direction.

Mentioning to Cheeboo that I had been in Peking, and was familiar with the appearance of the Lama priests there, whose attire was somewhat similar to that worn by him, I asked what relation they stood in to the sect of Lama Buddhists, to which he belonged? He said they were the same, any distinction between them being merely provincial.

Cheeboo sent for one of his servants to take the

letter he had written down to the Teesta, and on the man (a Mongol Lepcha) coming into the room he prostrated himself before Cheeboo, and went through an obeisance in exactly the same manner as the Kowtow is performed in China.

In reply to a query from Dr. Simpson as to what news he had had lately from Bhotan, he said that he had no knowledge as to what the feeling was in the eastern division of the country about the war, but that he was certain on the western side they were tired of it, and would be glad to bring matters to a peaceful issue if practicable. At first he said they were very bold and confident of success, and laughed at the idea of troops, clothed as ours are, being able to cope successfully with those partially clad in armour, as it appears the Bhotanese of the fighting class, to a certain extent, are. Now, however, he said, their opinion was entirely changed, as they had come to the conclusion that it was no use killing our people, because the more they killed the faster the others came on: a mode of warfare which they neither understood, nor considered altogether fair—the more so, as we encourage our men to do this by the sound of bugles at times, when, in accordance with Bhotanese notions of warfare, it was our duty to retire defeated; consequent on the occurrence of a few casualties. Under these circumstances, in the command at least of the Paro Penlow, the opinion was then prevailing that the time had come for ending war conducted in such an unreasonable manner.

On our rising to take our leave, Cheeboo got up, shook hands with us, and conducted us to the outside of his dwelling with that natural politeness, which, as a general rule, is one of the prominent characteristics of the Chinese as a people.

The same day as this interview with Cheeboo Lama occurred, a determined suicide was committed by a gunner of the Battery of Artillery at Julla Pahar. The man had purchased his discharge, and was waiting for the necessary formalities connected with it being completed. For a few days previously he had been noticed to be in low spirits, and early on the morning of the 6th May he got up, loaded his carbine, went out into the verandah, and discharged it against his chest. The wound proved fatal a few hours afterwards. No reason could be assigned for the act, and it is quite possible that the thick and foggy weather which was then—and had been for some time prevailing, may have had some share in developing the morbid condition of the mental faculty under which he was at the time, no doubt, labouring.

CHAPTER XIX.

Start for Dhalimkote—Our Coolie Transport—First Halt—State of the Road at the Rungeet after the Rains—Saul Wood—Arrival at the Teesta—Mode of crossing on a Bamboo Raft—Construction of the Houses of the Bhotan Peasantry—Country, Cultivation and Cattle at Kalimpoong—Annoyance from Leeches on the March—Wild Fruit—Buckwheat—A Monastery and Lama Priests—Butter Tea—Murwa—The Mystic Sentence of Thibet—Nature of the Country as we proceed—Paiongpoong—Scenes in Domestic Life in Bhotan—Mode of preparing Grain for Murwa—Effects of the latter on the "Laughing Pup."

On the 8th of May there was a sign of improvement in the weather, and having Cheeboo's assurance that with the change of the moon an interval of fine weather might be expected, we made up our minds to start for Dhalimkote that afternoon, provided coolies could be got together in time—procuring their services just as they are wanted, not being a very easy matter at Darjeeling, labour being so much in demand. After some little trouble two men were found who undertook to go with us themselves, and also to find the required number of coolies; making their own terms, however, in the first instance, which were eight rupees for the journey, paid in advance. These men were the representatives of two headmen of coolies, called Fool Sing and Gay Long—the one was a Sikim, the other a Dhurma Bhoteah. The name of the former was Kif-yu-Gulla, which translated into English, means "the Laughing Pup." He knew the road to Dhalimkote, having been there before, and agreed to act as guide and headman of the coolies on the journey. The number of coolies required was seven,—three to carry food and cooking utensils, while each of the party had one to carry bedding and change of clothing. Each coolie's load was limited by Kif-yu-Gulla to half a maund, which he said was as much as they could carry up steep ascents, and keep pace with the party at the rate we proposed to perform the journey, namely, three days from leaving Darjeeling.

This having been agreed to, the party, consisting of Major Miller, Captain Sullivan, Lieutenant Howard and myself, mustered at the mess-house at three o'clock in the afternoon, and found the "Laughing Pup" there, with Gay Long's representative and six other coolies. Their loads having been proportioned and secured on to the carrying apparatus, the next matter to be adjusted was paying each coolie, including the Kif Yu Gulla as guide, eight rupees, without which not one of them would start. This having been done they shouldered their loads and went on, accompanied by three Indian servants; namely, a Madras man, an up-country Mussulman, and a Bheastie, or water-carrier. Mr. Thomas Masson, the son of an old resident of Darjeeling, also formed one of our party, and was to overtake us the following day at the Rungeet.

Having allowed the coolies about a half an hour's start, we followed them towards the Rungeet, by the route through the village of Leebong which has been already described, and overtook them before they reached the place we had arranged to halt at for the night; namely, on the brow of a hill about 800 feet above the Rungeet, and overlooking it, where some hut barracks have been constructed, to which the detachments of the 17th Native Infantry at the Rungeet and the Teesta had been withdrawn, in consequence of the great heat and unhealthiness of the river posts. Here we rested for the night, and were hospitably entertained by Lieutenants Barlow and Dawes; whose detachments were now consolidated: 25 per cent. of the men being at the time laid up with fever.

It rained heavily all night, but cleared up towards morning, and at half-past six we continued our journey, reaching the bank of the Rungeet a few minutes before seven. Here we were joined by Mr. Masson, whose knowledge of the Bhotanese dialect proved of great service to us. The river was at this time much swollen, and the heavy rains had so damaged the road lately made on its bank, that it was almost impassable at several places—so much so that Messrs. Howard and Masson, who had brought ponies with them, had to send them back.

At several places on the bank of the Rungeet, we found natives employed felling saul trees, and cutting them up into sizes suited for railway sleepers; the experiment being about to be tried of floating this wood down the Teesta to the plains, supported on bamboo rafts: its weight being so great that unsupported by some buoyant material, it sinks in water. The local impression appears to be, that owing to the difficulties certain to be encountered connected with floating it down, it is likely to prove a costly experiment in search of an economical result.

At ten A.M. we reached the remains of the cane suspension bridge over the Teesta, at Pushok, and here we found about a dozen of Lepchas busy constructing a new one. Already several lines of cane creepers had been carried from one bank to the other, and formed the superstructure of the bridge from which the foot portion was about to be suspended. We also found that a light raft had been prepared formed of a few poles of bamboo lashed together in the shape of an acute-angled triangle. The current was running down very strong, and the Lepchas who were waiting to manage the raft, told us that only one of our party could be taken over at a time.

The mode of working the raft from one bank to the other of this deep and rapid river is simple, at the same time ingenious and effective. Two ropes made of cane creepers knotted together, each one about three hundred feet in length, are secured by one end to the bow, or acute angle of the raft; the other ends being respectively on the Sikim and the Bhotan banks of the river, in the hands of the ferrymen. The person who is under conveyance across, sits on a piece of bamboo work, forming a kind of stern seat placed about the middle third of the raft. His limbs are immersed in the river about half way to the knees, and the feet rest on three longitudinal poles forming the bottom of the raft. One of the ferrymen then gets on a part of the raft behind where the passenger is sitting, for the purpose of balancing it, to do which properly, some skill and experience is necessary, judging from what occurred in the course of our crossing. The passenger having steadied himself by grasping the longitudinal bamboo above water on each side, the men managing the rope on the bank where the raft at the time is, slack it slowly off, and the current immediately takes the raft with it. The down stream progress, however, is steadily counteracted by the ferryman in charge of the rope on the opposite bank;

who, by applying traction, bring the raft out into mid-stream, with its sharp angle meeting the current. Thus, from its wedge shape, the raft is easily worked against it and gradually drawn over to the opposite bank. In the same manner it is got back again to the side it started from.

I was the first that crossed, happening to be nearest the raft at the time it was ready to start. Major Miller crossed next, getting over as I did without mishap. Mr. Masson followed, then Captain Sullivan. By the time the latter crossed, the cane-rope on the Sikim side had got rubbed a good deal against a large boulder, which formed a kind of pier from which we got on to the raft, and snapped as Captain Sullivan was in the middle of the river; an unusually great strain having been put upon it, consequent on the balance of the raft having been in some way upset by the ‘ Laughing Pup,” (Kif Yu Gulla) who crossed at the same time, and had failed correctly to carry out the instructions given him by the ferrymen. The raft was consequently swept rapidly down the current. No accident however occurred, owing to the Bhotan rope maintaining its integrity, and the skilful way in which the natives managed it. About an hour and a half was occupied getting the party across, and no other mishap occurred.

We now commenced the ascent of the Bhotan mountains, and most fatiguing it proved; owing to the heat, the absence of anything like a road, and the extreme steepness of the narrow footpath we had to follow through the forest jungle. About two o'clock we reached a few huts constituting the hamlet of Kalimpoong at an elevation of between three and four thousand feet. The huts were supported on piles about four feet from the ground; the flooring being formed of roughly-hewn planks, and their walls of matting spread upon a framework of bamboo. The roofs were thatched. The huts contained no furniture, with the exception of a series of bamboo shelves suspended in three tiers from the roof. The first, or lower one, being used for smoking

BHOTANESE HUT, WITH LAMA MONASTERY ON THE HIGH GROUND.

meat on; the second, for the winter store of wood; and the third, as a general receptacle for domestic articles not in immediate use, such as baskets, earthen vessels, &c. The fireplace is an open hearth in the centre of the room, formed of clay and raised about three inches above the floor. The cooking utensils appear to be sometimes placed on a rude tripod formed of three stones, sometimes suspended over the fire. Wood is the only fuel used. The population of the hamlet consisted of two or three families looking very dirty and smoky. They were civil, but did not seem to be anxious to be on intimate terms with us, and kept as much aloof as possible. They declined to sell us fowls or eggs, but allowed us to occupy one of the houses, which was empty, as a dormitory for the night.

Towards sundown the cows belonging to the hamlet, eight in number, came home; having been loose in the jungle since the morning. Each one, prior to being milked, was tethered to a bamboo stake, by a rope passed round its horns, and thus secured for the night. They were then milked into bamboo tubes. These cows were the finest I have seen in the East, and closely resembled English ones.

The mountain slope about Kalimpoong is partially cleared, and a few plantain trees were growing near the huts. The soil is a rich black loam, capable of being rendered very productive. The only crop we saw, was a little rice, growing in small isolated patches. The peasantry differed in no perceptible way in appearance from those we had been accustomed to see on the opposite bank of the Teesta.

After the coolies had had their food, Kif Yu Gulla went off to a neighbouring hamlet in search of liquor; having been unable to get any where we halted. The Lepchas, it seems, are all more or less given to drinking—constituting another point of resemblance between them and the Mongolians. Their favourite liquor is a form of spirituous beer, made from the millet, and known amongst themselves as *che.* The Bhotanese also drink it, but not to the same extent, I am told, as the Lepchas do: tea being the principal beverage used by them—at the same time they are by no means free from habits of intemperance.

Having passed a somewhat uncomfortable night, consequent on the interest taken in us by the insect life with which the hut was exuberant, we started at a quarter to six on the morning of the 10th, and continuing to ascend, in a short time came to a deep nullah (small ravine) with a rivulet flowing through it. Crossing this, we turned due north by a narrow winding pathway, and passed through a considerable tract of light jungle, admitting of being readily cleared by burning. The ascent now became more gradual, and by seven o'clock we seemed to have reached the top of the hill, which, the previous day, we commenced to ascend immediately on crossing the Teesta. The ground at this part was undulating and covered with dense jungle of bamboo trees, wormwood, and ferns—a few good-sized trees appearing at intervals amongst it. The soil continued of the same rich dark character, and here and there small patches were cleared for rice cultivation. The kind of rice grown in the hills, I may remark, is of a more flat shape than that of the plains.

We now commenced to experience one of the disagreeables of Himalayan marshes, namely leeches. The paths hereabouts were swarming with them, and, notwithstanding every precaution, we were all more or less repeatedly bitten by them. They are of smaller size, but in other respects the same as those used for medicinal purposes in England. They work their way like needles through the thickest stockings, and may attain about six times their original size before the traveller is cognisant that he has been subjected to their operations—so imperceptibly do they bite and conduct the suction process. A slight, half itching, half smarting sensation usually draws his attention to his ankles, and, on looking at them, he will find himself bleeding freely from a half a dozen or more places, and a corresponding number of leeches inside his stockings in a state of plethoric engorgement. Pests as they no doubt are both at the time and afterwards; owing to the itching sensation which lasts for some ten or twelve days, I am nevertheless inclined to think that being freely bitten by them counteracts a certain painful feeling of lassitude in the limbs which is common after some hours' of mountain marching. The grounds on which this opinion is based will be alluded to further on.

About the ridge we had reached, wild strawberries and raspberries were plentiful. The former were of small size and destitute of taste. The latter had a good deal of flavour, and were of a pale yellow colour; their size being about the same as that of the English raspberry. Wormwood also, hereabouts, existed in large quantities.

Shortly after seven o'clock a second ridge was cleared, from which we had a fine view of the snowy range of Thibet. A little way on, we came to a cleared spot where buckwheat was growing. Flour made from this grain is extensively used by the Bhotanese as an article of food. The grain itself, in a state of fermentation, is also used by them, but for medicinal purposes only, such as those that we employ rhubarb and like vegetable drugs for. Near this place we passed a small farm, where a number of cows were confined inside a bamboo fence. From here we proceeded along a winding up and down pathway, and in about half an hour appeared for the time being to have got clear of mountain ridges; as a beautiful basin-shaped valley opened into view, along the slope of one side of which we passed by an undulating path, above a few detached houses, which we were told was the village of Dongra.

At eight o'clock we reached a two-storied building, with thatched roof and plastered walls—also two large projecting windows. This was Tusso Gimpa, or the monastery of Tusso.* On entering it by a doorway at the end of the building, we found the lower story unoccupied. The communication with the upper one was by a rude staircase, formed out of a large slab of wood with steps cut in it, and a bamboo pole on each side representing railings. We ascended to the upper story and found ourselves in a kitchen, where some nuns were engaged cooking. Passing through this, we came to the chief room of the monastery or the Lama Temple Proper. Here, three priests were sitting behind a small altar near the window, and fronting the principal altar, which was at the opposite end of the room. They were all dressed alike in dark red woollen robes: two of them had hand-bells before them; one was quite a youth. They were drinking tea from small shallow wooden cups, very similar to those that the highlanders of Scotland use for drinking whisky, and displayed most perfect indifference with reference to our intrusion upon them; the same liberality of sentiment, in regard to giving publicity to their religious institutions,

* "Gimpa," in the Bohtanese dialect, means "a monastery."

apparently existing in Bhotan as does in China —so different to the exclusiveness with respect thereto of most other Orientals.

The walls of the temple were decorated with a large number of coloured paintings of the same female deity; and, on the altar, behind which there was a figure of Buddha, I noticed a model of a Lama Buddhistic monument, exactly the same in shape as

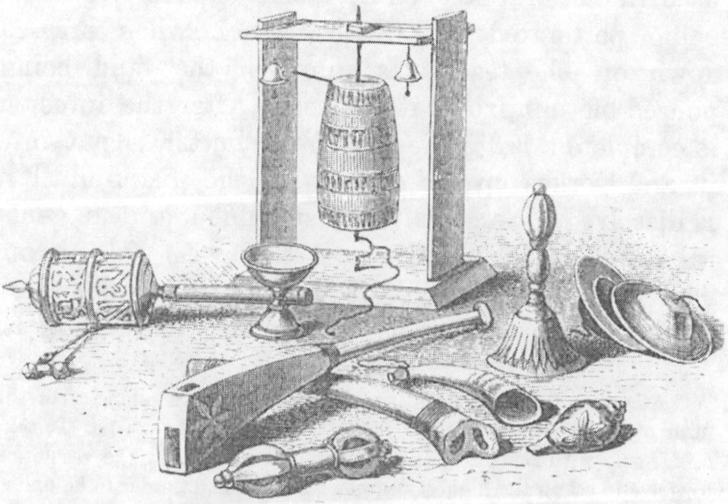

PRAYING CYLINDERS, SACRED MUSICAL INSTRUMENTS, AND TRUMPET MADE FROM A HUMAN THIGH-BONE.

two of those structures that form prominent objects in Peking, as seen from its wall. On the altar, also, a green-coloured European finger-glass was standing. Hanging up in different parts of the room there were musical instruments, including trumpets made of human thigh-bones, hollowed out and mounted with silver. Flagellators were also hanging up, with which the priests inflict self-punishment. They consisted of thongs of hide, arranged on a handle, in the same way as the "cats" used for flogging in the army and navy are.*

On passing through the kitchen on our way out the nuns were making butter tea, which is the usual way the latter is used as a beverage by the Bhotanese. The tea is first infused in a large bamboo tube, in which there is a wooden piston, such as is used in an ordinary churn: the expanded portion being perforated with holes, which when pressed down on the tea-leaves admit of the fluid being poured off unmixed with leaves. After the infusion is complete a large piece of fresh butter is put into it, and worked up and down with the piston until it is dissolved. Some salt is then added, and its general diffusion insured by agitation with the piston. The tea is then ready for use, and the nuns were kind enough to allow us the privilege of tasting it.

* According to Csoma de Korosi, the following is a summary of the form of Buddhism practised by the Lamas of Thibet:—1st. To take refuge only with Buddha. 2nd. To form in one's mind the resolution to strive to attain the highest degree of perfection, in order to be united with the supreme intelligence. 3rd. To prostrate oneself before the image of Buddha to adore him. 4th. To bring offerings before him, such as are pleasing to any of the six senses, as lights, flowers, garlands, incenses, perfumes, all kinds of edible and drinkable things, stuffs, cloths, &c., for garments and hanging ornaments. 5th. To make music, sing hymns, and utter the praises of Buddha, respecting his person, doctrine, love or mercy, perfections or attributes, and his acts or performances, for the benefit of all animal beings. 6th. To confess one's sins with a contrite heart, to ask forgiveness for them, and to resolve sincerely not to commit the like hereafter. 7th. To rejoice in the moral merits of all animal beings, and to wish that they may thereby obtain final emancipation or beatitude. 8th. To pray and entreat all Buddhas that are now in the world to turn the wheel of religion (in other words to teach their doctrines), and not to leave the world too soon, but to remain here for many ages or kalpas.

I cannot say that the majority of us were much enamoured with its flavour—tastes however differ, as one of our party seemed to enjoy it, and took a whole cupful.

Though the ground was well suited for cultivation in the neighbourhood of the monastery, the only crop we saw was a small patch of wheat. The paucity of population which hereabouts was very apparent is attributed to the oppressive character of the Government, causing the inhabitants to emigrate to Sikim, Nepaul, and the Darjeeling district. Shortly after leaving Tusso Gimpa, we met a mendicant priest named Chayboo Gylung, who belonged to the monastery we had just left, and was returning to it, after having been out on a professional tour. Though belonging to the mendicant class of ecclesiastics he looked in comfortable circumstances.

We halted for breakfast at a little stream about half a mile from Tusso Gimpa, and there got rid of a stock of leeches that had attached themselves to us on the road. During our halt Kif Yu Gulla and the coolies managed to get one of their national liquors into drinking order, namely that made from wheat in the first stage of fermentation, and locally known as murwa. It is prepared by putting some partially fermented wheat into a hollow bamboo or choonga, and pouring boiling water over it. The mode of imbibing it is by suction through a small wooden tube about the size of a goose-quill, the perforation being so arranged as to prevent any of the grain entering and obstructing the tube. Thus it would seem that the Americans are not the inventors of the tubular mode of imbibing, which has become so general in that country, and has of late years been introduced into our own.

The murwa has a slightly spirituous flavour, and is much the same as that referred to as prepared from the millet, and called by the Lepchas *che*. Both are made and drank in the same manner, that prepared from the millet however being considered the best.

At half-past ten we recommenced our march by a heavy ascent up a rocky pathway. The path shortly resumed its up and down character, the jungle on each side of it being very dense, consisting chiefly of wormwood and ferns. Hereabouts we met some cows going about loose in the jungle, and apparently rather wild. We also passed a patch of cultivation where some wheat was growing. A little ground near it had been recently cleared. From this place we had a good view of the opposite side of the valley —a small portion of Darjeeling also could be indistinctly seen in the distance.

At eleven o'clock we came to a rude stone structure, being a mengdong, sacred monument, having inscribed on each end of it the words, "Om Manee Padme Hom," the mystic sentence of Thibet, which constitutes the almost sole form of prayer said by the Bhotanese, as well as by the Lepchas, Thibetian and Mongolian. The coolies we noticed were very particular in passing on the right side of it, and repeating the words, "Om Manee Padme Hom." Each one also put a leaf or flower upon it. With reference to the meaning of the words, "Om Manee Padme Hom," which are commonly translated, "Oh! the jewel on the lotus," much diversity of opinion exists; no two authorities apparently agreeing about it. The interpretation of it given by Cheeboo Lama, and quoted by Mr. Eden, is that the six syllables represent the six states of future existence. The first, representing *Lha*, or the state of the gods; the second, *Mee*, or the state of human existence; the third, *Lhamayin*, or the state of neutral and mischievous spirits, to which men who die in war are regenerated; the fourth, *Tendro* or *Dado*, the state of beasts, in which lazy and indifferent Buddhists are born again; the fifth, *Yedag*, or state of wretched demons in a condition of suffering; and the sixth, *Myalwur*, or the state of punishment. "Those born in this latter state are exposed to tortures—heat, cold, and thirst; those who are sent there for abusing the priesthood are very suggestively punished with peculiar tortures; they are born with long tongues, which are perpetually lacerated with ploughshares. The constant repetition of these six syllables closes the entrance of the six states of metempsychosis, and procures the coveted condition of Nirvana, or exemption from all future metempsychosis, and absolute non-existence." The rendering of the words given by Dr. Hooker is, "Hail to him of the lotus and lewel."

About a mile further on we came to a place called Uchaka, distinguished by a single house, with a little cleared land near it. Beyond this a short distance two more mendongs were passed, the coolies again going through the form of repeating the sacred sentence. At noon we heard a succession of shots in the valley underneath, and the noise also of the barking deer. The path now became very rocky and bad: the vegetation on each side of it being dense in the extreme. The valley again came into sight, and from this aspect a small river was seen flowing through it. At one o'clock a fourth sacred structure was passed, about which the leeches were very troublesome; the path being literally alive with them. Beyond this we had to pass through a narrow, steep, and rugged ravine; on clearing which, we got on an uneven path on the mountain side: the view in every direction obstructed by the jungle.

No change of scenery now occurred for several miles, and after a fatiguing march of eight hours, at half-past three we came to an open piece of country on the mountain slope, called Paiong-poong, where there were a few detached houses. The first house we went to was kept by an old Bhotanese, with closely-cropped grey hair. He gave us a friendly reception, and undertook to supply us with milk as soon as the cows came home. As there were no buildings attached to this house, where we could sleep for the night, we went to the next one, a few hundred feet down the hill. At first the inmates seemed averse to give admission to any of the party, coolies included, and closed the door. After a little time a young woman came out, and objected to our staying there for the night, on the grounds that the coolies would make use of the bamboo fencing for firewood. Other members of the family having arrived, after a little conversation their scruples gave way, and they consented to our occupying a wood shed near the house for the night. They gave us some eggs and fresh butter, declining to fix a price for them, leaving that to ourselves—or, in the language of the East, making it a question of *bucksheesh*, or present.

Everything seemed very comfortable about this little farm. The cows came home at sundown and were milked, and the pigs were fed out of wooden troughs—the same as they are in England. The male head of the establishment had much the appearance of a Roman of old. His dress was made like the garb of old Gaul, in the form of a loose robe or doublet, descending to the knee, tightened by a waistband, from which was suspended a long, straight knife, in a wooden scabbard, not unlike the Roman sword. His bare legs, and a thick, short

BHOTANESE TEA-POTS, BRICK TEA, PEASANT'S KNIFE, FLINT, STEEL, PIPE, AND TOBACCO POUCH.

curly head of hair, added to the general resemblance. His family consisted of his mother, his wife, a sister-in-law, and three children.

After dinner, we went into the farm-house, and sat there on the floor for some time observing domestic life in Bhotan. The sister-in-law was busy preparing a mixture of boiled rice and warm water, which the old woman gave us to understand by signs was for the children. After the latter had their supper, they were undressed, and in a state of nudity retired to rest behind a bamboo partition. The nature of their bedclothing we had not an opportunity of seeing. After the children retired, the ladies resumed culinary operations, and presented each of us with a choonga full of murwa, and a tube to imbibe it. We all took a little of it, and found it rather palatable than otherwise. The farmer was determined not to be behind the female members of his establishment in hospitality, and went to a receptacle from which he produced an English bottle filled with Bhotan whisky, which he insisted on our tasting. It was by no means an ill-flavoured spirit, but not very strong. It is distilled from barley and rice mixed, and goes by the name of chong.

The mode of fermenting the wheat or the millet for the production of murwa is the following—The grain is first beaten in a wooden pail by a piece of solid bamboo. It is then wet, put into a basket, covered over, and subjected to pressure for three days : at the end of which, the fermentive process is sufficiently developed and the grain is fit for use. It is a decidedly economical liquor ; as fermentation continuing to go on in the grain, it imparts stimulating properties to several successive waterings. The refuse of the murwa is used for feeding pigs, and very good and wholesome food it seems to be for them. The kind of murwa made from the millet, which the Lepchas call *che*, the Bhotanese call *Been Chong* or honey spirit.

Honey, I may remark, is plentiful in Bhotan, and in the course of our journey we frequently saw the common honey-bee of the country—in appearance exactly the same as that of England. The Bhotanese collect the honey in choongas, and its flavour is very good. I have occasionally seen it offered for sale in Darjeeling.

The coolies having received permission to use the hearth, which was constructed the same as those described at Kalimpoong, and afforded accommodation for several fires, were also busy cooking. After supper, which consisted chiefly of rice, they regaled themselves with murwa, and the evening terminated by "The Laughing Pup" getting intoxicated and, by his boisterousness, disturbing us after we had retired to rest in the wood shed; the accommodation of which was very limited, and into which we had some difficulty in fitting ourselves.

CHAPTER XX.

A Bhotanese Witch Doctor—View of Dhumsong—Coolies resting—Meet some Natives—Halt at Labah—First View of Dhalimkote and the Dooars in the Distance—Approach to the Valley of Ambiok—The Chale River—Village of Ambiok—Ascent to Dhalimkote—Description of the Fort—Civil Jurisdiction—Bhotanese Arms—A Boa Constrictor—Dhalimkote as a Military Position—Question with respect to establishing our Frontier in the Bhotan Hills—Effects of Leech Bites in preventing sensations of Fatigue.

SHORTLY after five o'clock on the morning of the 11th of May we resumed our march, stopping a few minutes at a house where there was a sick child under the care of a witch doctor. Messrs. Howard and Masson had been there the previous evening and witnessed the ceremony of exorcising the evil spirit or demon of sickness from the child, which was effected by incantations and dances performed by the witch. The child was shown to me, it seemed to be in a very fair way for recovery, in fact it did not appear to have been seriously ill, therefore it is very probable that the form of treatment to which it had been subjected, from in no way interfering with nature, may have been that best suited to its case. The witch was still in the house, and had a wild gipsy look about her, very different to that of the other women.

Exactly an hour after leaving Paiong-poong, we reached the top of a ridge that we had seen from that place, and where we were told that the monastery of Rinchinsoong was concealed amongst the trees; its presence being indicated in the distance by a few flags overtopping the jungle. The ascent to the ridge was rugged and fatiguing; the only approach to it being through a watercourse. About half a mile before we came to the ridge, the path turning off to Dhumsong was pointed out to us. From this ridge we had a magnificent view of the snowy range. Going on from here about three quarters of a mile, we came to a ridge twelve feet broad, with almost perpendicular ravines of great depth on each side. On the left we looked down on Dhumsong, which has been already described, at page 66, as beautifully situated on a spur.

The march now consisted of a series of abrupt ups and downs until seven o'clock, when we reached a ridge called Miriam, where we halted for a short time to allow the coolies to come up: the steepness of the ascent having proved very trying to them. They made a short rest here, and refreshed themselves by smoking and eating dry a little coarse wheaten flour. Their mode of procuring a light is by flint and steel; the tinder used being the dried pith of the plantain. From this again they light a piece of rag and pass it from one to the other.

From here we passed along another ridge for about a mile, and then commenced a moderate ascent by a path completely shaded by forest. At the foot of it we met some natives, who told us that we were twelve miles from Dhalimkote. Some of them were dressed in brown woollen clothing, some in the variously striped garments which are frequently worn by the Lepchas, and by some people thought to be peculiar to them, which however I do not think is the case. After half an hour's steady ascent up a succession of steep uneven paths, we arrived at a point where the slope became more gradual, and here we met two more natives; one of whom was in the habit of visiting Darjeeling, and was recognised by Mr. Masson—"Is your body in health?" is the English of the Bhotanese salutation on meeting.

It was now nine o'clock—the paths had become very muddy, apparently from recent rain, and after a slight ascent for a short distance, which brought us to the top of the mountain of Labah, 6,922 feet in height. From here we steadily descended by a steep and slippery path, and exactly in one hour reached a small patch of grass, on every side surrounded by forest, and overlooked by a mountain between six and seven thousand feet high, called by the natives Choong Tassa Ga. Here there was a small matting hut as a resting-place for travellers, and a very fine herd of upwards of fifty English-looking cows were grazing about.

Shortly after arriving at this place, the weather, which had been fine since entering Bhotan, became overcast, distant thunder was heard, accompanied by lightning, and we were speedily enveloped in a thick mist, which shortly passed into steady heavy rain, in the midst of which, at noon, we proceeded on to the valley of Ambiok, descending by a rugged ravine, which the rain now falling in torrents had converted into a watercourse. After a steady descent of an hour and a half, here and there interrupted by some abrupt ascents to avoid impassable portions of the mountain slope—coincident with the reappearance of the sun, the richly-wooded valley of Ambiok suddenly burst on our view, and, on a spur running out from the opposite side, about 1,000 feet above the valley, with a winding path ascending to it, was seen a low line of works, containing within them some houses on the roofs of which we seemed to look down—this was our first view of the fort of Dhalimkote: surrounded on all sides and overtopped by densely-wooded mountain slopes. Looking from where we were to the south, a vast sea-like plain was seen, unbroken by any object that in the distance arrested the eye; this was the recently annexed territory: the Dooars of Bengal.

At twenty minutes to two, after having rested for ten minutes, looking at the scene underneath us, we proceeded on, and immediately re-entered forest jungle, and continued to descend by a rugged track, proving exceedingly trying to the limbs; some parts of it being almost precipitous. By half-past three we had approached within a short distance of the valley. The atmosphere was now very oppressive, and a death-like silence prevailed, unbroken even by the rustling of a leaf; so still had the air become. Here we killed a poisonous hill snake that was crawling amongst the leaves strewn on the path we were passing along. We also met three Lama priests coming up from Ambiok, accompanied by a coolie who was carrying on his back, seated in a sort of bamboo chair, a young man who looked in the last stage of malarious disease. The priests were taking him for change of air to some higher position than that in which he had contracted his malady. A waterfall on the opposite side of the valley, a long way up the mountain slope was now seen. A little way on, the fort of Dhalimkote again came into sight, but presenting a very different aspect to what it did when we first sighted it—now it was standing almost perpendicularly above us, and from its height and difficulty of access, it presented a decidedly formidable appearance.

A few minutes before four o'clock, after a continuous descent of nearly four hours, we reached a small stream running through the bottom of the valley, and here halted for half an hour, waiting for the coolies to come up; as they had fallen some distance behind. We also bathed here, and underwent a clearance of leeches. The coolies having all made their appearance, we went on a few hundred yards and found ourselves stopped by the Chale river, a swift stream, to ford which, we had to divest ourselves of our under garments a second time. The boulders in this river are very numerous and of huge size; the largest, in fact, I have seen in any part of the world.

From the bed of the Chale River, we ascended by a rugged zigzag to a path leading up a gentle ascent to the valley of Ambiok, which we reached a few minues after five o'clock. The village, the elevation of which is 2,922 feet above the sea, consisted of a few bamboo and matting huts, of similar construction to those described at Kalimpoong, and standing on rough stony ground, resembling the dry bed of a river. Near the village was a shed, in which some Government elephants were housed. A good many natives came round us and entered into conversation with the coolies. The women seemed much the same in appearance as those who go under the name of Lepcha females at Darjeeling. Viewed from the valley of Ambiok, the position of Dhalimkote is very imposing, but the fort itself is not so; the building having nothing of a striking character about it. At twenty minutes past five we commenced ascending to the fort by a winding path, and about a quarter of an hour afterwards reached one of a more level description, which proceeded round to the opposite side of the fort in the direction of the gate. From here we had a fine view of the Dooars, and the cool breeze which met us was most refreshing after the heat and fatigue attending the ascent. This was the ridge where the mortars operated from, and here we noticed two oblong mounds, with wooden crosses at the head of them—the graves of the three officers and the four men of the Royal Artillery killed by the explosion on the sixth of December previously.

We entered the fort at six o'clock, by a gateway on the opposite side to that which overlooks Ambiok. The officers at the garrison were at the time examining some wall-pieces which had been sent up by Government for the defences of the place, and their appearance was creating some amusement from the fact that they seemed to be but an improvement on the jingals of the Bhotanese themselves. They were intended to be supported on pivots fixed on the wall, and to be fired from the shoulder in the same manner as a musket; the projectile thrown by them being a small sized shell. We were very hospitably received and accommodated for the night. The garrison consisted of one division (two guns) of the Armstrong Mountain Train Battery, and one division of the 6th Battery of the 25th Brigade Royal Artillery, a Wing of the 31st Punjaub Infantry, and a company of Sebundy Sappers.

Dhalimkote has but few claims to be considered a fortification, apart from those which rest on its position, which is undoubtedly a very strong one. It is of irregular shape, being the top of the spur levelled and surrounded by a moderately thick wall, built of stones without mortar, within which there were formerly a few buildings, such as the Jungpen's house, a monastery, and a granary. These were destroyed by fire at the capture, and the remains only of the latter one now exist. The area enclosed by the walls is 76,000 superficial feet, which, with the necessary outbuildings, would not afford barrack accommodation for more than 300 British troops, according to the allowance of superficial space (upwards of 90 feet) which each soldier now-a-days is supposed to have.

The troops at the period of our visit were located in matting huts; some built round the walls, while others were built in the centre of the enclosure. They were all raised from the ground on bamboo supports, and in other respects constructed in the same manner as the Bhotanese dwellings. On an elevation of the spur about the same height as the fort, and a few hundred yards from it, called Dhalim Mow, Captain Lance, the Deputy Commissioner, had established his residence, in the form of a matting structure similar to those inside the fort.

Captain Lance's jurisdiction is intended to extend over what is to be styled the Dhalimkote Sub-division of the Western Dooars, in which he will exercise the powers of a Joint Magistrate and Deputy Collector; Dhalimkote being his head-quarters. In the first instance it has been very properly decided to restrict his judicial powers to criminal cases—those of a civil nature are to be disposed of by arbitrators, selected from among the inhabitants. Criminals sentenced by him are to undergo their terms of imprisonment in the Darjeeling jail. Appeals from his decisions are to be made to Colonel Haughton, the Political Agent, on the north-eastern frontier. The revenues of the

Dooar are to be collected for the present in the same manner as they have been by the Bhotanese, which would seem as if their system has not been so bad a one as Mr. Eden and other authorities have represented it. Collections of revenue thus made, are to be sent to the Government Treasury, recently established at Mynagoorie; which it is intended shall become the Civil station of the frontier, in place of Julpigorie, on the same principle as Julpesh has been made the Military one.

But little of interest was to be seen inside the fort, with the exception of the remains of a catapult, and a few specimens of Bhotanese arms and armour. The jingals were the same as those used by the Chinese. The specimens of armour were confined to the iron helmets with the padded flaps, and the shields made of hide, which have been described in the first chapter. The Bhotanese swords, however, are very creditable specimens of art. They are a trifle over two feet long, very heavy, and quite straight: the breadth of the blade being about an inch and three quarters. The handle is well made and covered with glistening green material, said to be the skin of the Thibetian lizard. The sword has no guard, and is enclosed in a well-made leathern sheath tipped with brass. An old and useless looking gun of native manufacture was lying on the ground. It was the only one found in the fort at the time of its capture. Another and more modern and effective one was afterwards found concealed in the valley of Ambiok: its progress towards the fort having apparently been arrested by the arrival of the force in December last. Lying amongst some rubbish I noticed a tin trumpet, between five and six feet long, exactly the same as I have seen used within walled cities in

China, by the Imperial troops, for giving the warning at sundown that the gates were about to be closed. I saw also the skin of a huge boa constrictor, which had been killed in the neighbourhood of the fort a day or two previously. It measured fifteen feet in length, and upwards of a foot in circumference. Serpents of this kind appear to be common in the lower Himalayas, and I have heard of their having been seen in the immediate vicinity of the Civil station of Darjeeling, especially on the part known as Birch Hill. The jungle in the neighbourhood of Dhalimkote is full of wild animals, including the elephant. Lieutenant Armstrong, of the Royal Engineers, while in the jungle near the fort, suddenly found himself face to face with a tiger, which looked at him and then slunk away. As a general rule, unless very hungry or provoked, they will rather avoid than attack an European.

As regards the supposition entertained by those at a distance, that the position of Dhalimkote is an important one, from its commanding the pass leading down to the plains, it appears to me to be erroneous, inasmuch as a large Bhotanese force might march easily through the valley of Ambiok to the Dooars, without the garrison of Dhalimkote being aware of the circumstance. So little does it command a view of the approaches to the Dooars, that the first notice the officers in the fort had of the approach of our party, was seeing us enter the gate, notwithstanding that there were sentries on the look-out at intervals along the wall. Whatever influence the occupation of Dhalimkote or any other post in the hills may be likely to exercise, it is pretty certain that it will be entirely of a moral nature, there being but little doubt that should the Bhotanese be so inclined, our occupation of them cannot prevent descents on the Dooars being made; owing to the numerous means which the Bhotanese have of getting at them through the hills, altogether beyond our scope of control. The idea that there are eighteen passes commanding a like number of Dooars, is a geographical epigram, which I am inclined to think has proved somewhat deceptive.

The opinion expressed by officers of local experience, with whom I have conversed on this subject, seems to be that it was a mistake on Mr. Eden's part recommending that our new frontier should be established in the hills, and that our having done so is likely to prove a source of chronic trouble. Military opinion appears to be strongly in favour of the plan adopted in respect of our northern frontier at Peshawur, which has proved very successful; namely, avoiding the hills, and establishing posts at convenient distances along the level ground at their foot. Recent events certainly tend to support this view and to demonstrate that with regard to Bhotan, it would have been better to have drawn our new frontier line south of the malarious Terai; which would thus have become a kind of neutral ground between British and Bhotan territory—the Terai, as a residence, being as much dreaded by the Bhotanese as it is by ourselves.*

* Since the above was written, and while the sheets are passing through the press, I have had an opportunity of perusing some parliamentary papers relating to Bhotan, wherein I find that prior to the military operations being commenced, opinions opposed to the annexation of hill territory were expressed by Major-General Jenkins, for many years Governor-General's agent in Assam, and by Captain Morton, Deputy-Commissioner of Assam, an officer also of extensive local experience. The opinion of General Jenkins was to the following effect—

The morning after my arrival at Dahlimkote, I was struck by the fact that I was enjoying a total absence of feeling of fatigue in my limbs, notwithstanding the long and difficult march of the previous day; abrupt

"As to the extent of annexation, this will probably depend much on circumstances, but I would not propose, in the first instance, going beyond the Dooars. Attempting to take up posts in the hills might bring you into a very unhealthy tract of forests, where it might be difficult to supply your detachments with necessary supplies. I should rather be inclined to give up to the Booteahs a wide margin under the hills for any use they would make of it, allowing them to hold as subject villagers and ryots who may voluntarily choose to remain under their authority. In tracing a boundary in the Assam Dooars, I gave a line from promontory to promontory, leaving all the villages within it. If you do not allow them a proportion of the population, they will find it difficult to get their supplies, and the people living close under the hills will be a sort of half savages, who have been principally employed as porters, and never paid any regular rents. On the Assam frontier such go-betweens are called Bohôteahs, who are not taxed by us." Captain Morton's views were even more decided—he stated—"I am strongly of opinion that for the present at least no steps should be taken to annex any portion of the hilly country. It will doubtless be necessary to take up posts a short distance within the hills to command the passes, but the occupation of these should be temporary. The annexation of the plains would be easy and profitable. We should meet with scarcely any opposition from the Booteahs, whereas an advance into the hills would be accompanied with much expense and harassment if not bloodshed, without, as far as I can see, any immediate advantage. Our Government is so situated that once a false step is taken it is difficult to retrace it. After annexing the plains if it were found necessary to enter the hills, there would be no greater difficulty than at present exists. Indeed, if whilst occupying the plains, we cultivated the friendship of the hillmen, we should at a future date advance into Bhotan proper with the good will of the people." These opinions were expressed in memoranda furnished respectively by General Jenkins and Captain Morton for the information of the Bengal Government, when arrangements were being made in 1864 for the annexation of the Dooars. Looking at the troubles we have already had since entering the hills, and considering those that, judging from the present aspect of affairs, are about to recommence, the observations of Captain Morton seem to be almost prophetic.

and rugged descents, as a general rule, being more felt during the ensuing twenty-four hours than up-hill journeys—attributable to the peculiar strain thrown on the muscles in descending. The immunity enjoyed by me on this occasion, I can only account for, by referring it to the bleeding I underwent from both my ankles the afternoon before, about half a dozen leeches having become attached to each of them between our halting place at Labah and the stream at Ambiok; notwithstanding that I was constantly on the watch and had pulled some dozens out of my stockings, as they were making their way through. As the natives of the hills generally, are liable to be attacked in the same way by them, to some it may seem as if they were a wise provision of nature placed on the hills to exercise their particular functions for the relief of the weary traveller :—be this as it may, I give the fact as experienced by myself; the occasion in question being the first, that, after having been exposed to fatigue of the nature referred to, I have not been physically sensible of it the next day.

CHAPTER XXI.

Leave Dhalimkote for the Dooars—Descent to the Terai—The Mechis and their physical Peculiarities—Remarks on Malaria—Mosquitoes at Ballabaree—Enter the Dooars—Kyrantee—Cattle—The Mechis of the Dooars—Details connected with them—Appearance of the Country—The Cantonment of Julpesh—Position and Soil—Affinity of Cholera for Water—The Bykantpore Family Temple—The Teesta at Julpigorie—Appearance of the Station—Two sides of the Question relating to Frontier Aggressions—Remarks thereon—Bhotanese Veracity—Discontent contingent on our Occupation of the Dooars—Their Products—Leave Julpigorie—Ambaree Fallacottah—Re-enter the Himalayas—Artillerymen at Kursiong—Return to Darjeeling.

THROUGH the kindness of Captain Huxham, of the 30th Punjaub Infantry, who had been temporarily commanding at Dhalimkote, and who was about to rejoin his regiment at Julpesh, I had the opportunity afforded me of going through the Dooars and returning to Darjeeling *viâ* Julpigorie, in place of by the same route that I came. Accordingly on the afternoon of the 12th of May, I started with Captain Huxham and Assistant-Surgeon Troup, in the midst of heavy rain which had been falling the greater portion of the day—our baggage having gone on some hours previously on elephants. We took exactly ten minutes to descend to the village of Ambiok, our pace exceeding four miles an hour. Here an elephant was waiting to accompany us, fitted with a pad, so as to be available for riding on when required.

At half-past two we left Ambiok, taking a track through the jungle leading south. The descent towards the plains, with a few exceptions, was gentle —very different indeed to that of the previous day. After crossing three streams, branches, I believe, of the Chale River, we came to the main stream itself at half-past four, which we forded on the elephant, and were now clear of the hills and fairly in the Terai. From here we had an hour and three-quarters ride on the elephant through forest jungle, and at a quarter past six reached Bullabaree, the site of a former Mechi village, where a matting hut and an elephant shed have recently been erected by the Government for the accommodation of officers travelling to and from Dhalimkote. Immediately on arriving here Captain Huxham was attacked with fever.

Though there is no marsh land in the neighbourhood, the position of Bullabaree is nevertheless very malarious looking; the vegetation being chiefly under-sized trees with tall grass and brushwood growing between them. This form of jungle is rife with malaria, and its effects have been very severely felt by the troops, both European and native, during the short time passed by them in the Dooars, as mention will be made of hereafter.

At Bullabaree, I had a good opportunity of observing the Mechi caste of countenance which is slightly Malayan, and not in the least Mongolian as some allege it to be. They seemed to me to be more allied to the Bengalee than to any other people I could call to mind, the difference in appearance between them being attributable chiefly to the Malay expression of the Mechi. They are a singular tribe, enjoying excellent health where other races, dark and fair, sicken and die—while again they contract malignant fevers when removed from their own locality into districts considered by us comparatively salubrious. They have consequently as great a dread of visiting such places, as we, in common with the Bhotanese, have of visiting theirs. What explanation can our so-called "Sanitary Science" of the present day offer of a fact in nature such as this?

The occurrence of similar phenomena in the history of malarious disease has frequently been noticed by me elsewhere in the East, and allusion to the anomalies connected with it have been casually noticed in speaking of the outbreak of it at Darjeeling under circumstances about as completely removed from what are usually considered malarious influences as it is possible to conceive. In the case of the Mechis, we have the unquestionable fact that they can reside as a healthy and robust race amongst the rankest vegetation and primitive jungle, and when removed from it suffer in exactly the same way as those who have resided in clear and cultivated localities do when exposed to the atmosphere of the jungle. However much we may be wedded to time-honoured medical theories, and epigrammatic explanations of malarious diseases, by referring them to poisoning of the blood by morbific exhalations from the soil or by the gaseous products of vegetable decomposition, I am sure that those who have had opportunities of observing the effects of malaria under varied circumstances of locality and climate, must feel as I do, the difficulty of avoiding the conclusion that there is a something connected with it that we have far from fathomed, and that in reality we are completely in the dark respecting its true nature.

As far as observation and experience enable me to throw any light on this obscure question, it is to the correlations between the nervous system and the atmospheric electricity that we must look for an explanation for the development of malarious disease in its active and cognisable form. The theory now-a-days entertained respecting the presence of an atmospheric poison, circulating indefinitely in the blood, is one failing altogether to account for a great deal connected with the natural history of ague, which is the type proper of ailments resulting from malaria; most other diseases traceable to that source being merely ague occurring under varied guises.*

* The following remarks made by me in "The British Arms in North China and Japan," show the occurrence of malarious disease amongst troops, under circumstances analogous to those under which the Mechis become liable to it. In a note dated 22nd October 1860, referring to a Wing of a Battalion of Royal Marines that I was on ship-board with from Shanghai to the Peiho, it is stated—"Out of 260 marines that embarked four days ago, there are now thirty on the sick list, suffering from ailments such as are usually referred to malaria. The medical officer in charge informs me that the men are now much more sickly than they were while on shore at Shanghai. This apparently injurious result of a change from a malarious locality and comparatively unhealthy atmosphere to conditions of an opposite kind, is quite in accordance with what I have frequently observed, and tends to confirm me in an impression I have formed since returning to China, to the effect that exposure to emanations from badly-drained soils, decaying vegetable matter, &c., is not the actual excitant of the train of symptoms familiar to us under the name of an ague fit, the exciting atmospheric cause being generally one of a contrary nature, namely, free currents of fresh air. This statement no doubt will seem at first paradoxical in the extreme, but it is not less in accordance with actual facts, and I believe admits the following explanation—namely, that a residence in malarious localities, though not the special exciting cause of the paroxysms of ague, still produces in particular constitutions a lowering of the vital power, characterised by organic changes of an obscure and frequently non-overt kind, which renders the individuals peculiarly susceptible of certain atmospheric influences, which, in constitutions thus predisposed,

The hut at Bullabaree was swarming with mosquitoes, of large size and voracious appetites, and during the night I had to adopt the native mode of

possess the power of generating paroxymal febrile action—the most potent of such atmospheric agents that I have observed being ordinary fresh breezes. This fact has been noticed particularly in Hong Kong, where invalids sent over from the extreme heat of Victoria to the sea breeze at Stanley on the opposite side of the island, have suffered more from ague and general sickness than they did at the less salubrious locality. Another illustration came under my notice lately. The men of the 67th Regiment, while in occupation of the city of Canton, had good apparent health, and freedom from ague, so long as they were quartered in the lower portion of the city, where they were a good deal shut in from the fresh air, but they were no sooner removed to the heights above the city, where they were freely exposed to the breeze, than they commenced to suffer from ague which was attributed to the malaria arising from the rice fields outside the city. The case of the marines is another illustration. The men are now suffering severely from malarious diseases, where there is no generating agent but that of the pure atmosphere which now surrounds them. Hence I think it not unreasonable to infer, that a residence in certain atmospheres, whether of the nature usually referred to malaria or not, developes a constitutional predisposition to intermittent and other diseases of a periodic type, which predisposition is brought into activity by meteorological conditions, which to those in actual health, are not only quite innocuous, but in reality invigorating. An account has lately been published by a Mr. Gougher, of an imprisonment he underwent a good many years ago in Burmah. He gives a frightful account of the disgusting nature of the atmosphere, which he, in common with the other prisoners, had to reside in; yet he describes his own health as having continued what seemed to him very good, until he was removed to a cell where he was exposed to the fresh breeze blowing on the banks of the Irrawaddy. Immediately he began to suffer from malarious disease, which was naturally referred by him to emanations from the banks of the river; the more so, as the symptoms disappeared as soon as he was replaced in the pestilential air of the interior of the prison." In further illustration I may add, that in a note to some remarks on cholera, contained in a report furnished to the Government of India at the end of 1864, I stated "My individual opinion in regard to filthy places not necessarily being visited by cholera during epidemic periods has been confined to China; the following however is a corroborative illustration occurring sleeping with the head under the bed-clothes, as the only means of escaping their buzzing and bites, sleep otherwise being impossible; and such as was thus procured was anything but sound and refreshing. The natives of India, I may observe, even in the hottest weather, cover their heads over at night, and exclude the access of air as much as possible, just as a bird puts its head under its wing during sleep.

At half-past five on the morning of the 13th of May we left Bullabaree by a path through a thick forest, and at ten minutes past seven, after fording a small stream, we found ourselves clear of the jungle at the foot of the hills, or what is usually called the Terai. We were now fairly in the Dooars—the characteristics of which, hereabouts, as far as the eye

in Calcutta. A few months ago, a committee of Government medical officers had to visit the filthiest part of the native town, where the slaughter-houses are, for the purpose of selecting a site for an abattoir. The stench was such as they had never before encountered, and they thought they had at last discovered the focus from which disease diffused itself over the place generally. On inquiring however amongst the inhabitants with reference to their sanitary condition, to their surprise they learned that there was no sickness in the place, that deaths were not common, and that the inhabitants had enjoyed immunity from cholera."

In making these observations I have no wish to decry the labours of sanitarians, but merely to show that the sweeping conclusions arrived at by them, from limited fields of observation, do not find support in the wide book of nature, and to caution the public against being deluded into the belief that the control of disease is that simple mechanical process which it has become the fashion now-a-days, for the most part, to represent it. There can be no question about the advantages of cleanliness of locality, attention to ventilation, improved drainage, &c., but we must not suppose that our acquaintance with morbific influences or their investigation, are to cease with the triumph of the ventilating or the scavenger arts.

could reach, being vast grassy plains, almost entirely free from timber. The malaria originating over ground of this kind, is that to which some of the troops have been chiefly exposed; and its effects are described to me as having been quite as hurtful as any experienced within the more dreaded Terai.

No change in the character of the country, or signs of population or cultivation were seen until nine o'clock, when some Mechi villages began to appear, and half an hour afterwards we reached that of Kyrantee, where accommodation for travellers, similar to that at Bullabaree, has been constructed—the distance between the two places being fourteen miles, and between the latter place and Dhalimkote thirteen miles.

Kyrantee is surrounded by beautiful pastoral land, and several fine herds of small-sized cattle were grazing in the neighbourhood. In appearance they were the same as those of Lower Bengal generally, and quite different to the cattle we had seen in Bhotan.

The villagers about Kyrantee are the class of Mechis, who have hitherto had to pay tribute to Bhotan, and have been subject to the jurisdiction of the Jungpen of Dhalimkote, and his subordinate Katma at Mynagoorie. Though from their name the Mechis might be supposed to have come originally from the Mechi River, they themselves state they are the aboriginal inhabitants of the Dooars and adjoining Terai. How far this is correct we have no means of knowing, but as they are the only tribe that has permanently resided there, it is as likely to be the case as not. How the term Mechi became their distinguishing appellation is not explained. They never live at elevations higher than from eight hundred to a thousand feet above the level of the sea, and as a general rule prefer cultivating clearances made in the Terai to the naturally cleared ground outside of it. They are fair agriculturists, and confine themselves chiefly to growing rice, tobacco, and cotton. Having an unlimited command of virgin soil they do not remain long at the same place, but change after a few successive crops—thus it is that there are so many indications of former cultivation in the Dooars, which I am inclined to think has been somewhat hastily attributed by casual observers to abandonment of villages, and depopulation directly attributable to Bhotanese oppression, while more than probably they are the consequences of the naturally gregarious habits of the people.

The Mechi language is peculiar to themselves, and is apparently derived chiefly from the Bengalee. It has no written character. Their religion is a form of Hindooism of a low caste, limited to occasional offerings before a clay figure of Kalee. They have neither temples, nor priests, nor caste distinctions; and eat all kinds of animal food, except the elephant, for which they have an extreme reverence.

The management of their households is left to their wives, who also assist in field labour, and attend the markets, which are periodically held in the neighbourhood of the villages, and there sell and barter their farm produce. In appearance they resemble both the Malay and the Bengalee female—most so however the latter.

At half-past four on the morning of the 14th May we left Kyrantee, where the heat had been very great the previous day, and proceeded along the bank of the Chale River, which flows past the place, until five o'clock, and then forded it. In this direction we passed extensive tracts of excellent pasture land, with herds of cattle grazing. At seven o'clock we crossed a small stream near a village, and at half-past eight passed through the newly-established civil station of Mynagoorie, near the village of that name, which is one of considerable extent. The Government buildings which have been constructed at this place are as yet few in number, and are composed of bamboo and matting. The Bhotanese stockade has been removed, and a bazaar and market-place established close to its site, which is indicated by a square surrounded by good-sized trees.

At nine o'clock we reached the cantonment of Julpesh, occupied by the 5th Bengal Cavalry, and the 30th Punjaub Infantry—the latter corps however being under orders to march the following morning for Cawnpore; the regiment having suffered so much from fever during the five months it had been in the Dooars, as to have rendered its removal from them very necessary.

Julpesh cantonment consists of two lines, four in each, of excellent bamboo bungalows, raised five feet from the ground on stakes; the roofs being thatched, and the walls formed of matting supported on split bamboo framework, making as it were matting panes about ten inches long by eight broad. The floors are formed by an interlacement of bamboos, which, while admitting of free ventilation, admit also the damp arising from the ground after dews and wet weather. These barracks were constructed for the Royal Artillery, and it was three days after taking possession of them that the men were attacked by cholera, and their removal to Darjeeling necessitated. They were then taken into occupation by the officers of the 5th Cavalry and 30th Punjaubees, who were glad to get them as a substitute for the tents they were then living under. With the exception of these buildings, a few outhouses and a line of matting sheds as stables for the cavalry horses, no others had yet been constructed, the troops being under canvas.

At noon, in the division of one of the Artillery barrack-rooms occupied by the Commandant, Major Gough, the thermometer stood at 90°, and in the afternoon was five degrees higher. The soil of Julpesh is a light sandy loam covered with a thin coating of grass. Judging from appearances it ought to be a healthy locality, being free from recognised sources of malaria. Like Putla Kowa, it was specially selected on sanitary grounds; a river flowing through it, and a large and well populated village in its vicinity, being viewed as auguring favourably for its salubrity. Both places, however, have proved the contrary, and Putla Kowa especially so; a heavy mortality having occurred there from cholera—and but for their prompt removal, a like disaster would most probably have happened to the European troops at Julpesh.

Although the position of the cantonment at Julpesh, owing to its freedom from ordinary malaria, superficially looked at, seems a satisfactory one in a sanitary point of view, I may observe however that the river, which is a running stream of moderate size, flows past within a few hundred feet of the barracks, and that though cholera occurs under all circumstances of locality, it nevertheless occasionally displays a marked tendency both to hover over and follow the course of water, several striking illustrations of which have come under my notice in China. I am, therefore, inclined to think, that, as a general rule, in the construction of barracks in a country such as India, where cholera may be said to be endemic to its atmosphere, the selection of sites in the immediate vicinity of water ought to be avoided as much as possible.

On the other side of the stream here referred to, about half way between Julpesh and Mynagoorie, there is an old temple which until lately was concealed by an earthen mound. The artillerymen, finding this out, removed the earth from the upper portion, and made excavations into the temple in search of treasure, but found none. Hearing from Major Gough of the existence of these ruins, I went over and looked at them. They consist of massive blocks of granite about fourteen inches square, and varying from ten to sixteen feet in length, resting on side walls of similar masses of granite, and also supported in the centre by four pillars formed after a style of architecture resembling the Grecian, Doric, and the Corinthian jumbled together; the shafts of the columns being a fair representation of the former, while the capitals are circular, and embrace an imitation of both orders; the one on the top of the other—the Corinthian being uppermost. This is the remains of the family temple of the Bykantpore Zemindars, alluded to at page 36, as the rightful possessors of the part of the Dooars in question.

At four o'clock on the morning of the 15th of May I left Julpesh with the 30th Punjaubees for Julpigorie, a march of about nine miles. A long line of elephants conveyed the baggage and a portion of the sick; the worst cases having gone on in dhoolies the previous day. The Seiks had a very rough and campaigning look about them; their coats being in tatters, and the condition of their nether garments non-apparent; inasmuch as they marched without them. The bank of the Teesta, opposite Julpigorie, was reached at seven o'clock. Here it is a shallow and wide stream, fully half a mile broad; presenting a marked contrast to the rolling torrent where I last saw it. We crossed the river in flat-bottomed boats, and a quarter of an hour was occupied in getting from one bank to the other.

The station and village of Julpigorie are prettily situated, and straggle along the bank of the Teesta for some two miles. All the houses, European and native, are built of the same material—namely, mats supported on framework of bamboo. More solid structures are considered dangerous; owing to the loose nature of the soil, and a liability which is stated to exist to the occasional occurrence of earthquakes.

After all that has been officially written on the subject of Bhotan and the oppressive character of its rule in the Dooars, I was hardly prepared to hear from a resident of Julpigorie, peculiarly well placed for obtaining reliable information, that the inhabitants of the Dooars, bordering on our frontier, state that they have no complaints to make of the Bhotanese, and that they have suffered much more from aggression from within our frontier (including that of Cooch Behar) than from oppression exercised over them on the part of Bhotan; raiding within the Dooars by natives living under British protection, having apparently been as common as it has been within our own frontier by the Bhotanese.

In reference to this point, the following extract from the memorandum dated 7th May 1864, addressed by Mr. Eden to the Indian Government, recommending the adoption of the measures quoted at page 155 appears to me worthy of notice. Mr. Eden states:—"Whatever else it may be considered expedient to do with a view of procuring satisfaction for the repeated insults offered to us, I think that the course which I have indicated (the annexation of the Bengal Dooars) is imposed upon Government, not only in assertion of its own dignity, and in execution of positive threats held out, but also in duty to its subjects resident on the frontier. The feeling of impatience which our forbearance has excited among our own subjects, may be gathered from a letter from the manager of Messrs. Dear & Co. to the Deputy Magistrate of Titalyah, dated the 5th March 1862, in which he says—'If the Government are unable to compel the Gopalgunge man (a Bhotanese officer) to restore my stolen elephant, would there be any objection to my trying to get her myself by any means in my power? I pay income tax to Government: I think I have a right to the protection of Government: if Government are able (I know they are willing) to protect me and my property, I am content to abide their time to do me justice, but if they are not able, then let them pay me the value of my elephant, or give me leave to protect and do justice to myself.' In taking possession of these Dooars, it would be necessary to do more than issue a formal notification that the Dooars were attached to the British territory, otherwise we shall render the position of the inhabitants of that tract worse than it has been before. Drawing all their supplies, as they do, from this tract, the Bhotanese will not probably surrender them without at least a formal show of resistance; and if the Dooars were left exposed to the raids of the Bhoteahs, they would become even more depopulated and devastated than they are now." This elephant case and the circumstances connected with it, are detailed in the latter of Appendix B, and it seems to me that the tone of the letter quoted by Mr. Eden is calculated to corroborate what the inhabitants of the Dooars state about aggressions from within the British frontier; inasmuch as the expressions used in it indicate the existence of—and the means of putting in force, the principle of "those taking who have the power and those keeping who can," on our side of the frontier. This is the interpretation at least, I put on the words "trying to get her back by any means in my power"—the conclusion that force is meant being unavoidable from the fact that the Bhotanese official at Gopalgunge, and also the Deb Raja, offered to give the elephant up for 300 rupees, a gun, and a telescope; considering, therefore, that the whole sum thus demanded did not exceed £35, it is clear that procuring the elephant back by force was thought practicable at a lower rate than that, otherwise the inference is that the terms offered would have been agreed to; as it is not probable that the permission of the Government would have been applied for to make an amicable adjustment of the matter; the more so as the Bhotanese declared that the elephant originally belonged to them. Though Mr. Eden characterises in his report this assertion as an act of insolence, yet of the impossibility of its being the case no shadow of evidence is adduced by him;

and therefore in a locality where rights of property have hitherto been so loosely respected, however apparently legitimately the elephant may have fallen into the complainant's hands, the possibility of the Bhotanese assertion having truth in it is not necessarily precluded.

Mr. Eden, at the time of writing his report, it must be remembered, can hardly be considered an impartial judge of the Bhotanese; and though, in his opinion, disregard of truth appears one of the prominent attributes of their character, more recent observers have nevertheless formed a more favourable impression. In an article relating to the military operations in Bhotan, in the "Calcutta Englishman" of the 29th March 1865, it is stated—"Our correspondents remark upon a most curious fact, that in no case have the Bhoteah prisoners, whom we have taken, given false information; everything they have said has been proved to be true. If this habit is general amongst the Bhoteahs, as our correspondents seem to think, we have indeed come upon a phenomenon in natural history—an Asiatic race addicted to speaking the truth, and possessing the other Persian virtue of using the bow well." Mr. Eden, in attributing "depopulation and desolation" in the Dooars specially to Bhotanese government, is hardly supported by facts; inasmuch as the most populated and most flourishing portions of them that I have seen, are those in the vicinity where the Bhotanese officials resided. The truth is, there is but a very scanty population in this part of Bengal, and as already shown, the Mechis, who form a considerable portion of it, are of unsettled agricultural habits—a fact which Mr. Eden himself makes reference to in his report, but apparently fails to see the probable connection it has with the neglected condition of the Dooars he describes.

Mentioning to Captain Huxham, who, as Wing officer and second in command of the 30th Punjaubees, has had extensive experience of the Western Dooars, what I had heard respecting the friendly feelings entertained by the inhabitants thereof towards the Bhotanese, he said that in his opinion it must be merely local, and confined to the vicinity of our frontier; as he had been careful to inquire amongst the people on the Bhotan side of the Dooars, and that without exception they had expressed gladness at coming under British rule: assigning as their reason, that they felt a degree of security with reference to the fate of their crops which they had hitherto been strangers to. Captain Huxham procured this information through the interpretorial aid of a Sebundy Sapper he had with him, who spoke the Mechi dialect. It would thus seem, from these conflicting statements, that on both borders of the Dooars analogous states of insecurity of property have prevailed; attributable on the one side to raids from within the British frontier, and on the other to raids from the Bhotan hills.

Without attempting to say what the general feeling of the inhabitants throughout the Dooars may be with reference to the change of Government, there was reason to believe, that, at the period of my visit to Julpigorie, those in the neighbourhood of the frontier in that direction would rather have remained as they were than come under our rule—a strong feeling of discontent prevailing respecting an order which had been issued by General Tytler, forbidding the villagers near Mynagoorie and Julpesh to wash or bathe in the parts of the river they had been hitherto in the habit of doing, and indicating a spot to them below Julpesh, to which for the future their ablutions were to be confined; sentries and policemen being at the same time stationed along the proscribed limits of the river to arrest any one infringing the order. This interference with their liberty of action the Bengalee villagers are stated to feel much; as it prevents their doing exactly as their forefathers have done before them: that they should continue to do so, being one of their most cherished customs.

From what I learned at Julpigorie about the produce of the Dooars, it appears that next to rice tobacco is their chief product, and is procurable in large quantities. The villagers however will not sell any of their produce, except at the fairs, which are held at fixed periods during the week. This I observed on the journey from Dhalimkote; our servants meeting with refusal on every occasion that they endeavoured to purchase provisions, such as eggs and fowls. A good deal of cotton also is grown in different parts, especially near the foot of the hills. It has a large pod, and is of good quality—but little care however is expended on its cultivation. In regard to this product I am told that a lucrative trade has—until lately arrested by our military operations—been carried on by Bengalees with the Bhotanese, the former taking up rice and bartering it weight for weight of cotton, thereby realizing enormous profits on their transactions; the commercial ignorance displayed by the latter in this matter apparently being nearly equal to that displayed by the Japanese at the commencement of our treaty intercourse in 1858, when gold could be purchased from them for but a few times its equivalent weight in silver.

Having left the coolie who carried my baggage from Darjeeling with the party at Dhalimkote, I had to procure a hackery at Julpigorie to convey it across country to Punkabarree; and having completed my arrangements I started in the afternoon for Ambaree Fallacottah, distant fifteen miles, and midway between Julpigorie and Silligoorie. I was now alone, with the exception of my native servant—a Madras man—who, though rejoicing in the euphonious name of Rung-go-sammy, had modestly adopted the Christian one of "James"—but had no other pretensions to that faith, which I cannot say was a source of regret to me; Madras Christians—or at least the class who take service with Europeans, and call themselves "Creest-awns," having the reputation of being, as a general rule, the worst of their kind; their conceptions of Christianity being chiefly confined to disregarding any control which their own religion may have formerly exercised over them; getting drunk, making use of English oaths, and copying such other peculiarities as constitute salient points of distinction between their own and the Christian race, with which they are associated.

The road to Ambaree Fallacottah is a somewhat intricate one, owing to numerous cross paths; and as the hackery man was not well acquainted with it, especially in the dark, frequent delays occurred procuring information from villagers in its vicinity, and though I left Julpigorie at five o'clock, I did not reach Ambaree Fallacottah until midnight. The only place I could find to sleep in was an outhouse, which seemed to have been used as a stable, attached to the establishment of the Raja of Julpigorie, who resides usually at this place. He was at the time absent, having taken a house at Darjeeling for the hot weather. I may here mention, with reference to him, that he is one of the many petty Rajas now under our protection, and that having been left a minor he was taken charge of as such, educated, and his affairs looked after until he became old enough to manage them himself. He consequently has received a thoroughly European education, of which he gave an illustration during his residence at Darjeeling; being at the time I left the station under medical treatment for symptoms considered a remarkably good imitation of delirium tremens. His establishment was left in charge of some sepoys, who occupied a guard-house at the gate, and one of them gave me the loan of a charpoy,* on which I slept soundly until daylight.

Ambaree Fallacottah I found to be a fine fertile district, well cultivated, and surrounded by villages. From its position it is difficult to understand how the Indian Government ever came voluntarily to cede it to Bhotan, seeing that it is some miles within our frontier proper. It is distant from Silligoorie about sixteen miles, and I left for that place at six in the morning. The road is both bad and difficult, and but for the aid of the natives the hackery man would

* The charpoy is the form of bed and bedstead in common use amongst the natives of India. It consists of a light wooden frame, filled up by an interlacement of rope work, and supported by four legs about a foot and a half from the ground. The better kinds have broad tape in lieu of rope work, and are in general use amongst Europeans in the up country districts as a substitute for the mattress bed, being cooler and less cumbrous.

have lost his way. The country I passed over was partly under rice cultivation, partly in pasturage, the latter being well stocked with cattle. The mode of harrowing adopted by the natives hereabouts is simple and rude. Three pieces of bamboo are ranged longitudinally, and fastened together by cross pieces. On this frame a man stands, and by his weight keeps it in firm contact with the ground as it is drawn along by bullocks. I reached Silligoorie at one o'clock, and halted at the dawk bungalow.

The following morning I re-entered the Terai, and got to Punkabaree at noon. Here I discharged the hackery, and left my servant to bring on my baggage and his own, on a pony that I hired from the native in charge of the dawk bungalow; no coolie being procurable. I then ascended to Kursiong, reaching the barracks there at five o'clock. On inquiring of the artillerymen who had recently come up from Julpesh, with reference to the circumstances under which they had been placed at the time cholera made its appearance amongst them, they complained of the ventilated bamboo flooring, of the huts referred to at page 354, stating that their clothes and bedding were invariably quite damp in the morning from the moisture which passed through the floors during the hours of dark; showing that, in the course of the varied circumstances under which the British soldier has to be located, improvements in ventilation may not always be improvements in sanitation. Even the Bhotanese, as far as my observation has extended, avoid this error, and form their floors of thick planking—in other respects their houses being the same as those in question, and raised the same height from the ground.

On the morning of the 18th of May, at half-past three o'clock, I left Kursiong, and made a long march of it into Darjeeling, arriving there at nine o'clock. The road I have already described as being a remarkably good one, with a slope so gentle as to be hardly perceptible until the ascent to Julla Pahar commences. This latter, however, is only a path for foot-travellers, palanquins, or ponies—a continuation of the level broad road running round Julla Pahar to Darjeeling on the left. It is not used at present, being some three miles longer than the other. It has been made with the view of forming the continuation of a cart-road communicating with the plains, and operations are now going on making a road, that it is expected will admit of hackeries coming right up from Silligoorie to Kursiong, and from thence of course along the road already made to Darjeeling. When this is effected the route by Punkabaree will cease.

CHAPTER XXII.

Further Observations on the Lepchas and their Language—Land Speculations operate unfavourably in developing Contentment with British Rule—Dress of the Lepchas—History, Progress and Prospects of the Darjeeling Mission for the Conversion of the Natives—Relations of Darjeeling with Thibet—Question of more extended Commerce with that Country—Treaty Provision for a Road through Sikim—Communication with Thibet through Bhotan—A conciliatory Policy towards the latter Country a Question of diplomatic Expediency—Note relating to the Position of our Affairs with Bhotan at the end of 1865.

A FEW days after returning to Darjeeling, I had a long and interesting conversation with the Reverend Mr. Niebel, a German Baptist Missionary, who has resided there twenty-two years, and is probably more intimately acquainted with the Lepchas than any other European. He has been studying their language, and engaged in the work of their conversion during the long period mentioned; but as far as refers to the latter with no results as yet of a satisfactory nature. Mr. Niebel, I found, had himself formed the idea that the Lepchas were emigrants from some other country, and was therefore the more ready to receive my view of their origin; namely, that they are sprung from the nomadic tribes of Mongols settled in Thibet, and not aboriginal to Sikim, as is supposed.* He confirmed what has already been

* In Nepaul, however, Mr. Niebel informed me that there is an undoubted aboriginal tribe to be found called the Newars: *ne* being the name of the country and *war* meaning people; *Paul* again in the lan-

quoted about their calling themselves Rong and not Lepchas, also that their written language is peculiar.* With reference to the latter point, it would be interesting to have it compared with the Mongolian, which could only be done through our Sinologues at Peking. Mr. Niebel scouted Cheeboo's statement about the Lepcha language being the product of the philological talents of one of their Rajas; as he says any information procured from the Lepchas as a class generally, however well educated or truthful they may be, which refers to periods beyond their own immediate epoch, is in no way reliable; as they have little or no idea of history. He also denies Cheeboo's assertion that the Lepcha language—or at least that which is recognised as such at Darjeeling—is free from admixture with Thibetian words, and gave as illustrations, that in the Lepcha, the word country is *Lee-ang*, while in the Thibetian it is *Ling*;† also that "kill" in the former is *say*—while, in the latter, it is *sat*. Mr. Niebel at the same time admits that the Lepcha language, as spoken at Darjeeling, contains much that is apparently original, and it is therefore quite possible that in saying what he did (see page 312), Cheeboo meant the language in its original state, before it became what is now known

guage of this tribe means country—hence Nepaul, the country of the *Ne*: conquered by the Goorkhas; the people we now call the Nepaulese.

* Thibet in the Lepcha language is called *Pooh*, but when written in ours it is spelt with B. The four letters given, however, convey the nearest approach to the word as pronounced by them. Bhotan again they call *Prooleang*. Their own country, as Cheeboo stated to me, is known to them as De jong— from *de* rice and *jong* producing.

† Yule, also, means country in the Thibetian language, but is employed as descriptive of larger tracts than Ling is supposed to imply.

as the Lepcha dialect—in other words, when it was pure Mongolian.

The Lepchas, it appears, in common with the Bhotanese, are a rather gregarious people; cultivating land for a certain number of years and then changing to another locality, accounting for the absence of towns which exists both in Sikim and Bhotan. They were much more contented under the rule of the Sikim Raja, than they now are under that of the British Government; having become dissatisfied in consequence of the inroad made on their lands by tea-culture speculation—their lands having been bought up from their headmen, and they themselves suddenly turned adrift to find new settlements where they can, or take to novel modes of employment, which are distasteful to them. At first, on coming under British rule they were contented; as they were given to understand that they would not be interfered with, further than being required to pay a tax which was not to exceed two rupees per house, This they did not object to in lieu of paying their annual tribute of rice and a pig to the Sikim Raja—though at the same time they made no complaint with respect to the latter. The only inconvenience which they admit attended this mode of paying for their land was the distance the tribute had to be conveyed—it was the custom, however, and, like all Orientals, for custom they had a great respect, and willingly conformed to it.* Now, however, things are altogether

* From officers whose experience of the Dooars has been confined to the Assam side, I have learned that sentiments very similar to the above pervade the inhabitants of the Dooars that they passed through during the late operations. No evidence being apparent of a desire to come under our protection on the part of the inhabitants of those

changed; the large tracts of land absorbed in the attempt to form tea-plantations having revolutionised their primitive state of society. In the inauguration of our Government in the Bhotan hills and the Bengal Dooars, it would therefore seem desirable that a similar cause of discontent should be anticipated, and some check imposed on native proprietors and village headmen selling land to foreign speculators, when such transactions involve the agricultural community being dispossessed of them, and their hereditary mode of livelihood interfered with. Waste land enough exists to afford scope for speculation without encroaching on, or even approaching a single acre of the agricultural and pastoral land now in use. Some landowners appear to recognise the injustice done their dependants by this mode of disposing of their land—Cheeboo Lama, for instance, who has refused lucrative offers made him for the purchase of the land given him by the British Government as a reward for his services—Cheeboo preferring going on cultivating it after the fashion of his forefathers, and getting his little tribute from his tenants. Tea speculation, I may here observe, is commencing to show a tendency to affect even the essential necessaries of life of the district. Formerly Darjeeling was noted for the goodness of its potatoes; now, however, judging from what I saw while with the 80th Regiment, it is likely not only to be distinguished for extreme badness of

portions of the Assam Dooars that were about to pass under our rule. While again in the portions that were accustomed to it, the people were slow to express any gratification at the change of government they had undergone, frequently saying that they saw no advantage in having to pay taxes to us in money, in place of giving up some of their produce to the Bhotanese, as they formerly had to do.

THE CHIEF LAMA PRIEST OF DARJEELING, ROSARY IN HAND, AND HIS ATTENDANT.
A PAHAREE AND LEPEHA SITTING DOWN.

[From a Photograph.]

quality but for scarcity of supply. The cause to which this deterioration is referred, is the fact that all the best land in the neighbourhood, including that on which potatoes used to be grown, is now taken up as tea-plantations. That the ultimate success as such, of a large proportion of the land thus occupied, is a matter of considerable doubt, I have already alluded to.

An opinion prevails in Darjeeling that dress is distinctive of the true Lepcha or Rong, and that neither the Bhotanese nor the Thibetians ever wear the many coloured striped garments that are characteristic of the former. My own observation hardly bears this out, and I may cite the following illustration. Walking in the bazaar on the 28th of May, I noticed in one of the groups loitering about two men dressed exactly alike, with the exception that one of them had on the yellow silk pork-pie hat. The dress consisted of an under garment, over which a striped cotton quilt was worn, somewhat after the manner of the shepherds' plaid, the arms being quite free, but the quilt so arranged as to hang loosely and descend a little below the knee. The long-bladed straight wooden-sheathed knife, or *ban*, as it is called, being worn on the right side, and suspended across the left shoulder. The one with the yellow hat said he was a Lepcha; the other described himself as a Sikim Bhoteah. To the European eye they were both Lepchas—they themselves, however, recognised a distinction in the term; the man who styled himself a Lepcha being a Rong or Mongolian—while the other was a Thibetian, whose family had settled in Sikim. The reader will probably ere this have fully recognised the ethnological confusion which the local adoption of the Nepaulese word Lepcha has created, and how difficult it is to avoid applying it as generic for two distinct people, when properly speaking it is

LEPCHA MODE OF CARRYING WATER IN BAMBOO TUBES OR CHOONGAS.

to distinguish a tribe *sui generis*, distinct from the Thibetians and other settlers in the Southern Himalayan range. The impression which has arisen respecting striped garments being peculiar to the

Lepchas, I think admits of the following explanation —namely, that while the striped cotton quilt (red and white, or blue and white) is that usually worn by the Rong tribe, the Sikim Bhoteahs wear a loose dressing-gown looking habiliment with wide sleeves, formed of a half woollen half cotton material, into which all the colours of the rainbow enter, arranged in stripes. It is girded at the waist, and with the exception of its showy pattern and material, is the same kind of outer garment as is worn by the Bhotanese or the Dhurma Bhoteahs, as they are called by the other tribes at Darjeeling. With respect to the dress of the Lama Priests—while at Peking, a yellow robe is its chief characteristic, at Darjeeling it is a red one with a yellow girdle—the later being the local distinguishing mark of the priesthood. Cheeboo, however, occasionally puts on a new yellow robe, and commands great respect when he appears abroad in it. The one he wears in ordinary was once yellow, but it is now so dirty and greasy, as to have completely obscured its original claim to that colour. Cheeboo is much liked and respected by the officals at Darjeeling, and I believe has had hints given him as to the probable advantages he would derive from the adoption of the foreign custom of regularly washing; but these hints have made no impression on Cheeboo, who adheres to the contempt for water distinctive of his tribe; Lepchas as a general rule rarely or never washing.

Having alluded to the Reverend Mr. Niebel's position as a missionary at Darjeeling, a notice of the circumstances under which he came to be settled there, may not be without interest to many—the following account of the origin of the mission is given by Captain Hathorn *:—"The Darjeeling mission was commenced, and has been, and is entirely supported by the Rev. William Start. This gentleman, a man of education and some substance, has devoted the whole of a long life and the greater part of his wealth to the cause of Indian missions. He is now (1862) in England, compelled by old age and ill-health to relinquish those personal labours in which his earlier years have been passed. Mr. Start came to Darjeeling for the first time in 1841, and then at once, with the view of forming a mission, commenced making a limited collection of Lepcha words. His original intention was to establish a mission at Darjeeling, on the Moravian, or self-supporting industrial system, and with this object he located several German missionaries at Tukvor (a spur to the west of Darjeeling station) in 1842. Mr. Treutler, Mr. Stoelke, the late Mr. Wernicke, and the Rev. C. G. Niebel, were amongst the number, but the experiment did not succeed, and the latter is the only one who continued to labour in connection with Mr. Start, which he has done, we believe, uninterruptedly from that time to the present. It has been remarked by a writer in the "Calcutta Review" with reference to the Darjeeling mission, that the Moravian system of missions is not suited to any part of India, because "Europeans cannot gain a livelihood as tradesmen in competition with natives." That this is a mistake so far as Darjeeling is concerned, is proved by the fact that the three Germans who left the mission work have without exception gained a livelihood as tradesmen, and one of them at least is now in comfortable if not affluent circumstances. We

* "Handbook of Darjeeling," published by La Page and Co., Calcutta.

must look elsewhere for the cause of failure. We are not disposed to enter on the subject at length, or to criticise the acts of so excellent a man as Mr. Start, but we conceive that some of his arrangements, however well intentioned, must have given umbrage to the Germans, and without coming to a positive rupture it was thought better to dissolve the connection, the mission being henceforth carried on conjointly by Mr. Start and Mr. Niebel. The Rev. Mr. Schultze also worked here during the year 1842, and the Rev. Mr. Cumley during 1848, 1849 and 1852. Mr. Start used to work at Darjeeling during the hot weather, and in the plains in the cold, until 1852, when he finally left the country; and though his intention was at the time to return, the medical men have positively forbidden it. Since 1852 Mr. Niebel has been alone.

"The chief object of the mission was the conversion of the Lepchas, and accordingly a dictionary of that language has been formed, as well as of the Nepaulese. In the Lepcha language Genesis, part of Exodus, and the Gospels of Matthew, Mark, and John, have been translated, and for the most part published. In Nepaulese, the Gospels of Luke and the Acts have been translated. Besides these, tracts both in Lepcha and Nepaulese have been distributed. For some years the work of the mission was confined to studying the language and compiling dictionaries; the latter, as we can testify from personal examination, are most voluminous; and the labour thus expended, although in itself obviously not of a nature to produce conversions, will ease the work of those who follow, and enable them with facility to learn and speak the language. Of late Mr. Niebel has also been preaching and itinerating, but we believe one conversion has been the only manifest result.

"Mr. Niebel is a married man with a large family, and his means of support, which are entirely derived from Mr. Start, are very small. We conceive that it is of great importance that this mission should be kept up. Darjeeling is on the high road from India to Lassa, the head-quarters of Boodhism, and is visited by Nepaulese, Thibetians, and hill tribes innumerable. These visitors, if instructed at Darjeeling, would carry away the seeds of Divine truth into their own lands, and act as the harbingers and forerunners of the missionaries who will one day follow. The southern foot of the Himalayas is a complete barrier to the spread of the gospel northwards. The Gospel taught in one part of the plains may spread from Calcutta to Peshawur, but the Himalayas as a huge breakwater, receives the truth and rolls it back again upon the plains. North of this barrier line are other races of the human family, and to affect them a mission must be established either in or north of the Himalayas. Twenty years have been spent in preparations, and now unless assistance of some kind is rendered, there is a strong probability of this labour being thrown away. For instance, what will become of the mission when good Mr. Start is taken from us? The Rev. Mr. Niebel is a Baptist, and as such the only society that could well adopt him is the Baptist or the London Missionary Society."

The mission at the present date continues as described in the foregoing extract, with the exception that the London Missionary Society has so far recognised Mr. Niebel as to temporarily give him an allowance of sixty rupees (£6) per month. With this exception his means of support are entirely derived from the rents of one or two houses in the station belonging to Mr. Start, and which of course form a precarious source of income.*

Some notice of the relations of Darjeeling with Thibet may not be out of place before bringing this narrative to a conclusion. At the present time no extent of trade exists, and what does, is carried on chiefly on sheep used as pack animals. Wool is the principal commodity brought from Thibet, cotton and tobacco being taken back in exchange. Ponies also, gold, silver, precious stones, coarse woollen and China goods are sometimes brought over from Thibet. The traders generally pass from Thibet about November before the snows set in, and return in spring after the melting of the snow has commenced: the passes in the mountains being impracticable in the interval. Judging however from the number of Thibetians seen about Darjeeling during the period I was there, they evidently either remain until later periods of the year or come across during the summer months as well.

In a report on Darjeeling written in 1853, Mr. Welby Jackson makes the following remarks with reference to the extension of trade between that place and Thibet.—"The flocks of Thibet are immensely numerous, and of the finest quality; it is as fine as the merino with a much longer staple, and its fineness is attributed to the same cause; the fine and succulent short pasture of the Thibet hills, while the cold climate has the usual effect on the fleece of supplying that peculiar quality which is found in the shawl wool

* While these sheets are passing through the press, I have, with much regret, heard of the Reverend Mr. Niebel's death; which took place at Darjeeling on the 9th of October 1865: its cause being dysentery, a disease when once developed, as formidable in the Himalayas, as it is in the plains of Bengal.

of the Thibet goats. The high plains on which these numerous flocks feed are of immense extent, and if the importation of the article could be facilitated, it would be a source of profit to our speculators and manufacturers, and of riches and civilisation to the steppes of Thibet which have hitherto been excluded from all possibility of improvement by rigid application of the exclusive policy of the Chinese. The Thibetian institutions are such as to admit without difficulty of the establishment of a consul of a foreign nation at Lassa, for the protection and control of the foreigners carrying on trade there. The Nimals of Nepaul, the Cashmeerees, the Ladakees, and the people of Bhotan have all headmen or consuls of this description at Lassa, as well as other states lying between China and Thibet. If, therefore, the traffic with Thibet could be extended by improvement of the communication, it would be easy to effect a commercial establishment in Lassa, if the opposition to the Chinese power now so much on the wane, could once be got over." With the view at some future period of extending our commerce in the direction of Thibet, the following clause was introduced into the treaty executed by Mr. Eden with the Sikim Raja in 1861 :—

"In the event of the British Government desiring to open out a road through Sikim with the view of encouraging trade, the Sikim Government will raise no objection thereto, and will afford every protection and aid to the party engaged in the work. If a road is constructed the Government of Sikim undertakes to keep it in repair, and to erect and maintain suitable travellers' rest-houses throughout its route."

The distance between Darjeeling and Lassa as the crow flies does not exceed 250 miles, but the nature of the ground which has to be travelled over, more than doubles that, and consequently the distance is usually estimated at about 600 miles. In the event of the formation of a road through Sikim being attempted, the portion of hill country between Darjeeling and the Choombi valley in Thibet, a distance of eighty-four miles, is that which will offer the greatest obstacles to its construction. As the difficulties likely to be encountered no doubt will be great, and the expense involved considerable, it is not probable that the measure will be carried out.

Though direct communication with Lassa, within a moderate period, may not be practicable, more extended commerce with Thibet than now exists is not necessarily precluded, and it occurs to me that our present relations with Bhotan might be turned to useful account with reference thereto—beneficial to all parties concerned. Before entering however further on the subject, it is as well to review what our present position with that country is. We have annexed the Bengal Dooars and abolished the annual compensation paid for those of Assam, which have been under jurisdiction since 1841. We have also annexed the lower range of the Bhotan mountains, constituting a hill frontier extending east and west 180 miles—the difficulties connected with the keeping of which have been already illustrated. Forbearance no doubt has been shown the Bhotanese, but in dealing with a class of Orientals such as they are, some allowance requires to be made, and things tolerated which would be inadmissible in European diplomacy. Now, however, their Government, if such a thing really exists, has been punished for past misconduct, and we can afford to be magnanimous. To the Bengal Dooars our right is as good as theirs; the power of the stronger to take them from the weaker having constituted their claim to the land in question. The hill territory however is a part of their country proper, inhabited by their own people, and while a source of encumbrance to us, it is also of questionable utility—to say nothing of the possibility of its being a source of often recurring trouble—its restoration to Bhotan might therefore, perhaps, be made the basis of friendly intercourse with the country, and the means of establishing a communication through it towards Thibet—the large commercial town of Phagri (referred to at page 101) being within a day's march of Paro, the capital of Western Bhotan; even laden coolies taking only two days to perform the journey. The route again to Paro is known to us both from Darjeeling, and from the plains *viâ* the Buxa Dooar.

Our own interests are more immediately involved in such a concession than may at first sight appear. The occupation of the Dooars has been attended with great sickness and mortality; a very large proportion of both the officers and men who have served in them having suffered to a greater or lesser extent from the effects of their unhealthy climate. So long therefore as the present unsatisfactory condition of affairs continues to exist with Bhotan—for we are virtually still at war with it, being constantly on the defensive—will it be necessary to keep up a much larger military establishment in this sickly locality, than were a more amicable adjustment of existing difficulties brought about. Were we even to resume paying the compensation for the Assam Dooars, and agree to pay one for the newly annexed Bengal Dooars also, on the understanding that in the event of any aggression from the Bhotan side, the value of the damage done would be stopped from the annual compensation, it would be a source of great saving of expense to the Government, and of health and life to the army. What now requires the services of a regular field force might probably be done by a few hundred police—that is to say, provided the Bhotan chiefs—for Government I believe to be a misnomer—being now convinced of our power to coerce, should recognise the advantage of acting reasonably in the matter. The number of unhealthy stations already existing in India, where necessity compels troops being kept, is such as to justify the adoption of means, however conciliatory they may be, to avoid having the number increased.*

* The narrative now concluded, was, as stated in the Preface, completed by me at sea, and three days after my arrival in England on the 17th of October last, it was placed in the hands of the eminent publisher through whom it goes forth to the public. The views expressed above, were consequently formed entirely from information locally acquired and from the study of the subject in such official documents as publicity had been given to prior to my leaving Calcutta on the 17th of June previously: therefore in total ignorance of the course events were taking on the spot—a brief allusion to which, appears to me now required.

During the few weeks which have elapsed since the printing of the work commenced, news has arrived from India, that an expedition on an extensive scale, amounting to upwards of 7,000 men, and including a considerable force of British infantry and artillery had been detailed to enter Bhotan, in two distinct columns, towards the end of the present year; the one to operate against the western and the other against the eastern divisions of the country—the former directed against the nominal seat of government at Poonakha—the latter specially against the Tongso Penlow. Since this news was received, intelligence (chiefly telegraphic) has reached this country, to the effect, that, the Deb Raja, overawed by the military preparations in course of being made, had conformed to all our demands, and had concluded a treaty with Colonel Bruce, the Civil Commissioner of the Dooars; one of its terms being that the Government of India, in consideration of the loss of territory sustained by Bhotan, consents to pay the Government of that country an annual sum of 25,000 rupees (£2500) to be increased to twice that amount in the event of the treaty obligations being faithfully acted up to. This satisfactory intelligence however, is somewhat negatived by the fact that the treaty refers only to the Deb Raja, and has no relation to the Tongso Penlow who appears to continue contumacious and determined to resist foreign aggression. The Deb Raja is stated to have requested two months to persuade or coerce this chief, at the expiry of which time, in the event of his still proving obstructive to peace, his chastisement is to be handed over to the Indian Government. Those who have read through this work, especially its first portion, and also Appendix B, will I think, have some difficulty in realising the value of any treaty entered into with any nominal ruler of Bhotan—whether Deb or Dhurma Raja or the two combined; seeing that both are merely puppets in the hands of whichever local chief happens for the time to be most powerful, and should the Penlow of Tongso continue to be so (as he was very recently) the probabilities are that the treaty now telegraphed as concluded is not worth the paper it is written on as far as any guarantee is concerned that our troubles with Bhotan are at an end. At the same time I think there can be no doubt (except probably in the minds of those having either a limited acquaintance with the subject or direct interests involved in the development of petty wars and their usual sequents—territorial increase) regarding the sound judgment characterising the policy which has been inaugurated of holding out, as it were, a pecuniary bait to our semi-civilised neighbours to behave themselves; particularly, as the payment is not to commence until the Tongso Penlow returns the two guns captured at Dewahgiri. It is even within the limits of possibility that more extended concessions may become a question of expediency; the more so, as it has yet to be proved that the military posts which it appears to be the intention to maintain in the range of hills overlooking the Dooars, will realise the expectations formed of them in a sanitary point of view, especially, as, before they can be reached, plains and jungle of unquestionably pestilential character have to be traversed. In conclusion I may state that the Deb and Dhurma Rajas having about as much control over what is passing in the country—the nominal Government of which they represent—as the figure-head has over the steering of a vessel, it is not improbable that the simplest way of bringing existing difficulties to a speedy and satisfactory issue, will be reducing the question to a matter of fact, by disregarding the idea of dealing with a central or practically responsible Government, and confining negotiations to the local chiefs who virtually rule Bhotan; namely, the Penlows of Paro and Tongso—paying a portion of the annual allowance of 50,000 rupees to the former for the Bengal Dooars, and a portion of it to the latter for those of Assam: the tribute formerly drawn from these sources having formed important items in their respective revenues—leaving it to them to settle accounts as they like with the nominal Government for the time being.

18*th December*, 1865.

APPENDIX A.

Translation of the Treaty made with Bhotan in 1774.

"ARTICLES of a Treaty between the Honourable English East India Company and the Deb Raja, or Raja of Bhotan.

"1. That the Honourable Company, wholly from consideration for the distress to which the Booteahs represent themselves to be reduced, and from the desire of living in peace with their neighbours, will relinquish the lands which belonged to the Deb Raja before the commencement of the war with the Raja of Cooch Behar, namely, to the eastward of the lands of Chichacotta and Pangolahaut, and to the westward of the lands of Kyrantee, Marraghaut, and Luckeepoor.

"2. That for the possession of the Chichacotta province the Deb Raja shall pay an annual tribute of five Tangun horses to the Honourable Company, which was the acknowledgment paid to the Cooch Behar Raja.

"3. That the Deb Raja shall deliver up Dudjind-Narrain, Raja of Cooch Behar, together with his brother, the Dewan Deo, who is confined with him.

"4. That the Booteahs, being merchants, shall have the same privileges of trade as formerly, without the payment of duties, and their caravan shall be allowed to go to Rungpore annually.

"5. That the Deb Raja shall never cause incursions to be made into the country, nor in any respect whatever molest the ryots that have come under the Honourable Company's subjection.

"6. That if any ryot or inhabitant whatever shall desert from the Honourable Company's territories, the Deb Raja shall cause them to be delivered up immediately upon application being made to him.

"7. That in case the Booteahs, or any one under the Government of the Deb Raja, shall have any demands upon, or disputes with any of the inhabitants of these or any part of the Company's territories, they shall prosecute them only by an application to the magistrate who shall reside here for the administration of justice.

"8. That whatever Suniasses* are considered by the English as an enemy, the Deb Raja will not allow to take shelter in any part of the districts now given up, nor permit them to enter into the Honourable Company's territories, or through any part of his; and if the Bhoteahs shall not of themselves be able to drive them out, they shall give information to the Resident on the part of the English in Cooch Behar, and they shall not consider the English troops pursuing the Suniasses into these districts as any breach of this treaty.

"9. That in case the Honourable Company shall have occasion for cutting timbers from any part of the woods under the hills, they shall do it duty free, and the people they send shall be protected.

"10. That there shall be a mutual release of prisoners.

"This treaty to be signed by the Honourable President and Council of Bengal, and the Honourable Company's seal to be affixed on the one part, and to be signed and sealed by the Deb Raja on the other part."†

APPENDIX B.

Narrative of the Relations existing between the Government of India and the Bhotanese, between the Years 1828 *and* 1861 : *being the Details of what has been summarised at Pages* 50 *and* 51.

THE first serious aggression against the newly established authority of the Indian Government in Assam was perpetrated by a Bhotanese official, named the Doompa Raja, who had charge of the Booree Goomah Dooar; the most eastern of the seven belonging to Assam. This officer, on the 22nd of October 1828 entered the district of Chatgarie adjoining the Dooar,‡ and carried off not

* A sect of Faqueers or hereditary mendicant priests.

† The following signatures on the part of the Government of India are appended to this treaty: Warren Hastings, William Andersey, P. M. Daires, J. Lawrell, Henry Goodwin, H. Graham, and George Vansitart.

‡ This Dooar was one of those held alternately by the British and the Bhotanese Governments, in accordance with the arrangement described at page 48, and the outrages occurred during the period of the year when the authority of the latter prevailed. In a despatch to the Government of India, dated 5th November 1828, detailing the particulars of the outrage, Mr. Scott states—"That disputes had long existed between the Assamese and the Booteahs respecting the right to certain frontier villages, of which Batta Koochee, the spot where this occurrence took place, was one; but that the lands had continued in undisturbed possession of the British Government from the year 1828, when we first occupied the country of Assam; and that the Deb Raja had some time before deputed an agent on his part to be present at an investigation into his claims, which were under consideration at the very time this attack was made; and with a perfect understanding that the lands were to remain in the interim, as heretofore, in the possession of the British Government."

only some natives who had fled from his jurisdiction, but also the owner of the house under whose protection they had been living. The Thannae Mohurrir (native police superintendent) wrote to the Doompa Raja, demanding the householder's release, and at the same time proceeded to Batta Koochee, a post on the frontier where a detachment of eight sepoys was stationed, to investigate the circumstances. The Doompa Raja came down with an armed force, attacked the guard, and caused some loss of life. In addition to the attack on the guard, a number of women and other natives were carried off into captivity, and remonstrances having failed to procure satisfaction, the Governor-General's agent in Assam addressed a letter to the Deb Raja, demanding the release of the prisoners and the surrender of the Doompa Raja.

No notice seems to have been taken of the representations thus made to the Bhotan Government. The release of the captives, however, was effected by a Jemadar (native lieutenant) and a party of Sebundies (native local militia), who had been ordered to occupy the Booree Goomah Dooar. The Jemadar having found out the place where the prisoners were confined, suddenly advanced upon it, and set them at liberty.

We continued to occupy the Booree Goomah Dooar for three years without any demand for its restoration being made by the Bhotan Government. In 1831 however, a letter was addressed to the Government of India by the Deb Raja, soliciting its restoration, and implying that the Doompa Raja, who was the party responsible for what had occurred, was dead. This letter was referred by the Government to the agent of the Governor-General in Assam, for his opinion in reference to the expediency of complying with the Deb Raja's request, and it was ultimately determined that on unquestionable proof being afforded by the Bhotanese Government that the Doompa Raja was dead—and on the payment of a fine of two thousand rupees as compensation to the families of the sepoys who had been killed in the attack on Batta Koochee, the Dooars would be restored. It was not however until the 31st July 1834 that the first of these conditions was fulfilled, and the remaining one being also agreed to, the Bhotanese were allowed to re-occupy the Booree Goomah Dooar.

The settlement of this affair was not followed by any prolonged tranquillity; as the following year an incursion was made from the Bijnee Dooar by a party of fifty armed men, who attacked a house belonging to a native called Moonoo Jauldah, from which ten persons were carried off into Bhotan. In the despatch to Government, dated 28th May 1835, reporting this outrage, the local authorities drew attention to the frequency of such occurrences, and stated that the Bhotanese officials in charge of the Bijnee Dooar had positively refused to pay the tribute for that year, or to make arrangements for paying off outstanding balances for previous years, which at that time amounted to 30,000 Narrain rupees—the equivalent of about 1,500*l.* sterling.

A general feeling of insecurity prevailed along the frontier, resulting from these Bhotanese raids, which rendered prompt and decisive action indispensable. A detachment of Assam Light Infantry under a native officer of distinction named Zalim Sing was accordingly sent to effect the rescue of the prisoners, with orders to do so if practicable by pacific means. Zalim Sing proceeded to the frontier and from thence to the stockade in which the prisoners were confined, and endeavoured to procure their release by negotiation. He failed in doing so, and immediately stormed the stockade; rescuing nine out of the eleven natives who had been carried off, and also capturing the Dooba Raja, a chief Bhotanese officer of the Dooar. This official fully admitted his participation in the act which had led to his stockade being attacked, and admitted that of the natives (British subjects) who had been carried off in the course of these incursions, several had been presented to the Tongso Penlow; affording strong proof of his connivance in these predatory proceedings. It appears that at this time (1835), altogether twenty-two British subjects had been carried off by raids made from Bijnee Dooar. Of these nine were retaken by Zalim Zing's party, four were subsequently delivered up by the Dooba Raja, and the remaining nine persons were satisfactorily accounted for, but in what manner we have no information. The Dooba Raja was then set at liberty.

Inquiries instituted at this period proved that several of the Bhotan frontier officers sheltered bands of regularly licensed robbers, who paid them both in money and in shares of the plunder, in consideration of the protection afforded them. This was officially reported by the Governor-General's agent to the Deb Raja; and the surrender of the robbers secreted in the Bijnee and Banska Dooars demanded, as well as the arrears of tribute—in default of which, the immediate attachment of the two Dooars being threatened. No reply was received to these demands, and it is a matter of doubt as to whether the letter containing them ever reached the Deb Raja; as it is natural to suppose that the local officers felt it conducive to their own interests that the central Government, such as it was, should know as little as possible about their proceedings. To effect this, they frequently intercepted the communications sent to the Deb Raja by the British authorities in

Assam. The threat with reference to attacking the Bijnee and Banska Dooars was therefore not put in force.

The Botanese now became so troublesome on the frontier, that it was necessary to organise a special corps for its protection; the climate being too unhealthy for ordinary troops. With respect to this necessity, Captain Pemberton observes—"A very considerable proportion of the detachment of Light Infantry which had been employed in Bijnee Dooar was destroyed by the extreme unhealthiness of the tract, and Zalim Sing, its gallant leader, who had rendered the most important services to the Government, in various situations from the first occupation of Assam, was included in the melancholy list of victims to the climate. So strong was the impression of the deadly nature of the duties of the Dooars to any but men born in the neighbourhood, that an additional corps, called Assam Sebundies, was raised for their performance, and was almost entirely composed, either of natives of that part of the country, or of men bred in tracts similar to those which they were now appointed to defend." Our military experience of the climate, thirty years later, has been equally confirmatory of its pestilential character.

The Bijnee affair had hardly been settled, when another incursion was made into the Durrung district from the Kalling Dooar. This occurred on the 16th November 1835, and the magistrate of Durrung, Captain Mathie, immediately advanced to the frontier with a detachment of sixteen men of the Assam Sebundy corps, and made a demonstration which so alarmed the officer in charge of the Dooar, that he delivered over thirteen men who had been engaged in the outrage.

The next event of importance occurred on the 14th of January 1836, when a daring robbery attended with loss of life and property to natives under British protection was committed in the north Kamroop district, by Bhotanese from the Banska Dooar, the most valuable of those on the Assam frontier. The perpetrators of this outrage were traced to the residence of the Bhotanese frontier officer, who was known by the name of the Boora Talookdar. The surrender of the robbers and the plundered property was demanded and refused. The magistrate, Captain Bogle, immediately advanced across the frontier with a detachment of eighty men of the Sebundy corps under the command of Lieutenants Mathews and Vetch. The Boora Talookdar fled to Dewangiri, and as stolen property was found in his house, a formal demand for satisfaction was addressed to the Bhotanese official at Dewangiri, and also to the Penlow of Tongso. A notification was likewise issued attaching the Banska Dooar and closing two of the passes communicating with the plains. The Dewangiri official who went under the name of Raja, immediately commenced to negotiate, and under pretence of furthering an amicable adjustment of the affair, came down from his post in the hills to meet Captain Bogle, accompanied however by a number of armed followers. Captain Bogle declined to grant him an interview until he had complied with that portion of the demands which had been made, having reference to the surrender of the robbers. This was done on the 1st of March; nineteen of the culprits being given up. He then visited Captain Bogle, attended by the Boora Talookdar the chief offender, whom he refused to surrender. He made professions of friendship, which seemed so much in earnest, that Captain Bogle reopened the passes to traders, but still demanded the immediate surrender of all the delinquents. This determination appears to have embarrassed him a good deal, and after a few days' delay he addressed a letter to Captain Bogle, agreeing to all his terms but the surrender of the Boora Talookdar, who being an officer appointed directly by the Deb Raja, he professed to be unable to give up without an express order. He then to all appearance returned to the hills, and Captain Bogle considered the matter settled as far as he was concerned. The following morning, however, it was found, that, instead of proceeding homewards as had been supposed, he had taken up two strongly stockaded positions, apparently with the intention of resisting the attachment of the Dooar. He was ordered to retire, but declined to do so, and coercive measures were at once adopted. On the approach of Captain Bogle's party, the Bhotanese abandoned their advanced stockade and fell back on the second one, where they answered the requisition that they should retire with shouts of defiance, and commenced firing at the elephant from the top of which Captain Bogle had been addressing them. Lieutenant Mathews then advanced at the head of his men, and firing a volley, they retired in disorder leaving a number of killed and wounded behind them. The result of this was, that the Boora Talookdar and the remainder of the offenders, six in number, were surrendered, and the Banska Dooar was restored to Bhotan. The Government declared it had never heard of the robberies committed on the frontier, and that the letters of remonstrance addressed to it connected therewith had never been received.

While such was the state of matters on the Assam side, the oppression of the Bhotan frontier officers had driven the inhabitants of the Bengal Dooars into open rebellion, and in the month of March 1836, Major Lloyd, who had been deputed to that part of the frontier to adjust some disputes, forwarded a petition to Government from the Bengalee Katmas, or subordinate officials of the Dooars, applying to be taken under British protection, but which could not be complied with. The month after this petition was forwarded, the magistrate of Rungpore received a complaint from the Jungpen of Dhalimkote, complaining that an aggression had been committed against peasantry under his jurisdiction at Kyrantee, a spot about twenty miles below the fort of Dhalimkote, by a rebellious Katma called Hurgovind,* whom he asserted, was aided in this and other acts of aggression, by adventurers organised within the British frontier, to which they fled, when pressed by the Bhotanese troops. Inquiries were made, into the correctness of this statement, and instructions were given to prevent, as much as possible, the assistance complained of being afforded either in troops or munitions of war.

Under the belief that the Bhotan Government was really in ignorance of the proceedings of its officers on the frontier, and that the communications thereto relating, from the British Government were either intercepted or withheld, it was determined in 1837 to send an envoy to the Court of Bhotan, to "settle the terms of commercial intercourse between the states, and, if possible, to effect such an adjustment of the tribute as might diminish the chances of misunderstanding arising from that source." Notification of this intention was sent to the Dhurma and Deb Rajas, whose replies clearly showed that the proposition was not an acceptable one. Three letters, contained in the same envelope, were received from the Deb Raja, dated on the 6th of April 1837. The first one proposed that no envoy should be sent to Bhotan, until an embassy on his (the Deb's) part should have reached Calcutta; or else that the proposed envoy should not be sent until fresh disturbances or disputes arose on the frontier, when in the event of such occurring, the Deb would have no objections to receive him. This letter also acknowledged certain presents which had been sent to the father of the Dhurma Raja, at the request of the agent of the Governor-General in Assam, and which the Deb alleged had been presented to the Dhurma Raja, who was represented as being much gratified

* This Katma Hurgovind, it appeared, was the nephew of a person called Hurry Doss, a Bengalee, who for many years had held an office in the household of the Deb Raja, and whose family possessed the estate of Mynagoorie in the Bengal Dooars under the Bhotan Government. He had been exposed to a good deal of oppression and injustice, to which he submitted for some time, and at last threw off his allegiance to Bhotan and seized upon some farms adjoining his property at Mynagoorie. He then hired a number of Hindostanee and Goorkha sepoys, and with their assistance, and arms procured from within the British frontier, he successfully resisted the Bhotanese. He then offered to pay the British Government 50,000 rupees annually, as tribute for its protection, but which it was not thought expedient to extend to him. The Bhotan Government ultimately came to terms with him, and he resumed his allegiance to it.

with them.* A second letter contained an account of the outrage committed by the Bengalee Katma, Hurgovind, and asking assistance in effecting his apprehension. The third communication requested that an order might be issued to render Bhotan money current in the East India Company's territories, or in the event of such not being practicable, the Deb requested the Government would furnish him with dies similar to those used in the Company's mint. On the 17th of April 1837, the Zinkaffs who had conveyed these letters left Calcutta with the Governor-General's reply to the effect that he adhered to his determination to send an envoy who would start on the termination of the rainy season.

This mission was entrusted to Captain Boileau Pemberton, accompanied by Ensign Blake, of the 56th Native Infantry, as Assistant and Commandant of the escort, and Dr. Griffiths, of the Madras Establishment, as Botanist and Medical Officer. The escort consisted of one Soubadar (captain), one Havildar (sergeant), and twenty-five sepoys of the Assam Sebundy corps.

The first question which presented itself to Captain Pemberton on assuming the charge of the mission, was the route by which it was to endeavour to reach the seat of government in Bhotan; past experience derived from the missions of Bogle and Turner rendering it probable that if left to the decision of the Bhotanese themselves it would be compelled to follow that taken by these officers, and enter the country by the Buxa Dooar, which runs so directly north and south as to afford but limited opportunities for making observations on the country. With the view therefore of doing so in a more satisfactory manner than it was practicable for either of the two previous missions to do, Captain Pemberton determined to enter Bhotan by one of the passes as far to the east as practicable, and selected that opening on the Banska Dooar, as the one least likely to be questioned; the Dooar having so recently been the subject of correspondence between the two Governments.

This course having been finally decided on, the mission proceeded direct from Calcutta by water to Gowhatty in Assam; intimation having previously been given of its intention to enter Bhotan from the Banska Dooar. Captain Pemberton arrived at Gowhatty on the 8th of December 1837, and was detained there until the twenty-first of the same month, waiting for a reply from the Deb Raja to the notification which had been sent of the route the mission intended taking. Captain Pemberton then pushed on to the frontier, and crossing the Berhampooter river about three miles be-

* It was subsequently ascertained that neither the Dhurma Raja nor his father received any of the presents; the whole having been intercepted and appropriated by the Deb.

low Gowhatty, commenced his march through the Kamroop district of Assam, which he thus describes—"The change now perceptible was most marked and delightful; from the northern bank of the Berhampooter to the frontier line which separated the British from the Bhotan territory, our march lay almost entirely through fields of the most luxuriant rice cultivation, and amongst villages which bore every appearance of being the dwellings of a happy and prospering people. All the fruit trees common to Bengal were found growing in profusion around the houses of the inhabitants; the herds of cattle were numerous and in the finest condition, and everything bespoke happiness and content. This general character of the country continued with little interruption as far as Dumduma, a village on the south bank of the Nao Nuddee, which here forms the boundary between the British and Bhotan possessions: but immediately after crossing it, a very marked change became apparent: extensively cultivated fields were no longer perceptible, and nearly the whole plain over which we travelled, from the nullah to the foot of the inferior heights of the Bhotan mountains, was covered with dense reed and grass jungle: the few villages were comparatively small and impoverished, and those which had been originally large and better inhabited had not recovered from the effects of the hostile invasion by our troops under Captain Bogle in 1836." After some delays at Dumduma, the mission continued its journey, and on the 3rd of January 1838, reached Dewangiri situated on the southern range of mountains immediately overlooking the valley of Assam.

At Dewangiri the mission was exposed to a delay of three weeks, caused by a succession of attempts which were made to induce Captain Pemberton to return to the plains, and re-enter Bhotan by the Buxa Dooar, and prosecute his journey by that route to the capital. This proposal, however, was resisted by Captain Pemberton, who, after being thus detained until the 23rd of January, was allowed to proceed by the route he had commenced.

During the detention of the mission at Dewangiri, a rebellion broke out, headed by the Daka Penlow (the Governor of Central Bhotan) against the Deb Raja, and as the direct route to Poonakha lay through the district of the Jungpen of Jonjar, who happened to be the brother and chief adviser of the rebellious Penlow, the Zinkaffs who had been appointed to accompany the mission recommended that the disaffected territories should be avoided. The mission was consequently compelled to adopt a circuitous route to Poonakha, extending over 250 miles, which occupied from the 23rd of January to the 1st of April; the delay arising from the unsettled state of the country, want of conveyance for baggage, and halts necessary to allow the followers to recover from the fatigue of long and severe marches. The number of days however actually employed in travelling was twenty-six.*

On reaching the quarters which had been provided for it at Poonakha and which were situated in front of the palace, the mis-

* I have not thought it necessary to weary the reader with the details of this tedious journey. Considering however the prominent part which the Governor of Eastern Bhotan (the Tongso Penlow) plays in another part of this narrative, a notice of Tongso, his seat of government, may not be uninteresting. Tongso, though usually considered the place of about third importance in Bhotan, is represented at this time (1838) as a miserable place, situated in a very narrow ravine drained by a petty stream. The village is 6,250 feet in altitude, and consisted of a few houses, the worst of which was rented to the mission. The castle of the Tongso Penlow is situated 1,200 feet lower down than the village, and stands on a tongue of land formed by the junction of the stream, above mentioned, with the large torrent of the Mateesam. It is described as a large, rather imposing-looking building sufficiently straggling to be relieved from heaviness of appearance, and so overhung by some of the nearest mountains, that it might be destroyed by rolling down rocks upon it. It is nominally defended, but in reality commanded by an outwork 400 feet above it. The surrounding country was found to be uninteresting, the vegetation consisting of a few low shrubs and some grasses. No woods could be reached without ascending from twelve to fifteen hundred feet. Barley was the chief cultivation seen; the crops being alternated with rice, which was cultivated here as high as 6,800 feet. In the gardens attached to the cottages, almond and pear trees in full blossom were seen. Of the arrival of the mission at Tongso on the 5th of March 1838, and its subsequent residence there, Dr. Griffiths gives the following brief but amusing account:—

"Our reception was by no means agreeable. I was roared to most insolently to dismount while descending to the castle, our followers were constantly annoyed, and in fact we got no peace until we had an interview with the Pillo (Penlow) on the 15th (ten days after arrival). Before the arrival of this personage, who had just succeeded to office, great efforts were made to bring about an interview with the ex-Pillo, and stoppage of supplies was actually threatened in case of a refusal. The firmness of Captain Pemberton was however proof against all this. It had been previously arranged that the former Pillo, the uncle of the present one, should be admitted at this interview on terms of equality; this kindness on the part of the nephew being prompted probably by the hopes of securing his uncle's presents afterwards. We were received with a good deal of state, but the apartments in which the meeting took place was by no means imposing or even well ornamented. The attendants were very numerous, and mostly well dressed, but the effects of this were lessened by the admission of an indiscriminate mob. We were not admitted however into the presence without undergoing the ordeals which the low impertinence of many Orientals imposes on those who wish for access to them. We were much struck with the difference in appearance between the old and new Pillos; the former was certainly the most aristocratic personage we saw in Bootan; the latter a mean bull-necked individual. A novel part of the ceremony consisted in the stirring up of a large can of tea and the general recital of prayers over it, after which a ladleful was handed to the Pillos who dipped their forefingers in it and so tasted it. The meeting passed off well, and afterwards several less ceremonies and more friendly meetings took place. We took leave on the 22nd (March). This interview was chiefly occupied in considering the list of presents which the Pillo requested the British Government would do themselves the favour of sending him. He begged most unconscionably, and I thought the list would never come to an end. And he was obliging enough to say that anything he might think of subsequently would be announced in writing. He was very facetious, and evidently rejoiced at the idea of securing so many good things at such a trifling expense as he had incurred in merely asking for them. Nothing could well exceed the discomfort we had to undergo during our tedious stay at this place. Our difficulties were increased subsequently to our arrival by the occurrence of unsettled weather, during which we had ample proofs that Bootan houses are not always waterproof. We were besides incessantly annoyed with a profusion of rats, bugs and fleas. Nor was there a single thing to counterbalance all these inconveniences, and we consequently left the place without the shadow of a feeling of regret."

sion was struck with the want of care and consideration shown with reference to the preparations for its reception, considering the long notice the Government had had of its coming. The quarters allotted to it had evidently been stables, and consisted of a square enclosure surrounded by low mud walls. Above the stables, small recesses, not much bigger than coffins, had been constructed as dormitories for the members of the mission, with the exception of Captain Pemberton, for whom a recess somewhat larger had been prepared. The whole was covered in by a roof of single mats, forming but an indifferent protection from the oppressive sun then prevailing, and, in addition, contained a profusion of every description of vermin. Captain Pemberton consequently determined on renting quarters in the village, and being willing to pay liberally, had no difficulty in hiring two houses, where the location of the mission, though improved, was by no means free from some of the discomforts of the quarters the Government had provided for it.

The winter capital of Bhotan was found to consist of some twelve or fifteen houses, half of which were on the left bank of the river; two-thirds of them being in a ruinous state. Around Poonakha, within the distance of a quarter of a mile, villages were seen, all of them bearing the stamp of poverty and oppression. "The palace is situated on a flat tongue of land formed by the confluence of the Patchoo and Matchoo rivers. To the west it is quite close to the west boundary of the valley, the river alone intervening. It is a very large building, but too uniform and too heavy to be imposing; it is upwards of two hundred yards in length, by perhaps eighty in breadth. Its regal nature is attested by the central tower and several coppered roofs." The climate had little to recommend it, and much annoyance was experienced from the strong winds which were more or less constantly blowing up the valley during the day, bringing with them clouds of dust.

The soil in the neighbourhood seemed very poor, and contained a large proportion of mica. Cultivation in the valley during the stay of the mission was limited to wheat and buckwheat, but scarcely any of the former seemed likely to come to maturity. Newly sown crops were liable to be eaten up by the swarms of sacred pigeons that were kept in the palace. Ground also was observed to be in course of preparation for the reception of rice. The agricultural work appeared to devolve chiefly on a number of Assamese slaves.

Nothing was seen indicative of any degree of trade being carried on at the place. People changing their residences frequently passed through from the north-east, generally accompanied by ponies, whose most common burdens appeared to be salt. No signs were seen of direct intercourse with Thibet, and even the tea, which seemed to be an article of large consumption, was said to have come from Thibet through Western Bhotan.

During the first few days after the mission arrived, it was much annoyed by the followers of the Deb Raja, who were continually having disputes with the sentries and the mission followers, and it was only after repeated messages had been sent to the palace, stating the probable consequences, if the system of annoyance was continued, that any respite from them was obtained. The first interview with the Deb Raja occurred on the 9th of April—Dr. Griffiths thus describes it—"Leaving our ponies, we crossed the bridge built over the Patchoo, which was lined with guards and defended by some large wretchedly constructed wall pieces. We then entered a paved yard, and thence ascended by some most inconvenient stairs to the palace, the entrance to which was guarded by a few household troops dressed in scarlet broadcloth. We then crossed the north quadrangle of the palace, which is surrounded with galleries and apartments, and was crowded with eager spectators, and ascending some still more inconvenient or even dangerous stairs reached a gallery along which we proceeded to the Deb's receiving room, which is on the west face of the palace. At the door of this the usual delays took place, these people supposing that their importance is enhanced by the length of delay they can manage to make visitors submit to. The Deb, who was an ordinary looking man in good condition, received us graciously, and actually got up and received his Lordship's letter standing. The usual conversation then took place by means of interpreting, and the Deb having received his presents and presented us with the usual plantains, ghee, and some walnuts, dismissed us. And this was the first and last time I had the honour of seeing him, as I was indisposed at the time of our leaving to return. The room was a good sized one, but rather low: it was supported by well ornamented pillars tastefully hung with scarfs and embroidered silks." Two days afterwards the Dhurma Raja, a good-looking boy of eight or ten years of age, and son of the Tongso Penlow, received the mission, which out of compliment to his religious character remained standing. The Dhurma Raja sat in a small recess, lighted chiefly by lamps, and was prompted by a venerable looking grey-headed priest. Around the room priests sat busily employed in muttering sacred sentences from handsome gilt-lettered black books.

Captain Pemberton in due course submitted the draft of a treaty such as he was instructed to negotiate—the terms of which, were not only extremely moderate, but favourable on the whole, to the

Bhotanese. It was apparently agreed to by the Dhurma and Deb Rajas, and all the council except the Tongso Penlow, whose interests were slightly affected by it. This however was made the ground for its final rejection by the Government. Captain Pemberton thus sums up the results of his mission—

"A mission was deputed from the supreme Government to the court of Bhotan under a belief that the rulers of that country were kept in ignorance of the proceedings of their local officers, and that when known some decisive steps would be taken to guard against the probability of interruption to those amicable relations the continuance of which was of vital importance to Bootan itself. In its progress through the country the mission was everywhere received with marked distinction, the Envoy was waited on by every Soubah (Jungpen) of the districts through which it passed, and nothing could have exhibited a more anxious desire to do honour to the power that deputed it than the extreme respect with which the letters and presents of the Governor-General of India were received by the Deb and Dhurma Rajas of Bootan. Yet so wholly impotent is the Government of the country, and so lamentable are the effects of the contests for supremacy which have devastated Bootan for the last thirty years, that its rulers dare not enter into engagements which, however calculated to promote the general welfare, may indirectly clash with the imaginary interests of a Pillo or Zimpe. During many protracted discussions held with the ministers of the Deb, every argument was used, and the most detailed explanations were offered, to arrest the attention of the Government, and to show the extreme hazard incurred by the misconduct of its officers. Various propositions were submitted and discussed, and the draft of a treaty was at last prepared with the avowed concurrence and approval of the Deb and his ministers, who repeatedly admitted, both in private and at the public durbars (state receptions), that its provisions were unobjectionable; they appointed a time for ratifying it by signature, and when the period for so doing arrived, evaded it on the most frivolous pretexts, the Deb to the last admitting that he had no valid objections to offer, and that it was calculated to benefit his country by removing many existing causes of disatisfaction. These opinions he held in common with the ex-Deb, the Paro Pillo, the Tassi Zimpe, Wandipoor Jungpen, and the Lam and Deb Zimpes; and yet he avowed he dare not sign it as the Tongso Pillo objected."

After a fruitless delay of upwards of five weeks, the mission left Poonakha on the 9th of May, just as a contest for the Debship was about to commence, the claimant being the ex-Deb, whose adherents had taken up a position in the fort of Telagong, about nine miles distant. On the morning of the mission's departure, a demonstration of defiance was made, though the enemy was miles away. The roof of the Deb's palace was covered with troops, who shouted, fired off matchlocks and waved banners for a considerable time—pretty much apparently after the 'awe-inspiring demonstrations' of the Chinese. The mission returned to the plains by the Buxa Pass, which was reached on the 18th of May. From thence it went on to Goalpara, on the Berhampooter, and from there returned to Calcutta.

No satisfactory result followed Captain Pemberton's visit to Poonakha, and things continued to go on on the frontier as they had done before. During the year 1839, twelve natives were carried off from British territory, one of whom died from his wounds, another was killed for attempting to escape, and a third was wounded and thrown down a precipice, because he would not work.

As the only means of protecting the frontier, and putting a stop to these continued aggressions, the Government of India determined to take the whole management of the Assam Dooars, attach them in fact, and pay the Bhotanese Government 10,000 rupees per annum as compensation for the loss of revenue sustained by the control of the Dooars in question passing into the hands of the Indian Government. This measure was carried out in conformity with an order from the Governor-General (Lord Auckland), dated 6th September 1841, and it proved on the whole successful, as far as the raids within the British frontier were concerned; but incursions from the hills on the villages in the Dooars themselves continued to go on for many years afterwards.

Having thus given a *résumé* of the relations which have existed between the British and Bhotan Governments regarding the Assam Dooars, those connected with the Dooars of Bengal require a similar notice; the disputes connected with them having given rise to more important results than those which originated with the former.

It has already been shown at page 36 that a large estate called Ambaree Fallacottah, situated within the British frontier, was taken from the Zemindar of Bykantpore, and made over to Bhotan in 1784. The year following the attachment of the Assam Dooars referred to above, it became the subject of correspondence between the British and Bhotan Governments; the latter having complained to the former of the conduct of a son of the Zemindar of Bykantpore, to whom it had let the estate in question:—apparently being unable to manage it through its own officers, consequent on its being some twenty miles inside our frontier. Referring to this matter Mr. Eden observes—"The

Bykantpore family always have considered that this land was wrongfully taken from them and given to the Bootanese; and the former, being a member of that family, took the opportunity of endeavouring to regain possession of it by withholding the rent, and refusing to obey the orders of the Booteah officers. He also was accused of making inroads into Bootan from the estate, and of there secreting the plunder obtained in these raids. It was in fact a kind of no-man's-land. We had no authority there, and the Government of Bootan was unable to enforce its orders on its own subordinates." Ambaree Fallacottah consequently became a constant source of disturbance on the frontier, particularly so, as the Bhotanese had no means of reaching it except by passing through British territory. The Government of Bhotan, in this matter seems to have acted sensibly, by requesting the Indian Government to take the estate under its charge, and hold itself responsible for the due payment to the former of the net annual proceeds of the property. This proposition was agreed to, and in 1842 Ambaree Fallacottah was taken under British management.

Outrages of a nature similar to those described on the Assam side, are stated to have been of periodical occurrence in the vicinity of the Bengal Dooars, scarcely a year passing without some of them taking place. The aggressors, it was believed, were either Bhotan officials, or robbers protected by them. An interval of ten years however occurs, wherein, in the records at my disposal, no details are given of specific outrages, though no doubt numbers occurred during that period. In 1852 an elephant valued at a thousand rupees was stolen from a native resident at Rungpore, by the Nieboo or Katma of Mynagoorie. The following year the same official stole an elephant of like value from a person called Ameeroodeen, and again in 1854 stole Enam Mahomed's elephant. In the latter year also, the house of one Daooreah Doss of Shaftbaree in Zillah Rungpore was attacked, the owner killed, his wife wounded, and fifty-two rupees' worth of property carried off. One of the offenders, a man named Roopa, found protection from the Katma of Mynagoorie, who treated the demands made for his surrender with contempt.

The next serious outrage occurring at this time is one having reference to the Assam Dooars. It appears that in March 1854, a mission was sent by the Bhotan Government to Gowhatty for the purpose of obtaining an increase to the amount of compensation annually paid by the British Government for the Assam Dooars. The Dewangiri Raja—as it has become the custom to call the Jungpen in charge of that pass—and an uncle of the Dhurma

Raja, both of them near connections of the Tongso Penlow, were the officials to whom this duty was entrusted. The mission proved unsuccessful, and on its way back to Bhotan committed a series of robberies on the Dooars under British protection.

The magistrate of Kamroop was directed to proceed to the scene of these robberies, with a company of the 2nd Assam Light Infantry, for the purpose of giving assurance and protection to the villagers, and while he was there, a party of the Dewangiri Raja's men were captured in the act of carrying off some Bhotanese who had settled in the Dooars. These men confessed to having perpetrated some of the robberies in conformity with direct orders from the Dewangiri Jungpen (Raja).

While these cases were under inquiry, fresh robberies continued. Amongst others, a party of forty Bhotanese plundered a merchant named Attum Chand of property to the value of between seven and eight thousand rupees. The robbers were believed to be in the service of the Dewangiri Raja, and the Governor-General's agent in Assam reported to Government, that there could be no longer any doubt that the official in question was not only implicated in the outrages, but kept organised bands of robbers for the purpose; and further, that there was a strong suspicion that in so doing he was acting under the authority of the Tongso Penlow.

The result of the representations made, and threats held out, to the Bhotan Government at this time, was, that it ordered the Tongso Penlow to pay into the Bhotanese treasury a sum of money in amount double that, which the value of the property plundered by his relative, the Dewangiri Raja, was estimated at.* The Tongso Penlow, on receiving the order from the Deb Raja to pay this fine, wrote two very insolent letters to the Governor-General's agent in Assam, abusing him for having addressed the Deb Raja direct with reference to the Dooar robberies, in place of having done so through him, making use of the following expression:—"I am a Raja like the Deb Raja—how can he injure me?" At the same time, however, he somewhat inconsistently intimated that the Dewangiri Jungpen had been removed, and requested the Governor-General's agent, Colonel (now General) Jenkins, to pay half the amount of the fine that had been imposed upon him.

Colonel Jenkins made a detailed report of recent occurrences to the Government of India, and recommended the immediate occupa-

* Mr. Eden states that it is a common proceeding in Bhotan, when a demand from the British Government is strongly pressed, for the officer responsible for the offence complained of—to be made to pay a sum of money as a fine, which is divided amongst the members of Council, and great credit claimed for the punishment thus inflicted; though probably, in the majority of instances, the members individually have connived at and profited by the offence.

tion of the Bengal Dooars as the only measure likely to be effective short of invading the country—also that the value of the property plundered by the Dewangiri Jungpen should be deducted from the compensation paid for the Assam Dooars, and submitted the question as to whether the whole of the compensation then due should not be entirely withheld until the whole of the offenders demanded by the magistrate had been surrendered.

In reply to this communication from Colonel Jenkins, the Governor-General (Lord Dalhousie) directed the following observations and instructions to be communicated to that officer, bearing date January 11th, 1856—

"The Governor-General in Council, although he is most anxious to avoid a collision with the Booteah Government, feels that it is impossible to tolerate the insolence and overbearing tone of the Tongso Penlow's communications to his representative on the north-east frontier, and if it be tolerated the motives of the Government may be, and probably will be, misconstrued, and the consequences will be more troublesome to the Government, and more injurious to the interests of its subjects, than if at once resented.

"His Lordship in Council therefore authorises the agent on the north-east frontier to point out to the Tongso Penlow the extremely unbecoming tone of his several communications, and the inadmissibility of the requisitions which they contain; to require him, on the part of the Governor-General in Council, to apologise for the disrespect which he has shown to his Lordship's representative, and in his person to the Government of India; and to inform him that, unless he forthwith accede to his demand, measures, which he will be unable to resist, and which will have the effect of crippling his authority on the frontier, will be put in force. The agent will, at the same time, inform the Tongso Penlow that, under any circumstances the value of the property plundered with the connivance of his brother, the late Dewangiri Raja, will be deducted from the Booteah share of the Dooar revenues. It is not thought expedient to go beyond this, and to declare that payment of the share of the Dooar revenue will be entirely withheld until all the offenders who have been demanded are surrendered.

"If the above remonstrance should be responded to in a becoming spirit, it will be sufficient for the agent to warn the Tongso Penlow that any repetition of the aggressive movements of which we have recently had to complain will be forthwith resented by the permanent occupation of the Bengal Dooars. It is possible that this menace may have the desired effect of bringing home to the mind of the Tongso Penlow the risk which he incurs by encouraging or permitting incursions into British territory; if not, and if there should be a recurrence of such incursions, the Governor-General in Council, deeming it a paramount duty to protect the subjects of the British Government, will have no alternative, and he authorises the agent, in the possible event supposed, to take immediate measures for the complete occupation of the Bengal Dooars, on the understanding that such occupation shall be permanent, and that the admission of the Booteahs to a share of the revenue of those Dooars, shall rest entirely with the discretion of the Governor-General in Council.

"His Lordship in Council is not unaware that the Deb Raja is the nominal head of the country, and that it is the conduct of the Tongso Penlow and his brother, the late Dewangiri Raja, and not the conduct of the Deb Raja, which has called for some measure of severity on the part of the British Government. But it is obvious that the Deb Raja, even though he may be ostensibly well disposed towards the Government, is unable, or unwilling, or remiss in his endeavours to restrain his subordinate chief, and it cannot be permitted that for this want of power, or want of will, or want of energy, the subjects of this Government should suffer. The Deb Raja must share in the penalty due to the delinquencies of those who own his authority, and for whose acts of aggression on British territory he must be considered responsible."

Colonel Jenkins immediately carried out these instructions, and forwarded a letter through the Dewangiri Raja to the Tongso Penlow, demanding an apology. The former at first reported having despatched the letter the moment it arrived, but subsequently, when the non-receipt of an answer led to inquiries, he apparently forgot what he had said before, and admitted having suppressed it, on the grounds that he was afraid of offending the Tongso Penlow by forwarding it. Letters of apology were ultimately received from the Bhotan Government, and on Colonel Jenkins's recommendation, accepted as sufficient. At the same time, the value of the property plundered by the men of the Dewangiri Raja, which was estimated at 2,868 rupees, was deducted from the Assam Dooar compensation money then due, and the balance paid over to the Bhotan Government.

Whilst these letters of apology were in course of transmission, a fresh aggression occurred, in the abduction of a person of considerable local importance, named Arun Sing, the hereditary Zemindar of Goomar Dooar, who had removed himself from Bhotanese protection and taken up his residence within British territory. He was carried off into Bhotan by an armed party from the Bhulka Pass, headed by the official in charge of it.

In reference to this case, the Governor-General directed the punishment of the offenders to be demanded from the Bhotan Government, as well as an apology for the aggression; warning it that on its failing to comply the Government of India would hold itself free to take permanent possession of the Bengal Dooars. The Bhotan Government however evaded complying, and the following curious reply was received from the Deb Raja—

"You have written to me to release the Zemindar and send him back, and that it will not be well if I do not do so. The Zemindar has all along been a servant of mine, and you write to say that there will be a quarrel if he is not sent back. I have not done an injury to any subject of your territory; there is no power greater than that exercised by the Honourable Company and the Dhurma Raja, and being on friendly terms, it is not proper to write about such trifles, but if the Zemindar has written to you, you will let me know, for even his doing so was improper."

In forwarding this reply to the Government, Colonel Jenkins observed that, "as the contention which appears to have existed for so many years amongst the chief families of Bhotan for supreme government of the country appears to be still continued," there was no reasonable expectation that any reform in its jurisdiction in the Dooars would be effected, and that he was of opinion that further reference was useless, and that the only measure open to Government was the annexation of the Bengal Dooars, but, as in the case of those of Assam, he proposed to allow the Bhotan Government a share of the revenue—expressing at the same time the conviction, that the annexation would be considered a great boon by the inhabitants of the tract of country in question.

While the Indian Government had this matter under consideration, two other outrages were reported to it, under date 21st November 1856. In the one case a native under British protection, named Salgaram Osawal, having gone across the frontier to Mynagoorie to trade, was seized and detained on the grounds, stated to be false, that he had in deposit, property belonging to a deceased Bhotanese. In the other case, a party of armed men employed by a Bhotanese official entered Cooch Behar and carried off three natives named Jubeel Doss, Ramdolall, and Hermohun; also three of their women, as well as cash and property valued at 2,176 rupees. The man first mentioned and all the women were released on the payment of 1,400 rupees as a ransom, and the promise of a thousand more at a future period; as security for the payment of which, three persons who negotiated their release were detained. In reply to a formal application for the release of the prisoners, made by the Governor-General's agent, he was told that Ramdolall owed money in Bhotan, and could not be released unless his son liquidated the debt.*

Coincident with these various acts of aggression, cattle lifting, including thefts of elephants, was of common occurrence. Between 1854 and 1857 seven cases were reported as having occurred on the Rungpore frontier, and in the latter year, five cases on the Cooch Behar frontier. The chief offender was believed to be the Katma of Mynagoorie, against whom fifteen distinct charges had been registered. The Government of India now determined to adopt active measures, and as the Lieutenant Governor of Bengal, Sir F. Halliday, was about to visit the north-eastern frontier, he was requested to report as to the course which seemed best suited to enforce better behaviour on the part of the Bhotanese:—the choice apparently lying between annexing the Bengal Dooars, or withholding the compensation for those of Assam. A regiment was at the same time ordered to the frontier.

Sir F. Halliday visited the frontier and after consulting with Colonel Jenkins and several intelligent natives of local experience, he came to the conclusion the withholding of the compensation for the Assam Dooars would be a punishment that would be more severely felt by the Tongso Penlow than the Government of Bhotan;† and he seemed to think that there were strong indications of an intention to adopt an improved foreign policy on the part of the Bhotan Government, the more so as certain obnoxious frontier officials had been dismissed, and the rebellion which had so long thrown the country into confusion had ceased. Sir F. Halliday therefore thought that the Deb Raja being now a more free agent would pay more attention to the administration of the country, and the season being too far advanced for any active operations, he suggested that a communication should be sent to the Dhurma and Deb Rajas, through the Tongso and Paro Penlows: "Solemnly warning them against trifling with the forbearance of the British Government, and once more, avowedly for the last time, calling upon them to deliver up Arun Sing and Ramdolall, or

* This man Ramdolall, as well as Salgaram Osawal and Hurmohun, and also three persons who remained as security for the thousand rupees due for the ransom of Jubeel Doss, have not been surrendered up to the present time. They are supposed to have been carried off into Bhotan as slaves, in which capacity, if still alive, they most probably continue to be.

† Mr. Eden, in reference to this view, states—"There seems to have arisen about this time a curious idea, that the Tongso Penlow was a man well disposed to our Government, and less to blame than the other officials. Why such a notion should have been entertained is not quite intelligible, for though there had been outrages on the western frontier as well as on the eastern, the Tongso Penlow had throughout treated our Government with unvarying insolence and ill-concealed contempt."

abide by such measures as the British Government may, in failure of full satisfaction, adopt on its own account towards the vindication of its right and powers." Failing compliance with the ultimatum, the course Sir F. Halliday proposed to adopt was the annexation of Ambaree Fallacottah and Jelpaish—territory, as already shown, ceded to Bhotan in 1784 and 1787 respectively.*

Sir F. Halliday thus describes the feelings of the people of the Dooars at this time in respect to their appreciation of the Bhotanese rule—"Various endeavours have been made by the heads of villages in the country opposite to Julpigoorie to persuade the British authorities to invade the Dooars, and free them from the oppressive Government of Bhotan. Messages to that effect have been sent across, and a deputation of heads of villages attempted to see me, probably with that object, but I declined to give them an interview. Assurances were conveyed through our own subjects, that the people of the Dooars were very anxious to come under our rule, and it was intimated that if we would only send troops, all supplies would be ready for them without expense." It was also asserted by the better informed natives on the frontier, that a very little encouragement would induce the people of the Dooars to rise upon their Bhotanese rulers. But to those and similar communications Sir F. Halliday gave no encouragement.

The Indian Government adopted the views of Sir F. Halliday with reference to the expediency of making one more demand, in the form of an ultimatum, for the surrender of the natives who had been abducted. Failing immediate compliance, it was determined to take permanent possession of Ambaree Fallacottah, within our own frontier line, and follow up the measure by the occupation and retention of Jelpaish within that of Bhotan. In the meantime the intention of stationing a military force on the frontier was carried out; a cantonment being established at Julpigorie, and the 73rd Native Infantry, with a detachment of the 11th Irregular Cavalry, was posted there.

At this period, however, the sepoy mutiny broke out, and it was improbable that any troops would be available to enforce the threats of the Government, it was deemed advisable at the time that this final demand should not be made: the more so, as the

* In reference to the cession of Jelpaish, Sir F. Halliday remarks that—"The Jelpaish tract on the left bank of the Teesta river in Bootan was undoubtedly part and parcel of the Bykantpore Zemindaree of Rungpore belonging to the Raja of Julpigorie, and it is still looked upon by that old family and its retainers and dependents, and indeed by the whole country side, as part of their old domain, improperly given up to the Booteahs, and likely some day or other to be recovered. Jelpaish itself, which is not far from the Bootan fort of Moinagoorie, is the site of the old family temple of the Bykantpore family."

attention of Government was absorbed by matters of much greater importance.

About this time a raid on rather an extensive scale was made into Cooch Behar by a party of between three and four hundred men commanded by Bhotan officials. In the first instance, 123 buffaloes and two herdsmen were carried off, and two days afterwards the house of Sakaloo Parmanick plundered, and property estimated at 20,936 rupees taken away. In this affair four native watchmen and two relatives of the owner of the house were carried into captivity.

A representation was now made to the Deb Raja requiring the release of all the British and Cooch Behar subjects then in confinement, in default thereof, punishment being threatened. The result of this was that the officer in charge of the Bhulka Dooar received an order from the Deb Raja to investigate the case, which ended in the official in question coming to the place of meeting attended by a considerable body of armed retainers, and after conducting himself in a violent manner, refusing to take any steps towards investigating the outrage complained of, until a revision was made of the frontier boundary. In a communication to Government, dated 9th March 1859, reporting the conduct of this official, Colonel Jenkins stated, "Nothing, I conceive, will effectually put a stop to these daring inroads, but the posting of a considerable force of Government troops, disposed in one or two detachments, on the frontier of Cooch Behar; but the mere presence of these guards will not be sufficient, I fear, to induce the Booteah authorities to give up the unfortunate individuals now detained in captivity, and the restitution of the value of the property which has from time to time been plundered from the border villages, except by the actual occupation of one or more of the Dooars until our demands are fully complied with. The superior officers of Bootan are possible well disposed towards our Government, but they have no control over the Soubahs or their subordinate Katmas, as I have often attempted to point out, and unless our Government themselves punish the Soubahs by the attachment of the Dooars, our captive subjects and dependents, who cannot escape or effect their own ransom, will end their days in confinement, and those who have been forcibly robbed will in vain look for the restoration of their property from the supreme Government of Bootan." As the year 1859 advanced, fresh aggressions were reported, and amongst other occurrences the Deb Raja in reply to a further demand about surrendering the prisoners, declared that Arun Sing had died, because his days were numbered.

Colonel Jenkins naturally considered any further attempts to obtain redress in a friendly manner hopeless, and urged the immediate annexation of Ambaree Fallacottah and Jelpaish. The then Lieutenant-Governor of Bengal (Sir J. Grant) however did not take so unfavourable a view of the Deb Raja's answer, and thought that the execution of the measure proposed should be kept in reserve for some new occasion; as he thought that there was some advantage in the Bhotanese possessing land, the annexation of which, in the event of misconduct, could be held out as a practical menace. These views did not meet with the support of the Governor-General (Lord Canning) who adopted the opinions of Colonel Jenkins, in as far as related to Fallacottah, and directed that the estate should be taken possession of, and a narrative of the circumstances which had rendered the measure necessary, sent to the Bhotan Government, coupled with a requisition for the restoration of the captives and punishment of the offenders;—full compliance with these demands being the only terms on which the territory would be given back to Bhotan.

The orders of the Governor-General were put in force in March 1860, but somewhat imperfectly carried out, through some misapprehension on the part of the local officers. Intimation that the territory had been seized was sent to the Bhotan authorities, but the letter giving them a chance of recovering it, was not sent, and the matter was allowed to stand as it was; the Government not deeming it expedient to disavow the acts of its agents. The Jungpen of Dhalimkote however made frequent demands for the rent of Ambaree Fallacottah, and was placed in full possession of the circumstances under which the attachment had been made; being given, at the same time, clearly to understand, that the payment would recommence as soon as the commands of the British Government had been complied with.

This measure (the attachment of Fallacottah) does not appear to have been productive of much improvement, as shown by the fact that early in January (1861) the Bhotan frontier official at Gopalgunge, sent over a party of his retainers into British territory, who took away a valuable elephant from a Mr. Pyne, the manager of a property belonging to Messrs. Dear and Co., at Silligoorie, on the road to Darjeeling. Mr. Pyne traced his elephant to Gopalgunge, where it was in the possession of the official referred to—who, far from attempting to deny the fact, not only admitted it, but declined to give the animal up unless he received a present of 300 rupees, a gun and a telescope—a proceeding in which he would seem to have been fully borne out by the Deb Raja; for in the month of April following, when Colonel Jenkins addressed the latter, demanding the release of the elephant, he declared that it belonged to Bhotan, but added, "if you be in need of the elephant give cash rupees 300 with gun and telescope, and you shall have it."* The authenticity of this letter was at the time doubted, but subsequent inquiries favoured the belief that it was actually written by the Deb Raja, establishing pretty clearly the fact that the forcible removal of property from within the British territory was not only sanctioned by the highest authority in Bhotan, but the profits also, accruing therefrom, apparently participated in by him.

In September 1861, a raid was made from the Banska Dooar into Cooch Behar, and four elephants and four Mahouts (elephant drivers) carried off, which however were recaptured by some of the Raja's people. The Raja of Cooch Behar however took advantage of this opportunity to submit to the British Government a list of seventeen elephants, which had been from time to time carried off from his territory.

Shortly after this last occurrence, the Jungpen of Dhalimkote wrote to Dr. Campbell, the Superintendent of Darjeeling, and stated that having represented to the Dhurma and Deb Rajas the circumstances connected with the attachment of Fallacottah, he had received instructions to arrange a meeting with the Superintendent for the purpose of making inquiries about the delinquents. Dr. Campbell consulted the Governor-General's agent (now Major Hopkinson), with reference to the propriety of complying with the request, who, seeing little or no hope of any satisfactory result from the interview, recommended that it should not be granted. At the same time however Major Hopkinson addressed a letter to the Bengal Government, recommending the appointment of a mission, and in so doing, thus expressed himself with reference to the political position of the Deb Raja—"I am myself inclined to think that it is almost unreasonable to expect any satisfaction from the Deb Raja, and though for some purposes, it may be a useful fiction to assume that we are in correspondence with him and nothing else, nothing short of our having a European functionary permanently stationed at the court of the Deb could give assurance to our communications reaching him." The establishment of such a permanent agent, Major Hopkinson also thought would be the best means of paving the way for friendly intercourse with Lassa.

* A demand which was made at the same time for the surrender of British and Cooch Behar subjects detained in captivity met with no better success than the application for the release of the elephant.

The Bengal Government approved of Major Hopkinson's suggestion respecting the dispatch of a mission, and the appointment of an agent at the Bhotan court, and recommended the same to the supreme Government of India:—the mission of the Hon. Ashley Eden was the result of this recommendation.

APPENDIX C.

Translation of the Document which Mr. Eden signed under compulsion.

Agreement.

That from to-day there shall always be friendship between the Feringees (English) and the Bhotanese. Formerly the Dhurma Raja and the Company's Queen were of one mind, and the same friendship exists to the present day. Foolish men on the frontier having caused a disturbance, certain men belonging to the British power, living on the frontier have taken Bulisusan (Julpigorie?) between Cooch Behar and the Kam Raja, and Ambaree, near the border of Sikim, and then between Banska and Gowalparah, Rangamuttee, Bokalibaree, Motteeamaree, Papareebaree, Arioetta, and then the seven Eastern Dooars. Then certain bad men on the Bhoteah side stole men, cattle, and other property, and committed thefts and robberies, and the Feringees' men plundered property and burnt down houses in Bhotan. By reason of these bad men remaining, the ryots suffered great trouble; and on this account the Governor-General, with a good intention, sent an envoy, Mr. Eden, with letters and presents, and sent with him Cheeboo Lama, the Minister of Sikim, and on their coming to the Dhurma and Deb Rajas, making petition, a settlement of a permanent nature has been made by both parties. The Dhurma Raja will send one agent to the east and one to the west; when they shall arrive on the frontier of the Company's territory, they shall, after an interview with the Feringees' agents, receive back the tracts above mentioned belonging to Bhotan, and after these shall be given back, and on full proof being given against persons charged with cattle stealing, &c., the Feringees will surrender such offenders to the Bhotanese, and the Bhotanese will in like manner surrender offenders to the Feringees. After that each shall take charge of his own territory, look after his own ryots, and remain on friendly terms, and commit no aggressions, and the subjects of either State going into the neighbouring State shall be treated as brothers.

If, notwithstanding, any bad men on either side shall commit any aggression, the rulers of the place in which the offender lives shall seize and punish him. And as Cheeboo Lama is the interpreter between the Feringees and the Bhoteahs, the Sikimese are therefore henceforth to assist the Bhoteahs. We have written above that the settlement is permanent; but who knows, perhaps this settlement is made with one word in the mouth and two in the heart. If, therefore, this settlement is false, the Dhurma Raja's demons (names omitted) will, after deciding who is true or false, take his life, and take out his liver and scatter it to the winds like ashes. The Bhotan army will take possession of Sikim, and if the Raja of Cooch Behar shall attempt to take any land belonging to Bhotan, the Bhotan Government, the Sikim Government, and the Company will invade Cooch Behar. If the Feringees attempt to take land from Bhotan, the Bhoteahs, Sikimese, and Beharees will invade the Company's territory; and if the Behar Raja shall invade Sikim, the Bhotanese, Sikimese, and the Company shall invade Behar. Whichever of the four States, Bhotan, Feringee, Behar, Sikim, commit aggression, the other three shall punish it; and if, whilst this agreement remains, any other enemy shall arise to any of the States, the others shall all assist him. This agreement is made between the Feringees and the Bhotanese. And this is the seal of the Dhurma and Deb Rajas.

Seal here attached.

(Signed) ASHLEY EDEN.
(Under compulsion.)

The year Singee, 21st month, Danopipa.

THE END.

LONDON
PRINTED BY SPOTTISWOODE AND CO.
NEW-STREET SQUARE

ALBEMARLE STREET, LONDON,
January, 1866.

MR. MURRAY'S

GENERAL LIST OF WORKS.

ALBERT (PRINCE). THE SPEECHES AND ADDRESSES of H.R.H. THE PRINCE CONSORT, on Public Occasions; with an Introduction giving some Outlines of his Character. Portrait. 8vo. 10*s*. 6*d*.; or Popular Edition. Portrait. Fcap. 8vo, 1*s*.

ABBOTT'S (REV. J.) Philip Musgrave; or, Memoirs of a Church of England Missionary in the North American Colonies. Post 8vo. 2*s*.

ABERCROMBIE'S (JOHN) Enquiries concerning the Intellectual Powers and the Investigation of Truth. 14*th Edition*. Fcap. 8vo. 6*s*. 6*d*.

——— Philosophy of the Moral Feelings. 13*th Edition*. Fcap. 8vo. 4*s*.

ACLAND'S (REV. CHARLES) Popular Account of the Manners and Customs of India. Post 8vo. 2*s*.

ÆSOP'S FABLES. A New Translation. With Historical Preface. By Rev. THOMAS JAMES. With 100 Woodcuts, by TENNIEL and WOLF. 50*th Thousand*. Post 8vo. 2*s*. 6*d*.

AGRICULTURAL (THE) JOURNAL. Of the Royal Agricultural Society of England. 8vo. *Published half-yearly*.

AIDS TO FAITH: a Series of Theological Essays. By various Writers. Edited by WILLIAM THOMSON, D.D., Lord Archbishop of York. 8vo. 9*s*.

CONTENTS.

Rev. H. L. MANSEL—*Miracles*.

BISHOP OF KILLALOE—*Christian Evidences*.

Rev. DR. McCAUL—*Prophecy and the Mosaic Record of Creation*.

Rev. CANON COOK—*Ideology and Subscription*.

Rev. GEORGE RAWLINSON—*The Pentateuch*.

ARCHBISHOP OF YORK—*Doctrine of the Atonement*.

BISHOP OF ELY.—*Inspiration*.

BISHOP OF GLOUCESTER AND BRISTOL.—*Scripture and its Interpretation*.

AMBER-WITCH (THE). The most interesting Trial for Witchcraft ever known. Translated from the German by LADY DUFF GORDON. Post 8vo. 2*s*.

ARMY LIST (THE). *Published Monthly by Authority*. 18mo. 1*s*. 6*d*.

ARTHUR'S (LITTLE) History of England. By LADY CALLCOTT. 150*th Thousand*. Woodcuts. Fcap. 8vo. 2*s*. 6*d*.

ATKINSON'S (MRS.) Recollections of Tartar Steppes and their Inhabitants. Illustrations. Post 8vo. 12*s*.

AUNT IDA'S Walks and Talks; a Story Book for Children. By a LADY. Woodcuts. 16mo. 5*s*.

AUSTIN'S (JOHN) LECTURES ON JURISPRUDENCE; or, the Philosophy of Positive Law. 3 Vols. 8vo. 39*s*.

——— (SARAH) Fragments from German Prose Writers. With Biographical Notes. Post 8vo. 10*s*.

ADMIRALTY PUBLICATIONS; Issued by direction of the Lords Commissioners of the Admiralty:—

A MANUAL OF SCIENTIFIC ENQUIRY, for the Use of Travellers. Edited by Sir JOHN F. HERSCHEL, and Rev. ROBERT MAIN. *Third Edition.* Woodcuts. Post 8vo. 9*s.*

AIRY'S ASTRONOMICAL OBSERVATIONS MADE AT GREENWICH. 1836 to 1847. Royal 4to. 50*s.* each.

——— ASTRONOMICAL RESULTS. 1848 to 1858. 4to. 8*s.* each.

——— APPENDICES TO THE ASTRONOMICAL OBSERVATIONS.

1836.—I. Bessel's Refraction Tables.
II. Tables for converting Errors of R.A. and N.P.D. into Errors of Longitude and Ecliptic P.D. } 8*s.*
1837.—I. Logarithms of Sines and Cosines to every Ten Seconds of Time.
II. Table for converting Sidereal into Mean Solar Time. } 8*s.*
1842.—Catalogue of 1439 Stars. 8*s.*
1845.—Longitude of Valentia. 8*s.*
1847.—Twelve Years' Catalogue of Stars. 14*s.*
1851.—Maskelyne's Ledger of Stars. 6*s.*
1852.—I. Description of the Transit Circle. 5*s.*
II. Regulations of the Royal Observatory. 2*s.*
1853.—Bessel's Refraction Tables. 8*s.*
1854.—I. Description of the Zenith Tube. 3*s.*
II. Six Years' Catalogue of Stars. 10*s.*
1856.—Description of the Galvanic Apparatus at Greenwich Observatory. 8*s.*
1862.—I. Seven Years' Catalogue of Stars. 10*s.*
II. Plan of the Building and Ground of the Royal Observatory, Greenwich.
III. Longitude of Valentia. } 3*s.*

——— MAGNETICAL AND METEOROLOGICAL OBSERVATIONS. 1840 to 1847. Royal 4to. 50*s.* each.

——— ASTRONOMICAL, MAGNETICAL, AND METEOROLOGICAL OBSERVATIONS, 1848 to 1863. Royal 4to. 50*s.* each.

——— ASTRONOMICAL RESULTS. 1848 to 1863. 4to.

——— MAGNETICAL AND METEOROLOGICAL RESULTS. 1848 to 1863. 4to. 8*s.* each.

——— REDUCTION OF THE OBSERVATIONS OF PLANETS. 1750 to 1830. Royal 4to. 50*s.*

——————— LUNAR OBSERVATIONS. 1750 to 1830. 2 Vols. Royal 4to. 50*s.* each.

——————— 1831 to 1851. 4to. 20*s.*

BERNOULLI'S SEXCENTENARY TABLE. *London,* 1779. 4to.

BESSEL'S AUXILIARY TABLES FOR HIS METHOD OF CLEARING LUNAR DISTANCES. 8vo.

——— FUNDAMENTA ASTRONOMIÆ: *Regiomontii,* 1818. Folio. 60*s.*

BIRD'S METHOD OF CONSTRUCTING MURAL QUADRANTS. *London,* 1768. 4to. 2*s.* 6*d.*

——— METHOD OF DIVIDING ASTRONOMICAL INSTRUMENTS. *London,* 1767. 4to. 2*s.* 6*d.*

COOK, KING, AND BAYLY'S ASTRONOMICAL OBSERVATIONS. *London,* 1782. 4to. 21*s.*

ENCKE'S BERLINER JAHRBUCH, for 1830. *Berlin,* 1828. 8vo. 9*s.*

GROOMBRIDGE'S CATALOGUE OF CIRCUMPOLAR STARS. 4to. 10*s.*

ADMIRALTY PUBLICATIONS—*continued.*

HANSEN'S TABLES DE LA LUNE. 4to. 20*s.*

HARRISON'S PRINCIPLES OF HIS TIME-KEEPER. PLATES 1797. 4to. 5*s.*

HUTTON'S TABLES OF THE PRODUCTS AND POWERS OF NUMBERS. 1781. Folio. 7*s.* 6*d.*

LAX'S TABLES FOR FINDING THE LATITUDE AND LONGITUDE. 1821. 8vo. 10*s.*

LUNAR OBSERVATIONS at GREENWICH. 1783 to 1819. Compared with the Tables, 1821. 4to. 7*s.* 6*d.*

MASKELYNE'S ACCOUNT OF THE GOING OF HARRISON'S WATCH. 1767. 4to. 2*s.* 6*d.*

MAYER'S DISTANCES of the MOON'S CENTRE from the PLANETS. 1822, 3*s.*; 1823, 4*s.* 6*d.* 1824 to 1835, 8vo. 4*s.* each.

——— THEORIA LUNÆ JUXTA SYSTEMA NEWTONIANUM. 4to. 2*s.* 6*d.*

——— TABULÆ MOTUUM SOLIS ET LUNÆ. 1770. 4to. 5*s.*

——— ASTRONOMICAL OBSERVATIONS MADE AT GOTTINGEN, from 1756 to 1761. 1826. Folio. 7*s.* 6*d.*

NAUTICAL ALMANACS, from 1767 to 1869. 8vo. 2*s.* 6*d.* each.

——— SELECTIONS FROM THE ADDITIONS up to 1812. 8vo. 5*s.* 1834-54. 8vo. 5*s.*

——— SUPPLEMENTS, 1828 to 1833, 1837 and 1838. 8vo. 2*s.* each.

——— TABLE requisite to be used with the N.A. 1781. 8vo. 5*s.*

POND'S ASTRONOMICAL OBSERVATIONS. 1811 to 1835. 4to. 21*s.* each.

RAMSDEN'S ENGINE for DIVIDING MATHEMATICAL INSTRUMENTS. 4to. 5*s.*

——— ENGINE for DIVIDING STRAIGHT LINES. 4to. 5*s.*

SABINE'S PENDULUM EXPERIMENTS to DETERMINE THE FIGURE OF THE EARTH. 1825. 4to. 40*s.*

SHEPHERD'S TABLES for CORRECTING LUNAR DISTANCES. 1772. Royal 4to. 21*s.*

——— TABLES, GENERAL, of the MOON'S DISTANCE from the SUN, and 10 STARS. 1787. Folio. 5*s.* 6*d.*

TAYLOR'S SEXAGESIMAL TABLE. 1780. 4to. 15*s.*

——— TABLES OF LOGARITHMS. 4to. 3*l.*

TIARK'S ASTRONOMICAL OBSERVATIONS for the LONGITUDE of MADEIRA. 1822. 4to. 5*s.*

——— CHRONOMETRICAL OBSERVATIONS for DIFFERENCES of LONGITUDE between DOVER, PORTSMOUTH, and FALMOUTH. 1823. 4to. 5*s.*

VENUS and JUPITER: OBSERVATIONS of, compared with the TABLES. *London*, 1822. 4to. 2*s.*

WALES' AND BAYLY'S ASTRONOMICAL OBSERVATIONS. 1777. 4to. 21*s.*

WALES' REDUCTION OF ASTRONOMICAL OBSERVATIONS MADE IN THE SOUTHERN HEMISPHERE. 1764—1771. 1788. 4to. 10*s.* 6*d.*

BAIKIE'S (W. B.) Narrative of an Exploring Voyage up the Rivers Quorra and Tshadda in 1854. Map. 8vo. 16*s.*

BANKES' (THE HON. GEORGE) STORY OF CORFE CASTLE, with documents relating to the Time of the Civil Wars, &c. Woodcuts. Post 8vo. 10*s*. 6*d*.

BARBAULD'S (MRS.) Hymns in Prose for Children. With 112 Original Designs. Small 4to. 5*s*. Or Fine Paper, 7*s*. 6*d*.

BARROW'S (SIR JOHN) Autobiographical Memoir, including Reflections, Observations, and Reminiscences at Home and Abroad. From Early Life to Advanced Age. Portrait. 8vo. 16*s*.

——— Voyages of Discovery and Research within the Arctic Regions, from 1818 to the present time. 8vo. 15*s*.

——— Life, Exploits, and Voyages of Sir Francis Drake. With numerous Original Letters. Post 8vo. 2*s*.

BARRY'S (SIR CHARLES) Life. By his Son, Rev. Alfred Barry, D.D. With Illustrations. 8vo. (*In the Press.*)

BATES' (H. W.) Records of a Naturalist on the River Amazons during eleven years of Adventure and Travel. *Second Edition*. Illustrations. Post 8vo. 12*s*.

BEES AND FLOWERS. Two Essays. By Rev. Thomas James. Reprinted from the "Quarterly Review." Fcap. 8vo. 1*s*. each.

BERTHA'S Journal during a Visit to her Uncle in England. Containing a Variety of Interesting and Instructive Information. *Seventh Edition*. Woodcuts. 12mo.

BIRCH'S (SAMUEL) History of Ancient Pottery and Porcelain: Egyptian, Assyrian, Greek, Roman, and Etruscan. With 200 Illustrations. 2 Vols. Medium 8vo. 42*s*.

BLUNT'S (REV. J. J.) Undesigned Coincidences in the Writings of the Old and New Testament, an Argument of their Veracity: containing the Books of Moses, Historical and Prophetical Scriptures, and the Gospels and Acts. *9th Edition*. Post 8vo. 6*s*.

——— History of the Church in the First Three Centuries. *Third Edition*. Post 8vo. 7*s*. 6*d*.

——— Parish Priest; His Duties, Acquirements and Obligations. *Fourth Edition*. Post 8vo. 7*s*. 6*d*.

——— Lectures on the Right Use of the Early Fathers. *Second Edition*. 8vo. 15*s*.

——— Plain Sermons Preached to a Country Congregation. *Second Edition*. 3 Vols. Post 8vo. 7*s*. 6*d*. each.

——— Essays on various subjects. 8vo. 12*s*.

BISSET'S (ANDREW) History of England during the Interregnum, from the Death of Charles I. to the Battle of Dunbar, 1648—50. Chiefly from the MSS. in the State Paper Office. 8vo. 15*s*.

BERTRAM'S (JAS. G.) Harvest of the Sea: a Contribution to the Natural and Economic History of British Food Fishes. With 50 Illustrations. 21*s*.

BLAKISTON'S (CAPT.) Narrative of the Expedition sent to explore the Upper Waters of the Yang-Tsze. Illustrations. 8vo. 18*s*.

BLOMFIELD'S (BISHOP) Memoir, with Selections from his Correspondence. By his Son. *2nd Edition*. Portrait, post 8vo. 12*s*.

BOOK OF COMMON PRAYER. Illustrated with Coloured Borders, Initial Letters, and Woodcuts. A new edition. 8vo. 18*s.* cloth; 31*s.* 6*d.* calf; 36*s.* morocco.

BORROW'S (GEORGE) Bible in Spain; or the Journeys, Adventures, and Imprisonments of an Englishman in an Attempt to circulate the Scriptures in the Peninsula. 3 Vols. Post 8vo. 27*s.*; or *Popular Edition*, 16mo, 3*s.* 6*d.*

——— Zincali, or the Gipsies of Spain; their Manners, Customs, Religion, and Language. 2 Vols. Post 8vo. 18*s.*; or *Popular Edition*, 16mo, 3*s.* 6*d.*

——— Lavengro; The Scholar—The Gipsy—and the Priest. Portrait. 3 Vols. Post 8vo. 30*s.*

——— Romany Rye; a Sequel to Lavengro. *Second Edition.* 2 Vols. Post 8vo. 21*s.*

——— WILD WALES: its People, Language, and Scenery. *Popular Edition.* Post 8vo., 6*s.*

BOSWELL'S (JAMES) Life of Samuel Johnson, LL.D. Including the Tour to the Hebrides. Edited by MR. CROKER. Portraits. Royal 8vo. 10*s.*

BRACE'S (C. L.) History of the Races of the Old World. Post 8vo. 9*s.*

BRAY'S (MRS.) Life of Thomas Stothard, R.A. With Personal Reminiscences. Illustrated with Portrait and 60 Woodcuts of his chief works. 4to.

BREWSTER'S (SIR DAVID) Martyrs of Science, or the Lives of Galileo, Tycho Brahe, and Kepler. *Fourth Edition.* Fcap. 8vo. 4*s.* 6*d.*

——— More Worlds than One. The Creed of the Philosopher and the Hope of the Christian. *Eighth Edition.* Post 8vo. 6*s.*

——— Stereoscope: its History, Theory, Construction, and Application to the Arts and to Education. Woodcuts. 12mo. 5*s.* 6*d.*

——— Kaleidoscope: its History, Theory, and Construction, with its application to the Fine and Useful Arts. *Second Edition.* Woodcuts. Post 8vo. 5*s.* 6*d.*

BRINE'S (Capt.) Narrative of the Rise and Progress of the Taeping Rebellion in China. Plans. Post 8vo. 10*s.* 6*d.*

BRITISH ASSOCIATION REPORTS. 8vo. York and Oxford, 1831-32, 13*s.* 6*d.* Cambridge, 1833, 12*s.* Edinburgh, 1834, 15*s.* Dublin, 1835, 13*s.* 6*d.* Bristol, 1836, 12*s.* Liverpool, 1837, 16*s.* 6*d.* Newcastle, 1838, 15*s.* Birmingham, 1839, 13*s.* 6*d.* Glasgow, 1840, 15*s.* Plymouth, 1841, 13*s.* 6*d.* Manchester, 1842, 10*s.* 6*d.* Cork, 1843, 12*s.* York, 1844, 20*s.* Cambridge, 1845, 12*s.* Southampton, 1846, 15*s.* Oxford, 1847, 18*s.* Swansea, 1848, 9*s.* Birmingham, 1849, 10*s.* Edinburgh, 1850, 15*s.* Ipswich, 1851, 16*s.* 6*d.* Belfast, 1852, 15*s.* Hull, 1853, 10*s.* 6*d.* Liverpool, 1854, 18*s.* Glasgow, 1855, 15*s.*; Cheltenham, 1856, 18*s.*; Dublin, 1857, 15*s.*; Leeds, 1858, 20*s.* Aberdeen, 1859, 15*s.* Oxford, 1860, 25*s.* Manchester, 1861, 15*s.* Cambridge, 1862, 20*s.* Newcastle, 1863, 25*s.* Bath, 1864, 25*s.*

BROUGHTON'S (LORD) Journey through Albania and other Provinces of Turkey in Europe and Asia, to Constantinople, 1809—10. *Third Edition.* Illustrations. 2 Vols. 8vo. 30*s.*

——— Visits to Italy. *3rd Edition.* 2 vols. Post 8vo. 18*s.*

BRITISH CLASSICS. A New Series of Standard English Authors, printed from the most correct text, and edited with notes. 8vo.

Already Published.

I. GOLDSMITH'S WORKS. Edited by PETER CUNNINGHAM, F.S.A. Vignettes. 4 Vols. 30*s.*

II. GIBBON'S DECLINE AND FALL OF THE ROMAN EMPIRE. Edited by WILLIAM SMITH, LL.D. Portrait and Maps. 8 Vols. 60*s.*

III. JOHNSON'S LIVES OF THE ENGLISH POETS. Edited by PETER CUNNINGHAM, F.S.A. 3 Vols. 22*s.* 6*d.*

IV. BYRON'S POETICAL WORKS. Edited, with Notes. 6 vols. 45*s.*

In Preparation.

LIFE AND WORKS OF POPE. Edited by REV. WHITWELL ELWIN.

HUME'S HISTORY OF ENGLAND. Edited, with Notes.

LIFE AND WORKS OF SWIFT. Edited by JOHN FORSTER.

BUBBLES FROM THE BRUNNEN OF NASSAU. By an Old MAN. *7th Edition*, with Illustrations. Post 8vo. 7*s.* 6*d.*

BUNYAN (JOHN) and Oliver Cromwell. Select Biographies. By ROBERT SOUTHEY. Post 8vo. 2*s.*

BUONAPARTE'S (NAPOLEON) Confidential Correspondence with his Brother Joseph, sometime King of Spain. *Second Edition.* 2 vols. 8vo. 26*s.*

BURGON'S (Rev. J. W.) Christian Gentleman; or, Memoir of Patrick Fraser Tytler. *Second Edition.* Post 8vo. 9*s.*

——— Letters from Rome, written to Friends at Home. Illustrations. Post 8vo. 12*s.*

BURN'S (COL.) Dictionary of Naval and Military Technical Terms, English and French, and French and English. *Fourth Edition.* Crown 8vo. 15*s.*

BURR'S (G. D.) Instructions in Practical Surveying, Topographical Plan Drawing, and on sketching ground without Instruments. *Fourth Edition.* Woodcuts. Post 8vo. 6*s.*

BUTTMAN'S LEXILOGUS; a Critical Examination of the Meaning of numerous Greek Words, chiefly in Homer and Hesiod. Translated by Rev. J. R. FISHLAKE. *Fifth Edition.* 8vo. 12*s.*

——— CATALOGUE OF IRREGULAR GREEK VERBS. With all the Tenses extant—their Formation, Meaning, and Usage, accompanied by an Index. Translated, with Notes, by Rev. J. R. FISHLAKE. *Fifth Edition.* Revised by Rev. E. VENABLES. Post 8vo.

BUXTON'S (SIR FOWELL) Memoirs. With Selections from his Correspondence. By his Son. Portrait. 8vo. 15*s.* *Abridged Edition,* Portrait. Fcap. 8vo. 2*s.* 6*d.*

——— (CHARLES, M.P.) IDEAS OF THE DAY ON POLICY. 8vo.

BYRON'S (LORD) Life, Letters, and Journals. By THOMAS MOORE. Plates. 6 Vols. Fcap. 8vo. 18*s*.

——— Life, Letters, and Journals. By THOMAS MOORE. Portraits. Royal 8vo. 9*s*.

——— Poetical Works. Portrait. 6 Vols. 8vo. 45*s*.

——— Poetical Works. Plates. 10 Vols. Fcap. 8vo. 30*s*.

——— Poetical Works. 8 Vols. 24mo. 20*s*.

——— Poetical Works. Plates. Royal 8vo. 9*s*.

——— Poetical Works. Portrait. Crown 8vo. 6*s*.

——— Childe Harold. With 80 Engravings. Small 4to. 21*s*.

——— Childe Harold. With 30 Vignettes. 12mo. 6*s*.

——— Childe Harold. 16mo. 2*s*. 6*d*.

——— Childe Harold. Vignettes. 16mo. 1*s*.

——— Childe Harold. Portrait. 16mo. 6*d*.

——— Tales and Poems. 24mo. 2*s*. 6*d*.

——— Miscellaneous. 2 Vols. 24mo. 5*s*.

——— Dramas and Plays. 2 Vols. 24mo. 5*s*.

——— Don Juan and Beppo. 2 Vols. 24mo. 5*s*.

——— Beauties. Selected from his Poetry and Prose. Portrait, Fcap. 8vo. 3*s*. 6*d*.

CARNARVON'S (LORD) Portugal, Gallicia, and the Basque Provinces. From Notes made during a Journey to those Countries. *Third Edition*. Post 8vo. 3*s*. 6*d*.

——— Recollections of the Druses of Lebanon. With Notes on their Religion. *Third Edition*. Post 8vo. 5*s*. 6*d*.

CAMPBELL'S (LORD) Lives of the Lord Chancellors and Keepers of the Great Seal of England. From the Earliest Times to the Death of Lord Eldon in 1838. *Fourth Edition*. 10 Vols. Crown 8vo. 6*s*. each.

——— Lives of the Chief Justices of England. From the Norman Conquest to the Death of Lord Tenterden. *Second Edition*. 3 Vols. 8vo. 42*s*.

——— Shakspeare's Legal Acquirements Considered. 8vo. 5*s*. 6*d*.

——— Life of Lord Chancellor Bacon. Fcap. 8vo. 2*s*. 6*d*.

——— (GEORGE) Modern India. A Sketch of the System of Civil Government. With some Account of the Natives and Native Institutions. *Second Edition*. 8vo. 16*s*.

——— India as it may be. An Outline of a proposed Government and Policy. 8vo. 12*s*.

——— (THOS.) Short Lives of the British Poets. With an Essay on English Poetry. Post 8vo. 3*s*. 6*d*.

CALLCOTT'S (LADY) Little Arthur's History of England. 150*th Thousand*. With Woodcuts. Fcap. 8vo. 2*s*. 6*d*.

CASTLEREAGH (The) DESPATCHES, from the commencement of the official career of the late Viscount Castlereagh to the close of his life. Edited by the Marquis of Londonderry. 12 Vols. 8vo. 14s. each.

CATHCART'S (Sir George) Commentaries on the War in Russia and Germany, 1812-13. Plans. 8vo. 14s.

CAVALCASELLE and CROWE'S History of Painting in Italy, from the Second to the Sixteenth Century, from recent researches, as well as from personal inspection of the Works of Art in that Country. With 70 Illustrations. Vols. I. and II. 8vo. 42s.

——— Notices of the Lives and Works of the Early Flemish Painters. Woodcuts. Post 8vo. 12s.

CHARMED ROE (The); or, The Story of the Little Brother and Sister. By Otto Speckter. Plates. 16mo. 5s.

CHORLEY'S (H. F.) STUDIES OF THE MUSIC OF MANY NATIONS; including the Substance of a Course of Lectures delivered at the Royal Institution. 8vo. (*In the Press.*)

CHURTON'S (Archdeacon) Gongora. An Historical Essay on the Age of Philip III. and IV. of Spain. With Translations. Portrait. 2 Vols. Small 8vo. 15s.

CICERO: HIS LIFE AND TIMES. With his Character viewed as a Statesman, Orator, and Friend. With a Selection from his Correspondence and Orations. By William Forsyth, Q.C. With Illustrations, 2 vols. Post 8vo. 18s.

CLAUSEWITZ'S (Carl Von) Campaign of 1812, in Russia. Translated from the German by Lord Ellesmere. Map. 8vo. 10s. 6d.

CLIVE'S (Lord) Life. By Rev. G. R. Gleig, M.A. Post 8vo. 3s. 6d.

COLCHESTER (The) PAPERS. The Diary and Correspondence of Charles Abbott, Lord Colchester, Speaker of the House of Commons, 1802-1817. Edited by his Son. Portrait. 3 Vols. 8vo. 42s.

COLERIDGE (Samuel Taylor). Specimens of his Table-Talk. *New Edition.* Portrait. Fcap. 8vo. 6s.

COLONIAL LIBRARY. [See Home and Colonial Library.]

COOK'S (Rev. Canon) Sermons Preached at Lincoln's Inn Chapel, and on Special Occasions. 8vo. 9s.

COOKERY (Modern Domestic). Founded on Principles of Economy and Practical Knowledge, and adapted for Private Families. By a Lady. *New Edition.* Woodcuts. Fcap. 8vo. 5s.

CORNWALLIS (The) Papers and Correspondence during the American War,—Administrations in India,—Union with Ireland, and Peace of Amiens. Edited by Charles Ross. *Second Edition.* 3 Vols. 8vo. 63s.

COWPER'S (Mary, Countess) Diary while Lady of the Bedchamber to Caroline Princess of Wales, 1714—20. Edited by Hon. Spencer Cowper. *Second Edition.* Portrait. 8vo. 10s. 6d.

CRABBE'S (Rev. George) Life, Letters, and Journals. By his Son. Portrait. Fcap. 8vo. 3s.

——— Life and Poetical Works. Plates. 8 Vols. Fcap. 8vo. 24s.

——— Life and Poetical Works. Plates. Royal 8vo. 7s.

CROKER'S (J. W.) Progressive Geography for Children. *Fifth Edition.* 18mo. 1*s.* 6*d.*

———— Stories for Children, Selected from the History of England. *Fifteenth Edition.* Woodcuts. 16mo. 2*s.* 6*d.*

———— Boswell's Life of Johnson. Including the Tour to the Hebrides. Portraits. Royal 8vo. 10*s.*

———— Essays on the Early Period of the French Revolution. 8vo. 15*s.*

———— Historical Essay on the Guillotine. Fcap. 8vo. 1*s.*

CROMWELL (OLIVER) and John Bunyan. By ROBERT SOUTHEY. Post 8vo. 2*s.*

CROWE'S AND CAVALCASELLE'S Notices of the Early Flemish Painters; their Lives and Works. Woodcuts. Post 8vo. 12*s.*

———— History of Painting in Italy, from 2nd to 16th Century. Derived from Historical Researches as well as inspection of the Works of Art in that Country. With 70 Illustrations. Vols. I. and II. 8vo. 42*s.*

CUMMING'S (R. GORDON) Five Years of a Hunter's Life in the Far Interior of South Africa; with Anecdotes of the Chace, and Notices of the Native Tribes. *New Edition.* Woodcuts. Post 8vo. 5*s.*

CUNNINGHAM'S (ALLAN) Poems and Songs. Now first collected and arranged, with Biographical Notice. 24mo. 2*s.* 6*d.*

CURETON (REV. W.) Remains of a very Ancient Recension of the Four Gospels in Syriac, hitherto unknown in Europe. Discovered, Edited, and Translated. 4to. 24*s.*

CURTIUS' (PROFESSOR) Student's Greek Grammar, for the use of Colleges and the Upper Forms. Translated under the Author's revision. Edited by DR. WM. SMITH. Post 8vo. 7*s.* 6*d.*

———— Smaller Greek Grammar for the use of the Middle and Lower Forms, abridged from the above. 12mo. 3*s.* 6*d.*

———— First Greek Course; containing Delectus, Exercise Book, and Vocabularies. 12mo. 3*s.* 6*d.*

CURZON'S (HON. ROBERT) ARMENIA AND ERZEROUM. A Year on the Frontiers of Russia, Turkey, and Persia. *Third Edition.* Woodcuts. Post 8vo. 7*s.* 6*d.*

———— Visits to the Monasteries of the Levant. *Fifth Edition.* Illustrations. Post 8vo. 7*s.* 6*d.*

CUST'S (GENERAL) Annals of the Wars of the 18th & 19th Centuries. 9 Vols. Fcap. 8vo. 5*s.* each.

———— Lives and Characters of the Warriors of the 17th Century who have Commanded Fleets and Armies before the Enemy. 2 Vols. Post 8vo. 16*s.*

DARWIN'S (CHARLES) Journal of Researches into the Natural History of the Countries visited during a Voyage round the World. Post 8vo. 9*s.*

———— Origin of Species by Means of Natural Selection; or, the Preservation of Favoured Races in the Struggle for Life. Post 8vo. 14*s.*

———— Fertilization of Orchids through Insect Agency, and as to the good of Intercrossing. Woodcuts. Post 8vo. 9*s.*

———— Domesticated Animals and Cultivated Plants; or, the Principles of Variation, Inheritance, Re-version, Crossing, Interbreeding, and Selection under Domestication. With Illustrations. Post 8vo. (*In Preparation.*)

DAVIS'S (NATHAN) Visit to the Ruined Cities of Numidia and Carthaginia. Illustrations. 8vo. 16*s.*

———— (SIR J. F.) Chinese Miscellanies: a Collection of Essays and Notes. Post 8vo. 6*s.*

DAVY'S (SIR HUMPHRY) Consolations in Travel; or, Last Days of a Philosopher. *Fifth Edition.* Woodcuts. Fcap. 8vo. 6*s.*

———— Salmonia; or, Days of Fly Fishing. *Fourth Edition.* Woodcuts. Fcap. 8vo. 6*s.*

DELEPIERRE'S (OCTAVE) History of Flemish Literature. From the Twelfth Century. 8vo. 9*s.*

DENNIS' (GEORGE) Cities and Cemeteries of Etruria. Plates. 2 Vols. 8vo. 42*s.*

DERBY'S (EDWARD, EARL OF) Translation of the Iliad of Homer into English Blank Verse. *Fifth Edition, Revised.* 2 Vols. 8vo. 24*s.*

DIXON'S (W. HEPWORTH) Story of the Life of Lord Bacon. Portrait. Fcap. 8vo. 7*s.* 6*d.*

DOG-BREAKING; the Most Expeditious, Certain, and Easy Method, whether great excellence or only mediocrity be required. With a Few Hints for those who Love the Dog and the Gun. By LIEUT.-GEN. HUTCHINSON. *Fourth Edition.* With 40 Woodcuts. Crown 8vo. 15*s.*

DOMESTIC MODERN COOKERY. Founded on Principles of Economy and Practical Knowledge, and adapted for Private Families. *New Edition.* Woodcuts. Fcap. 8vo. 5*s.*

DOUGLAS'S (GENERAL SIR HOWARD) Life and Adventures; From Notes, Conversations, and Correspondence. By S. W. FULLOM. Portrait. 8vo. 15*s.*

———— Theory and Practice of Gunnery. *5th Edition.* Plates. 8vo. 21*s.*

———— Military Bridges, and the Passage of Rivers in Military Operations. *Third Edition.* Plates. 8vo. 21*s.*

———— Naval Warfare with Steam. *Second Edition.* 8vo. 8*s.* 6*d.*

———— Modern Systems of Fortification, with special reference to the Naval, Littoral, and Internal Defence of England. Plans. 8vo. 12*s.*

DRAKE'S (SIR FRANCIS) Life, Voyages, and Exploits, by Sea and Land. By JOHN BARROW. *Third Edition.* Post 8vo. 2*s.*

DRINKWATER'S (JOHN) History of the Siege of Gibraltar, 1779-1783. With a Description and Account of that Garrison from the Earliest Periods. Post 8vo. 2*s.*

DU CHAILLU'S (PAUL B.) EQUATORIAL AFRICA, with Accounts of the Gorilla, the Nest-building Ape, Chimpanzee, Crocodile, &c. Illustrations. 8vo. 21*s.*

DUFFERIN'S (LORD) Letters from High Latitudes, being some Account of a Yacht Voyage to Iceland, &c., in 1856. *Fourth Edition.* Woodcuts. Post 8vo.

———— Lispings from Low Latitudes, or the Journal of the Hon. Impulsia Gushington. With 24 Plates. 4to. 21*s.*

DYER'S (THOMAS H.) History of Modern Europe, from the taking of Constantinople by the Turks to the close of the War in the Crimea. 4 Vols. 8vo. 60*s.*

EASTLAKE'S (SIR CHARLES) Italian Schools of Painting. From the German of KUGLER. Edited, with Notes. *Third Edition.* Illustrated from the Old Masters. 2 Vols. Post 8vo. 30*s.*

EASTWICK'S (E. B.) Handbook for Bombay and Madras, with Directions for Travellers, Officers, &c. Map. 2 Vols. Post 8vo. 24*s.*

EDWARDS' (W. H.) Voyage up the River Amazon, including a Visit to Para. Post 8vo. 2*s.*

ELDON'S (LORD) Public and Private Life, with Selections from his Correspondence and Diaries. By HORACE TWISS. *Third Edition.* Portrait. 2 Vols. Post 8vo. 21*s.*

ELLIS (REV. W.) Visits to Madagascar, including a Journey to the Capital, with notices of Natural History, and Present Civilisation of the People. *Fifth Thousand.* Map and Woodcuts. 8vo. 16*s.*

——— (MRS.) Education of Character, with Hints on Moral Training. Post 8vo. 7*s.* 6*d.*

ELLESMERE'S (LORD) Two Sieges of Vienna by the Turks. Translated from the German. Post 8vo. 2*s.*

——— Campaign of 1812 in Russia, from the German of General Carl Von Clausewitz. Map. 8vo. 10*s.* 6*d.*

——— Poems. With Illustrations. Crown 4to.

——— Essays on History, Biography, Geography, and Engineering. 8vo. 12*s.*

ELPHINSTONE'S (HON. MOUNTSTUART) History of India—the Hindoo and Mahomedan Periods. *Fifth Edition, Revised.* Map. 8vo. 18*s.*

ENGEL'S (CARL) Music of the Most Ancient Nations; particularly of the Assyrians, Egyptians, and Hebrews; with Special Reference to the Discoveries in Western Asia and in Egypt. With 100 Illustrations. 8vo. 16*s.*

ENGLAND (HISTORY OF) from the Peace of Utrecht to the Peace of Versailles, 1713—83. By LORD MAHON (Earl Stanhope). *Library Edition,* 7 Vols. 8vo. 93*s.*; or *Popular Edition,* 7 Vols. Post 8vo. 35*s.*

——— From the First Invasion by the Romans, down to the Present Year of Queen Victoria's Reign. By MRS. MARKHAM. *New and Cheaper Edition.* Woodcuts. 12mo. 4*s.*

——— (THE STUDENT'S HUME). From the Invasion of Julius Cæsar to the Revolution of 1688. By DAVID HUME. Corrected and continued to 1858. Edited by WM. SMITH, LL.D. Woodcuts. Post 8vo. 7*s.* 6*d.*

——— A Smaller History of England for Young Persons. By DR. WM. SMITH. Woodcuts. 18mo. 3*s.* 6*d.*

——— Little Arthur's History of England. By LADY CALLCOTT. Woodcuts. 18mo. 2*s.* 6*d.*

ENGLISHWOMAN IN AMERICA. Post 8vo. 10*s.* 6*d.*

ESKIMAUX and English Vocabulary, for Travellers in the Arctic Regions. 16mo. 3*s.* 6*d.*

ESSAYS FROM "THE TIMES." Being a Selection from the LITERARY PAPERS which have appeared in that Journal. *Seventh Thousand.* 2 vols. Fcap. 8vo. 8s.

ETHNOLOGICAL SOCIETY OF LONDON, TRANSACTIONS. New Series. Vols. I., II., and III. 8vo.

EXETER'S (BISHOP OF) Letters to the late Charles Butler, on the Theological parts of his Book of the Roman Catholic Church; with Remarks on certain Works of Dr. Milner and Dr. Lingard, and on some parts of the Evidence of Dr. Doyle. *Second Edition.* 8vo. 16s.

FAMILY RECEIPT-BOOK. A Collection of a Thousand Valuable and Useful Receipts. Fcap. 8vo. 5s. 6d.

FARRAR'S (REV. A. S.) Critical History of Free Thought in reference to the Christian Religion. Being the Bampton Lectures, 1862. 8vo. 16s.

——— (F. W.) Origin of Language, based on Modern Researches. Fcap. 8vo. 5s.

FEATHERSTONHAUGH'S (G. W.) Tour through the Slave States of North America, from the River Potomac to Texas and the Frontiers of Mexico. Plates. 2 Vols. 8vo. 26s.

FERGUSSON'S (JAMES) Palaces of Nineveh and Persepolis Restored. Woodcuts. 8vo. 16s.

——— History of Architecture in all Countries: from the Earliest Times to the Present Day. With 1200 Illustrations. 2 Vols. 8vo. Vol. I. 42s.

——— History of the Modern Styles of Architecture: forming the Third and Concluding Volume of the above work. With 312 Illustrations. 8vo. 31s. 6d.

——— Holy Sepulchre and the Temple at Jerusalem; being the Substance of Two Lectures delivered at the Royal Institution, 1862 and '65. Woodcuts. 8vo. 7s. 6d.

FISHER'S (REV. GEORGE) Elements of Geometry, for the Use of Schools. *Fifth Edition.* 18mo. 1s. 6d.

——— First Principles of Algebra, for the Use of Schools. *Fifth Edition.* 18mo. 1s. 6d.

FLOWER GARDEN (THE). By REV. THOS. JAMES. Fcap. 8vo. 1s.

FONNEREAU'S (T. G.) Diary of a Dutiful Son. Fcap. 8vo. 4s. 6d.

FORBES' (C. S.) Iceland; its Volcanoes, Geysers, and Glaciers. Illustrations. Post 8vo. 14s.

FORSTER'S (JOHN) Arrest of the Five Members by Charles the First. A Chapter of English History re-written. Post 8vo. 12s.

——— Grand Remonstrance, 1641. With an Essay on English freedom under the Plantagenet and Tudor Sovereigns. *Second Edition.* Post 8vo. 12s.

——— Sir John Eliot: a Biography, 1590—1632. With Portraits. 2 Vols. Crown 8vo. 30s.

——— Biographies of Oliver Cromwell, Daniel De Foe, Sir Richard Steele, Charles Churchill, Samuel Foote. *Third Edition.* Post 8vo. 12s.

FORD'S (RICHARD) Handbook for Spain, Andalusia, Ronda, Valencia, Catalonia, Granada, Gallicia, Arragon, Navarre, &c. *Third Edition.* 2 Vols. Post 8vo. 30*s.*

——— Gatherings from Spain. Post 8vo. 3*s.* 6*d.*

FORSYTH'S (WILLIAM) Life and Times of Cicero. With Selections from his Correspondence and Orations. Illustrations. 2 Vols. Post 8vo. 18*s.*

FORTUNE'S (ROBERT) Narrative of Two Visits to the Tea Countries of China, 1843-52. *Third Edition.* Woodcuts. 2 Vols. Post 8vo. 18*s.*

——— Third Visit to China. 1853-6. Woodcuts. 8vo. 16*s.*

——— Yedo and Peking. With Notices of the Agriculture and Trade of China, during a Fourth Visit to that Country. Illustrations. 8vo. 16*s.*

FOSS' (Edward) Judges of England. With Sketches of their Lives, and Notices of the Courts at Westminster, from the Conquest to the Present Time. 9 Vols. 8vo. 114*s.*

FRANCE (HISTORY OF). From the Conquest by the Gauls to Recent Times. By MRS. MARKHAM. *New and Chaper Edition.* Woodcuts. 12mo. 4*s.*

——— (THE STUDENT'S HISTORY OF). From the Earliest Times to the Establishment of the Second Empire, 1852. By W. H. PEARSON. Edited by WM. SMITH, LL.D. Woodcuts. Post 8vo. 7*s.* 6*d.*

FRENCH (THE) in Algiers; The Soldier of the Foreign Legion—and the Prisoners of Abd-el-Kadir. Translated by Lady DUFF GORDON. Post 8vo. 2*s.*

GALTON'S (FRANCIS) Art of Travel; or, Hints on the Shifts and Contrivances available in Wild Countries. *Third Edition.* Woodcuts. Post 8vo. 7*s.* 6*d.*

GEOGRAPHY, ANCIENT (THE STUDENT'S MANUAL OF). By Rev. W. L. BEVAN. Woodcuts. Post 8vo. 7*s.* 6*d.*

——— MODERN (THE STUDENT'S MANUAL). By Rev. W. L. BEVAN. Woodcuts. Post 8vo. *In the Press.*

——— Journal of the Royal Geographical Society of London. 8vo.

GERMANY (HISTORY OF). From the Invasion by Marius, to Recent times. By MRS. MARKHAM. *New and Cheaper Edition.* Woodcuts. 12mo. 4*s.*

GIBBON'S (EDWARD) History of the Decline and Fall of the Roman Empire. Edited, with Notes, by DEAN MILMAN and M. GUIZOT. *A New Edition.* Preceded by his Autobiography. And Edited, with Notes, by Dr. WM. SMITH. Maps. 8 Vols. 8vo. 60*s.*

——— (The Student's Gibbon); Being an Epitome of the above work, incorporating the Researches of Recent Commentators. By Dr. WM. SMITH. Woodcuts. Post 8vo. 7*s.* 6*d.*

GIFFARD'S (EDWARD) Deeds of Naval Daring; or, Anecdotes of the British Navy. New Edition. Fcap. 8vo. 3*s.* 6*d.*

GOLDSMITH'S (OLIVER) Works. A New Edition. Printed from the last editions revised by the Author. Edited by PETER CUNNINGHAM. Vignettes. 4 Vols. 8vo. 30*s.*

GLADSTONE'S (RIGHT HON. W. E.) Financial Statements of 1853, 60, 63, and 64; also his Speeches on Tax-Bills, 1861, and on Charities, 1863. *Second Edition*. 8vo. 12*s*.

——— Address on the Place of Ancient Greece in the Providential Order of the World. *Fourth Edition*. 8vo. 2*s*. 6*d*.

——— Wedgwood: an Address delivered at Burslem. Woodcuts. Post 8vo. 2*s*. *A Cheap Edition*, 1*s*.

GLEIG'S (REV. G. R.) Campaigns of the British Army at Washington and New Orleans. Post 8vo. 2*s*.

——— Story of the Battle of Waterloo. Post 8vo. 3*s*. 6*d*.

——— Narrative of Sale's Brigade in Affghanistan. Post 8vo. 2*s*.

——— Life of Robert Lord Clive. Post 8vo. 3*s*. 6*d*.

——— Life and Letters of Sir Thomas Munro. Post 8vo 3*s*. 6*d*.

GONGORA; An Historical Essay on the Times of Philip III. and IV. of Spain. With Illustrations. By ARCHDEACON CHURTON. Portrait. 2 vols. Post 8vo. 15*s*.

GORDON'S (SIR ALEX. DUFF) Sketches of German Life, and Scenes from the War of Liberation. From the German. Post 8vo. 3*s*. 6*d*.

——— (LADY DUFF) Amber-Witch: A Trial for Witchcraft. From the German. Post 8vo. 2*s*.

——— French in Algiers. 1. The Soldier of the Foreign Legion. 2. The Prisoners of Abd-el-Kadir. From the French. Post 8vo. 2*s*.

GOUGER'S (HENRY) Personal Narrative of Two Years' Imprisonment in Burmah. *Second Edition*. Woodcuts. Post 8vo. 12*s*.

GRAMMARS (LATIN and GREEK). See CURTIUS; SMITH; KING EDWARD VITH., &c. &c.

GREECE (THE STUDENT'S HISTORY OF). From the Earliest Times to the Roman Conquest. By WM. SMITH, LL.D. Woodcuts. Post 8vo. 7*s*. 6*d*.

——— (A SMALLER HISTORY OF, FOR YOUNG PERSONS). By DR. WM. SMITH. Woodcuts. 16mo. 3*s*. 6*d*.

GRENVILLE (THE) PAPERS. Being the Public and Private Correspondence of George Grenville, including his PRIVATE DIARY. Edited by W. J. SMITH. 4 Vols. 8vo. 16*s*. each.

GREY (EARL) on Parliamentary Government and Reform; with Suggestions for the Improvement of our Representative System, and an Examination of the Reform Bills of 1859—61. *Second Edition*. 8vo. 9*s*.

——— (SIR GEORGE) Polynesian Mythology, and Ancient Traditional History of the New Zealand Race. Woodcuts. Post 8vo. 10*s*. 6*d*.

GRUNER'S (LEWIS) Brick and Terra-Cotta Buildings of Lombardy, Fourteenth and Fifteenth Centuries. From careful Drawings and Restorations. Engraved and printed in Colours. Illustrations. Small folio. *Nearly Ready*.

GUIZOT'S (M.) Meditations on the Essence of Christianity, and on the Religious Questions of the Day. Post 8vo. 9*s*. 6*d*.

GROTE'S (GEORGE) History of Greece. From the Earliest Times to the close of the generation contemporary with the death of Alexander the Great. *Fourth Edition.* Maps. 8 vols. 8vo. 112*s.*

——— PLATO, and the other Companions of Socrates. 3 Vols. 8vo. 45*s.*

——— (MRS.) Memoir of Ary Scheffer. Post 8vo. 8*s.* 6*d.*

——— Collected Papers. 8vo. 10*s.* 6*d.*

HALLAM'S (HENRY) Constitutional History of England, from the Accession of Henry the Seventh to the Death of George the Second. *Seventh Edition.* 3 Vols. 8vo. 30*s.* Or Popular Edition, 3 Vols., Post 8vo, 18*s.*

——— History of Europe during the Middle Ages. *Tenth Edition.* 3 Vols. 8vo. 30*s.* Or Popular Edition, 3 Vols., Post 8vo, 18*s.*

——— Literary History of Europe, during the 15th, 16th and 17th Centuries. *Fourth Edition.* 3 Vols. 8vo. 36*s.* Or Popular Edition, 4 Vols., Post 8vo., 24*s.*

——— Literary Essays and Characters, Extracted from the above Work. Fcap. 8vo. 2*s.*

——— Historical Works. Containing History of England, —Middle Ages of Europe,—Literary History of Europe. 10 Vols. Post 8vo. 6*s.* each.

——— (ARTHUR) Remains; in Verse and Prose. With Preface, Memoir, and Portrait. Fcap. 8vo. 7*s.* 6*d.*

HAMILTON'S (JAMES) Wanderings in North Africa. With Illustrations. Post 8vo. 12*s.*

HART'S ARMY LIST. (*Quarterly and Annually.*) 8vo. 10*s.* 6*d.* and 21*s.* each.

HANNAH'S (REV. DR.) Bampton Lectures for 1863; the Divine and Human Elements in Holy Scripture. 8vo. 10*s.* 6*d.*

HAY'S (J. H. DRUMMOND) Western Barbary, its wild Tribes and savage Animals. Post 8vo. 2*s.*

HEAD'S (SIR FRANCIS) Horse and his Rider. Woodcuts. Post 8vo. 5*s.*

——— Rapid Journeys across the Pampas. Post 8vo. 2*s.*

——— Bubbles from the Brunnen of Nassau. With Illustrations. Post 8vo.

——— Emigrant. Fcap. 8vo. 2*s.* 6*d.*

——— Stokers and Pokers; or, N.-Western Railway. Post 8vo. 2*s.*

——— Fortnight in Ireland. Map. 8vo. 12*s.*

——— (SIR EDMUND) Shall and Will; or, Future Auxiliary Verbs. Fcap. 8vo. 4*s.*

HEBER'S (BISHOP) Journey through the Upper Provinces of India, from Calcutta to Bombay, with an Account of a Journey to Madras and the Southern Provinces. *Twelfth Edition.* 2 Vols. Post 8vo. 7*s.*

——— Poetical Works, including Palestine, Europe, The Red Sea, Hymns, &c. *Sixth Edition.* Portrait. Fcap. 8vo. 6*s.*

HERODOTUS. A New English Version. Edited, with Notes and Essays, historical, ethnographical, and geographical, by Rev. G. RAWLINSON, assisted by SIR HENRY RAWLINSON and SIR J. G. WILKINSON. *Second Edition.* Maps and Woodcuts. 4 Vols. 8vo. 48*s.*

HAND-BOOK—TRAVEL-TALK. English, French, German, and Italian. 18mo. 3s. 6d.

——— NORTH GERMANY, HOLLAND, BELGIUM, and the Rhine to Switzerland. Map. Post 8vo. 10s.

——— KNAPSACK GUIDE—BELGIUM AND THE RHINE. Post 8vo. (*In the Press.*)

——— SOUTH GERMANY, Bavaria, Austria, Styria, Salzberg, the Austrian and Bavarian Alps, the Tyrol, Hungary, and the Danube, from Ulm to the Black Sea. Map. Post 8vo. 10s.

——— KNAPSACK GUIDE—THE TYROL. Post 8vo. (*In the Press.*)

——— PAINTING. German, Flemish, and Dutch Schools. Edited by DR. WAAGEN. Woodcuts. 2 Vols. Post 8vo. 24s.

——— LIVES OF THE EARLY FLEMISH PAINTERS, with Notices of their Works. By CROWE and CAVALCASELLE. Illustrations. Post 8vo. 12s.

——— SWITZERLAND, Alps of Savoy, and Piedmont. Maps. Post 8vo. 9s.

——— KNAPSACK GUIDE—SWITZERLAND. Post 8vo. 5s.

——— FRANCE, Normandy, Brittany, the French Alps, the Rivers Loire, Seine, Rhone, and Garonne, Dauphiné, Provence, and the Pyrenees. Maps. Post 8vo. 10s.

——— KNAPSACK GUIDE—FRANCE. Post 8vo. (*In the Press.*)

——— PARIS AND ITS ENVIRONS. Map. Post 8vo. 5s.

——— SPAIN, Andalusia, Ronda, Granada, Valencia, Catalonia, Gallicia, Arragon, and Navarre. Maps. 2 Vols. Post 8vo. 30s.

——— PORTUGAL, LISBON, &c. Map. Post 8vo. 9s.

——— NORTH ITALY, Piedmont, Liguria, Venetia, Lombardy, Parma, Modena, and Romagna. Map. Post 8vo. 12s.

——— CENTRAL ITALY, Lucca, Tuscany, Florence, The Marches, Umbria, and the Patrimony of St. Peter's. Map. Post 8vo. 10s.

——— ROME AND ITS ENVIRONS. Map. Post 8vo. 9s.

——— SOUTH ITALY, Two Sicilies, Naples, Pompeii, Herculaneum, and Vesuvius. Map. Post 8vo. 10s.

——— KNAPSACK GUIDE—ITALY. Post 8vo. 6s.

——— SICILY, Palermo, Messina, Catania, Syracuse, Etna, and the Ruins of the Greek Temples. Map. Post 8vo. 12s.

——— PAINTING. The Italian Schools. From the German of KUGLER. Edited by Sir CHARLES EASTLAKE, R.A. Woodcuts. 2 Vols. Post 8vo. 30s.

——— LIVES OF THE EARLY ITALIAN PAINTERS, AND PROGRESS OF PAINTING IN ITALY, from CIMABUE to BASSANO. By Mrs. JAMESON. *A New Edition.* Woodcuts. Post 8vo. *In the Press.*

——— NORWAY. Map. Post 8vo. 5s.

——— DENMARK, SWEDEN, and NORWAY. Maps. Post 8vo. 15s.

HAND-BOOK—GREECE, the Ionian Islands, Albania, Thessaly, and Macedonia. Maps. Post 8vo. 15*s.*

———— TURKEY, Malta, Asia Minor, Constantinople, Armenia, Mesopotamia, &c. Maps. Post 8vo.

———— EGYPT, Thebes, the Nile, Alexandria, Cairo, the Pyramids, Mount Sinai, &c. Map. Post 8vo. 15*s.*

———— SYRIA AND PALESTINE, Peninsula of Sinai, Eidom, and Syrian Desert. Maps. 2 Vols. Post 8vo. 24*s.*

———— BOMBAY AND MADRAS. Map. 2 Vols. Post 8vo. 24*s.*

———— RUSSIA, POLAND, and FINLAND. Maps. Post 8vo. 12*s.*

———— MODERN LONDON. A Complete Guide to all the Sights and Objects of Interest in the Metropolis. Map. 16mo. 3*s.* 6*d.*

———— WESTMINSTER ABBEY. Woodcuts. 16mo. 1*s.*

———— KENT AND SUSSEX, Canterbury, Dover, Ramsgate, Sheerness, Rochester, Chatham, Woolwich, Brighton, Chichester, Worthing, Hastings, Lewes, Arundel, &c. Map. Post 8vo. 10*s.*

———— SURREY AND HANTS, Kingston, Croydon, Reigate, Guildford, Winchester, Southampton, Portsmouth, and Isle of Wight. Maps. Post 8vo. 10*s.*

———— BERKS, BUCKS, AND OXON, Windsor, Eton, Reading, Aylesbury, Uxbridge, Wycombe, Henley, the City and University of Oxford, and the Descent of the Thames to Maidenhead and Windsor. Map. Post 8vo. 7*s.* 6*d.*

———— WILTS, DORSET, AND SOMERSET, Salisbury, Chippenham, Weymouth, Sherborne, Wells, Bath, Bristol, Taunton, &c. Map. Post 8vo. 7*s.* 6*d.*

———— DEVON AND CORNWALL, Exeter, Ilfracombe, Linton, Sidmouth, Dawlish, Teignmouth, Plymouth, Devonport, Torquay, Launceston, Truro, Penzance, Falmouth, &c. Maps. Post 8vo. 10*s.*

———— NORTH AND SOUTH WALES, Bangor, Carnarvon, Beaumaris, Snowdon, Conway, Menai Straits, Carmarthen, Pembroke, Tenby, Swansea, The Wye, &c. Maps. 2 Vols. Post 8vo. 12*s.*

———— SOUTHERN CATHEDRALS OF ENGLAND—Winchester, Salisbury, Exeter, Wells, Chichester, Rochester, Canterbury. With 110 Illustrations. 2 Vols. Crown 8vo. 24*s.*

———— EASTERN CATHEDRALS OF ENGLAND—Oxford, Peterborough, Norwich, Ely, and Lincoln. With 90 Illustrations. Crown 8vo. 18*s.*

———— WESTERN CATHEDRALS OF ENGLAND—Bristol, Gloucester, Hereford, Worcester, and Lichfield. With 50 Illustrations. Crown 8vo. 16*s.*

———— FAMILIAR QUOTATIONS. From English Authors. *Third Edition.* Fcap. 8vo. 5*s.*

HESSEY (REV. DR.). Sunday—Its Origin, History, and Present Obligations. Being the Bampton Lectures for 1860. *Second Edition.* 8vo. 16*s.* Or *Third and Popular Edition.* Post 8vo.

HICKMAN'S (WM.) Treatise on the Law and Practice of Naval Courts-Martial. 8vo. 10*s.* 6*d.*

HOME AND COLONIAL LIBRARY. A Series of Works adapted for all circles and classes of Readers, having been selected for their acknowledged interest and ability of the Authors. Post 8vo. Published at 2*s.* and 3*s.* 6*d.* each, and arranged under two distinctive heads as follows:—

CLASS A.

HISTORY, BIOGRAPHY, AND HISTORIC TALES.

1. SIEGE OF GIBRALTAR. By JOHN DRINKWATER. 2*s.*
2. THE AMBER-WITCH. By LADY DUFF GORDON. 2*s.*
3. CROMWELL AND BUNYAN. By ROBERT SOUTHEY. 2*s.*
4. LIFE OF SIR FRANCIS DRAKE. By JOHN BARROW. 2*s.*
5. CAMPAIGNS AT WASHINGTON. By REV. G. R. GLEIG. 2*s.*
6. THE FRENCH IN ALGIERS. By LADY DUFF GORDON. 2*s.*
7. THE FALL OF THE JESUITS. 2*s.*
8. LIVONIAN TALES. 2*s.*
9. LIFE OF CONDE. By LORD MAHON. 3*s.* 6*d.*
10. SALE'S BRIGADE. By REV. G. R. GLEIG. 2*s.*
11. THE SIEGES OF VIENNA. By LORD ELLESMERE. 2*s.*
12. THE WAYSIDE CROSS. By CAPT. MILMAN. 2*s.*
13. SKETCHES OF GERMAN LIFE. By SIR A. GORDON. 3*s.* 6*d.*
14. THE BATTLE OF WATERLOO. By REV. G. R. GLEIG. 3*s.* 6*d.*
15. AUTOBIOGRAPHY OF STEFFENS. 2*s.*
16. THE BRITISH POETS. By THOMAS CAMPBELL. 3*s.* 6*d.*
17. HISTORICAL ESSAYS. By LORD MAHON. 3*s.* 6*d.*
18. LIFE OF LORD CLIVE. By REV. G. R. GLEIG. 3*s.* 6*d.*
19. NORTH - WESTERN RAILWAY. By SIR F. B. HEAD. 2*s.*
20. LIFE OF MUNRO. By REV. G. R. GLEIG. 3*s.* 6*d.*

CLASS B.

VOYAGES, TRAVELS, AND ADVENTURES.

1. BIBLE IN SPAIN. By GEORGE BORROW. 3*s.* 6*d.*
2. GIPSIES OF SPAIN. By GEORGE BORROW. 3*s.* 6*d.*

3 & 4. JOURNALS IN INDIA. By BISHOP HEBER. 2 Vols. 7*s.*

5. TRAVELS IN THE HOLY LAND. By IRBY and MANGLES. 2*s.*
6. MOROCCO AND THE MOORS. By J. DRUMMOND HAY. 2*s.*
7. LETTERS FROM THE BALTIC. By a LADY. 2*s.*
8. NEW SOUTH WALES. By MRS. MEREDITH. 2*s.*
9. THE WEST INDIES. By M. G. LEWIS. 2*s.*
10. SKETCHES OF PERSIA. By SIR JOHN MALCOLM. 3*s.* 6*d.*
11. MEMOIRS OF FATHER RIPA. 2*s.*

12, 13. TYPEE AND OMOO. By HERMANN MELVILLE. 2 Vols. 7*s.*

14. MISSIONARY LIFE IN CANADA. By REV. J. ABBOTT. 2*s.*
15. LETTERS FROM MADRAS. By a LADY. 2*s.*
16. HIGHLAND SPORTS. By CHARLES ST. JOHN. 3*s.* 6*d.*
17. PAMPAS JOURNEYS. By SIR F. B. HEAD. 2*s.*
18. GATHERINGS FROM SPAIN. By RICHARD FORD. 3*s.* 6*d.*
19. THE RIVER AMAZON. By W. H. EDWARDS. 2*s.*
20. MANNERS & CUSTOMS OF INDIA. By REV. C. ACLAND. 2*s.*
21. ADVENTURES IN MEXICO. By G. F. RUXTON. 3*s.* 6*d.*
22. PORTUGAL AND GALLICIA. By LORD CARNARVON. 3*s.* 6*d.*
23. BUSH LIFE IN AUSTRALIA. By Rev. H. W. HAYGARTH. 2*s.*
24. THE LIBYAN DESERT. By BAYLE ST. JOHN. 2*s.*
25. SIERRA LEONE. By a LADY. 3*s.* 6*d.*

*** Each work may be had separately.

HILLARD'S (G. S.) Six Months in Italy. 2 Vols. Post 8vo. 16s.

HOLLWAY'S (J. G.) Month in Norway. Fcap. 8vo. 2s.

HONEY BEE (The). An Essay. By Rev. Thomas James. Reprinted from the "Quarterly Review." Fcap. 8vo. 1s.

HOOK'S (Dean) Church Dictionary. *Ninth Edition.* 8vo. 16s.

———— (Theodore) Life. By J. G. Lockhart. Reprinted from the "Quarterly Review." Fcap. 8vo. 1s.

HOOKER'S (Dr. J. D.) Himalayan Journals; or, Notes of an Oriental Naturalist in Bengal, the Sikkim and Nepal Himalayas, the Khasia Mountains, &c. *Second Edition.* Woodcuts. 2 Vols. Post 8vo. 18s.

HOPE'S (A. J. Beresford) English Cathedral of the Nineteenth Century. With Illustrations. 8vo. 12s.

HORACE (Works of). Edited by Dean Milman. With 300 Woodcuts. Crown 8vo. 21s.

———— (Life of). By Dean Milman. Woodcuts, and coloured Borders. 8vo. 9s.

HOUGHTON'S (Lord) Poetical Works. Fcap. 8vo. 6s. 6d.

HUME'S (The Student's) History of England, from the Invasion of Julius Cæsar to the Revolution of 1688. Corrected and continued to 1858. Edited by Dr. Wm. Smith. Woodcuts. Post 8vo. 7s. 6d.

HUTCHINSON (Gen.) on the most expeditious, certain, and easy Method of Dog-Breaking. *Fourth Edition.* Enlarged and revised, with 40 Illustrations. Crown 8vo. 15s.

HUTTON'S (H. E.) Principia Græca; an Introduction to the Study of Greek. Comprehending Grammar, Delectus, and Exercise-book, with Vocabularies. *Third Edition.* 12mo. 3s. 6d.

IRBY AND MANGLES' Travels in Egypt, Nubia, Syria, and the Holy Land. Post 8vo. 2s.

JAMES' (Rev. Thomas) Fables of Æsop. A New Translation, with Historical Preface. With 100 Woodcuts by Tenniel and Wolf. *Forty-eighth Thousand.* Post 8vo. 2s. 6d.

JAMESON'S (Mrs.) Lives of the Early Italian Painters, from Cimabue to Bassano, and the Progress of Painting in Italy. *New Edition.* With Woodcuts. Post 8vo.

JESSE'S (Edward) Gleanings in Natural History. *Eighth Edition.* Fcp. 8vo. 6s.

JOHNSON'S (Dr. Samuel) Life. By James Boswell. Including the Tour to the Hebrides. Edited by Mr. Croker. Portraits. Royal 8vo. 10s.

———— Lives of the most eminent English Poets. Edited by Peter Cunningham. 3 vols. 8vo. 22s. 6d.

JOURNAL OF A NATURALIST. Woodcuts. Post 8vo. 9s. 6d.

KEN'S (Bishop) Life. By a Layman, Author of "Life of the Messiah." *Second Edition.* Portrait. 2 Vols. 8vo. 18s.

———— Exposition of the Apostles' Creed. Extracted from his "Practice of Divine Love." Fcap. 1s. 6d.

———— Approach to the Holy Altar. Extracted from his "Manual of Prayer" and "Practice of Divine Love." Fcap. 8vo. 1s. 6d.

KENNEDY'S (GENERAL SIR J. SHAW) Notes on the Battle of Waterloo. With a Memoir of his Life and Services, and a Plan for the Defence of Canada. With Map and Plans. 8vo. 7*s.* 6*d.*

KING'S (REV. S. W.) Italian Valleys of the Alps; a Tour through all the Romantic and less-frequented "Vals" of Northern Piedmont. Illustrations. Crown 8vo. 18*s.*

——— (REV. C. W.) Antique Gems; their Origin, Use, and Value, as Interpreters of Ancient History, and as illustrative of Ancient Art. Illustrations. 8vo. 42*s.*

KING EDWARD VITH'S Latin Grammar; or, an Introduction to the Latin Tongue, for the Use of Schools. *Seventeenth Edition.* 12mo. 3*s.* 6*d.*

——— First Latin Book; or, the Accidence, Syntax, and Prosody, with an English Translation for the Use of Junior Classes. *Fifth Edition.* 12mo. 2*s.* 6*d.*

KIRK'S (J. FOSTER) History of Charles the Bold, Duke of Burgundy. Portrait. 2 Vols. 8vo. 30*s.*

KERR'S (ROBERT) GENTLEMAN'S HOUSE; OR, HOW TO PLAN ENGLISH RESIDENCES, FROM THE PARSONAGE TO THE PALACE. With Tables of Accommodation and Cost, and a Series of Selected Views and Plans. *Second Edition.* 8vo. 24*s.*

——— Ancient Lights; a Book for Architects, Surveyors, Lawyers, and Landlords. 8vo. 5*s.* 6*d.*

KING GEORGE THE THIRD'S CORRESPONDENCE WITH LORD NORTH, 1769-82. Edited, with Notes and Introduction, by W. BODHAM DONNE. 2 vols. 8vo. Published by permission. From the Royal Library at Windsor. (*In the Press.*)

KUGLER'S Italian Schools of Painting. Edited, with Notes, by SIR CHARLES EASTLAKE. *Third Edition.* Woodcuts. 2 Vols. Post 8vo. 30*s.*

——— German, Dutch, and Flemish Schools of Painting. Edited, with Notes, by DR. WAAGEN. *Second Edition.* Woodcuts. 2 Vols. Post 8vo. 24*s.*

LAYARD'S (A. H.) Nineveh and its Remains. Being a Narrative of Researches and Discoveries amidst the Ruins of Assyria. With an Account of the Chaldean Christians of Kurdistan; the Yezedis, or Devil-worshippers; and an Enquiry into the Manners and Arts of the Ancient Assyrians. *Sixth Edition.* Plates and Woodcuts. 2 Vols. 8vo. 36*s.*

——— Nineveh and Babylon; being the Result of a Second Expedition to Assyria. Plates 8vo. 21*s.* On *Fine Paper,* 2 Vols. 8vo. 30*s.*

——— Popular Account of Nineveh and Babylon. A New Edition. With Woodcuts. Post 8vo. (*In the Press.*)

LESLIE'S (C. R.) Handbook for Young Painters. With Illustrations. Post 8vo. 10*s.* 6*d.*

——— Autobiographical Recollections, with Selections from his Correspondence. Edited by TOM TAYLOR. Portrait. 2 Vols. Post 8vo. 18*s.*

——— Life of Sir Joshua Reynolds. With an Account of his Works, and a Sketch of his Cotemporaries. By C. R. LESLIE and TOM TAYLOR. Illustrations. 2 Vols. 8vo. 42*s.*

LETTERS FROM THE BALTIC. By a LADY. Post 8vo. 2s.

——— MADRAS. By a LADY. Post 8vo. 2s.

——— SIERRA LEONE. By a LADY. Edited by the HONOURABLE MRS. NORTON. Post 8vo. 3s. 6d.

LEWIS' (SIR G. C.) Essay on the Government of Dependencies. 8vo. 12s.

——— Glossary of Provincial Words used in Herefordshire and some of the adjoining Counties. 12mo. 4s. 6d.

——— (M. G.) Journal of a Residence among the Negroes in the West Indies. Post 8vo. 2s.

LIDDELL'S (DEAN) History of Rome. From the Earliest Times to the Establishment of the Empire. With the History of Literature and Art. 2 Vols. 8vo. 28s.

——— Student's History of Rome, abridged from the above Work. With Woodcuts. Post 8vo. 7s. 6d.

LINDSAY'S (LORD) Lives of the Lindsays; or, a Memoir of the Houses of Crawfurd and Balcarres. With Extracts from Official Papers and Personal Narratives. *Second Edition.* 3 Vols. 8vo. 24s.

——— Report of the Claim of James, Earl of Crawfurd and Balcarres, to the Original Dukedom of Montrose, created in 1488 Folio. 15s.

——— Scepticism; a Retrogressive Movement in Theology and Philosophy. 8vo. 9s.

LISPINGS from LOW LATITUDES; or, the Journal of the Hon. Impulsia Gushington. Edited by LORD DUFFERIN. With 24 Plates, 4to. 21s.

LITTLE ARTHUR'S HISTORY OF ENGLAND. By LADY CALLCOTT. *150th Thousand.* With 20 Woodcuts. Fcap. 8vo. 2s. 6d.

LIVINGSTONE'S (DR.) Popular Account of his Missionary Travels in South Africa. Illustrations. Post 8vo. 6s.

——— Narrative of an Expedition to the Zambezi and its Tributaries; and of the Discovery of Lakes Shirwa and Nyassa. 1858-64. By DAVID and CHARLES LIVINGSTONE. Map and Illustrations. 8vo. 21s.

LIVONIAN TALES. By the Author of "Letters from the Baltic." Post 8vo. 2s.

LOCKHART'S (J. G.) Ancient Spanish Ballads. Historical and Romantic. Translated, with Notes. *New Edition.* Illustrations. 4to. 21s. *Or Popular Edition,* Post 8vo. 2s. 6d.

LONDON'S (BISHOP OF) Dangers and Safeguards of Modern Theology. Containing Suggestions to the Theological Student under present difficulties. *Second Edition.* 8vo. 9s.

LOUDON'S (MRS.) Instructions in Gardening for Ladies. With Directions and Calendar of Operations for Every Month. *Eighth Edition.* Woodcuts. Fcap. 8vo. 5s.

LUCAS' (SAMUEL) Secularia; or, Surveys on the Main Stream of History. 8vo. 12s.

LUCKNOW: a Lady's Diary of the Siege. Fcap. 8vo. 4s. 6d.

LYELL'S (SIR CHARLES) Elements of Geology; or, the Ancient Changes of the Earth and its Inhabitants considered as Illustrative of Geology. *Sixth Edition.* Woodcuts. 8vo. 18s.

——— Geological Evidences of the Antiquity of Man. *Third Edition.* Illustrations. 8vo. 14s.

LYTTELTON'S (Lord) Ephemera. Post 8vo. 10s. 6*d.*

LYTTON'S (Sir Edward Bulwer) Poems. *New Edition.* Post 8vo. 10s. 6*d.*

MACPHERSON'S (Major S. C.) Memorials of Service in India, while Political Agent at Gwalior during the Mutiny, and formerly employed in the Suppression of Human Sacrifices in Orissa. Edited by his Brother. With Portrait and Illustrations. 8vo. 12s.

MAHON'S (Lord) History of England, from the Peace of Utrecht to the Peace of Versailles, 1713—83. *Library Edition.* 7 Vols. 8vo. 93s. *Popular Edition*, 7 Vols. Post 8vo. 35s.

——— "Forty-Five;" a Narrative of the Rebellion in Scotland. Post 8vo. 3s.

——— History of British India from its Origin till the Peace of 1783. Post 8vo. 3s. 6d.

——— Spain under Charles the Second; 1690 to 1700. *Second Edition.* Post 8vo. 6s. 6d.

——— Historical and Critical Essays. Post 8vo. 3s. 6*d.*

——— Story of Joan of Arc. Fcap. 8vo. 1s.

——— Addresses. Fcap. 8vo. 1s.

——— Life of William Pitt, with Extracts from his MS. Papers. *Second Edition.* Portraits. 4 Vols. Post 8vo. 42s.

——— Miscellanies. *Second Edition.* Post 8vo. 5s. 6*d.*

——— Condé, surnamed the Great. Post 8vo. 3s. 6*d.*

——— Belisarius. *Second Edition.* Post 8vo. 10s. 6*d.*

McCLINTOCK'S (Capt. Sir F. L.) Narrative of the Discovery of the Fate of Sir John Franklin and his Companions in the Arctic Seas. *Twelfth Thousand.* Illustrations. 8vo. 16s.

McCULLOCH'S (J. R.) Collected Edition of Ricardo's Political Works. With Notes and Memoir. *Second Edition.* 8vo. 16s.

MacDOUGALL (Col.) On Modern Warfare as Influenced by Modern Artillery. With Plans. Post 8vo. 12s.

MAINE (H. Sumner) On Ancient Law: its Connection with the Early History of Society, and its Relation to Modern Ideas. *Third Edition.* 8vo. 12s.

MALCOLM'S (Sir John) Sketches of Persia. Post 8vo. 3s. 6*d.*

MANSEL (Rev. H. L.) Limits of Religious Thought Examined. Being the Bampton Lectures for 1858. *Fourth Edition.* Post 8vo. 7s. 6d.

MANSFIELD (Sir William) On the Introduction of a Gold Currency into India: a Contribution to the Literature of Political Economy. 8vo. 3s. 6*d.*

MANTELL'S (Gideon A.) Thoughts on Animalcules; or, the Invisible World, as revealed by the Microscope. *Second Edition.* Plates. 16mo. 6s.

MANUAL OF SCIENTIFIC ENQUIRY, Prepared for the Use of Officers and Travellers. By various Writers. Edited by Sir J. F. Herschel and Rev. R. Main. *Third Edition.* Maps. Post 8vo. 9s. (*Published by order of the Lords of the Admiralty.*)

MARKHAM'S (MRS.) History of England. From the First Invasion by the Romans, down to Recent Times. *New and Cheaper Edition.* Woodcuts. 12mo. 4s.

———— History of France. From the Conquest by the Gauls, to Recent Times. *New and Cheaper Edition.* Woodcuts. 12mo. 4s.

———— History of Germany. From the Invasion by Marius, to Recent Times. *New and Cheaper Edition.* Woodcuts. 12mo. 4s.

———— (CLEMENTS, R.) Travels in Peru and India, for the purpose of collecting Cinchona Plants, and introducing Bark into India. Maps and Illustrations. 8vo. 16s.

MARKLAND'S (J. H.) Reverence due to Holy Places. *Third Edition.* Fcap. 8vo. 2s.

MARRYAT'S (JOSEPH) History of Modern and Mediæval Pottery and Porcelain. With a Description of the Manufacture. *Second Edition.* Plates and Woodcuts. 8vo. 31s. 6d.

———— (HORACE) Jutland, the Danish Isles, and Copenhagen. Illustrations. 2 Vols. Post 8vo. 24s.

———— Sweden and Isle of Gothland. Illustrations. 2 Vols. Post 8vo. 28s.

MATTHIÆ'S (AUGUSTUS) Greek Grammar for Schools, abridged from the Larger Grammar. By Blomfield. *Ninth Edition.* Revised by EDWARDS. 12mo. 3s.

MAUREL'S (JULES) Essay on the Character, Actions, and Writings of the Duke of Wellington. *Second Edition.* Fcap. 8vo. 1s. 6d.

MAYNE'S (CAPT.) Four Years in British Columbia and Vancouver Island. Its Forests, Rivers, Coasts, and Gold Fields, and Resources for Colonisation. Illustrations. 8vo. 16s.

MELVILLE'S (HERMANN) Typee and Omoo; or, Adventures amongst the Marquesas and South Sea Islands. 2 Vols. Post 8vo. 7s.

MILLS' (REV. JOHN) Three Months' Residence at Nablus, with an Account of the Modern Samaritans. Illustrations. Post 8vo. 10s. 6d.

MILMAN'S (DEAN) History of the Jews, from the Earliest Period, brought down to Modern Times. *New Edition.* 3 Vols. 8vo. 36s.

———— Christianity, from the Birth of Christ to the Abolition of Paganism in the Roman Empire. *New Edition.* 3 Vols. 8vo. 36s.

———— Latin Christianity; including that of the Popes to the Pontificate of Nicholas V. *New Edition.* 9 Vols. 8vo. 84s.

———— Character and Conduct of the Apostles considered as an Evidence of Christianity. 8vo. 10s. 6d.

———— Translations from the Agamemnon of Æschylus and Bacchanals of Euripides; with Passages from the Lyric and Later Poets of Greece. With Illustrations, crown 8vo. 12s.

———— Life and Works of Horace. With 300 Woodcuts. 2 Vols. Crown 8vo. 30s.

———— Poetical Works. Plates. 3 Vols. Fcap. 8vo. 18s.

———— Fall of Jerusalem. Fcap. 8vo. 1s.

———— (CAPT. E. A.) Wayside Cross. A Tale of the Carlist War. Post 8vo. 2s.

MEREDITH'S (Mrs. Charles) Notes and Sketches of New South Wales. Post 8vo. 2*s*.

MESSIAH (THE): A Narrative of the Life, Travels, Death, Resurrection, and Ascension of our Blessed Lord. By a Layman. Author of the "Life of Bishop Ken." Map. 8vo. 18*s*.

MICHIE'S (Alexander) Siberian Overland Route from Peking to Petersburg, through the Deserts and Steppes of Mongolia, Tartary, &c. Maps and Illustrations. 8vo. 16*s*.

MODERN DOMESTIC COOKERY. Founded on Principles of Economy and Practical Knowledge and adapted for Private Families. *New Edition*. Woodcuts. Fcap. 8vo. 5*s*.

MOORE'S (Thomas) Life and Letters of Lord Byron. Plates. 6 Vols. Fcap. 8vo. 18*s*.

——— Life and Letters of Lord Byron. Portraits. Royal 8vo. 9*s*.

MOTLEY'S (J. L.) History of the United Netherlands: from the Death of William the Silent to the Synod of Dort. Embracing the English-Dutch struggle against Spain; and a detailed Account of the Spanish Armada. Portraits. 2 Vols. 8vo. 30*s*.

MOUHOT'S (Henri) Siam, Cambojia, and Lao; a Narrative of Travels and Discoveries. Illustrations. 2 vols. 8vo. 32*s*.

MOZLEY'S (Rev. J. B.) Treatise on Predestination. 8vo. 14*s*.

——— Primitive Doctrine of Baptismal Regeneration. 8vo. 7*s*. 6*d*.

MUNDY'S (General) Pen and Pencil Sketches in India. *Third Edition*. Plates. Post 8vo. 7*s*. 6*d*.

——— (Admiral) Account of the Italian Revolution, with Notices of Garibaldi, Francis II., and Victor Emmanuel. Post 8vo. 12*s*.

MUNRO'S (General Sir Thomas) Life and Letters. By the Rev. G. R. Gleig. Post 8vo. 3*s*. 6*d*.

MURCHISON'S (Sir Roderick) Russia in Europe and the Ural Mountains. With Coloured Maps, Plates, Sections, &c. 2 Vols. Royal 4to. 5*l*. 5*s*.

——— Siluria; or, a History of the Oldest Rocks containing Organic Remains. *Third Edition*. Map and Plates. 8vo. 42*s*.

MURRAY'S RAILWAY READING. Containing:—

Wellington. By Lord Ellesmere. 6*d*.
Nimrod on the Chase, 1*s*.
Essays from "The Times." 2 Vols. 8*s*.
Music and Dress. 1*s*.
Layard's Account of Nineveh. 5*s*.
Milman's Fall of Jerusalem. 1*s*.
Mahon's "Forty-Five." 3*s*.
Life of Theodore Hook. 1*s*.
Deeds of Naval Daring. 3*s*. 6*d*.
The Honey Bee. 1*s*.
James' Æsop's Fables. 2*s*. 6*d*.
Nimrod on the Turf. 1*s*. 6*d*.
Art of Dining. 1*s*. 6*d*.
Hallam's Literary Essays. 2*s*.
Mahon's Joan of Arc. 1*s*.
Head's Emigrant. 2*s*. 6*d*.
Nimrod on the Road. 1*s*.
Croker on the Guillotine. 1*s*.
Hollway's Norway. 2*s*.
Maurel's Wellington. 1*s*. 6*d*.
Campbell's Life of Bacon. 2*s*. 6*d*.
The Flower Garden. 1*s*.
Lockhart's Spanish Ballads. 2*s*. 6*d*.
Taylor's Notes from Life. 2*s*.
Rejected Addresses. 1*s*.
Penn's Hints on Angling. 1*s*.

MUSIC AND DRESS. By a Lady. Reprinted from the "Quarterly Review." Fcap. 8vo. 1*s*.

NAPIER'S (Sir Chas.) Life; chiefly derived from his Journals and Letters. By Sir W. Napier. *Second Edition*. Portraits. 4 Vols. Post 8vo. 48*s*.

——— (Sir Wm.) Life and Letters. Edited by H. A. Bruce, M.P. Portraits. 2 Vols. Crown 8vo. 28*s*.

——— English Battles and Sieges of the Peninsular War. *Fourth Edition*. Portrait. Post 8vo. 9*s*.

NAUTICAL ALMANACK. Royal 8vo. 2*s.* 6*d.* (*By Authority.*)

NAVY LIST. (*Published Quarterly, by Authority.*) 16mo. 2*s.* 6*d.*

NEW TESTAMENT (THE) Illustrated by a Plain Explanatory Commentary, and authentic Views of Sacred Places, from Sketches and Photographs. Edited by ARCHDEACON CHURTON and REV. BASIL JONES. With 110 Illustrations. 2 Vols. Crown 8vo. 30*s.* cloth; 52*s.* 6*d.* calf; 63*s.* morocco.

NICHOLLS' (SIR GEORGE) History of the English, Irish and Scotch Poor Laws. 4 Vols. 8vo.

——— (REV. H. G.) Historical Account of the Forest of Dean. Woodcuts, &c. Post 8vo. 10*s.* 6*d.*

NICOLAS' (SIR HARRIS) Historic Peerage of England. Exhibiting the Origin, Descent, and Present State of every Title of Peerage which has existed in this Country since the Conquest. By WILLIAM COURTHOPE. 8vo. 30*s.*

NIMROD On the Chace—The Turf—and The Road. Reprinted from the "Quarterly Review." Woodcuts. Fcap. 8vo. 3*s.* 6*d.*

O'CONNOR'S (R.) Field Sports of France; or, Hunting, Shooting, and Fishing on the Continent. Woodcuts. 12mo. 7*s.* 6*d.*

OXENHAM'S (REV. W.) English Notes for Latin Elegiacs; designed for early Proficients in the Art of Latin Versification, with Prefatory Rules of Composition in Elegiac Metre. *Fourth Edition.* 12mo. 3*s.* 6*d.*

PARIS' (DR.) Philosophy in Sport made Science in Earnest; or, the First Principles of Natural Philosophy inculcated by aid of the Toys and Sports of Youth. *Ninth Edition.* Woodcuts. Post 8vo. 7*s.* 6*d.*

PEEL'S (SIR ROBERT) Memoirs. Edited by EARL STANHOPE and Right Hon. E. CARDWELL. 2 Vols. Post 8vo. 7*s.* 6*d.* each.

PENN'S (RICHARD) Maxims and Hints for an Angler and Chessplayer. *New Edition.* Woodcuts. Fcap. 8vo. 1*s.*

PENROSE'S (F. C.) Principles of Athenian Architecture, and the Optical Refinements exhibited in the Construction of the Ancient Buildings at Athens, from a Survey. With 40 Plates. Folio. 5*l.* 5*s.*

PERCY'S (JOHN, M.D.) Metallurgy of Iron and Steel; or, the Art of Extracting Metals from their Ores and adapting them to various purposes of Manufacture. Illustrations. 8vo. 42*s.*

PHILLIPP (CHARLES SPENCER MARCH) On Jurisprudence. 8vo. 12*s.*

PHILLIPS' (JOHN) Memoirs of William Smith, the Geologist. Portrait. 8vo. 7*s.* 6*d.*

——— Geology of Yorkshire, The Coast, and Limestone District. Plates. 4to. Part I., 20*s.*—Part II., 30*s.*

——— Rivers, Mountains, and Sea Coast of Yorkshire. With Essays on the Climate, Scenery, and Ancient Inhabitants. *Second Edition*, Plates. 8vo. 15*s.*

PHILPOTTS' (BISHOP) Letters to the late Charles Butler, on the Theological parts of his "Book of the Roman Catholic Church;" with Remarks on certain Works of Dr. Milner and Dr. Lingard, and on some parts of the Evidence of Dr. Doyle. *Second Edition.* 8vo. 16*s.*

POPE'S (ALEXANDER) Life and Works. *A New Edition.* Containing nearly 500 unpublished Letters. Edited, with a NEW LIFE, Introductions and Notes, by REV. WHITWELL ELWIN. Portraits. 8vo. (*In the Press.*)

PORTER'S (Rev. J. L.) Five Years in Damascus. With Travels to Palmyra, Lebanon and other Scripture Sites. Map and Woodcuts. 2 Vols. Post 8vo. 21s.

——— Handbook for Syria and Palestine: including an Account of the Geography, History, Antiquities, and Inhabitants of these Countries, the Peninsula of Sinai, Edom, and the Syrian Desert. Maps. 2 Vols. Post 8vo. 24s.

PRAYER-BOOK (Illustrated), with 1000 Illustrations of Borders, Initials, Vignettes, &c. Edited, with Notes, by Rev. Thos. James. Medium 8vo. 18s. cloth; 13s. 6d. calf; 36s. morocco.

PRECEPTS FOR THE CONDUCT OF LIFE. Extracted from the Scriptures. *Second Edition.* Fcap. 8vo. 1s.

PUSS IN BOOTS. With 12 Illustrations. By Otto Speckter. 16mo. 1s. 6d. or Coloured, 2s. 6d.

QUARTERLY REVIEW (The). 8vo. 6s.

RAMBLES in the Syrian Deserts among the Turkomans and Bedaweens. Post 8vo. 10s. 6d.

RAWLINSON'S (Rev. George) Herodotus. A New English Version. Edited with Notes and Essays. Assisted by Sir Henry Rawlinson and Sir J. G. Wilkinson. *Second Edition.* Maps and Woodcut. 4 Vols. 8vo. 48s.

——— Historical Evidences of the truth of the Scripture Records stated anew. *Second Edition.* 8vo. 14s.

——— Five Great Monarchies of the Ancient World, Chaldæa, Assyria, Media, Babylonia, and Persia. Illustrations. 4 Vols. 8vo. 16s. each.

REJECTED ADDRESSES (The). By James and Horace Smith. Fcap. 8vo. 1s.

RENNIE'S (D. F.) British Arms in Peking, 1860; Kagosima, 1862. Post 8vo. 12s.

——— Peking and the Pekingese: Being a Narrative of the First Year of the British Embassy in China. Illustrations. 2 Vols. Post 8vo. 24s.

——— Story of Bhotan and the Dooar War; including Sketches of a Residence in the Himalayas and Visit to Bhotan in 1865. Map and Woodcut. Post 8vo.

REYNOLDS' (Sir Joshua) Life and Times. Commenced by C. R. Leslie, R.A., continued and concluded by Tom Taylor. Portraits and Illustrations. 2 Vols. 8vo. 42s.

——— Descriptive Catalogue of his Works. With Notices of their present owners and localities. By Tom Taylor and Charles W. Franks. With Illustrations. Fcap. 4to. (*In the Press.*)

RICARDO'S (David) Political Works. With a Notice of his Life and Writings. By J. R. M'Culloch. *New Edition.* 8vo. 16s.

RIPA'S (Father) Memoirs during Thirteen Years' Residence at the Court of Peking. From the Italian. Post 8vo. 2s.

ROBERTSON'S (Canon) History of the Christian Church, from the Apostolic Age to the Concordat of Worms, A.D. 1123. *Second Edition.* 3 Vols. 8vo. 38s.

ROBINSON'S (Rev. Dr.) Later Biblical Researches in the Holy Land. Being a Journal of Travels in 1852. Maps. 8vo. 15*s.*

——— Physical Geography of the Holy Land. Post 8vo. 10*s.* 6*d.*

ROME (The Student's History of). From the Earliest Times to the Establishment of the Empire. By Dean Liddell. Woodcuts. Post 8vo. 7*s.* 6*d.*

——— (A Smaller History of, for Young Persons). By Wm. mith, LL.D. Woodcuts. 16mo. 3*s.* 6*d.*

ROWLAND'S (David) Manual of the English Constitution; Its Rise, Growth, and Present State. Post 8vo. 10*s.* 6*d.*

——— Laws of Nature the Foundation of Morals. Post 8vo. 6*s.*

RUNDELL'S (Mrs.) Domestic Cookery, adapted for Private Families. *New Edition.* Woodcuts. Fcap. 8vo. 5*s.*

RUSSELL'S (J. Rutherfurd) History of the Heroes of Medicine. Portraits. 8vo. 14*s.*

RUXTON'S (George F.) Travels in Mexico; with Adventures among the Wild Tribes and Animals of the Prairies and Rocky Mountains. Post 8vo. 3*s.* 6*d.*

SALE'S (Sir Robert) Brigade in Affghanistan. With an Account of the Defence of Jellalabad. By Rev. G. R. Gleig. Post 8vo. 2*s.*

SANDWITH'S (Humphry) Siege of Kars. Post 8vo. 3*s.* 6*d.*

SCOTT'S (G. Gilbert) Secular and Domestic Architecture, Present and Future. *Second Edition.* 8vo. 9*s.*

——— (Rev. Robert, D.D., Master of Baliol) Sermons, preached before the University of Oxford. Post 8vo. 8*s.* 6*d.*

SCROPE'S (G. P.) Geology and Extinct Volcanoes of Central France. *Second Edition.* Illustrations. Medium 8vo. 30*s.*

SENIOR'S (N. W.) Suggestions on Popular Education. 8vo. 9*s.*

SHAFTESBURY (Lord Chancellor); Memoirs of his Early Life. With his Letters, &c. By W. D. Christie. Vol. I. Portrait. 8vo. 10*s.* 6*d.*

SHAW'S (T. B.) Student's Manual of English Literature. Edited, with Notes and Illustrations, by Dr. Wm. Smith. Post 8vo. 7*s.* 6*d.*

——— Specimens of English Literature. Selected from the Chief English Writers. Edited by Wm. Smith, LL.D. Post 8vo. 7*s.* 6*d.*

SIERRA LEONE; Described in Letters to Friends at Home. By A Lady. Post 8vo. 3*s.* 6*d.*

SIMMONS (Capt. T. F.) on the Constitution and Practice of Courts-Martial; with a Summary of the Law of Evidence as connected therewith, and some Notice of the Criminal Law of England, with reference to the Trial of Civil Offences. *5th Edition.* 8vo. 14*s.*

SOUTH'S (John F.) Household Surgery; or, Hints on Emergencies. *Seventeenth Thousand.* Woodcuts. Fcp. 8vo. 4*s.* 6*d.*

SMILES' (SAMUEL) Lives of British Engineers; from the Earliest Period to the Death of Robert Stephenson; with an account of their Principal Works, and a History of Inland Communication in Britain. Portraits and Illustrations. 3 Vols. 8vo. 63*s*.

——— Lives of Boulton and Watt. Comprising a History of the Invention and Introduction of the Steam Engine. With Portraits and 70 Illustrations. 8vo. 21*s*.

——— Story of George Stephenson's Life, including a Memoir of Robert Stephenson. With Portraits and 70 Woodcuts. Post 8vo. 6*s*.

——— James Brindley and the Early Engineers. With Portrait and 50 Woodcuts. Post 8vo. 6*s*.

——— Self-Help. With Illustrations of Character and Conduct. Post 8vo. 6*s*.

——— Industrial Biography: Iron-Workers and Tool Makers. companion volume to "Self-Help." Post 8vo. 6*s*.

——— Workmen's Earnings—Savings—and Strikes. Fcap. 8vo. 1*s*. 6*d*.

SOMERVILLE'S (MARY) Physical Geography. *Fifth Edition.* Portrait. Post 8vo. 9*s*.

——— Connexion of the Physical Sciences. *Ninth Edition.* Woodcuts. Post 8vo. 9*s*.

STANLEY'S (DEAN) Sinai and Palestine, in Connexion with their History. Map. 8vo. 16*s*.

——— Bible in the Holy Land. Woodcuts. Fcap. 8vo. 2*s*. 6*d*.

——— St. Paul's Epistles to the Corinthians. 8vo. 18*s*.

——— History of the Eastern Church. Plans. 8vo. 12*s*.

——— Jewish Church. ABRAHAM TO THE CAPTIVITY. 2 Vols. 8vo. 16*s*. each.

——— Historical Memorials of Canterbury. Woodcuts. Post 8vo. 7*s*. 6*d*.

——— Sermons in the East, with Notices of the Places Visited. 8vo. 9*s*.

——— Sermons on Evangelical and Apostolical Teaching. Post 8vo. 7*s*. 6*d*.

——— ADDRESSES AND CHARGES OF BISHOP STANLEY. With Memoir. 8vo. 10*s*. 6*d*.

SOUTHEY'S (ROBERT) Book of the Church. *Seventh Edition.* Post 8vo. 7*s*. 6*d*.

——— Lives of Bunyan and Cromwell. Post 8vo. 2*s*.

SPECKTER'S (OTTO) Puss in Boots. With 12 Woodcuts. Square 12mo. 1*s*. 6*d*. plain, or 2*s*. 6*d*. coloured.

——— Charmed Roe; or, the Story of the Little Brother and Sister. Illustrated. 16mo.

SMITH'S (DR. WM.) Dictionary of the Bible; its Antiquities, Biography, Geography, and Natural History. Illustrations. 3 Vols. 8vo. 105*s.*

——— Concise Dictionary of the Bible, condensed from the above Dictionary for Families and Students. Illustrations. Medium, 8vo. 21*s.*

——— Dictionary of Christian Antiquities: from the Times of the Apostles to the Age of Charlemagne. Illustrations. Medium. 8vo. (*In preparation.*)

——— Greek and Roman Antiquities. Woodcuts. 8vo. 42*s.*

——— Greek and Roman Biography and Mythology. Woodcuts. 3 Vols. 8vo. 5*l.* 15*s.* 6*d.*

——— Greek and Roman Geography. Woodcuts. 2 Vols. 8vo. 80*s.*

——— Classical and Biblical Atlas. Small folio. (*In preparation.*)

——— Classical Dictionary for the Higher Forms in Schools, compiled from the above works. With 750 Woodcuts. 8vo. 18*s.*

——— Smaller Classical Dictionary, abridged from the above Work. Woodcuts. Crown 8vo. 7*s.* 6*d.*

——— Smaller Dictionary of Greek and Roman Antiquities, compiled from the larger Work. Woodcuts. Crown 8vo. 7*s.* 6*d.*

——— Latin-English Dictionary for the Higher Forms in Schools. Based on the Works of FORCELLINI and FREUND. With Tables of the Roman Calendar, Measures, Weights, and Money. 8vo. 21*s.*

——— Smaller Latin-English Dictionary, abridged from the above Work. 12mo. 7*s.* 6*d.*

——— New English-Latin Dictionary, compiled from original sources. 8vo. and 12mo. (*In the Press.*)

——— Small Classical Mythology for Schools. With Illustrations. 12mo.

——— Latin-English Vocabulary; for Phædrus, Cornelius Nepos, and Cæsar. *2nd Edition.* 12mo. 3*s.* 6*d.*

——— Principia Latina—Part I. A Grammar, Delectus, and Exercise Book, with Vocabularies. *6th Edition.* 12mo. 3*s.* 6*d.*

——— Part II. A Reading-book of Mythology, Geography, Roman Antiquities, and History. With Notes and Dictionary. *3rd Edition.* 12mo. 3*s.* 6*d.*

——— Part III. A Latin Poetry Book. Hexameters and Pentameters; Eclog. Ovidianæ; Latin Prosody, &c. *2nd Edition.* 12mo. 3*s.* 6*d.*

——— Part IV. Latin Prose Composition. Rules of Syntax, with Examples, Explanations of Synonyms, and Exercises on the Syntax. *Second Edition.* 12mo. 3*s.* 6*d.*

——— Student's Greek Grammar for the Higher Forms. By Professor CURTIUS. Post 8vo. 7*s.* 6*d.*

——— Smaller Greek Grammar, abridged from the above Work. 12mo. 3*s.* 6*d.*

——— Student's Latin Grammar for the Higher Forms. Post 8vo. 7*s.* 6*d.*

——— Smaller Latin Grammar, abridged from the above Work. 12mo. 3*s.* 6*d.*

STANHOPE'S (EARL) Life of William Pitt. With Extracts from his MS. Papers. *Second Edition.* Portraits. 4 Vols. Post 8vo. 42*s*.

——— Miscellanies. *Second Edition.* Post 8vo. 5*s*. 6*d*.

——— Life of Belisarius. Post 8vo. 10*s*. 6*d*.

——— Life of Condé. Post 8vo. 3*s*. 6*d*.

——— History of England, from the Peace of Utrecht to the Peace of Versailles, 1713-83. *Library Edition.* 7 vols. 8vo. 93*s*. *Or Popular Edition.* 7 vols. Post 8vo. 5*s*. each.

——— History of British India, from its origin till the Peace of 1783. Post 8vo. 3*s*. 6*d*.

——— "Forty-Five;" a Narrative of the Rebellion in Scotland. Post 8vo. 3*s*.

——— Spain under Charles the Second. Post 8vo. 6*s*. 6*d*.

——— Historical and Critical Essays. Post 8vo. 3*s*. 6*d*.

STUDENT'S HUME. A History of England from the Invasion of Julius Cæsar to the Revolution of 1688. By DAVID HUME. Corrected and continued to 1858. Woodcuts. Post 8vo. 7*s*. 6*d*. Questions on, 2*s*.
⁎ A Smaller History of England. 12mo. 3*s*. 6*d*.

——— HISTORY OF FRANCE; from the Earliest Times to the Establishment of the Second Empire, 1852. By W. H. PEARSON, M.A. Woodcuts. Post 8vo. 7*s*. 6*d*.

——— HISTORY OF GREECE; from the Earliest Times to the Roman Conquest. With the History of Literature and Art. By WM. SMITH, LL.D. Woodcuts. Crown 8vo. 7*s*. 6*d*. (Questions. 2*s*.)
⁎ A SMALLER HISTORY OF GREECE. 12mo. 3*s*. 6*d*.

——— HISTORY OF ROME; from the Earliest Times to the Establishment of the Empire. With the History of Literature and Art. By Dean LIDDELL. Woodcuts. Crown 8vo. 7*s*. 6*d*.
⁎ A SMALLER HISTORY OF ROME. 12mo. 3*s*. 6*d*.

——— GIBBON; an Epitome of the History of the Decline and Fall of the Roman Empire. By EDWARD GIBBON. Incorporating the Researches of Recent Commentators. Woodcuts. Post 8vo. 7*s*. 6*d*.

——— MANUAL OF ANCIENT GEOGRAPHY. By REV. W. L. BEVAN, M.A. Woodcuts. Post 8vo. 7*s*. 6*d*.

——— MODERN GEOGRAPHY. By Rev. W. L. BEVAN. Woodcuts. Post 8vo. (*In the Press.*)

——— ENGLISH LANGUAGE. By GEORGE P. MARSH. Post 8vo. 7*s*. 6*d*.

——— ENGLISH LITERATURE. By T. B. SHAW, M.A. Post 8vo. 7*s*. 6*d*.

——— SPECIMENS OF ENGLISH LITERATURE. Selected from the Chief Writers. By THOMAS B. SHAW, M.A. Post 8vo. 7*s*. 6*d*.

——— SCRIPTURE HISTORY: the Old and New Testament. Maps and Woodcuts. 2 Vols. Post 8vo. 7*s*. 6*d*. each.

——— BLACKSTONE: a Systematic Abridgment of the Entire Commentaries. By R. MALCOLM KERR, LL.D. Post 8vo. 7*s*. 6*d*.

ST. JOHN'S (CHARLES) Wild Sports and Natural History of the Highlands. Post 8vo. 3*s*. 6*d*.

———— (BAYLE) Adventures in the Libyan Desert and the Oasis of Jupiter Ammon. Woodcuts. Post 8vo. 2*s*.

STEPHENSON (GEORGE and ROBERT). The Story of their Lives. By SAMUEL SMILES. With Portraits and 70 Illustrations. Medium. 8vo. 21*s*. Or Popular Edition, Post 8vo. 6*s*.

STOTHARD'S (THOS.) Life. With Personal Reminiscences. By Mrs. BRAY. With Portrait and 60 Woodcuts. 4to. 21*s*.

STREET'S (G. E.) Gothic Architecture in Spain. From Personal Observations during several journeys through that country. Illustrations. Medium 8vo. 50*s*.

———— Brick and Marble Architecture of Italy in the Middle Ages. Plates. 8vo. 21*s*.

SWIFT'S (JONATHAN) Life, Letters, Journals, and Works. By JOHN FORSTER. 8vo. (*In Preparation.*)

SYME'S (PROFESSOR) Principles of Surgery. *5th Edition.* 8vo. 12*s*.

TAIT'S (BISHOP) Dangers and Safeguards of Modern Theology, containing Suggestions to the Theological Student under Present Difficulties. 8vo. 9*s*.

TAYLOR'S (HENRY) Notes from Life, in Six Essays on Money, Humility and Independence, Wisdom, Choice in Marriage, Children, and Life Poetic. Fcap. 8vo. 2*s*.

THOMSON'S (ARCHBISHOP) Sermons, Preached in the Chapel of Lincoln's Inn. 8vo. 10*s*. 6*d*.

THREE-LEAVED MANUAL OF FAMILY PRAYER; arranged so as to save the trouble of turning the Pages backwards and forwards. Royal 8vo. 2*s*.

TREMENHEERE'S (H. S.) The Franchise a Privilege and not a Right, proved by the Political Experience of the Ancients. Fcap. 8vo. 2*s*. 6*d*.

TRISTRAM'S (H. B.) Great Sahara. Wanderings South of the Atlas Mountains. Map and Illustrations. Post 8vo. 15*s*.

TWISS' (HORACE) Public and Private Life of Lord Chancellor Eldon, with Selections from his Correspondence. Portrait. *Third Edition.* 2 Vols. Post 8vo. 21*s*.

TYLOR'S (E. B.) Researches into the Early History of Mankind, and the Development of Civilization. Illustrations. 8vo. 12*s*.

TYNDALL'S (JOHN) Glaciers of the Alps. With an account of Three Years' Observations and Experiments on their General Phenomena. Woodcuts. Post 8vo. 14*s*.

TYTLER'S (PATRICK FRASER) Memoirs. By REV. J. W. BURGON, M.A. 8vo. 9*s*.

VAUGHAN'S (REV. DR.) Sermons preached in Harrow School. 8vo. 10*s*. 6*d*.

VENABLES' (Rev. R. L.) Domestic Scenes in Russia. Post 8vo. 5*s.*

WAAGEN'S (Dr.) Treasures of Art in Great Britain. Being an Account of the Chief Collections of Paintings, Sculpture, Manuscripts, Miniatures, &c. &c., in this Country. Obtained from Personal Inspection during Visits to England. 4 Vols. 8vo.

WALSH'S (Sir John) Practical Results of the Reform Bill of 1832. 8vo. 5*s.* 6*d.*

VAMBERY'S (Arminius) Travels in Central Asia, from Teheran across the Turkoman Desert, on the Eastern Shore of the Caspian to Khiva, Bokhara, and Samarcand in 1863. Map and Illustrations. 8vo. 21*s.*

WELLINGTON'S (The Duke of) Despatches during his various Campaigns. Compiled from Official and other Authentic Documents. By Col. Gurwood, C.B. 8 Vols. 8vo. 21*s.* each.

———— Supplementary Despatches, and other Papers. Edited by his Son. Vols. I. to XII. 8vo. 20*s.* each.

———— Selections from his Despatches and General Orders. By Colonel Gurwood. 8vo. 18*s.*

———— Speeches in Parliament. 2 Vols. 8vo. 42*s.*

WILKINSON'S (Sir J. G.) Popular Account of the Private Life, Manners, and Customs of the Ancient Egyptians. *New Edition.* Revised and Condensed. With 500 Woodcuts. 2 Vols. Post 8vo. 12*s.*

———— Handbook for Egypt.—Thebes, the Nile, Alexandria, Cairo, the Pyramids, Mount Sinai, &c. Map. Post 8vo. 15*s.*

———— (G. B.) Working Man's Handbook to South Australia; with Advice to the Farmer, and Detailed Information for the several Classes of Labourers and Artisans. Map. 18mo. 1*s.* 6*d.*

WILSON'S (Bishop Daniel) Life, with Extracts from his Letters and Journals. By Rev. Josiah Bateman. *Second Edition.* Illustrations. Post 8vo. 9*s.*

———— (Genl. Sir Robert) Secret History of the French Invasion of Russia, and Retreat of the French Army, 1812. *Second Edition.* 8vo. 15*s.*

———— Private Diary of Travels, Personal Services, and Public Events, during Missions and Employments in Spain, Sicily, Turkey, Russia, Poland, Germany, &c. 1812-14. 2 Vols. 8vo. 26*s.*

———— Autobiographical Memoirs. Containing an Account of his Early Life down to the Peace of Tilsit. Portrait. 2 Vols. 8vo. 26*s.*

WORDSWORTH'S (Canon) Journal of a Tour in Athens and Attica. *Third Edition.* Plates. Post 8vo. 8*s.* 6*d.*

———— Pictorial, Descriptive, and Historical Account of Greece, with a History of Greek Art, by G. Scharf, F.S.A. *New Edition.* With 600 Woodcuts. Royal 8vo. 28*s.*

BRADBURY, EVANS, AND CO., PRINTERS, WHITEFRIARS.